KT-594-431

GREAT MOVIES

This edition published exclusively for
Marks and Spencer p.l.c.
in 1985 by
Octopus Books Limited
59 Grosvenor Street, London W1

Produced by Mandarin Publishers Limited
22a Westlands Road, Quarry Bay, Hong Kong
Printed in Hong Kong
ISBN 0 86273 237 9

GREAT MOVIES

Editor: Nick Roddick
Text by:
John Douglas Eames
Vernon Harbin
Clive Hirschhorn
Richard B. Jewell
Nick Roddick
Foreword by James Mason

Page 1:
Fred Astaire in the limelight;
pages 2-3:
Christopher Plummer and
Julie Andrews in silhouette in a
scene from *The Sound of Music*

CONTENTS

FOREWORD

It is indeed a privilege to become part of so comprehensive a lexicon of great films, but I feel that I have earned it, having been an actor throughout most of my working life and having been, from the age of seven, a bona fide Movie Buff.

The first film I ever watched was a newsreel special called *British Tanks in Action*, which had been rushed into circulation to encourage morale on the home front during World War I. I was suitably impressed, of course, but other images were so firmly printed in my mind on that first visit to the cinema that they still survive to this day, colour and all. They emanated from a segment of the main feature which occupied the screen immediately prior to the *Tanks in Action*. For the night time sequences the screen went blue and for the thrilling climax, when the factory in which our heroine was working was set alight by the villain's cigar butt tossed carelessly (or purposely?) into a heap of wood shavings, the screen, of course, became red.

Since my parents were non-moviegoers, I was not often able to indulge my addiction. But every red-blooded boy had to see Doug Fairbanks, and, while still in short trousers, I was striding around Huddersfield with straw hat and horn-rimmed glasses and the notion that I resembled Harold Lloyd. Or else at school we smeared our hair with a special grease and glowered into the mirror like Valentino.

But when I became a serious moviegoer in the late twenties, it was all those classic silents from Europe that enthralled me. Film became recognized as an art: it was no longer just a matter of going to the pictures. And my preference remained firmly entrenched in this rut through my early acting years until I made off to the U.S. in 1946, my lofty tastes having been gratified at least in *Odd Man Out*, a film which I am glad to see included in this book.

Clara Bow excepted, the ingredient that I had admired most of all in American movies was the wit. I suppose that Frank Capra and Preston Sturges were the wittiest directors and it was wit that made immortal such films as Keaton's *The Cameraman*. And the wit was not only in the movies, the entire American scene erupted with it: *The New Yorker*, the silent movie comedies, Dorothy Parker, James Thurber, Ogden Nash, the Crazy comedies, Thornton Wilder, the list is endless. It was this, more than anything else, that drew me to Hollywood. While in America, I learned how the powerful movie machine worked and I learned the nature of the men who had the power, which in those days meant the men who controlled the studios, though by the time I left Hollywood it was already the agents and the entrepreneurs who had taken over.

This same much admired wit was later to abandon Hollywood and reappear in England, losing very little in translation—at least as far as films were concerned. There was Alec Guinness, the Ealing comedies of Michael Balcon, the Goon Show and the Boulting Brothers films with Peter Sellers.

From the look of Mr Roddick's list, it might seem that each year the number of 'great movies' has become smaller and that that alone might be enough to reduce the number of film buffs. But it takes more than a little statistic to upset a card-carrying buff. And there is another large group who are as happy as clams while they sit blank-eyed and wait. Wait for what? Why, for the next segment of their favourite soap opera! What else? I was sitting next to this duchess at a party. She said to me, 'Movies are much better than they used to be, you know. Have you seen *Dynasty*? It's wonderful!'

May 1984

James Mason

Sadly James Mason died two months after writing this.

HOORAY FOR HOLLYWOOD

A collection of great movies is not like a list of great plays or an anthology of great books. For one thing, the critical standards which govern their selection are nowhere near as firmly established as they are in the theatre or in literature. For another, the selection is bound to be more personal, since movies deal with dreams and desires. They are also a mass entertainment: people who have never had a favourite novel have a memory full of favourite movies. Theatre audiences have always been restricted—at first because theatres were only to be found in the great cities, later because theatre has become the preserve of the educated classes. And reading novels has always been a private experience—something done in the home, with the action taking place in the reader's head.

Films are communal experiences, seen (or supposed to be seen) in great gilt palaces with hundreds or even thousands of other people. In them, the dreams are certainly acted out, many times larger than life in actual scale, and nearly always larger than life in terms of emotion. Films have been, for many of us, important things, fixing key moments in our lives like landmarks in the memory; they have given a special kind of pleasure. Whether they will continue to do so in the future, as their scale diverges to the two extremes of the spectrum, is another matter. Now that television has won the battle—about that, there can be no doubt—cinema films will increasingly be either blockbusters that play the holiday dates and bring in (as *Return of the Jedi* did) some $30 million in a week; or they will be small films, destined for television, but being given a showcase in a cinema first, to appease the film-makers and make them something of an event. When that has happened, cinemas will have become like theatres, catering for a minority audience, not entertaining the weekly millions they used to reach.

Not that the pleasures of cinema have always been entirely innocent. Without citing *A Clockwork Orange*, beloved of our self-appointed moral guardians as an example of a film which drives the already depraved to specific acts of depravity, there can be no doubt that ordinary, mainstream cinema has had a profound influence on the way in which three or four generations of people view themselves, their lives and their responsibilities. There is nothing particularly sinister about this: films which do not touch off some response in the moviegoer are unlikely to be successful. And touching off a response means more than simply appealing to pre-existing ideas: it means picking up those ideas and running with them. The films we love are, by and large, the films that tell us what we want to hear, that show us people doing things we would like to do or believe we could do, and which in general portray a world which is how we think it ought to be. John Wayne is in his saddle and all's well with the West. Movie companies sink or swim by their ability to touch off such responses.

Of course, they can't do it every time: Hollywood is quite full enough of box office horror stories and fractured careers to prove that. Yet in the Golden Age of the cinema, which stretched from the birth of the talkies to the definitive advent of television in the late 1940s and early 1950s, families went to the pictures twice a week. The movies were then the world's greatest socializing force, introducing new clothes and new dances, teaching behaviour—anything from what to do on your first date to how to deal with a giant ape—and, in a word, *influencing* people in a way that used to be done, in a simpler, less 'nuclear' age, by the village square and the extended family.

This, then is a book of dreams. But they were dreams produced in a factory. They cost a lot of money to make and they were made with one overwhelming aim: to get that money back with a profit on top. The American film industry started off as a sideshow activity on the East Coast in the declining years of the 19th century: films would be shown as speciality items in musical halls and at travelling fairs. Before long—by around 1905—there were regular places of showing, called nickelodeons because of what (for a short time) it cost to get in. As the industry grew, Thomas Alva Edison, the man who had invented it and a businessman as much as he was an innovator, sought to control its growth. He also wished to ensure that he reaped the profits that were to be made from a brainchild he had not expected to be much more than a passing craze.

For Edison, the important thing was the machine: films were things that had to be made to encourage people to buy projectors. But as the short-lived craze began its long reign as a major entertainment form, a new generation of entrepreneurs moved in. They sensed the money to be made from showing films, and they resented the control exercised by Edison and his hastily assembled Motion Picture Patents Company (MPPC), which asserted its right to license every cinematograph show and to take a percentage of the profits. This new generation had names like William Fox and Samuel Goldfish (later changed, for reasons of euphony, to Goldwyn), the brothers Harry, Albert, Sam and Jack Warner, Adolph Zukor (who called his company Paramount) and Carl Laemmle (who dubbed his, with what seemed monstrous pride, Universal). When they tried to hold out against the MPPC, they found themselves deprived of films. The only solution was to make their own. They started proceedings against the MPPC under Federal anti-trust legislation; but such things take time

John Wayne (middle); Fairbanks and Mary Pickford (top); (bottom, left to right) DeMille, Goldwyn, Zukor and Lasky on Zukor's 80th birthday

LLYWOOD
80

and, if they were not to go out of business, they would have to break the law. The MPPC employed some fairly effective arguments to enforce their monopoly—men who used sledgehammers rather than writs—and the new independents searched around for a place where they would be out of the reach of such irritants. Cuba seemed a possibility, but there were all sorts of problems, like supply and customs regulations. Then someone came back with a brochure from the relatively small West Coast city of Los Angeles, which praised its constant sunshine. Los Angeles was a long way from New York and it was, as a last resort, within comparatively easy driving distance of the Mexican border.

Out of such chance events, Hollywood was born, since it was in the unbuilt-up Los Angeles suburb of Hollywood that the filmmakers settled. They have long since moved on—Universal to the other side of the Hollywood Hills, MGM to nearby Culver City, 20th Century-Fox a few miles west to Westwood. But the name has stuck: Hollywood means the American film industry. It also means a great deal more in most people's minds: glamour and extravagance and a strong hint of scandal—all things on which the film industry has played to attract audiences to its product.

The case against the MPPC was won in 1915, but by then it didn't matter: the original companies were fading into insignificance, and the new ones were taking over. The fact that, in 1915, the rest of the filmmaking world—basically Europe—had other things on its mind helped Hollywood to establish a commanding position in world cinema from which it has never looked back. By the late 1920s, Hollywood accounted for around 95 per cent of all American filmmaking, and America for 75 per cent of the world's cinematic output. During the 1920s, Hollywood was one of the United States' major growth industries, after steel and the motor car. The days of that exclusively 20th-century phenomenon, the entertainment industry, had well and truly arrived. The 1920s were years of extravagance and glamour in Hollywood, but also of consolidation and technical innovation. The second generation of film companies merged into five majors—MGM, Fox, Warner Bros, Paramount and a latecomer, RKO—backed up by two 'mini-majors', Universal and Columbia.

It was a coincidence of circumstances, however, that brought about the biggest change in the nature of Hollywood. This was the fact that the advent of sound happened at around the same time as the great Wall Street Crash of 1929. All the studios had borrowed huge sums to invest in their reorganization and in the development of talking pictures, and the Crash called for economies. The Depression which followed the Crash also meant that audiences had less money to spend. While it didn't necessarily mean that they stopped spending it on the movies (the opposite was in fact the case: the proportion of a family's budget spent on moviegoing actually increased), it did mean that the studios had to be more careful about meeting their needs. The days of the great fight to get people into the picture houses—which was after all the bottom line of the movie industry—had arrived.

The 1930s were the Golden Age of Hollywood, not just because of the classic films that were produced during this decade, but also because, in the early part, the major companies all perfected a form of streamlined organization. This was the age of the studio system. The company that made the films was linked with the company that showed them, and a more or less permanent circle of feedback ensured that the audience got what it wanted. The automatic corollary of such an equation in the entertainment business being that it also wanted what it got. Individual studios' profit and loss sheets fluctuated as the decade progressed (RKO in particular, having been a corporate creation and not, like the other studios, the brainchild of one man or one family). But the movies were a firmly established part of American life.

They stayed that way throughout the early and middle 1940s. The war years were boom ones for Hollywood, though new export markets had temporarily to be found, which accounts for the plethora of South American-oriented pictures which came out at the time. But as the GI's began to come home, a number of things conspired to end the Golden Age. First, the majors found themselves faced with the same kind of anti-trust legislation they had inaugurated against the MPPC; and, with the so-called 'Paramount Decrees' of 1948, they had to sever the corporate links between studios and theatre chains. Secondly, four years' worth of eager husbands returning from the war, produced a baby boom, which kept the crucial young adult audience home at night. Finally, there was TV. The figures tell it all. In 1947, there were 14,000 TV sets in use. Next year, there were 172,000. By 1949 there were a million, by 1950 four million and by 1954 32 million. By the end of the decade, 90 per cent of US homes had a set.

The movie business began a scramble to reorganize and grab the dwindling audience from which it has never entirely recovered. One of the majors, RKO, which had become the personal plaything of millionaire Howard Hughes, languished and died. The others tried everything to win the audiences back: bigger screens, 3-D, colour (which had been around for a while but which now became almost universal), horror, sex, scandal.... In the years since then, Hollywood has withstood one onslaught after another. It has become part of the world of the conglomerate, with every Hollywood studio now owned by some massive corporation of which it represents only a small part of the turnover. Both 20th Century-Fox and MGM have sold off large sections of their lot for real estate development, and Universal now makes a good part of its income from showing people round on organized tours.

More and more American films are now made outside Hollywood, by independent American or even foreign companies, many of them constituted for the sole purpose of making a particular film and disbanded immediately afterwards. In some strange way, however, Hollywood remains the centre of the world's film industry: projects are discussed and deals are done there, films are previewed there and get their prizes there. We still know what we mean when we say 'Hollywood'. Almost all the majors have gone into television in a big way, and they have adapted just as quickly (and just as painfully) to the more recent developments of cable TV. For all the upheavals and corporate wheeling and dealing, Hollywood is still the centre of the cinematic universe—the place from which the great movies come or through which the great movies pass on their way to us.

This book is a fascinating collection of those great movies, from the very early days (it includes the first film to be made at Universal City in 1914, *Damon and Pythias*) through to the corporate present—the production credit on the most recent film in the book, *Never Say Never Again* reads as follows: 'A Taliafilm production, in association with Producer Sales Organisation, for European Banking Co., Manufacturers Hanover, MFI Furniture Group, Midland Montagu Leasing, First National Bank of Chicago (London Branch) and B.A. Turner Ltd.'. It is perhaps as well to know where our dreams come from.

Stars from near and far: left: Return of the Jedi *and below Sean Connery in* Never Say Never Again

OUT OF THE PAST

The proposition that you have to spend a lot to make a lot is one that Hollywood has viewed with a certain amount of caution—if only because, in the movies, it is quite possible to lay out a great deal and get very little back. Costume epics—costume pictures of any kind—are generally expensive to make, because not only do you have to dress all your actors in specially made period clothes, but you have to put them in front of period sets too.

The trips taken by filmmakers back through the mists of time and the pages of the research department bibles tend to be more sporadic than regular. If one sword-and-sandal epic is a success, there is probably time to squeeze in a few more before audience tastes switch to something else.

The silent screen saw quite a few excursions into the ancient world, from D. W. Griffith's mammoth *Intolerance* (1916), through to the major studio spectacles like *The Ten Commandments* (1923) and *Ben-Hur* (1925). The 1930s and 1940s had other things on their minds, but the threat of television in the 1950s brought out all the old BC showmanship once more, and there was quite a revival in films from the forum. The two 1920s epics were remade along with *Quo Vadis* (1951), *Spartacus* (1960), and even a big-budget version of Shakespeare's *Julius Caesar* (1953).

In the interim, when the movies first found their tongue, the plots of costume dramas turned to thoughts of love. Warner Bros.' very first picture with a degree of synchronized sound, *Don Juan* (1926), dealt with the greatest romantic hero (or villain) of all time, and Greta Garbo's costume roles throughout the 1930s kept the tradition alive. In some ways, the big 1930s costume pictures were the last refuge for the romance which had dominated the silent screen. While audiences had adored the Valentino films, they seemed to find the same thing laughable in the early days of the talkie. But placing heavily romantic plots and situations far away and long ago somehow made them more acceptable. Silent lovers could never sound silly. But since people in funny costumes *looked* a bit silly already, audiences seemed prepared to let them talk in a different way from the folks next door. Or perhaps it was just Garbo. In any case it all died out with the war and it wasn't really until *Dr Zhivago* (1965) that the massive widescreen romance returned to Hollywood. When it did it was with a vengeance: 'Lara's Theme' rang in our ears and fur-covered people thundered across the snow.

Screen biographies—or biopics, as they were generally known—were a favourite at Warners, and two of their best are included here: *The Story of Louis Pasteur* (1936) and *The Life of Emile Zola* (1937). However, the decision to expend money and prestige on a famous life from the past was one that was taken at regular intervals by a number of film producers. Two striking examples find a place in this chapter: John Ford's marvellous piece of Americana, *Young Mr Lincoln* (1939); and Richard Attenborough's epic triumph, *Gandhi* (1982)—the most successful British film ever when it came to Oscars.

Hollywood has always fought a little shy of the history of its own country. Few subsequent producers took up the challenge, issued by D. W. Griffith: to chart the birth of the nation. Two highly conventionalized periods of history have dominated Hollywood's look at America's past: the Civil War and the frontier days.

The Civil War, which left its mark on the real America for a century, wasn't taken all that seriously by Hollywood. It tended to occur in the background as it did in RKO's *Little Women* (1933), the Bette Davis picture *Jezebel* (1938), *The Little Foxes* (1941), *The Little Colonel* (1935)—which spirited Shirley Temple back to the Reconstruction era—and, of course, *Gone With The Wind* (1939). The attraction of the Civil War was less for what it was than for what it brought to an end. It was regarded as rather a romantic age, and the dominant emotion in films from the period tends to be nostalgia for the lost elegance of the Old South—all those magnolias and mint juleps and gentlemen callers. But audiences loved it: the Old South was the young nation's only home-grown nostalgic myth, romanticized in much the same way as Victorian London is romanticized on Christmas cards. And if Hollywood's versions turned out looking like *Jezebel* or *Gone With the Wind*, it was hard to care that they weren't strictly true.

Hollywood's main myth, though, was the myth of the Old West. The Western is the film capital's one undoubted contribution to the history of American culture, derided by Dwight Macdonald in 1929 as 'one of the most vapid and infantile art forms ever conceived', hailed by Jorge Luis Borges in 1967 as the genre which had saved the epic from destruction. The Hollywood West was a place where the men were brave and strong, the women sweet and gentle (and occasionally quite strong too), and a time when the country was young, new and uncomplicated. The western landscape gave an extra resonance to the simplest of stories, and audiences loved the fact that they could recognize the world to which the movies took them back again and again. The West was America as it never really was, but as it certainly ought to have been.

In fact, the 1950s were the great age of the Western. Before that, with one or two exceptions like *Cimarron* (1931) and the magnificent *Stagecoach* (1939), Westerns were for the most part cheaply made B features. Unlike other costume pictures, they were cheaper than the modern-day variety: the actors wore old clothes, and no one seemed to mind that the sets were nearly always the same. In the 1950s, though, the need to compete with television brought the widescreen, Technicolor Western, which offered the sorts of landscapes and the kind of action that TV, with its poor picture definition, could at that time only dream of. This chapter contains some of the high spots of the genre, from *Red River* (1948) through to *Gunfight at the O.K. Corral* (1957), as well as the first real 'psychological' Western, *The Left-Handed Gun* (1958), which actually started life as a TV play. In the 1960s, Westerns grew more and more elegiac, portraying the waning of an era. There was *Ride the High Country* (1962), which brought together those two old warhorses of the West, Joel McCrea and Randolph Scott, for the last time and *Butch Cassidy and the Sundance Kid* (1969), an affectionate farewell to the Old West.

Hollywood's picture of the past may have varied in quality and accuracy, but the aim was always entertainment, with only a little historical comment. Though filmmakers dealing with contemporary subjects had to keep their productions true to life, such constraints did not apply quite so strictly to those dealing with the past. For Hollywood, the past was a sort of cinematic Disneyland, in which anything was possible. But above all costume pictures had bigger emotions, bigger battles, bigger promises, bigger sets, bigger budgets and, ideally, bigger box-office receipts.

• THROW • THEM • TO • • THE • LIONS •

The first feature film to be made at Universal City in Hollywood, and completed before the studio's official opening in 1915, **Damon And Pythias** (1914) was a six-reel epic that employed a cast of a thousand extras, as well as William Worthington (who dropped his director's mantle to play Damon) and Herbert Rawlinson (centre) as Pythias. Frank Lloyd (right), later to be a very successful film director, played the ambitious Dionysius, while the women in this familiar story of a self-sacrificing friendship between two men were Anna Little (left) and Cleo Madison (behind). All the performances were commensurate with the not-too-exacting demands of the scenario, and the direction, by Otis Turner, was at its best in the 'spectacle' sequences such as the battle outside the walls of Agrigentum—as well as an exciting chariot race in Syracuse, which city was impressively constructed on the large Universal City backlot. Particularly praised on its release was 'its fascinating and dramatic scenario, its splendid portraying company, its great scenes and perfection in photography'. At its glittering opening on November 30, 1914, the public resoundingly cheered its wholehearted approval.

Cecil B. De Mille made the first emergence, on a major scale, from his long preoccupation with glamorous infidelities and indiscretions in 1923, when **The Ten Commandments** arrived. Starting with a budget of $600,000, generous for its time, he had planned to precede a modern melodrama by Jeanie Macpherson with a biblical prologue showing Moses announcing to Israel the laws of God, the penalties for breaking which formed the main story. A rearrangement, in fact, of the De Mille formula of interrupting a wages-of-sin drama with a flashback to ancient times. But this 'prologue' gripped his imagination and was enlarged to include the death of Pharaoh's son, the adoration of the golden calf, the flight of the Israelites through the Red Sea, enormous crowd scenes, colossal sets and a doubled budget. Such wanton expenditure sent the Paramount board into a corporate swoon, from which it recovered only when the company's costliest production rapidly proved to be also its biggest moneymaker. It was the biblical spectacle that drew and thrilled vast audiences, though the much longer modern tale which followed certainly kept them enthralled. This contrasted a good brother (Richard Dix) with a bad one (Rod La Rocque) who cheated both his wife (Leatrice Joy) with an adventuress (Nita Naldi), and his church with shoddy materials used in constructing a cathedral. Little did Rod know, during his assorted commandment-breakings, that the voluptuous Nita had escaped from a leper colony; that he would kill her after discovering that she had infected him; that his mother would perish in the collapsing cathedral; that he would die in a speedboat escape from the police, leaving brother Richard to enjoy the fade-out with Leatrice. De Mille propelled his players—including also Agnes Ayres, Theodore Roberts, Estelle Taylor, and Charles de Roche—through all this with such gusto that nobody thought of laughing.

Facing page: Damon and Pythias*; above: Ramon Novarro and Francis X. Bushman in* Ben-Hur

The biggest gamble of MGM's first year was inherited from the Goldwyn company. In 1923 that organization (Samuel Goldwyn had no connection with it by then) had propped up its tottering prestige by obtaining movie rights to **Ben-Hur**. Lew Wallace's fabulous best-seller was also a huge moneymaker on the stage, and Goldwyn had had to sign away an unheard-of 50 per cent of the film's future income to get it. A massive production budget had been required: a company headed by director Charles Brabin, writer-supervisor June Mathis and star George Walsh trekked to Rome. Cameras had been rolling spasmodically for three months when Goldwyn became part of MGM. News of sluggish progress so disquieted the new firm that president Marcus Loew himself sailed to the rescue with replacements: director Fred Niblo, writers Bess Meredyth and Carey Wilson, and star Ramon Novarro (here as Ben-Hur, with Francis X. Bushman as the villainous Messala). But before long there were signs that the new key people were having as disastrous a time as the old, and early in 1925 MGM executives Louis B. Mayer and Irving Thalberg prevailed upon Loew to order the whole enterprise back to California where they could keep an eye on it. They did so with such efficiency—and lavish expenditure—that **Ben-Hur** emerged as the greatest world-wide success the movie industry had ever produced (except, possibly, *Birth of a Nation*). However, its $6 million cost was never entirely recouped, thanks to that original 50 per cent royalty deal. Also cast: May McAvoy, Carmel Myers, Mitchell Lewis, Betty Bronson, Nigel de Brulier.

Colossal **Quo Vadis**—the adjective was part of the billing—generated the greatest cash flow into MGM's coffers since *Gone with the Wind*, its world-wide rentals exceeding an incredible $25 million. Despite old *Ben-Hur* disasters, the company still chose to make it in Rome, where the newly built Cinecitta studio offered cheap facilities, not least in extras: a useful point since 5,500 were used in the particular sequence for the triumphal march to Nero's palace as director Mervyn LeRoy envisaged it. LeRoy and producer Sam Zimbalist did well to bring the Technicolor super-spectacle in for $7 million in six months' shooting in 1950, followed by 1951 editing, scoring and tidying up at MGM British and Culver City. Robert Taylor, Deborah Kerr, Peter Ustinov and Leo Genn starred, with Patricia Laffan, Finlay Currie, Abraham Sofaer, Marina Berti, Buddy Baer, Felix Aylmer, Nora Swinburne, Norman Wooland, Rosalie Crutchley, twenty lions to eat Christians and two cheetahs to flank Miss Laffan's Poppaea. The script from Henryk Sienkiewicz's book (filmed silent three times) by John Lee Mahin, S. N. Behrman and Sonya Levien was straight movie drama, representing a victory for Mayer, who ironically was fired before it reached the screen. His rival at the studio, Dore Schary had wanted the film to take a political slant, equating Nero

with modern dictators: a false start had been made on it in 1949, also in Rome. John Huston directing, Arthur Hornblow producing, with Gregory Peck and Elizabeth Taylor.

Marlon Brando was an unexpectedly accomplished Mark Antony in **Julius Caesar** (MGM, 1953). A fine classical actor, syllable-perfect (coached by John Gielgud), had replaced mumblin' Marlon, and his fans helped to make it commercially viable. Also cast: Louis Calhern as Caesar, Brando, Greer Garson as Calpurnia and Deborah Kerr as Portia (behind them, Michael Patel, Alan Napier and John Hoyt) in John Houseman's clean-cut, forceful production of Shakespeare's drama. Director Joseph L. Mankiewicz took care to project the beauty of the language as clearly as the excitement of the plot, aided in this respect by Gielgud (Cassius) and James Mason (a magnificent Brutus). The Academy was less then generous with its Oscars, awarding only the art direction of Cedric Gibbons and Edward Carfagno. Among the vast cast were Edmond O'Brien, George Macready, Tom Powers, Ian Wolfe, Lumsden Hare, Morgan Farley, Douglas Watson, Rhys Williams, John Lupton and Douglass Dumbrille.

Rendering unto Caesar: facing page: Nero's Palace in Quo Vadis *(top) and Louis Calhern as Caesar and Marlon Brando as Mark Antony in* Julius Caesar *(bottom); below: Charlton Heston and Yul Brynner in* The Ten Commandments

Cecil B. De Mille's second crack at **The Ten Commandments** was so festooned with publicity superlatives and money records that its audiences expected to be not so much entertained as stupefied. It was the longest (3 hours, 39 minutes), most expensive (over $13 million) picture in Paramount's history, and by topping $80 million world-wide, it returned more than three times the company's previous record receipts (with De Mille's *Greatest Show on Earth*) and beat all other pictures except *Gone with the Wind*. Production began in October 1954, when De Mille headed an immense location troupe at Mount Sinai, south of Cairo, where cinematographer Loyal Griggs trained four Technicolor-VistaVision cameras on 12,000 people for the exodus sequence. Shooting continued into 1955 on twelve sound stages in Paris and eighteen in Hollywood, spilling over from Paramount to the RKO studio next door, and in 1956 De Mille's perennial film editor, Anne Bauchens, completed nine months' work on it. The story of Moses, which in the producer-director's 1923 *The Ten Commandments* was little more than a prologue for a modern tale, had been expanded by Aeneas MacKenzie, Jesse Lasky Jr, Jack Garris and Frederic Frank, whose script was 'based on the Holy Scriptures and other ancient and modern writings'. Charlton Heston, unsurpassed among Hollywood actors in giving biblical epics credibility, led the Israelites and a cast including Yul Brynner, Anne Baxter, Edward G. Robinson, Yvonne De Carlo, John Derek, Debra Paget, Sir Cedric Hardwicke, Nina Foch, Judith Anderson, Vincent Price, Henry Wilcoxon (also associate producer), Martha Scott, John Carradine, H. B. Warner, Ian Keith, Douglass Dumbrille and John Miljan. And the verdict on the film itself? Undeniably impressive, even when the story seemed to be lasting as long as it took Moses to live it.

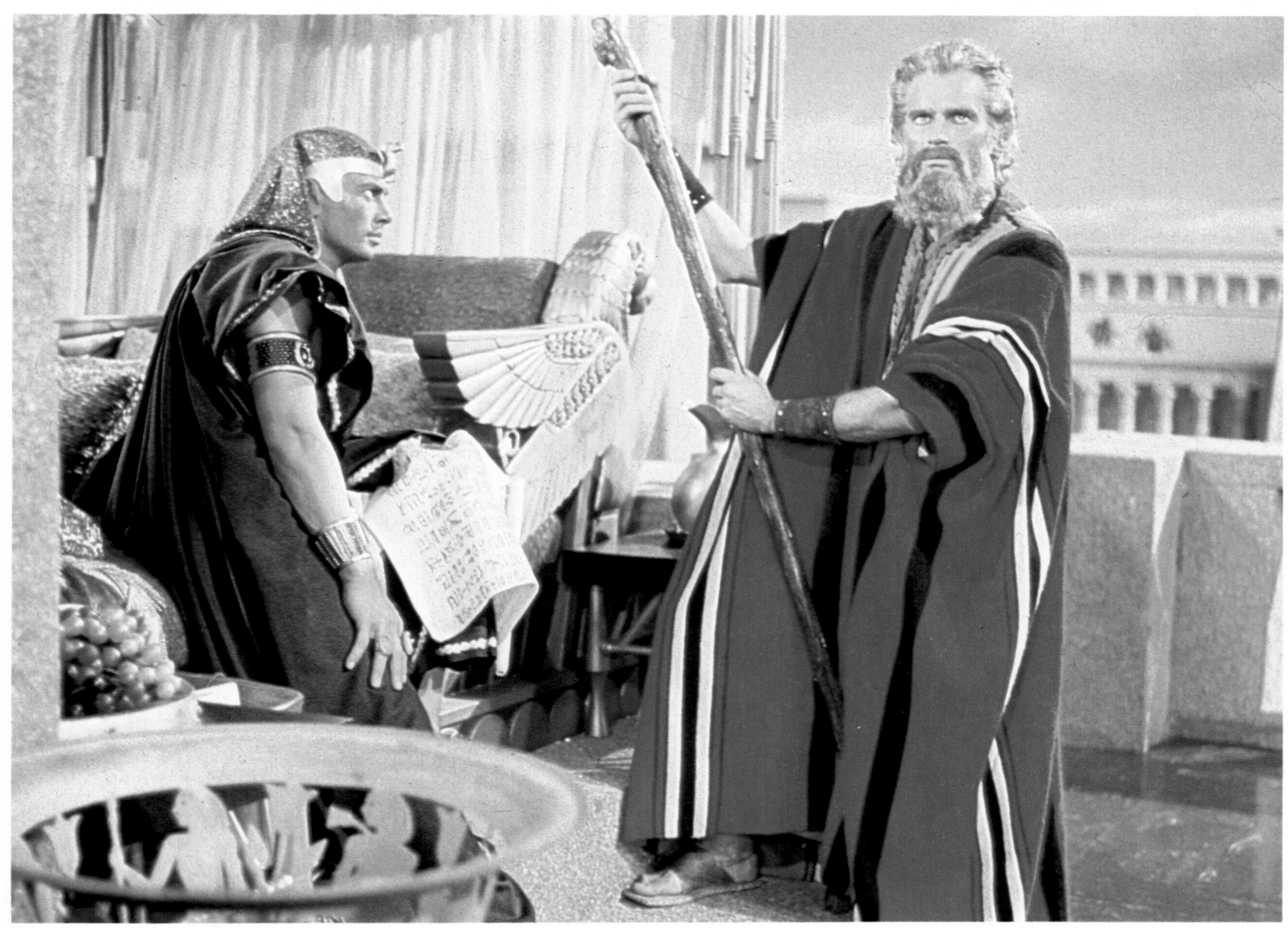

Two of the greatest strokes of good fortune in MGM's history were called **Ben-Hur**. In 1958 the continuance of MGM's prestige and its financial stability were risked with a $15 million investment in a remake of the same subject. A flop would have been disastrous. But its triumph was even more overwhelming than the original one; it brought MGM over $80 million in world-wide rentals. Then, in 1971, it had the biggest audience for a single screening of any film when it was seen by 32,630,000 Americans on TV. Those who pigeonhole it as just an inflated supercolossal may be surprised to know that it was received by the critics, almost without exception, as a masterly piece of film-making; praise was showered on every aspect of its production, and this welcome was echoed in the Academy's 1959 prizegiving. A record twelve Oscars were voted to it as the year's best picture and for best direction (William Wyler); actor (Charlton Heston in a portrayal of great spiritual and physical strength); supporting actor (Hugh Griffith); cinematography (Robert Surtees); scoring (Miklos Rozsa); editing (Ralph Winters, John Dunning); costumes (Elizabeth Haffenden); art direction (William Horning, Edward Carfagno); sound recording (Franklin Milton): visual effects (Arnold Gillespie, Robert MacDonald); and sound effects (Milo Lory). Those special effects were greatly responsible for the spectacular sea battle and the breathtaking chariot race sequences; they in turn were prime reasons for the phenomenal crowds it drew. It was produced in Rome by Sam Zimbalist, whose making of *Quo Vadis* there was a picnic in comparison; the mounting pressure of producing this now-or-never winner hastened his death shortly before its completion. Karl Tunberg got solo credit for a script also worked on by Christopher Fry (who was on the set with Wyler throughout), Maxwell Anderson, S. N. Behrman and Gore Vidal. Six 65-millimetre cameras were focused on its (give or take a thousand) 3,000 sets and 50,000 people, who included Stephen Boyd (at left, clashing with Heston in the chariot race) and Jack Hawkins, Haya Harareet, Martha Scott, Cathy O'Donnell, Sam Jaffe, Finlay Currie, Frank Thring, Terence Longdon, André

Morell, Marina Berti, George Relph, Lawrence Payne and Duncan Lamont. Important contributions were made by second unit directors Andrew Marton, Yakima Canutt and Mario Soldati.

It took $12 million and two years of intensive planning to bring Howard Fast's stirring novel, **Spartacus** (Universal, 1960), to the screen. Photographed by Russell Metty in Technicolor, and starring Kirk Douglas (illustrated foreground) as the eponymous hero, the end results justified the enormous expense. Directing a cast of heavyweight marquee names such as Laurence Olivier (as the sadistic patrician general Crassus), Jean Simmons (the slave girl Varinia), Charles Laughton (Republican senator Gracchus), Peter Ustinov (Batiatus, the fleshy dealer in gladiators) and Tony Curtis (Crassus' Italian houseboy Antoninus), Stanley Kubrick (then aged 31), in his fifth feature, brought as much visual sweep and dramatic emphasis to his epic subject as the Technirama 70 screen could comfortably contain, as well as some excessively violent scenes which it could not—such as Crassus' callous puncturing of a gladiator's neck, and the severing of a warrior's arm in a battle between Roman legions and slaves. For most of its fairly extensive running time, however, Kubrick wisely concentrated on the development of the personal relationships described in both the novel and in Dalton Trumbo's literate, deeply moving screenplay (his first since his blacklisting and imprisonment a decade earlier by the House Un-American Activities Committee) relegating the spectacle, if not exactly to the background (there was far too much of it for that), certainly to second place. What interested him more was his hero's courageous and inspiring struggle for freedom from a tyrannical and pagan regime; and, aided by Douglas' granite-strong performance, he succeeded. A Bryna Production (produced by Edward Lewis), it was filmed partially on location outside Madrid (where 8,000 Spanish soldiers doubled as Roman legionnaires) and in Hollywood. Secondary roles featured John Gavin, Herbert Lom, John Ireland, John Dall, and the physically overpowering Woody Strode who, in one of the film's most memorable sequences, unwillingly engages in a fight to the death with Spartacus, the latter wielding a stunted Thracian sword, the former a trident and net, to the sadistic delight of Roman noblewomen Nina Foch and Joanna Barnes. The film netted a massive $14,600,000.

Roman revels and rebels: top and inset left: the chariot race in Ben Hur*; above: Kirk Douglas as Spartacus leads the slaves in revolt*

• THE • ROMANTIC • AGE •

John Barrymore (right) gave Douglas Fairbanks' reputation as the screen's foremost acrobat and lover a decided jolt with **Don Juan**. Warner Bros.' first full-length Vitaphone excursion into sound (a music track by William Axt, appropriate sound effects, but no spoken dialogue). Theatres not wired for sound screened a silent version. Whether leaping on and off balconies to vouchsafe a promised rendezvous, scaling walls or thrusting himself bodily on to an opponent from the top of a flight of stairs, Barrymore cut a dashing figure and swashbuckled his way into the hearts of audiences across the country. A statistic-prone press agent recorded that, in the course of his romantic exploits, he favoured the women who comprised the cast with 191 kisses. Bearing the brunt of his adoration was Mary Astor seen here as Adriana della Varnese, with Estelle Taylor (as Lucretia Borgia), Myrna Loy, Phyllis Haver, and June Marlowe all getting their share of love as well. Also cast were Warner Oland as Caesar Borgia, and Willard Louis as Don Juan's faithful servant. Hedda Hopper appeared in a small

role. Barrymore wanted Dolores Costello to play Adriana, but as Mary Astor was already signed the studio did not wish to risk a second breach of contract suit and he was forced to capitulate. Opinions about the film itself were mixed, but as the hero and heroine literally rode off into the sunset, Jack Warner knew he was on to a winner. The film made a fortune and spurred the brothers in their efforts to pioneer sound pictures. Alan Crosland directed with just the right amount of dash and bravado. It was written by Bess Meredyth and beautifully photographed by Byron Haskin.

MGM's Barrymore idolatry reached its summit with **Rasputin and the Empress/Rasputin the Mad Monk** (1932), for which Irving Thalberg enticed Ethel Barrymore into the movies for the first time in fourteen years—and for the only time with her two brothers. Despite much frequent publicity fiction about their temperamental clashes, they worked together like good professionals, even when filming caught up with Charles MacArthur's rewrites. Director Richard Boleslawski allowed Lionel to do some scenery-chewing as Rasputin, and the Bernard Hyman production had a mixed reception. Diana Wynyard, Edward Arnold, C. Henry Gordon and Gustav von Seyffertitz also featured in the cast. There have been at least six other movies on the same subject; this one had the misfortune to be the cause of a celebrated libel suit brought against MGM in London by Prince and Princess Yousoupoff. They won record damages after convincing the court that, while the Prince was Rasputin's killer, as portrayed by John Barrymore, the Princess's rape by Rasputin was invented.

Barrymore at large: left: with Mary Astor in Don Juan*; below: with sister Ethel in* Rasputin and the Empress

Rouben Mamoulian had Garbo's movements timed to a metronome like a ballet for the lyrical 'I am memorizing this room' scene in **Queen Christina** (1933). After making *As You Desire Me* Garbo had taken a year off, mostly in Sweden, leaving the world (and not least MGM) in suspense about her possible retirement. A new and lucrative contract, with script, director, photographer and cast approval rights, brought her back. The romanticized story of Sweden's 17th-century queen became the star vehicle *in excelsis*; it was still getting profitable bookings 40 years later. Script was by Garbo's friend Salka Viertel (with S. N. Behrman and H. M. Harwood), direction by Mamoulian, photography by her favourite William Daniels; her leading man was John

Gilbert (replacing newcomer Laurence Olivier because she wanted to restore her old co-star's prestige). Production was by Walter Wanger. All was as Garbo desired it, and she responded with her finest performance to date. Lewis Stone, Ian Keith, C. Aubrey Smith, Akim Tamiroff and Reginald Owen supported reverently.

Camille: tragedy on the screen, tragedy at the studio. Before its completion, its producer, Irving Thalberg, died in September 1936 at the age of 37 and at the peak of his creative power. His associate and best friend, Bernard Hyman, finished the picture, with George Cukor continuing his superlative direction. Aware of their film's excellence and in tribute to Thalberg, an unprecedented MGM contingent attended its première, including Loew's Inc. President Schenck, Louis B. Mayer and—rarest of public appearances—Garbo. The applause has continued ever since and some consider that Garbo's performance is the finest on film. Certainly it was her best. The range of feeling expressed by the subtle play of her features and voice, from the flirtatious gaiety of the early sequences (here, with Robert Taylor respectfully passionate as Armand) to the feverish exhaustion of her dying, was screen acting of the highest order. In the best scene of all she and Henry Daniell, as her protector, bait each other with the knowledge that her new lover is waiting outside her door; their barbed dialogue, his piano playing and her sardonic laughter rise to a brilliant crescendo. Daniell delighted critics in the role Thalberg had intended for John Barrymore, who was ill; brother Lionel was present, though, to play Taylor's father. Jessie Ralph as the motherly maid and Lenore Ulric as the rival strumpet won praise, and minor roles were filled by Elizabeth Allan, Russell Hardie, E. E. Clive and Douglas Walton. The screenplay by Zoe Atkins, Frances Marion and James Hilton oiled the creaks out of the old Dumas story, and William Daniels surpassed himself in photographing the star.

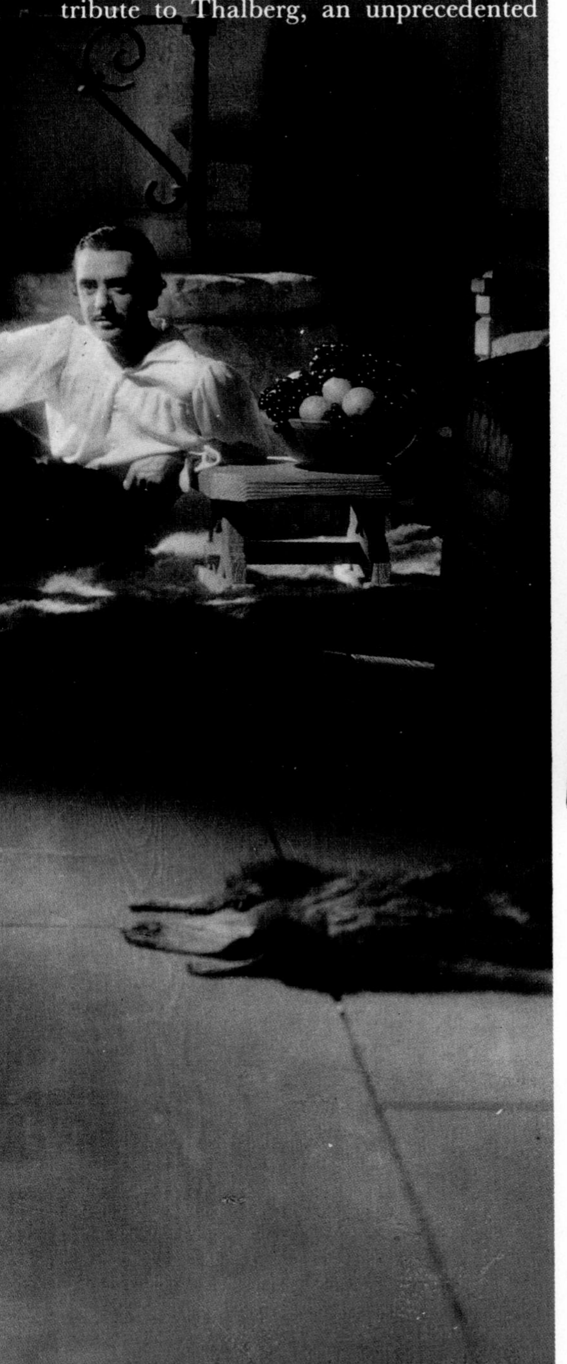

Garbo and two of her leading men: left with John Gilbert in Queen Christina, *above: with Robert Taylor in* Camille

Adapted for the screen by Casey Robinson from Rachel Field's best-seller, **All This and Heaven Too** (Warner Bros., 1940) took its time (140 minutes) to recount, in flashback, the true story of Henriette Desportes, a governess accused of having an affair with her employer, the Duc de Praslin, and participating in the murder of his wife. A subdued Bette Davis (below right) played the governess, Charles Boyer returned from France especially to appear as the Duc, and the supporting roles were filled by Virginia Weidler (on loan from MGM), Helen Westley, Walter Hampden, Henry Daniell, Harry Davenport, George Coulouris, June Lockhart (left) and Ann Todd (the American child actress, not the British star). Budgeted at $1,370,000 (the rights alone cost $100,000), producer Hal B. Wallis and his associate David Lewis had every confidence in director Anatole Litvak's ability to deliver them a hit. He did. (First National.) Song: *All This And Heaven Too* (by M. K. Jerome and Jack Scholl).

Carlo Ponti's 1965 production of Boris Pasternak's **Doctor Zhivago** gave MGM a selling problem: at first the masses couldn't pronounce the title or care less about Russian literature, and the discriminating were put off by decidedly mixed reviews. But gradually the movie was rescued by that most potent show-business asset, word-of-mouth praise, and it eventually became the company's second biggest moneymaker, ranking between *GWTW* and *Ben-Hur* with returns approaching $100 million. Even David Lean's genius for covering a lot of dramatic territory in one film was taxed by the vast scale of the novel and its abundance of characters and events. But he and his screenwriter Robert Bolt kept a firm grip on both the narrative and the audience's emotions for $3\frac{1}{4}$ hours, with very few lapses through over-condensing. Bolt's script, Freddie Young's photography, John Box's and Terry Marsh's art direction, Maurice Jarre's score (the theme was a best-seller) and Phyllis Dalton's costumes won Academy Awards. A huge cast included Omar Sharif as Zhivago, Geraldine Chaplin and Julie Christie (with him above), Rod Steiger, Alec Guinness, Tom Courtenay, Siobhan McKenna, Ralph Richardson, Rita Tushingham, Adrienne Corri, Geoffrey Keen, Gerard Tichy, Noel Willman. While its makers were mostly British, it was shot in Spain and Finland.

Below: All This and Heaven Too*; above and right: epic romance in* Doctor Zhivago

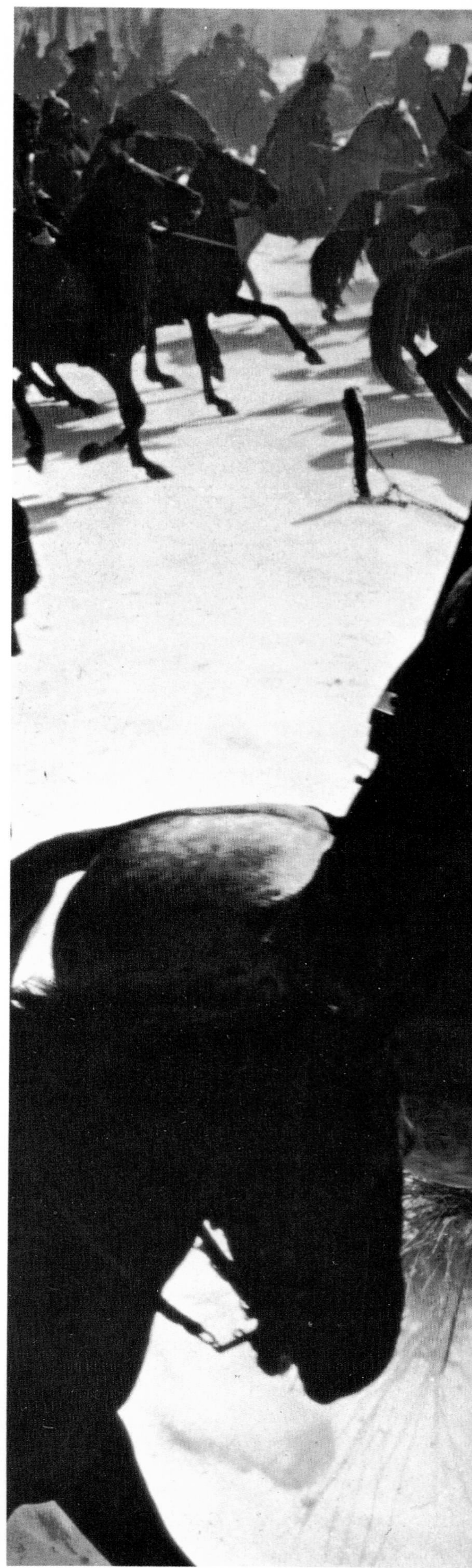

· OLDE · WORLDE ·

The RKO advertising department called **Gunga Din** (1939), 'too big for words!', and, for once, the hypercole was only slightly inflated. The studio had been endeavouring to make the film since 1936. Howard Hawks was originally scheduled to direct but casting difficulties postponed production, and Hawks lost out when company executives decided (during the filming of *Bringing up Baby*) that the director was too slow and too expensive for this epic. The dependable George Stevens inherited the project and was even slower and more painstaking than Hawks had ever been. When the dust settled, the final cost was a staggering $1,915,000, making **Gunga Din** the most expensive film RKO had ever made. Thankfully, it proved to be worth every cent. Composed of equal parts spectacle, adventure, suspense, humour and action, the picture remains one of the prime examples of the cinema of exhilaration. Its story seems remarkably coherent when one considers how many different writers contributed (final script credit was shared by Joel Sayre and Fred Guiol, based on a story by Ben Hecht and Charles MacArthur and inspired by Rudyard Kipling's poem). The story told of sergeants McChesney (Victor McLaglen, centre) and Cutter (Cary Grant, left) of the Royal Sappers who are faced with the loss of their closest fighting and drinking pal, Ballantine (Douglas Fairbanks Jr, right) who is determined to marry Emmy Stebbins (Joan Fontaine) and quit the military. Interfering with Ballantine's plans is the revolt of the Thuggees, a murderous sect of religious fanatics, which threatens the safety of the British regiment, the surrounding area and, indeed, all of India itself. At the climax, Gunga Din (Sam Jaffe), a native water boy, blows a warning signal on his bugle, thus saving the lives of the three heroes as well as their regiment, but losing his own. Ballantine decides to remain in the army with his friends, and Gunga Din is made a posthumous corporal and buried with full military honours. A list of the important contributors to this film could go on forever, but a few names must be singled out: Henry Berman and John Lockert, whose dynamic editing heightened the excitement; Joseph August, whose photography transformed the area around Lone Pine, California, into authentic-looking Indian settings; and Alfred Newman, for the musical score. Also cast: Eduardo Ciannelli, Montagu Love, Robert Coote, Abner Biberman and Lumsden Hare.

Writer-producer-director Stanley Kubrick's long and loving adaptation of Thackeray's novel **Barry Lyndon** (Warner Bros., 1975) proved to be one of the screen's most sophisticated recreations of the 18th century sensibility. The novel itself was written by a 19th century writer

Right: pipe dreams for Ryan O'Neal (with Marisa Berenson) in Barry Lyndon*; below: dreams of Empire for Cary Grant, Victor McLaglen and Douglas Fairbanks Jr in* Gunga Din

with Kubrick adding an extra dimension to it. What emerged, therefore, was a 20th century view of 18th century England. By relying on the great English landscape and portrait painters of the 18th century for his inspiration, Kubrick was forced to break new technical ground in order to capture the lighting of the canvases and the glow of candlelit rooms, and to this end he was magnificently assisted by production designer Ken Adam, cameraman John Alcott and art-director Roy Walker. However, the film was not only a pictorial, but also a social document, as could be seen from Kubrick's technique of starting almost every sequence with a long-shot then gradually moving in to close-up to show that the life within those frames was often hard and cruel. The picaresque story concerns a young Irish lad, Barry Lyndon (Ryan O'Neal, above) trying to gain a higher place in life. His adventures begin when he flees from a duel and enlists in the British army. Motivated by ambition but without much sense of morality, he deserts the army, and by marrying a wealthy widow (Marisa Berenson) whom he badly mistreats, finds himself the owner of a great stately home. But greed, egotism and his unbridled ambition soon get the better of him, and thus begins his downfall—as spectacular, in its own way, as his rise. He ends in ruin, alone, destitute and minus a leg. There were splendid supporting performances from Patrick Magee as a double dealer and Murray Melvin as the Reverend Runt—with good work, too, from Frank Middlemass, Hardy Kruger, Steven Berkoff, Andre Morell, Leonard Rossiter and Michael Hordern. Ryan O'Neal, however, was miscast in the title role, and totally unable to suggest the ambiguities at the heart of the character. And for a film whose keynote was authenticity, O'Neal's accent was a severe blemish on Kubrick's otherwise meticulously prepared canvas.

• LET • US • NOW • PRAISE • FAMOUS • MEN • AND • WOMEN •

Paul Muni's portrayal of the passionate struggle against prejudice and hostility in **The Story of Louis Pasteur** (1936) kindled the studio's faith in prestige biopics, an area of film-making hitherto held in disregard by the Warner hierarchy. In fact, so certain was Jack Warner that the Pasteur film would fail, he allocated a budget of no more than $330,000 to supervisor Henry Blanke—a pitifully small amount for an important production. Even the sets were doctored leftovers, including the Academy of Science amphitheatre which was a re-dressed nightclub from a Busby Berkeley production number. But Muni's (illustrated) dedicated, awesomely intelligent performance as the scientist pursuing a cure for anthrax and hydrophobia, aligned to Sheridan Gibney and Pierre Collings' dignified screenplay resulted in triumph for all concerned—on both sides of the camera. The superb photography was by Tony Gaudio and the purposeful direction by William Dieterle. Josephine Hutchinson co-starred as Madame Pasteur. Anita Louise was his daughter Annette, with other roles going to Donald Woods, Fritz Leiber, Henry O'Neill, Porter Hall, Akim Tamiroff and six-year-old Dickie Moore.

Paul Muni as Louis Pasteur (below) and (top right) as Emile Zola. Opposite page: Henry Fonda as the future President in Young Mr Lincoln

Hal B. Wallis' superb production of **The Life of Emile Zola**, in which Paul Muni gave a towering performance as Zola under William Dieterle's intensely-felt direction, emerged as that *rara avis*: a prestigious as well as a financially successful film. No expense was spared in the recreation of period detail, and the film was the first ever to win an Academy Award as Best Film of 1937 for Warner Bros. If only for its powerful recreation of the 'I accuse' courtroom scene, it deserved the soubriquet 'classic'. It was written by Norman Reilly Raine, Geza Herczeg and Heinz Herald whose screenplay elicited flawless performances from Joseph Schildkraut (as Dreyfus), Gale Sondergaard, Gloria Holden, Donald Crisp, Erin O'Brien Moore, John Litel, Henry O'Neill, Morris Carnovsky, Louis Calhern and Ralph Morgan. Henry Blanke supervised. An interesting sideline is that not once, throughout the Dreyfus affair, was the word 'Jew' mentioned.

Young Mr Lincoln (Fox, 1939) was the film which did more than any other to make a star out of Henry Fonda. Up to this point he had been very definitely No. 3 at Fox, behind Tyrone Power and Don Ameche. Director John Ford's casting of him as the future President was an inspired gamble: not only does he turn in a low-key performance which preserves Lincoln's dignity without embalming it in reverence, but the resemblance is close enough for the actor not to have to disappear behind excessive make-up. The screenplay, by Lamar Trotti, is about the young Abe Lincoln, a country lawyer pleading his first case (he defends two brothers on a murder charge and gets them off), whose first love ends in tragedy when his sweetheart, Ann Rutledge (Pauline Moore) dies. An ordinary country boy, in fact. But hints of destiny are there too, in Alfred Newman's musical score, and in the marvellous closing sequence. Here Ford makes use of a fortuitous thunder storm for an image of the gangling figure riding away in his stove-pipe hat—an image which dissolves into a shot of the Lincoln Memorial in Washington. Ford claimed that Fox cut his best moment of hinted destiny, though—a chance encounter between the young Lincoln and the young John Wilkes Booth, his future assassin. Bert Glennon was behind the camera, Kenneth Macgowan produced with Darryl F. Zanuck as Executive Producer, and Alice Brady, Marjorie Weaver and Ward Bond in the cast.

Gandhi (Indo-British Films, 1982), the life story of the father of modern India, represented the culmination of a 20-year dream for its director, Sir Richard Attenborough. After years of struggling to raise the money for what everyone thought a hopelessly uncommercial idea, the film was finally launched with the help of the Indian Film Development Corporation—something which raised a few hackles in India. It went on to record-breaking successes at the world's box offices and at the Oscar ceremony, where it won more statuettes than had ever been awarded to a non-American film (Best Picture, Director, Actor, Original Screenplay, Cinematography, Editing, Costume Design and Art Direction). John Briley's screenplay brilliantly compresses the Mahatma's life, sometimes at the expense of detailed historical understanding but never at odds with the spirit of its subject. What really accounted for the film's success—apart from the tenacious sincerity which Attenborough's direction endowed on it—was Ben Kingsley's extraordinary performance in the title role. Kingsley, a virtually unknown stage actor in his forties, had in fact been born in India, and his performance exactly captures the saintly obstinacy of Gandhi. Other Oscar winners were Billy Williams and Ronnie Taylor (Cinematography), John Bloom (Editing), John Mollo and Bhanu Athaiya (Costumes) and Bob Laing (Art Direction). Candice Bergen, Edward Fox, John Gielgud, Trevor Howard, John Mills, Martin Sheen, Ian Charleson and Athol Fugard headed the cast.

Ben Kingsley as the Mahatma; facing page: Henry B. Walthall and Mae Marsh in Birth of a Nation

• BIRTH • OF • A • NATION •

Produced by the aptly named Epoch Production Corporation (a company set up by director D. W. Griffith and the Rev. Thomas Dixon Jr with the express purpose of filming the latter's novel, *The Klansman*) **Birth of a Nation** (1916) was the most distinctive milestone in the early history of the cinema. As the *New York Times* noted rather sourly, it marked the advent of the two-dollar movie. More importantly, the $100,000 Griffith reckoned it would take to make the story was unheard of by 1914 standards, and most established companies baulked at the cost, despite Griffith's enormous reputation as a director of prestige silent films. Dixon's novel tells the story of the Civil War and Reconstruction in the South from a frankly segregationist viewpoint: the Ku Klux Klan is the real hero of the film. As a result, the Boston opening was attended by a riot (which, of course, did nothing to harm the picture's box-office prospects!). The story of two families, the Camerons and the Stonemans, is interwoven with the history of the South. The Camerons are Southerners, and the Stonemans abolitionists. Phil Stoneman (Elmer Clifton) falls for Margaret Cameron (Miriam Cooper). Ben Cameron (Henry B. Walthall)—the ''Little Colonel'—is smitten with Elsie Stoneman (Lillian Gish), and finally rides to her rescue at the head of a detachment of Klansmen when she is besieged by a horde of marauding negroes. Though the message of the film 70 years on, is hard to take, Griffith's production still looks as impressive as ever. This is due to the massive, set-piece battle scenes; the historical facsimiles of Appomattox; the assassination of Abraham Lincoln and the burning of Atlanta. The cinematic technique is also years ahead of its time in the scene in which the 'little sister' (Mae Marsh) is pursued through the woods to her death. Griffith's regular cameraman, G. W. 'Billy' Bitzer, was responsible for the monumental task of photographing **Birth of a Nation**, and two future Hollywood directors can be glimpsed in small roles: Raoul Walsh as John Wilkes Booth, the man who shoots Lincoln; and Erich von Stroheim as a man who falls off a roof.

Innocent joys, juleps and Jezebel*: above:* Little Women*; below: Lionel Barrymore and Shirley Temple in* The Little Colonel. *Opposite: Bette Davis as the Southern siren*

Little Women was a smash hit in 1933, and one of the most important pictures ever produced by RKO. It revitalized interest in the 'classics' and in costume pictures, driving most of the Hollywood companies into a mad scramble to acquire similar type material. Production chief David O. Selznick decided to film Louisa May Alcott's episodic novel about the highs and lows of a New England family during the Civil War era, but he departed for MGM before it went into production. His successor Merian C. Cooper kept the project alive, assigned Kenneth Macgowan to produce, and squeezed extra funding to upgrade the cast. Returning from MGM to direct was George Cukor. He handled the Academy Award-winning adaptation by Sarah Y. Mason and Victor Heerman with such finesse that it firmly established his reputation as a major cinematic talent. Katharine Hepburn (above, back centre) topped the cast, playing tomboyish Jo, and received first class support from Joan Bennett (centre), Frances Dee (right) and Jean Parker (left) as her sisters Amy, Meg and Beth respectively. Paul Lukas, Douglas Montgomery, Edna May Oliver, Spring Byington, Henry Stephenson, John Davis Lodge, Samuel Hinds, Mabel Colcord and Marion Ballou also appeared in this nostalgic triumph, photographed in the style of finely-etched ferrotypes by master cinematographer Henry Gerrard. For once, RKO's timing was impeccable. Depression audiences were ripe for the film's evocation of life in a simpler, more innocent and auspicious world. In addition, the movie business had come under fire in 1932 and 1933 for presenting an abundance of violent and sexually titillating material. **Little Women** was just the kind of film the bluenoses felt should be produced. They proclaimed it, sent their children to see it, and made it part of school curricula. RKO was the ultimate beneficiary, amassing notable profits of $800,000 on this irresistibly entertaining picture.

The Little Colonel (Fox, 1935) was the Shirley Temple movie to end all Shirley Temple movies—the one in which, having watched tap-dancer Bill 'Mr Bojangles' Robinson do his famous routine up and down the stairs, the little superstar gets right in there and does a duet with him. Blessed with the largest budget yet to be lavished by 20th Century-Fox on their prodigy, it tells a simple tale of heartbreak and reconciliation during the Civil War. Lionel Barrymore plays the crusty old grandpa who disowns his daughter (Evalyn Venable) for consorting with a Yankee (John Lodge). Much to the puzzlement of the audience, he consistently resists the pleas of the Little Colonel to reunite the family. But soon his lips, like those of the audience, are trembling and tears are running down into his moustache. 'God, he made her just all by herself', comments 'Uncle Bill' Robinson on Miss Temple. The film does, in fact, amply demonstrate Miss Temple's unique qualities—an extraordinary professional skill (for anyone, let alone a six-year-old), both as an actress and as a dancer; and a warmth which, while never less than cute, was always short of being mawkish. The screenplay was by William Conselman, from a story by Annie Fellows Johnston. B. G. de Sylva produced and David Butler directed, doing his second in a stint of four Temple movies. The talented Arthur Miller was the cameraman.

'Half-angel, half-siren, all woman!' proclaimed the ads for **Jezebel**, the highly successful award-winning drama which Warner Bros. fashioned in 1938 for their frequently ill-used star Bette Davis. The film was the actress's compensation for Jack Warner's refusal to loan her to David O. Selznick for *Gone with the Wind.* Determined to out-Scarlett Scarlett, Davis totally committed herself to the role of Julie Marston, a wilful Southern belle who does everything in her considerable power to goad her fiancé (Henry Fonda) into jealousy, but who reforms when he is stricken with the plague. Fortunately, director William Wyler, aware of his leading lady's tendency to chew the scenery if given half a chance, restrained her mannerisms and toned down the energy quotient of her performance, while at the same time allowing none of the essential Davis magnetism to disappear in the process. The result was her finest performance to date and a second Oscar. In less talented hands, there can be little doubt that the rather trite story, based on a stage flop by Owen Davis and scripted by Clements Ripley, Abem Finkel and John Huston, with assistance from Robert Buckner, would have been faintly ludicrous. Apart from Wyler's painstaking attention to atmosphere and detail reflected in the overall quality of the film, and Miss Davis' towering central performance, the rather soggy plot was kept this side of credibility by Fay Bainter's sterling, Oscar-winning performance as Aunt Belle. George Brent was miscast as the rejected Buck Cantrell (but then, when wasn't he!). Margaret Lindsay once again played the part of the 'other woman', without much impact, while Spring Byington, Henry O'Neill, Gordon Oliver and John Litel contributed their usual solid performances. Max Steiner wrapped it all up in one of his most memorable scores. Hal B. Wallis was the executive producer, Henry Blanke his associate. The film cost the studio $1,073,000 to make, but its success justified the expense.

When **Gone with the Wind** had its world premiere in Atlanta on December 14, 1939, the movie event, despite the real tragedy that started its long run three months earlier, was news everywhere. It was the culmination of the most intensively publicized production ever filmed. The furore began in June 1936 when Margaret Mitchell's 1,037-page novel was published with instantaneous success (it passed the million-copy mark in six months). David O. Selznick bought the film rights four weeks later for $50,000—which eventually seemed so inadequate that he gave Miss Mitchell another $50,000. Although he intended it as the supreme achievement of the independent studio he founded in 1935 after leaving MGM, Selznick was soon forced to turn to Mayer for aid. It appeared that, while casting Scarlett O'Hara, the stormy heroine, had become an international pastime, no one would accept any actor but Clark Gable in the male lead—and he was firmly tied to Metro. Presented with these needs of his son-in-law, Mayer made one of his greatest business deals: for Gable and an investment of $1,250,000—less than a third of the total cost—MGM got the distribution rights and retained half the profits. (In 1944, after the demise of Selznick International, MGM acquired the film outright. By 1974 its estimated rentals totalled $150 million.) Meanwhile, Selznick had assigned George Cukor to direct and playwright Sidney Howard to do the screenplay, and launched a talent hunt for Scarlett that involved testing 1,400 unknowns and half the actresses in Hollywood. The first choice was Norma Shearer; a month later she announced her refusal, and the *New York Times* published an editorial regretting her decision! Leslie Howard and Olivia de Havilland were signed for the second leads. At last, in January 1939, Scarlett was won by Vivien Leigh, the English girl who had unknowingly tested for the

Selznick's south: Vivien Leigh and Clark Gable in GWTW. *Inset: Olivia de Havilland, Ward Bond, Gable and Leslie Howard. Opposite: RKO's south: Herbert Marshall, Teresa Wright and Bette Davis in* The Little Foxes

part by playing the flirt (and incurring Mayer's wrath) in *A Yank at Oxford*. By this time dozens of writers ranging from Ben Hecht to Scott Fitzgerald had worked on the script (it remained chiefly Sidney Howard's, but he died in an accident before it was screened and never saw the result) and scenes of Atlanta burning in the Civil War had been shot. Main production began on January 26 and ended on July 1. After the first few weeks Selznick replaced Cukor with Victor Fleming, who had a nervous breakdown ten weeks later; Sam Wood took over while he recovered, then they co-directed. Like Cukor, both were borrowed from MGM. Also working overtime under Selznick's painstaking supervision were William Cameron Menzies, production design; Ernest Haller, camera; Lyle Wheeler, art direction; Hal Kern and James Newcom, editing; Max Steiner, music; and more than 4,000 others including actors Thomas Mitchell, Barbara O'Neil, Victor Jory, Laura Hope Crews, Hattie McDaniel, Ona Munson, Harry Davenport, Ann Rutherford, Evelyn Keyes, Carroll Nye, Paul Hurst, Isabel Jewell, Cliff Edwards, Ward Bond, Butterfly McQueen, Rand Brooks, Violet Kemble-Cooper, Eric Linden and George Meeker. Among the many records it established were length (3 hours, 42 minutes, plus interval), Academy Awards (ten: to Selznick, Miss Leigh, Fleming, Sidney Howard, Miss McDaniel—the first black winner of an Oscar—Menzies, Haller, Wheeler, Kern and Newcom jointly, and the picture itself); and long runs (four years at London's Ritz, for example, with queues even during air raids). Having attracted more viewers to cinema and television screens than any other film ever made and given carefully spaced re-issues (with re-processed enlarged Technicolor prints in recent years), **Gone with the Wind** continues in its fifth decade to fill MGM's coffers.

RKO's association with famed producer Samuel Goldwyn began on a high note with **The Little Foxes** (1941), a picture meriting consideration as one of the finest adaptations of a play ever to be filmed The source was Lillian Hellman's brooding drama about greed and treachery eating away at a genteel Southern family. William Wyler's impeccable direction gave free rein to the manifold talents of Herbert Marshall, Teresa Wright, Richard Carlson, Dan Duryea and, especially, Bette Davis, who jolted Miss Hellman's characters to life in brilliant fashion. Although Tallulah Bankhead had created the central role of Regina Giddens on Broadway, the part seemed written for Davis, and she performed it with a relentless iciness that was heartstopping—and appropriate to the portrayal of a woman who, when her husband (who has refused her the money for a sordid business arrangement) has a coronary, stands back and allows him to die rather than fetch his medicine. It was one of the greatest achievements of a great actress. Patricia Collinge, Charles Dingle, Carl Benton Reid, John Marriott and Duryea all repeated their stage roles, and Jessie Grayson, Russell Hicks, Lucien Littlefield, Virginia Brissac, Terry Nibert, Henry 'Hot Shot' Thomas and Charles R. Moore were other cast members. Miss Hellman wrote the sulphuric screenplay with additional scenes and dialogue by Arthur Kober, Dorothy Parker and Alan Campbell, and Gregg Toland's deep-focus camerawork facilitated the stage to screen translation. Inspired by the Biblical reference to 'the little foxes which spoil the vines', the tale was cruel, cold and cynical but extraordinarily vivid and compelling. It towered above most of the other stabs at drama that issued from Hollywood studios during the year.

· FRONTIER · DAYS ·

Director Jack (John) Ford chose Western star Harry Carey (seen below) for his leading man in **The Outcasts of Poker Flat** (Universal, 1919), an adaptation, by H. Tipton Steck, of Bret Harte's celebrated story. Utilizing a plot-within-a-plot technique, the film featured Carey as the proprietor of a gambling hall in Arizona who cannot make up his mind whether to sacrifice the love he feels for his pretty ward (Gloria Hope) who he believes is in love with his buddy Tommy (Cullen Landis), or to try to win her for himself. Stumbling upon a copy of *The Outcasts Of Poker Flat*, he soon identifies with Harte's hero, John Oakhurst, whose predicament is similar to his own and, after reading all about Oakhurst (who befriends a girl on a steamboat, then magnanimously relinquishes her when a younger man claims her attention), Carey decides to fight for Miss Hope who, it turns out, has loved him all along. Ford was more successful with his re-creation of

a California mining colony circa 1850 than in his handling of the film's big set-piece—a patently phoney studio-bound snow sequence; but on this occasion action took second place to the slow development of the plot, the principal interest being in the eventual outcome of the narrative, and in the dual roles played by the three principals. It was remade in 1937 (RKO) and in 1952 (20th Century-Fox).

Cimarron, written by Howard Estabrook from the best-selling novel by Edna Ferber, was conceived as an epic project and its final cost ($1,433,000) far surpassed any previous RKO budget. Ambition was rewarded when the 131-minute film won the 1931 'Best Picture' Oscar, picked up two other Academy Awards (for Estabrook's script and Max Ree's art direction), and received many additional accolades (sadly, it would be the only RKO picture—with the exception of Sam Goldwyn's *The Best Years of Our Lives*, which the studio distributed in 1946—to win the top industry honour). Set in Oklahoma during the great land rush of 1889, and spanning its development to 1929, **Cimarron** top-starred Richard Dix (above, centre) as Yancey Cravat. Cravat, an American knight errant who champions the cause of the downtrodden (Indians included) through his actions and through the influential newspaper he publishes, is also a restless wanderer. He periodically leaves for years at a time, while his patient wife Sabra (Irene Dunne) carries on his newspaper and his fight for justice. Much of the film rested on Miss Dunne's able shoulders, and audiences were encouraged to suffer with her during her extended periods of abandonment, and to marvel at her spirit and fortitude. Obviously Edna Ferber, producer William Le Baron, and director Wesley Ruggles believed that the combination of Yancey's passion and Sabra's indomitability made America great. The large cast included Edna May Oliver, Estelle Taylor, Nance O'Neil, William Collier Jr, Rosco Ates, George E. Stone, Stanley Fields and Robert McWade. Despite all the publicity and kudos, the depressed business climate of the day wrecked the film's box-office performance, and **Cimarron** recorded a $565,000 loss. A major reissue in 1935 helped redress the balance. MGM later bought the property and remade it for release in 1960 with Glenn Ford and Maria Schell.

Destry Rides Again (Universal, 1939) is remembered as the one in which Marlene Dietrich, as saloon singer Frenchy, immortalized Frank Loesser and Frederick Hollander's song *See What The Boys In The Backroom Will Have*. It was also the one in which la Dietrich and Una Merkel tore into each other in a most unladylike manner over Mischa Auer's trousers. And, you may remember, it was the one in which second-billed James Stewart, cast as a mild-mannered sheriff's deputy with a dislike of guns, proved that underneath this sensitive exterior beat the heart of one of the West's true heroes! Though Felix Jackson, Gertrude Purcell and Henry Myers' screenplay (from the novel by Max Brandt) told a story no more powerful than how law and order were restored to the frontier town of Bottleneck, it was written with enough brio to disguise its basic thinness, directed by George Marshall with such unbridled gusto, and so irresistibly performed by its two stars that, in the end, it was not *what* happened but *how* it happened, that mattered. Brian Donlevy (foreground left) was in fine form as the villain of the piece, Charles Winninger played the local sheriff, and Samuel S. Hinds did well as the town's mayor, with other roles in producer Joe Pasternak's solid gold winner being played by Irene Hervey, Allen Jenkins, Warren Hymer, Billy Gilbert, Tom Fadden, Jack Carson, Dickie Jones and Ann Todd (not to be confused with the English actress). Two other numbers by Loesser and Hollander were also featured—*Little Joe The Wrangler* and *You've Got That Look.* The movie had been previously made in 1932 with Tom Mix. It was remade in 1950 as *Frenchie* with Shelley Winters as the singer and again, as *Destry,* with Audie Murphy

The brothers Frank and Jesse James, the villainous Bob Ford who betrayed them, the Glenville train and the Northfield, Minnesota, Raid have figured in at least a dozen films. All these elements are also included in 20th Century-Fox's 1939 **Jesse James**, brilliantly held together by director Henry King working from a script by Nunnally Johnson. But what made this film extra special was that it was based on historical facts assembled by Rosalind Shaffer and Jo Frances James, the great Jesse's granddaughter. She liked the finished film, but was heard to remark at the première that, 'it isn't Jesse'. And, indeed, it isn't: it is Tyrone Power; with Henry Fonda as Frank, John Carradine as Bob Ford and Randolph Scott as Will Wright. Darryl Zanuck produced it as a prestige film for his new star, Tyrone Power, using the expensive 'improved' Technicolor process. The James Gang are strongly romanticized, becoming mid-Western Robin Hood figures who are driven outside the law by the ruthless St Louis Midland Railroad (headed by a more than usually unpleasant Donald Meek), which takes the family's land and generally persecutes the simple folk of Missouri. In the film's more elegiac second half, the brothers are trapped by their own notoriety and are unable to turn from the paths of unrighteousness. Henry Hull, Nancy Kelly, Slim Summerville and Lon Chaney Jr (as a member of the gang) also figure. There was a 1940 sequel, *The Return of Frank James*, directed by Fritz Lang, and a remake, *The True Story of Jesse James/The James Brothers*, directed by Nicholas Ray in 1956.

Gone West: facing page: Harry Carey at Poker Flat (bottom) and Richard Dix in Cimarron *(top); above: Marlene Dietrich in* Destry Rides Again, *and below: Tyrone Power and Henry Fonda as the James Brothers*

'In one superbly expressive gesture', wrote the *New York Times'* Mordaunt Hall, a man rarely given to such eulogies, 'John Ford has swept away ten years of artifice and has made a motion picture that sings a song of camera.' **Stagecoach** (Walter Wanger, 1939) is the quintessential Western. It has John Wayne in his first real starring role and it is directed by John Ford, who had a great understanding of the genre. It has Indian attacks, Cavalry, a showgirl called Dallas with a heart of gold (Claire Trevor) and an old doctor (performed by Thomas Mitchell who won the Oscar for Best Supporting Actor), more interested in whisky than medicine, but able to extract a bullet or deliver a baby if the need arises. Above all, it is the first Ford Western to be shot among the mesas of Monument Valley, which is to the genre what Wembley is to soccer. The basic story—a stagecoach full of misfits crossing the New Mexico territory from Tonto to Lordsburg in 1884, right through Geronimo country—is not all that special. But Dudley Nichols' screenplay, from a story, *Stage to Lordsburg*, by Ernest Haycox, brought out all the basic conflicts around which great Westerns are built, and which can generally be resolved by honour and action—two things in which Wayne's Ringo Kid is an expert. The music, by Richard Hageman, Frank Harling, John Leipold and Leo Shuken, won an Oscar and the inimitable Andy Devine drove the stage. The film was remade by Gordon Douglas for 20th Century-Fox in 1966 with an expensive but wasted cast.

Until **They Died with their Boots on** (Warner Bros.) no film had attempted to tell the full story of George Armstrong Custer and his famous last stand. The part of Custer was a natural for Errol Flynn, whose salary in 1941 totalled $240,000, and whose ability to combine roguish spoilt-boy pranks with manly acts of heroism and valour, perfectly equipped him to fill the shoes of Custer, at least as seen by writers Wally Kline and Aeneas MacKenzie in their highly romanticized version of one of the most stirring (and futile) incidents in American history. Though Michael Curtiz was originally offered the directorial chores, Flynn's continuing vendetta with the fiery director resulted in Raoul Walsh being signed instead. Like Curtiz, Walsh was very much an action director: the climactic charge at the end of the film more than

On the move: below: Red River*; above: Flynn and De Havilland on the eve of Little Big Horn. Facing page: the stagecoach's passengers (Claire Trevor and John Wayne on the right)*

justified its build-up and was most effectively stage-managed. Appearing with Errol Flynn for the last time was Olivia de Havilland cast as his loving wife. Their scenes together had a poignancy matched only by their work together in *The Adventures of Robin Hood* (1938). Others in the cast included Arthur Kennedy, Charles Grapewin, Gene Lockhart, Anthony Quinn, Sydney Greenstreet, Regis Toomey, Hattie McDaniel and, in a small part, a newcomer called Byron Barr who soon changed his name to Gig Young. Hal B. Wallis produced: the associate producer was Robert Fellows.

Red River (Monterey Productions, 1948) was initially received by critics with restrained admiration, though it has latterly acquired the status of a classic. In general, they liked the scope, the action and the scenes with the cattle, but found the love interest rather soppy. Director Howard Hawks felt differently: 'After **Red River**,' he said, 'I'd had enough of all those cows, and wanted to work with human beings for a while.' The film tells the story of two men, Dunton (John Wayne) and Matt (Montgomery Clift), who have a kind of rumbustious father-son relationship. Dunton dreams of taking a herd of cattle from Texas, where beef is plentiful, to Missouri, where it commands a lot of money and can be shipped back East. When things come to a head, Matt takes over the cattle drive and diverts it to Abilene, where he has heard talk of a new railhead. Matt is thus responsible for one of the great breakthroughs of the West—the opening up of the Chisholm Trail. Like all great Westerns, **Red River** deals with simple situations but quite complex emotions. But it is the backgrounds—the ever-shifting sea of cattle, the big skies of the West, the physical obstacles that men and beasts have to overcome—that lift the film way above its rivals. The script was by Borden Chase and Charles Schnee from the former's novel, and the film was photographed by Russell Harlan. Joanne Dru, Walter Brennan, John Ireland, Noah Beery (Sr *and* Jr for good measure) and Hank Worden made up the cast.

Shortly after taking charge of RKO in 1948, Howard Hughes sold **The Outlaw**, a film he had produced independently, to his new company. The transaction would become a matter of controversy in later years, partially because **The Outlaw** was already one of the most controversial films in Hollywood history. The film was actually finished in 1941, but its release was postponed while producer-director Hughes fought an acrimonious battle with Joseph Breen's Production Code Administration which refused to grant the movie a Code Seal. Hughes arranged a token San Francisco exhibition in February 1943, and United Artists handled limited bookings in 1946. The RKO distribution was, in actuality, a re-release. All the *sturm und drang* revolved around the portrayal of the ample-bosomed Hughes discovery Jane Russell (illustrated). The picture's high-voltage scenes with Miss Russell, including one in which she got undressed and climbed into bed 'to warm' sickly Jack Buetel (his debut) had been excised by the time RKO became the distributor. This left a picture that was not very sexy, but was extremely bizarre. Jules Furthman's screenplay depicted the relationship between Billy the Kid and 'Doc' Holliday (Walter Huston). Before the story begins, Billy has stolen Holliday's horse, and the entire film becomes a contest between the two men for possession of the animal. Though both characters have the advantage of Rio's (Miss Russell's) affections, they consider her much less important than the sacred steed. Overlong, disjointed, weirdly parodic in its approach to Western movie conventions, and misogynistic to the core, **The Outlaw** was also visually stunning and eccentrically provocative. Gregg Toland shot the supple, mood-setting cinematography and Victor Young composed the generous musical score. Also cast: Thomas Mitchell as Sheriff Pat Garrett, Mimi Aguglia, Joe Sawyer and Gene Rizzi. Note: Howard Hawks directed the film for a short time before Hughes fired him and took over.

Winchester '73 (1950), Universal's answer to Warner's *Colt .45* (1950), was an altogether superior Western. Though basically little more than an oater which might accurately be summarized as man gets gun, man loses gun, man gets gun, it starred frontiersman James Stewart as the proud possessor of a Winchester model 73 rifle, won in a Dodge City marksmanship contest. It is stolen, however, by his own murderous brother (Stephen McNally), from whence it passes to an Indian chief, a gun trader, a pair of bank robbers, back to McNally, and, finally, after a showdown on a mountain precipice, into the hands of Stewart (below right, with rifle), its rightful owner. None of it was meant to be taken too seriously, and the result was an hour and a half of unfaltering entertainment, niftily scripted by Robert L. Richards and Borden Chase (from a story by Stuart N. Lake), with direction to match by Anthony Mann who, with a cast that also included Shelley Winters as a dancehall girl (and the rifle's only rival for Stewart's affections), Dan Duryea as a trigger-happy cut-throat (what else?), Will Geer as the marshal of Dodge City, John McIntire as a no-good Indian trader, and Jay C. Flippen as a cavalry sergeant, helped turn the picture into one of the year's most enjoyable Westerns. Aaron Rosenberg produced. It was remade for TV in 1970.

The Pacific Northwest in all its scenic splendour looked marvellous in Technicolor, and provided the handsome backdrop to Universal's **Bend of the River** (1952), an exciting, continually gripping outdoor actioner starring James Stewart (above, left) as the leader of a wagon train who, together with a group of settlers, moves through the wilderness into Oregon. Arthur Kennedy (on his right), as a former Missouri raider rescued from the gallows by Stewart, joins the group and, together with Stewart, picks off some marauding Indians en route; so does Rock Hudson (as a gambler). Julia Adams was second-billed as the (romantic) female lead, and shared Borden Chase's screenplay (based on Bill Gulick's novel *Bend Of The Snake*) with Lori Nelson, Jay C. Flippen, Stepin Fetchit, Henry Morgan, Chubby Johnson and Howard Petrie. The all-involving direction was by Anthony Mann and Aaron Rosenberg produced.

Guns and fast women: left: Jane Russell in The Outlaw*; above: James Stewart and Arthur Kennedy in* Bend of the River*, and below: Stewart in* Winchester '73

High Noon (Stanley Kramer, 1952) was that very rare thing—a Western which was a box-office triumph *and* won virtually boundless praise from critics and historians of the cinema. Its appeal as a popular winner relies on the superb way in which the director, Fred Zinnemann, builds up the tension as the clock ticks away the minutes to noon and the arrival of the train bearing the Miller boys. Dimitri Tiomkin and Ned Washington's Oscar-winning song ('Do Not Forsake Me, O My Darling..'), sung by Tex Ritter, helped too. What won **High Noon** its critical acclaim, though, was its psychological depth and the fact that, because it was written by Carl Foreman, who was blacklisted just after he completed it, it was bound to be seen as an indictment of the McCarthy era. The sheriff, Will Kane (Gary Cooper), stands up for what he believes is right while everyone else hides or flees (there is a wonderful shot of the Judge wrapping up his scales of justice, his law books and the American flag prior to departure). Having dispatched the Millers—with a little help from his new bride, Amy (Grace

Kelly)—Cooper flings his tin star into the dust and rides out. Miss Kelly's performance, much praised at the time, is rather overshadowed these days by that of Katy Jurado as Helen Ramirez, the firebrand he ditches for cool, clean Amy. Thomas Mitchell and Lloyd Bridges also feature, and future spaghetti Western star Lee Van Cleef may be glimpsed as a member of the feared Miller gang. Gary Cooper, the score, the song and the editing were all Oscar winners.

The fifth collaboration between producer Aaron Rosenberg, director Anthony Mann and star James Stewart resulted in **The Far Country** (Universal, 1955), a rugged and exhilarating Western whose entertainment value derived from Stewart's central performance, Borden Chase's intelligent screenplay, Mann's gritty direction and the stunning scenery (in Technicolor) provided by the Canadian Rockies, the Columbia ice-fields and Jaspar National Park. Stewart (right, standing), together with his partner Walter Brennan, arrives in Canada via Wyoming with a herd of cattle. The pair hope to sell the herd at inflated prices to the gold-crazy citizens of Dawson and Skagway, thus pocketing enough money to return to Utah and open a ranch. They haven't, however, reckoned with John McIntire, the self-styled 'lawman' of Skagway, who grabs hold of Stewart's herd before it reaches Dawson. Then, when Brennan is shot by one of McIntire's claim-jumpers, the hitherto laid-back, characteristically laconic Stewart lets rip in time for a rootin'-tootin'-shoot-out that climaxes the film. Ruth Roman plays a saloon keeper with a yen for Stewart, but the woman who finally nabs him is Corinne Calvet as a hoydenish French-Canadian girl of the goldfields. Jay C. Flippen was prominently featured as a booze-loving pal of the hero, with other roles going to Henry Morgan, Steve Brodie, Connie Gilchrist and Chubby Johnson.

One of John Ford's best films, **The Searchers** (Warner Bros., 1956), eschewed the fast-developing trend towards psychological Westerns and concentrated instead on all the traditional elements of the genre. It did, however, make a tentative attempt to deal with the problem of racism and, in that respect, was something of a breakthrough for its aggressively right-wing director. And, in a sense, for its star John Wayne who, in the role of Ethan Edwards, gave his most densely-conceived performance to date—better, even, than his work in Howard Hawks' *Red River*. Wayne joins forces with Jeffrey Hunter (a half-breed) in a five-year search for his young niece (Natalie Wood) who was abducted by Indians two years after the Civil War. Ford's handling of all the relationships was subtler, more economical than anything he had done previously, and the performances he got from Jeffrey Hunter, Natalie Wood, Vera Miles and Ward Bond were excellent. Written by Frank S. Nugent (from the novel by Alan Le May) and filmed in VistaVision and Technicolor, the C. V. Whitney Production, under Merian C. Cooper's supervision, was one of the great Westerns of the decade.

Running, but not scared: left: Gary Cooper (with Bridges, Jurado and Kelly) in High Noon*; below: James Stewart in* The Far Country. *Inset: John Wayne in* The Searchers

The irresistible combination of two such high-powered stars as Burt Lancaster and Kirk Douglas and a title as stimulating as **Gunfight at the O.K. Corral** (Paramount, 1957) had all but Western-haters lining up at box-offices around the world. The oft-told tale of intrepid Marshal Wyatt Earp and tubercular gambler Doc Holliday joining forces against the wicked Clanton gang has not oft been told as well as this. Producer Hal Wallis surrounded Lancaster as Earp and Douglas as Holliday (both actors he had helped starwards in the Forties) with equally strong talents: John Sturges, who had recently scored with *Bad Day at Black Rock*, directed; best-selling novelist Leon Uris wrote the script; and Oscar-winning Jo Van Fleet was memorable as the woman who had a hard time with Doc. Rhonda Fleming, John Ireland, Earl Holliman, Lyle Bettger, Frank Faylen and Kenneth Tobey were others on hand. The promise of the big showdown in the title was fulfilled: the Clantons needing enough bullets and blood-letting for a small war before they bit the dust—in Technicolor and VistaVision of course.

Originally a television play by Gore Vidal, **The Left-Handed Gun** (Warner Bros., 1958) was a 'psychological' Western whose lack of action in telling how a homosexual Billy the Kid goes after the four men who killed his pal was slow-moving, and somewhat 'arty'. Producer Fred Coe and director Arthur Penn's intentions to turn what was basically a routine revenge story into something more significant, were to be respected, but not the way they went about it. Paul Newman (above, right) starred as Billy. His performance was the victim not only of the direction and screenplay (by Leslie Stevens), but of his own 'method' mumblings which slowed down the proceedings even further. A Harroll Production, it also featured Lita Milan, John Dehner. Hurd Hatfield, John Dierkes, James Best and Colin Keith-Johnston.

Winners and losers: above: The Left-Handed Gun; *below:* Gunfight at the O.K. Corral.

Cinerama joined forces with MGM to tell a story: **How the West was Won**. After ten years of cashing in on sheer size, it needed a shot in the arm. This widest of wide-screen processes (using three linked cameras in production and three projectors in specially adapted theatres to fill the field of vision) had exhausted its travelogue possibilities. Completed in 1962, the massive production by Bernard Smith covered the adventures of a pioneering family with enough plot twists to equip a dozen movies. It was a prodigious money's worth—and worth about $50 million in world rentals. Much of this came from non-Cinerama theatres, which were provided with conventional reels for one projector. Unfortunately they still showed the joins necessitated by Cinerama's triple width; incredibly, no single-camera version had been shot. Spencer Tracy's voice linked the episodes directed by Henry Hathaway, John Ford and George Marshall and enacted by a large cast including Karl Malden, Carroll Baker, Debbie Reynolds and Agnes Moorehead and not forgetting the following: Henry Fonda, James Stewart, Gregory Peck, John Wayne, George Peppard, Richard Widmark, Robert Preston, Carolyn Jones, Lee J. Cobb, Eli Wallach, Raymond Massey, Thelma Ritter, Walter Brennan, Brigid Bazlen, David Brian, Andy Devine, Russ Tamblyn, Henry Morgan and Mickey Shaughnessy. Writer James R. Webb, film editor Harold Kress and the MGM sound department won Academy Awards.

Ride the High Country/Guns in the Afternoon (MGM, 1962) has a special place in the history of Westerns. After joining forces for it, Randolph Scott and Joel McCrea, two of the most durable stars, went into wealthy retirement—

top: How the West was Won, *and bottom:* Ride the High Country

Scott was reputed to be Hollywood's richest actor. And it was also the first cinema success for director Sam Peckinpah, long a maker of television Westerns. Unexpectedly a winner of critics' raves and international awards, it had wry humour in its N. B. Stone Jr script about two tired lawmen going into action again and finding many excitements in their last adventure. Richard Lyons produced, with Mariette Hartley, Ronald Starr, Edgar Buchanan, R. G. Armstrong, John Anderson, L. Q. Jones, Warren Oates, James Drury and John Davis Chandler in the cast.

Into his super-spaghetti Western's 165 minutes of shoot-'em-up action director Sergio Leone crammed elements of virtually every similar winner ever filmed, not least the violence of his Clint Eastwood *Dollar* movies. The resulting **Once Upon a Time in the West** (Paramount, 1969) fell short of his epic goal, but crowded audiences enjoyed a feast of blood-splattered excitement. Claudia Cardinale and Charles Bronson starred. There is also a big surprise among the clichés: Henry Fonda cast as a vicious villain, coldly wiping out an entire family to be finally confronted with the only one left, a child. Killer and innocent stare at each other then Fonda coldly blasts him point blank and rides away, leaving Jason Robards to be falsely accused of the slaughter. Leone actually shot some scenes in America for the first time but his sociological approach still held the film apart from the homegrown Western. Keenan Wynn, Lionel Stander, Paolo Stoppa and Jack Elam acted in the Leone-Sergio Donati screenplay, produced by Fulvia Morsella.

Butch Cassidy and the Sundance Kid (Campanile Productions, 1969) was the kind of mixture that could hardly fail. It had two superstars (Paul Newman and Robert Redford) at the peak of their fame, a girl (Katherine Ross) who could shoot as well as cook and who rode around on a new-fangled contraption called a bicycle, plus an Oscar-winning song, *Raindrops Keep Fallin' On My Head* (by Burt Bacharach and Hal David) which has become part of the musical wallpaper. William Goldman's Oscar-winning screenplay is based on the supposedly true tale of two outlaws at the turn of the century. Butch is a talkative romantic, Sundance a more conventional Western hero (though one who can't swim!), but their career of crime is as likely to lead to fiasco as to financial reward. When they attempt to blow up a safe on a train, they blow up the whole railroad car instead. When the US gets too civilized and they emigrate to Bolivia, their first bank hold-up is thwarted because their Spanish phrase book omits such useful instructions as, 'Hands up!' and, 'Over against the wall!' In common with other 1960s Westerns, the film has a distinct end-of-an-era feel to it: the great days of the West—and the Western— are over. But audiences flocked to see it, and it was one of the decade's most successful films, creating a whole new vogue for drooping moustaches. A rather engaging prequel, *Butch and Sundance: The Early Days* was made by Richard Lester in 1979, but it didn't cause many ripples. John Foreman produced. Conrad Hall won an Oscar for cinematography. Henry Jones, Jeff Corey and Cloris Leachman provided the supporting cast.

CRIME & PUNISHMENT

There is one place where crime has always paid, and that is at the cinema box office. Ever since D. W. Griffith had the degenerate Snapper Kid terrorize the Little Lady (Lillian Gish) and her beloved in his 1912 two-reeler, *The Musketeers of Pig Alley*, audiences have flocked in for their trips to the underworld. On the face of it, crime movies have generally been socially conscious things, with the Production Code ensuring that the criminals get their come-uppance in the end, and that the good guys get the girl. But the criminals somehow seemed more attractive than their victims, and not infrequently more honourable than the cops: who, after all, has ever heard the phrase 'There's honour among cops'?

Ever since then, Hollywood has carried out a kind of ambiguous flirtation with the world of the criminal: gangsters are, after all, people who appreciate the good things in life, like money and drink and fast cars. The other guys are rather dull. As Tommy Powers (James Cagney) says dismissively of his hard-working, up-standing brother in *The Public Enemy* (1931), 'Ah, that sucker! He's too busy going to school. He's learning how to be poor!' Audiences didn't want to be poor, even when, in the heyday of the great gangster films, during the days of the Depression, they almost invariably were.

More to the point, audiences didn't want to be suckers, and for quite a while in the early 1930s it looked as though playing it by the rules was a sucker's game. Al Capone was earning a reputed $2 million a week while working folk queued for handouts. Wasn't there a lesson there somewhere? It was not, of course, a lesson that Hollywood ever explicitly taught. All the gangster films end badly for their gangster heroes (until *The Getaway* in 1972, that is). And just in case the message wasn't quite clear, the Hays Office—Hollywood's own censor—often insisted that a title appear before or after the film, sometimes both. Having first insisted that the initial release title be changed from the punchy *Scarface* to the soggy *Scarface: The Shame of the Nation*, for instance, the Hays Office also insisted that the following title should be shown at the start of the 1932 film: 'Every incident in this picture is a reproduction of an actual incident. What are you going to do about it? The Government is your Government. What are you going to do about it?' With a neat side-step, the producers of *Scarface* managed to suggest that the film was a plea for the Government to move against organized crime. It wasn't, of course, or at best was so only in part. What it really did was play on the public's interest in crime in order to get the public to part with its dollars at the paybox. Quite a good little con in its own right, in fact.

There was another, more deeply-rooted, reason for the public's fascination with crime movies. It is not by chance that the great crime movies stem from the heart of the Great Depression. American society had been more or less built on the notion of continuous growth, and of every man's chance to succeed if he worked hard enough. The Depression disproved that dream, or at the very least put it on ice for a few years. And those were the years of the gangster film. In the world of the gangster—of *The Public Enemy*'s Tommy Powers, *Scarface*'s Tony Camonte and *Little Caesar*'s Rico Bandello (played, respectively, by James Cagney, Paul Muni and Edward G. Robinson)—effort still paid dividends. Even (or especially) if the

effort was not channelled along the strictest of legal lines. The gangsters always got it in the end, but somehow that was not the important bit. At least they were *doing* something. In the best American tradition, they were not letting the system beat them. In Britain, there has never been quite the same concern with beating the system (though the intense interest which surrounded the Great Train Robbery of 1963 had some of that about it). American audiences, however, have responded with something close to admiration to those who wouldn't lie down, giving rise to what a Federal agent in a 1935 movie (*Special Agent*) refers to disparagingly as 'the public's half-baked hero worship of the tough guy'.

At the core of this chapter is a portrait gallery of vicious hoods who somehow caught the public's imagination in a vice-like love-hate relationship, starting with a pair of Warner Bros. films that were shot simultaneously in the company's two Los Angeles studios in early 1931—*Little Caesar* and *The Public Enemy*. It is no coincidence that most of the films in this section (and nearly half those in the chapter as a whole) come from Burbank. Warners developed and refined the crime movie in the 1930s just as MGM developed and refined the musical in the 1950s. In less attractive vein come a psychopath: Jimmy Cagney in *White Heat* (1949), for whom the love-hate relationship is with his Ma and a pair of pretty people on the run and killing with gay abandon (*Bonnie and Clyde*, 1967).

America, of course, is the home of private enterprise, and the private detective has always been more popular there than the cop. No moviegoer, after all, has ever been booked for speeding by a private eye. So, here we have a gallery of the best—and the worst—from Nick and Nora Charles (not forgetting Asta the Dog) in *The Thin Man* (1934) to Sam Spade (*The Maltese Falcon*, 1941), along with a couple of Philip Marlowes—Dick Powell (*Murder, My Sweet*, 1945) and Humphrey Bogart (*The Big Sleep*, 1946), the appalling Mike Hammer (*Kiss Me Deadly*, 1955), that screwed-up child of the 1960s, John Klute (1971) and the bemused J. J. Gittes (Jack Nicholson), lifting the lid off LA's civic corruption in *Chinatown* (1974).

As if to prove that women needed men more than men needed women, Hollywood produced occasional sagas of women trying to make it alone and getting into trouble. By far the best of these is *Mildred Pierce* (1945) in which Joan Crawford's performance carried a much stronger message than the film's ending. With *The Postman Always Rings Twice* (1948), Lana Turner helped to establish beyond a doubt that a bad woman will always bring a good man down. To balance the books in Miss Turner's case her version of *Madame X* (1966) is also included in this chapter.

The chapter ends with a group of films which have criminal behaviour of one kind or another as their theme—whether the subject is the American gutter press or robbery in Northern Ireland—but which use it as a metaphor for something bigger. Of course, all crime movies could probably be called metaphors, both for the problems of society against which, in a particularly dramatic way, the criminal is rebelling, and for the inadequacies of the individual which the criminal simply has on a larger scale than the rest of us. Audiences obviously love crime movies because they are exciting and full of action. But, often we love them because the people in them are, to use the title of a great crime novel from the late 1940s (twice filmed), *Thieves Like Us*.

· TALES · FROM · THE · · UNDERWORLD ·

The uplifting message of **Outside the Law** (1921), an eight-reel Jewel Production written, produced and directed by Tod Browning, was 'virtue is its own reward'. It starred Priscilla Dean (below, left) as a society crook known as 'Silky Moll'. Her co-star was Wheeler Oakman (centre) and, for much of Lucien Hubbard's scenario (story by Browning), the couple can't decide whether to continue their crooked life-styles or to go straight. In reel eight they opt for the latter. Plot took second place to Browning's vigorous depiction of his underworld milieu, with an all-out, no-expense-spared brawl in a Chinese restaurant being the film's big set-piece. Miss Dean received some of the best notices of her career for her work as 'Silky', but, thief though she was, couldn't quite match third-billed Lon Chaney (right) when it came to scene-stealing. In the dual role of arch-hood Black Mike Sylva, and Ah Wing, a Confucius disciple who teaches Dean and Oakman how to play it straight, Chaney notched up his greatest triumph to date, proving, at the same time, what a wizard he was with make-up (a climactic double exposure scene at the film's close has Black Mike stopping a bullet fired by Ah Wing). A child actor called Stanley Goethals, referred to as 'that kid' in the credits, also received critical attention, and the cast was completed by Ralph Lewis (as Miss Dean's father, a one-time crook), E. A. Warren, Melbourne McDowell and Wilton Taylor. It was remade in 1930.

When MGM opened shop, it found some problem items on the shelves stocked by former proprietors. A major one was Erich von Stroheim's **Greed**, which he had finished shooting for the Goldwyn company in 1923. A year passed before its release, during which time it was cut from its original, impossible 42 reels (about four times as long as a long film should be) to 24. At this stage von Stroheim baulked, saying that this was his masterpiece and it would be ruined by further editing. He was half right: it was his masterpiece, but it wasn't ruined even after he allowed Rex Ingram to cut six reels and June Mathis, without his permission, whittled off eight more. It was an unremittingly realistic filming of a sordid novel, Frank Norris' *McTeague*, first done by World Films in 1915, and dealt with sleazy characters obsessed by money-love to the point of insanity. In a company and an industry dedicated to mass entertainment, **Greed** was a freak, and, just as Louis B. Mayer predicted, audiences found it repellent: it never recovered its cost. Nevertheless, it stands among the memorable artistic achievements of Hollywood. ZaSu Pitts (facing page, left with Dale Fuller) gave a dramatic performance of harrowing intensity as McTeague's wife, murdered for the money she hoarded. Von Stroheim's script also spotlighted Gibson Gowland (McTeague) and Jean Hersholt.

Right: a scene from Erich von Stroheim's Greed.
Below: the very early Outside the Law

The Godfather (1972), the picture that raised the gangster drama to epic proportions, had two outstanding performances: Marlon Brando as the patriarch of a family which dominated organized crime in America, and Al Pacino as his youngest son, a college boy who had to take a post-graduate course in killing. An instantaneous smash-hit, it returned about $150 million in world-wide rentals to Paramount, making it not only the company's, but also the whole industry's biggest money-maker up to that time. Some critics deplored the romantic glow it cast over what was really a bunch of bloodthirsty criminals, but none could deny its dramatic strength, its ability to rivet attention for nearly three hours in the details of domestic and Mafia power-plays, and its occasional nerve-jolting shocks. Albert S. Ruddy's production gathered ten Academy Award nominations, three of them winners: the film itself as the year's best, Brando as best actor (despite the distractions of a stuffed-cheeks make-up and an almost inaudible hoarse whisper), and the screenplay by Mario Puzo (author of the original novel) and Francis Ford Coppola, also its masterly director. Brando caused an uproar by refusing to accept his Oscar, on the curious grounds that Hollywood was unfair to the American Indian. Three of the five nominees as best supporting actor were named for this one picture (a record): Pacino, Robert Duvall and James Caan. Scarcely less memorable were Diane Keaton, Talia Shire (Coppola's sister), Sterling Hayden, Richard Conte, John Cazale, Abe Vigoda, Gianni Russo, Morgana King, Al Lettieri, Richard Costellano, John Marley, and Al Martino in a role rumoured to have been based on Frank Sinatra. **The Godfather's** early history paralleled *Gone with the Wind's* in that the book was bought from galley proofs for what turned out to be a bargain price when it became a runaway best-seller; and there was much publicity about casting the lead (Laurence Olivier and Edward G. Robinson were most strongly tipped) before Brando accepted a percentage deal that brought him $1 million.

Al Pacino and Simonetta Stefanelli in The Godfather*; facing: Chester Morris in* The Big House

• THE • BIG • HOUSE •

Chester Morris went into solitary in **The Big House**, one of the first and best of all prison movies, and a knockout at the 1930 box office. Although it was one of the year's top money-makers, MGM did not follow it up with a burst of violence: neither Mayer nor Thalberg relished that genre. Under George Hill's direction, Morris' tough, forceful performance was matched by Wallace Beery's as a condemned convict (a role intended for Lon Chaney), and Robert Montgomery extended his acting range as a cowardly informer. Others sharing the all-round praise it received were Lewis Stone, Leila Hyams, J. C. Nugent, Karl Dane, and writer Frances Marion who won an Oscar for it. So did Douglas Shearer's sound recording.

Sex, melodrama and gangsterism were some of the ingredients that went into producer Mark Hellinger's **Brute Force** (Universal, 1947), a prison movie with a vengeance! Apart from a planned jail break which provided the film with its climax, Richard Brooks' entertaining and taut screenplay (from a story by Robert Patterson) was underpinned by four stories concerning a quartet of 'insiders' and their 'outside' women. Thus (via flashback) we saw how Whit Bissell, a book-keeper, embezzled $3,000 to give his avaricious wife (Ella Raines) a mink coat; how Howard Duff (below, left), an ex-army corporal, took the rap for a murder committed by his bride (Yvonne De Carlo); how top-starred Burt Lancaster's love for his invalided wife Ann Blyth landed him in jail, and how John Hoyt, a crapshooter, was 'hijacked' by Anita Colby. Hume Cronyn was monstrously effective as the sadistic Wagner-loving prison captain, with good performances, too, from Charles Bickford, Sam Levene, Jeff Corey, Jack Overman, Roman Bohnen (as the weak-willed warden) and Sir Lancelot (as a Trinidadian songwriter). The virile direction was by Jules Dassin.

Cool Hand Luke (1967), coming 35 years after *I am a Fugitive from a Chain Gang*, was more eloquent about prisoners and their problems than any of its screen predecessors. Starring Paul Newman (right) as a reticent, psychologically disturbed loner picked up by the police for decapitating parking meters, it charted the vicissitudes of his life in a correctional camp from outsider to camp hero as a result of eating fifty hard-boiled eggs in one uninterrupted session. Working from Donn Pearce and Frank R. Pierson's trenchant screenplay, Stuart Rosenberg's probing, intimate direction almost amounted to an invasion of the prisoners' privacy. The result was a tough, unsentimental drama which worked not only as social comment but as marvellous screen entertainment. Apart from Newman's powerful central performance, the film was expertly served by George Kennedy, J. D. Cannon, Lou Antonio, Robert Drivas, Strother Martin and Jo Van Fleet. It was produced in Technicolor and Panavision by Gordon Carroll for Jalem Productions with Carter De Haven Jr as associate producer.

Devil's Island has the dubious privilege of being one of the world's most famous prisons, and Henri Charrière (Papillon) is probably its most famous inmate. **Papillon** (Papillon Partnership) was based on Charrière's best-selling novel, with a screenplay by two of Hollywood's top writers, Lorenzo Semple Jr and former blacklistee, Dalton Trumbo. The hero (Steve McQueen), sentenced to life imprisonment for a murder he did not

Right and inset: Paul Newman and George Kennedy in Cool Hand Luke. *Below: Burt Lancaster and Howard Duff in* Brute Force

commit, becomes friendly with a forger called Louis Dega (Dustin Hoffman). He becomes Dega's bodyguard, and together they work on a series of escapes, each of which fails, landing them in solitary confinement for long spells. At the end of the film, they have been released on to Devil's Island to become colonists. Papillon makes one last escape bid. The film leaves him on his tiny coconut-matting raft, but a voice-over informs us he made it back to France (how else would we have the novel?). **Papillon** the movie is an epic, 150-minute prison drama, covering a period of over thirty years. It is part adventure story (the various escape bids), part reflection on the horrors of prison life (McQueen crouching in his cell, seeking the one tiny beam of light and hallucinating about the stains on his cell wall), part humorous observation of the associations that spring up in jail. Here, Schaffner is aided by two undoubtedly star performances. Hoffman is weak, myopic and crotchety, McQueen tenacious and unbowed, even when two years' solitary has reduced him to a shadow of his former self. By the end, the relationship is a little strained. 'I wish you hadn't come,' mutters Hoffman, and goes back to tending his carrots. **Papillon** was one of the year's top-grossing movies and has continued to be popular. It has been regularly revived since it opened in 1973. Fred Koenekamp filmed it, and Victor Jory, Don Gordon and Anthony Zerbe provided the acting support.

A 1983 poll by a London commercial radio station revealed **Midnight Express** to be its listeners' favourite film of all time. This popularity has extended beyond the capital: Alan Parker's massively successful movie has, at one time or another, headed box-office lists in almost every country in the world. Its storyline is loosely based on the prison experiences of a young American, Billy Hayes, played in the film by Brad Davis. Hayes is arrested at Istanbul Airport in 1970 with two kilos of hashish. He is sentenced to four years in the city's notorious Sagamilcar prison. The film follows those years, during which Hayes is subjected to various forms of brutality at the hands of prison officials and other inmates. Produced by Alan Marshall, Parker's regular producer, and David Puttnam—working under the Casablanca FilmWorks banner and releasing through Columbia—**Midnight Express** is unrelenting, nasty but breathlessly exciting. It is a sort of inferno in which the hero goes from one form of degradation to another until he finally, almost by chance, escapes, taking the metaphorical 'midnight express' to freedom. Visually magnificent with Michael Seresin's glowing cinematography, **Midnight Express** is prison drama at its very best, and is the film which did more than any other to establish its director and producer as major figures in the international film world. Oliver Stone's screenplay—his first—won an Oscar, as did Giorgio Moroder's score. Parker himself won the 1978 British Film and Television Academy Award as Best Director, with John Hurt (above, left, with Brad Davis) getting the Best Supporting Actor Award for his remarkable portrayal of a dissipated Englishman who has adjusted to prison life.

Jail birds in France and in Turkey: Dustin Hoffman and Steve McQueen on Devil's Island in Papillon*; and above: Brad Davis and John Hurt incarcerated in Istanbul's Sagamilcar prison in* Midnight Express

• LOVE-HATE • • RELATIONSHIPS •

Edward G. Robinson (right) snarled, 'No buzzard like you' will ever put the cuffs on Rico,' in **Little Caesar** (1931), the first of the Warner Bros.' great 'social conscience' crime offerings. And he was right. After almost fifty years, the film remains unmanacled by time. Though Francis Edward Faragoh's screenplay, adapted from the novel by W. R. Burnett, was restricted by economy measures characterizing the studio in the early part of the Thirties (especially in crime films) forcing much of the action to take place in sleazy, low-budget settings, it managed to make a virtue of its limitations and was largely responsible for convincing Jack Warner that quality and quantity were not synonymous. Clearly based on the character of Al Capone, **Little Caesar** chronicled with such impact the rise and fall of an Italian gangster that, despite the many other parts he played, Robinson was always associated with the role of Rico. Against all odds, Robinson—who was not attractive in the traditional Hollywood sense and had a voice to match his looks—became a star. If anything, his slight, unglamorous appearance enhanced his popularity during the Depression era of the underdog, and if **Little Caesar** made a star of its hero (who in reality was afraid of guns and had to have eyelids taped to prevent him from blinking every time he pulled the trigger), it also bestowed on Warner Bros. a quality status it had hitherto rarely managed to achieve, established Darryl Zanuck (in charge of production) and Hal Wallis as producer as major talents in the industry and gave Mervyn Le Roy ('a great director, with a small g', according to Jack Warner) the kind of recognition he was waiting for. The enormous success of **Little Caesar**, (budgeted at $700,000) which also starred Douglas Fairbanks Jr, William Collier Jr, Ralph Ince and Glenda Farrell, led to a wave of socially committed films that enhanced Warner Bros.' reputation. (First National.)

The Public Enemy (1931) (released in Britain as **Enemies of the Public**) took a clinical look at the criminal mind, made a super-star out of James Cagney (below) and also a minor star of Mae Clarke who, in one of the film's most celebrated scenes, has a grapefruit twisted into her face. The shock registered on Miss Clarke's face was completely genuine, for she had been assured by Cagney

The everyday life of the hood: top left: Edward G. Robinson at work in Little Caesar*; bottom left: James Cagney at home in* The Public Enemy *and right: Paul Muni at play in* Scarface

that the grapefruit would not touch her, although the scene would be shot in such a way as to give the impression that it did. The story of Tom Powers (Cagney), a Chicago slum kid whose childhood dabbling in petty thievery was to find full expression during Prohibition, it etched an accurate picture of the ferocious criminal underworld in the late twenties, and by starting its story in 1909 when Powers was still a boy, gave audiences a documentary-like look at the environmental influences that helped turn him into the fully-fledged hood he eventually became. Though typical of Warner Bros.' many society-versus-the-criminal melodramas. **The Public Enemy**, together with *Little Caesar*, remains a classic of the genre. Directed by William A. Wellman with a toughness that never resorts to sensationalism (most of the killings are done off camera) and with a focal performance from Cagney that is compulsively watchable (and which, despite the 'comeuppance' ending, glamorizes violence through the sheer forcefulness of the star's personality), it remains as strong today as it was nearly 50 years ago. Kubec Glasmon, John Bright and Harvey Thew wrote it from Bright's original story *Beer and Blood* (whose title did not find favour with the Hays office). Jean Harlow, Joan Blondell, Beryl Mercer, Donald Cook and Leslie Fenton were also cast.

In late 1930, rumours abounded that Al Capone was to appear in a movie about his life. It didn't happen, but the news was enough to galvanize Howard Hughes into pulling together the plans for his gangster saga based on Capone. The script was by former Chicago newspaperman Ben Hecht, with additional dialogue by three more of Hollywood's greatest screenwriters, Seton I. Miller, John Lee Mahin and W. R. Burnett. To direct the picture, which was finally called **Scarface** (Caddo Productions), Hughes hired Howard Hawks, whose earlier *Dawn Patrol* he had tried to ban because it resembled his own cherished flying picture, *Hell's Angels*. It was a wise move: as directed by Hawks, **Scarface** is one of the greatest gangster movies of all time. Capone becomes Tony Camonte, superbly played by Paul Muni, who rises ruthlessly to power on the South Side of Chicago. But it is his extreme jealousy of his sister, Cesca—a relationship with more than a hint of incest—that causes his downfall. Infuriated when she 'abandons' him to marry his aide Guino Rinaldo (George Raft), Camonte murders Rinaldo. He, in turn, is gunned down by the police beneath the Cooks Tours sign which has also been his motto: 'The world is yours'. Tony Camonte is an unlikely tragic hero, but his rise and fall has all the purity of a classical tragedy. New York audiences who wanted to see the 'pure' version, however, had to cross the river to Newark, New Jersey, because the New York censors insisted that Tony be seen to go to the gas chamber. The film was remade as a violent and rather ridiculous gangster melodrama in 1983 by Brian de Palma, with Al Pacino in the lead. The 1932 cast also had Ann Dvorak as Cesca, Karen Morley as Tony's mistress, and Osgood Perkins, C. Henry Gordon, Vince Barnett and Boris Karloff in support. Lee Garmes was responsible for the moodily stark photography.

Returning to Warners after a five-year absence, James Cagney was given **White Heat** (1949) which turned out to be one of the great crime films, and the apotheosis of his dazzling career. He played Cody Jarrett, who, in the studio's words was a 'homicidal paranoiac with a mother fixation', under Raoul Walsh's *macho* direction. A scene in prison in which he hears of the death of his mother (Margaret Wycherley) and goes berserk, was shattering in its intensity and totally convincing. Basically the story of a ruthless killer who gets himself jailed on a minor charge to avoid a murder rap, it contained all the necessary ingredients of the genre, and quite a few more. Technically more proficient than the studio's raw but effective efforts of the early thirties, and with a screenplay (by Ivan Goff and Ben Roberts, based on a story by Virginia Kellogg) that catered as much for thrills as for character development, it was a solid winner. Virginia Mayo (above, left) played Cagney's (right) sluttish wife. Steve Cochran was his two-timing henchman and Edmond O'Brien the undercover Treasury agent who deliberately sets out to win Cagney's confidence in prison, in order to betray him later. Others cast were John Archer, Wally Cassell, Mickey Knox and Fred Clark. The producer was Louis F. Edelman.

Returning to the depression years of the thirties, an era inextricably linked with Warner Bros., **Bonnie and Clyde** (1967) was arguably the best American film of the last 25 years. Director Arthur Penn's highly personal vision of the period melded with the grim story of the Barrow gang and their murderous exploits. Criticized for turning its protagonists into cult heroes and for glorifying violence (the climactic final scene in which Clyde Barrow and Bonnie Parker are reduced to marionettes as a thousand rounds of ammunition jerk their bodies into a grotesque dance of death, was as romantic as it was shocking), the film nevertheless appealed to a nostalgia-prone America. Apart from Faye Dunaway and Warren Beatty as Bonnie and Clyde, there were also marvellous performances from Michael J. Pollard as C. W. Moss, Gene Hackman as Clyde's brother Buck, Estelle Parsons as his wife Blanche, Denver Pyle as a cop, and, making his movie debut, Gene Wilder as an innocent bystander whose car the Barrow gang requisition. David Newman and Robert Benton wrote the screenplay, Charles Strouse was responsible for the evocative period music, and Burnett Guffey's superb Technicolor photography captured to perfection the look, mood and feel of the era. Warren Beatty produced.

Produced for 20th Century-Fox in 1968 by Robert Fryer, **The Boston Strangler** is very much a late-1960s thriller; tight, cynical, visually experimental and with a definite edge of perversity. Scripted by Edward Anhalt (then one of Hollywood's highest paid writers) from a case study by Gerrold Frank, it is the largely true story of a Boston plumber, Albert de Salvo (Tony Curtis), who murdered thirteen women in the city between June 1962 and January 1964. De Salvo, a schizophrenic, was apparently completely unaware of what he had done. And the scene in which the police investigator—an authoritative and steely performance by Henry Fonda—confronts him with irrefutable evidence of his guilt, is one of the most disturbing in the history of crime films. The room is white, Curtis' hospital overalls are white, and he seems to want to shrink into the walls in self-loathing and horror. The rest of the film is handled with superior efficiency by director Richard Fleischer (son of the pioneer animator Max Fleischer), whose career is riddled with tautly impressive thrillers. **The Boston Strangler** is one of his finest. He treats the subject virtually head-on, neither voyeuristically nor sensationally. The first half of the film, which makes abundant use of split-screen to show the murders, is a whodunnit. The second half—the interrogation—puts us in the uncomfortable position of observing a terrified caged animal for whose blood we had earlier, like everyone else, been baying. With Mike Kellin, George Kennedy, Hurd Hatfield and Sally Kellerman in support, **The Boston Strangler** is a first-rate, semi-documentary thriller, finely photographed by Richard Kline.

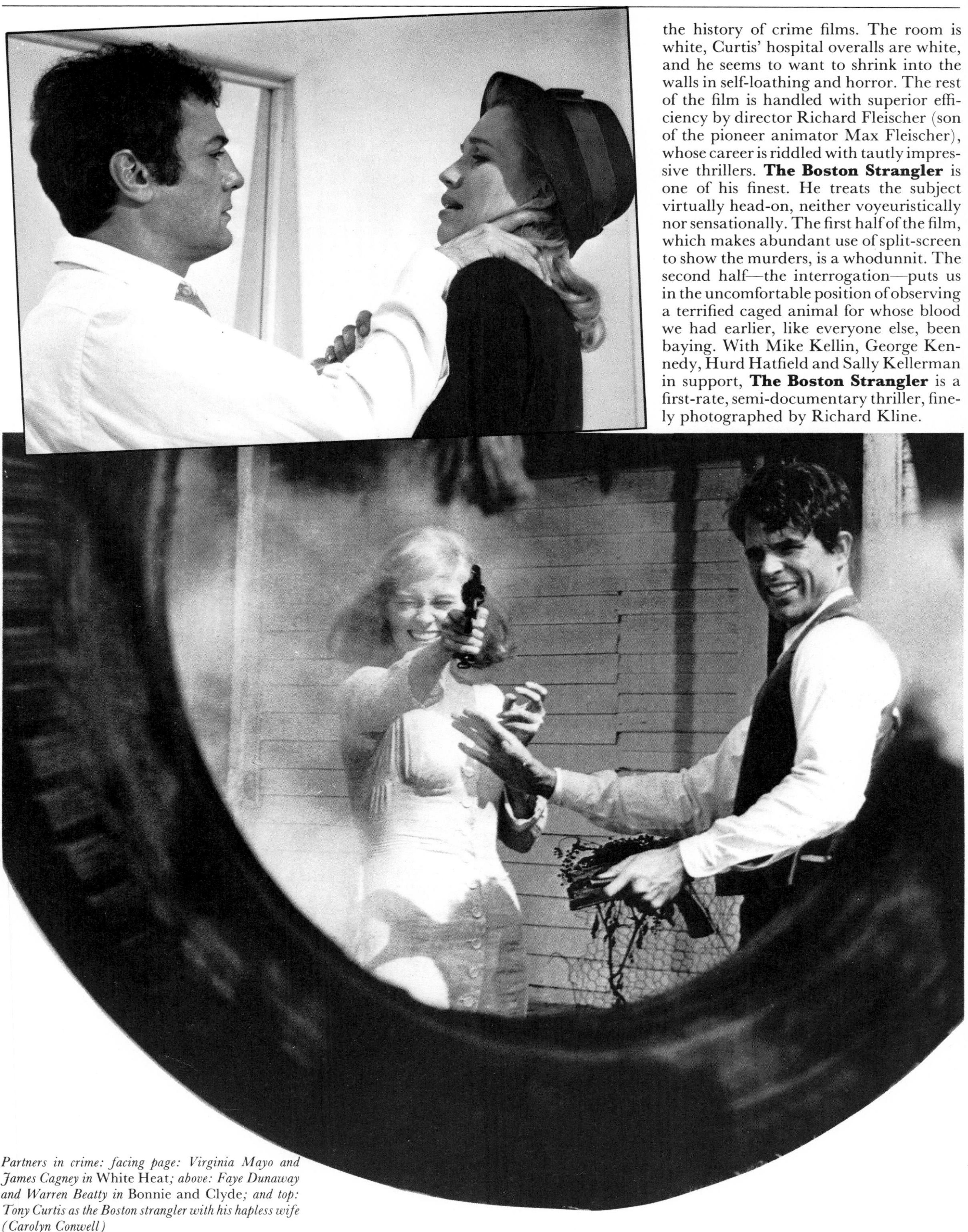

Partners in crime: facing page: Virginia Mayo and James Cagney in White Heat*; above: Faye Dunaway and Warren Beatty in* Bonnie and Clyde*; and top: Tony Curtis as the Boston strangler with his hapless wife (Carolyn Conwell)*

• CALL • THE • COPS •

In 1933 the Production Code Authority insisted that gangsterism should in no way be glorified. This, coupled with the Catholic Legion of Decency's demands on the film industry, resulted in crime movies taking on a slightly different complexion. Stars such as James Cagney and Edward G. Robinson were, in the immediate future, to be seen squarely on the side of Uncle Sam. Cagney (right), whose salary at Warner Bros. was now $4,500 a week, was cast in **G-Men** (which cost $450,000 to make) as a lawyer who joins the Justice Department and becomes a G-Man for the sole purpose of avenging the murder of a friend. His tough, staccato delivery complemented William Keighley's well paced, action-filled direction and he gave his most celebrated performance since *Public Enemy* (1931). Feminine interest, as supplied by Ann Dvorak and Margaret Lindsay, took a backseat in his exciting 1935 roller-coaster ride of a movie, though supporting players Barton MacLane, Robert Armstrong, Lloyd Nolan and William Harrigan each managed to make his presence felt. Seton I. Miller wrote the screenplay and the production was supervised by Lou Edelman. Song: *You Bother Me An Awful Lot* (by Irving Kahal and Sammy Fain). (First National.)

Painting an alarming picture of the extent to which organized crime had infiltrated the fabric of American life in the mid-Thirties, Warners' **Bullets or Ballots** (1936) was a tough, hard-hitting, well-scripted (by Seton I. Miller from his and Martin Mooney's story), well acted, tautly directed (by William Keighley) melodrama that certainly made the most of its 81 action-packed minutes. It told the all-involving story of a New York strong-arm squad detective Edward G. Robinson (below, right) who ostensibly goes to work for an underworld racketeer (Barton MacLane) after demotion from the force. In reality, however, he has not been demoted but only made to look as though he has been in order to help uncover the racket-game's top man. It was typical of the type of economical first-rate crime melodrama so closely associated with the studio, especially its 'March of Time'-like opening. Also featured were Joan Blondell, Humphrey Bogart (below, left), Frank McHugh, Joseph King, Richard Purcell, George E. Stone, Joseph Crehan, Henry O'Neill and Henry Kolker. The production was supervised by Lou Edelman. (First National.)

On Dangerous Ground (RKO, 1952) was the story of a thug cop—a man so dehumanized by his experience with the 'garbage' of the world that he takes pleasure in bashing suspects until they tell him what he wants to hear. Sent into the country on a case involving the murder of a schoolgirl, the man is slowly regenerated by his relationship with two people: the dead girl's father whose thirst for revenge provides a mirror image of the policeman's own brutality, and the neurotic killer's blind sister, a sensitive, perceptive woman who understands the cop's loneliness. The film's awkward, two-part structure, and its emphasis on mood and character rather than plot and action, failed to capture the fancy of audiences (box-office loss $425,000). Those who gave it a chance discovered an honest, probing and worthwhile experience, as gripping as it was intelligent and as emotionally involving as it was realistic. Robert Ryan played the thug cop with his usual excellence, Ida Lupino was the blind girl who 'sees' more than any of the other characters, and Ward Bond portrayed the blood-thirsty father who dreams of emptying his shotgun into the slayer of his daughter. Behind the camera were producer John Houseman, executive producer Sid Rogell and, most importantly, director Nicholas Ray. Bernard Herrmann composed the beautiful musical score and A. I. Bezzerides wrote the screenplay, based on an adaptation by himself and director Ray of Gerald Butler's novel *Mad With Much Heart*. Also cast: Sumner Williams (the killer), Charles Kemper, Anthony Ross, Ed Begley.

A thriller set on a train, RKO's 1952 **The Narrow Margin** sizzled all the way from Chicago to Los Angeles, thanks to Earl Felton's crafty screenplay (based on a story by Martin Goldsmith and Jack Leonard) and the stimulating direction of Richard O. Fleischer. Charles McGraw played a hardened police detective trying to protect a gangster's widow who is scheduled to testify before a grand jury on the West Coast. Out to snuff her are a trio of gangsters who aren't sure which passenger is their target. The tension approaches

Behind the badge: above: Cagney (with Ann Dvorak) in G-men*; below: Bogart and Robinson in* Bullets or Ballots *and inset: Ryan and Lupino in* On Dangerous Ground. *Facing page, top: Orson Welles in* Touch of Evil, *and bottom right: Charles McGraw and Marie Windsor in* The Narrow Margin

the upper limits as the hoodlums eliminate various suspects before killing the woman whom McGraw thinks is the witness. In fact, the murder victim is an undercover policewoman whose mission was to lead the thugs astray and to test McGraw's honesty. This sets up more suspense as both cop and killers discover the truth and begin their deadly conflict all over again. Marie Windsor (right), given some of the script's most pungent dialogue, was outstanding as the undercover policewoman. Her performance was well matched by McGraw's and by Jacqueline White's (the real widow), and the rest of the cast—including Gordon Gebert, Queenie Leonard, David Clarke, Peter Virgo, Don Beddoe, Paul Maxey and Harry Harvey—also attacked their roles with exceptional vigour. Produced by Stanley Rubin at a $230,000 negative cost, **The Narrow Margin** was a streamlined sleeper, one of the best in the studio's history.

Writer/director/actor Orson Welles (above) made a remarkable return to form in all three capacities for **Touch of Evil** (Universal, 1958), which he adapted from Whit Masterson's novel *Badge Of Evil*, and in which he appeared as Hank Quinlan, ruthless, twisted Texas cop in a Mexican border town who, after framing a young man for murder, clashes with top-billed Charlton Heston as a coolly indignant Mexican government official on honeymoon with Janet Leigh. Not only does Heston have to cope with the machinations of the evil Mr Welles, but his honeymoon is further blighted by a gang of narcotics racketeers who, in one of the most chilling, nightmarish scenes in the film, give Miss Leigh a really tough time. From the marathon opening tracking shot (Russell Metty's camerawork was particularly stunning throughout), to the macabre closing sequence in which the dead body of Welles is seen floating whale-like in the water, the movie was a stylistic triumph, with Welles again exploring the infinite possibilities the medium of film offers for personal expression. There was not a tired set-up throughout and, as a pierce of atmospheric cinema, it was an unqualified winner, relying far more on its baroque style than on its often melodramatic content. Also appearing with

Heston, Leigh and Welles were Joseph Calleia, Akim Tamiroff, Joanna Moore, Ray Collins, Dennis Weaver, Valentin de Vargas, Mort Mills and, in unbilled guest spots, Zsa Zsa Gabor, Joseph Cotten, Mercedes McCambridge, Keenan Wynn and, as the madam of a Mexican bordello, a gypsy-like Marlene Dietrich, who had the best line of all when, talking about Welles after his death, she remarks, 'What can you say about anybody? He was some kind of a man'. It could also be said that **Touch of Evil**, produced by Albert Zugsmith, was some kind of a film.

Steve McQueen had his work cut out for him in **Bullitt** (1968). He plays a police lieutenant bucked not only by an ambitious politician (Robert Vaughn), but by the Mafia as well. A straightforward, but undeniably stylish Technicolor thriller, its main plot line has McQueen (illustrated) picking at the knotted threads of a murder involving a Grand Jury witness. Set in San Francisco (stunning use of which is made by director Peter Yates), it was awash with exciting moments, all of them climaxed by that hoary chestnut, the car-chase. But this time a chase with a difference, and possibly the most thrilling ever committed to film. Jacqueline Bisset is cast as Bullitt's attractive girlfriend, with other roles going to Don Gordon, Robert Duvall, Simon Oakland and Norman Fell. It was written by Alan R. Trustman and Harry Kleiner from the story *Mute Witness* by Robert L. Pike. Philip D'Antoni produced for Solar productions (Warner Bros.) and came up with a winner all the way.

This page: Bullitt*; opposite: Eastwood performing on cue in* Coogan's Bluff

The combination of Clint Eastwood and director Don Siegel proved explosive in **Coogan's Bluff** (1968) a hard-hitting police melodrama in which law enforcement as practised in the Old West and its more sophisticated urban counterpart, clashed forcibly. Eastwood played a sheriff from Arizona who is sent to New York to extradite hippie Don Stroud for an unspecified crime; Lee J. Cobb was the city detective whose methods are vastly different from those of Eastwood's. How the taciturn out-of-towner eventually apprehends Stroud after the latter's escape provided the violent content of Herman Miller, Dean Riesner and

Howard Rodman's no-punches-pulled screenplay (story by Miller) which might have been improved by putting more flesh on its central character rather than taking it off his victims! In a cast also including Susan Clark as a probation officer who falls for Clint, Tisha Sterling (daughter of Ann Sothern and Robert Sterling) as Stroud's girlfriend, and Betty Field as his mother—the standout performance was Cobb's. Siegel also produced (the executive producer for Universal was Richard E. Lyons), in Technicolor.

Assault on Precinct 13 was a low-budget thriller aimed at the US drive-in market. It has since become a cult movie in Europe (it received a Special Award in 1977 from the British Film Institute, which normally gives its prizes to experimental or art films) and it launched its young director John Carpenter on a meteorically successful career. It is a simple enough story of an isolated Los Angeles police precinct which is due to be closed down but which, after a shoot-out, is besieged by a youth gang. Gradually, those inside the precinct, police as well as prisoners, unite against the outside threat. Carpenter's film, independently produced by an outfit called CKK Productions (Carpenter, his executive producer, Joseph Kaufman, and his producer, J. S. Kaplan), fuses tension and humour with amazing skill. He draws out the suspense to a quite uncanny extent, both in the opening sequence where the police ambush the *cholo* gang, and in the scene in which a little girl is gunned down at an ice cream truck, when she has gone back to complain that she has been given the wrong flavour. Written by Carpenter, edited by him (under the name of John T. Chance) and shot in Panavision by Douglas Knapp, **Assault on Precinct 13** is all the more convincing for being performed almost entirely by unknowns: the cast is headed by Austin Stoker, Darwin Joston, Laurie Zimmer, Martin West, Tony Burton and Nancy Loomis.

Hemmed in by the cholo*: Darwin Joston in* Assault on Precinct 13

• THE • PRIVATE • SECTOR •

You can find many an oldster whose all-time favourite team is William Powell, Myrna Loy and Asta. Bill and Myrna were so easy, natural and affectionately insulting together that a large section of the public believed they were married in life, as in **The Thin Man** (1934). Nothing quite like this relationship had been screened before: critics and customers were totally captivated. The never failing MGM producer-director-writers team of Hunt Stromberg, W. S. Van Dyke and Francis Goodrich/Albert Hackett filmed Dashiell Hammett's vivid novel, with Maureen O'Sullivan, Nat Pendleton, Minna Gombell, Porter Hall, Henry Wadsworth, William Henry, Harold Huber, Cesar Romero, Natalie Moorhead and Edward Brophy. Edward Ellis played the thin man, a murder victim.

Through the good offices of producer Henry Blanke, John Huston, hitherto a scriptwriter at the studio, finally got to direct a film: **The Maltese Falcon** (1941). The fact that Dashiell Hammett's novel had already been filmed twice (in 1931, and again in 1936 as *Satan Met A Lady*), was of little consequence to Jack Warner who firmly believed you couldn't keep a good yarn down; and when he read Huston's scene-by-scene breakdown of Hammett's novel, which he mistook as the final draft screenplay, Warner was so delighted that the flavour of the book had been retained that he immediately set a production date. George Raft was asked to play the role of Sam Spade, but turned it down on the grounds that he did not want to work with an inexperienced director. So, as had been the case with *High Sierra*, Humphrey Bogart inherited it. Other roles were played by Mary Astor, Peter Lorre, Gladys George, Barton MacLane, Lee Patrick, Ward Bond, Jerome Cowan, Elisha Cook Jr, and, making his film debut at the age of 61, the 280 lb. 'Fat Man' from Britain, Sydney Greenstreet. Without having the foggiest notion that a masterpiece was about to emerge, Warner gave Huston the usual 'gangster flick' budget of $300,000, plus a shooting schedule of six weeks, while associate producer Henry Blanke just gave advice: 'Make every shot count,' he told Huston. 'No detail can be overlooked.' After completion, a written foreword describing the history of the Falcon was added at Warner's request (he felt that the story was confusing without it) and in 1941, the film was released. It set new standards in thrillers and turned Bogart into a star.

Above: The Maltese Falcon*; and below:* The Thin Man

Raymond Chandler regarded RKO's 1945 **Murder, My Sweet** (GB: **Farewell, My Lovely**, the title of the original novel) as the best film adaptation of any of his works, and considered Dick Powell the nearest cinematic equivalent to his own conception of Philip Marlowe. Powell (above, right) was surprisingly good in the role, abandoning his song-and-dance man persona to become one of the classic hard-boiled heroes. Director Edward Dmytryk explored the full vocabulary of film to convey the descent of private eye Marlowe into a nether world of homicide, blackmail, charlatanism, thievery, sadistic violence, sexual enslavement and, above all else, mystery. The film's dream and drug sequences (cinematography by Harry J. Wild; special effects by Vernon L. Walker) were especially effective in their visualization of Marlowe's confused and paranoiac state of mind. One of the refreshing aspects of **Murder, My Sweet** was its notable lack of clean-living, soft-spoken heroes and heroines. Here we find two-faced Claire Trevor, cretinous giant Mike Mazurki (left, playing Moose Malloy who sets the plot in motion), boozy old floozy Esther Howard, psychoanalytic blackmailer Otto Kruger and angry and scornful Anne Shirley. It was performed wholeheartedly by the leading stars, and supported by Miles Mander, Douglas Walton, Don Douglas and Ralf Harolde. John Paxton's screenplay remained reasonably faithful to its source and to Chandler's exceptional dialogue. Adrian Scott produced, working with executive producer Sid Rogell. Elements of the basic story had been used in *The Falcon Takes Over* (1942); it would be remade as *Farewell, My Lovely* in 1975 with Robert Mitchum playing Marlowe in the Avco-Embassy release.

Not even scriptwriters William Faulkner, Leigh Brackett and Jules Furthman could make head or tail of the screenplay they fashioned from Raymond Chandler's novel **The Big Sleep** (Warner Bros., 1946). Under normal circumstances, this would have placed them and the prospective audience at something of a disadvantage. But in one of the screen's greatest examples of style triumphing over content, disentangling the plot (Private Eye Philip Marlowe is hired by the father of a nymphomaniac daughter to rid him of a blackmailer, but it wasn't as simple as that) offered only an incidental pleasure next to the stylish performances of Humphrey Bogart cast as Marlowe and Lauren Bacall (by now Mrs Bogart in real life) as a sexy young divorcée with whom he falls in love. The 'Big Sleep' of the title was death—a commodity the thriller was not short on—and producer-director Howard Hawks brilliantly choreographed the film's numerous killings with awesome inventiveness. Confusing it may have been, but dull it certainly wasn't. Aside from the film's visual elegance, Max Steiner's score contributed much to its overall success, as indeed did Sid Hickox's photography. If *Little Caesar* (1931) was the studio's quintessential crime melodrama, this was its most characteristic thriller with the look, feel, and the sound of Warner Bros. Also cast were John Ridgely, Martha Vickers, Dorothy Malone (below), Peggy Knudsen, Regis Toomey and Elisha Cook Jr.

Kiss Me Deadly (Parklane Productions) was hailed as a masterpiece by critics in France when it opened there, after a very poor reception in America. It is a characteristic work by the maverick American director, Robert Aldrich, which takes a well-known right-wing pulp thriller by the crime novelist Mickey Spillane, and turns it into a subversive look at

the underside of 1950s America, ending with a nuclear explosion. ('What the hell are you going to do with another jewel heist?' demanded Aldrich, explaining the changes he had made in the plot with veteran thriller scenarist A. I. Bezzerides.) Aldrich's Mike Hammer, played by the unprepossessing Ralph Meeker, is a product of the gutter he investigates. The film portrays, with consistency, a world without values, where no one is to be trusted. No worse than anyone else, Hammer is certainly no better either. In one unforgettable scene, he interrogates a harmless old opera lover by snapping, one by one, his priceless collection of Caruso 78s. **Kiss Me Deadly** deserves a place in any anthology of great American crime movies, if only for its unrelenting vision of the world of crime and criminals, whose rough edges are generally filed by other films. Albert Dekker, Paul Stewart, Wesley Addy, Maxine Cooper, Cloris Leachman, and Nick Dennis accompanied Hammer, with photography by Ernest Laszlo and music by Frank DeVol.

Andy and Dave Lewis' story **Klute** (Warners, 1971), which grossed over $6 million and was all about a prostitute who helps a private detective to solve a mysterious case involving the disappearance of an out-of-towner last seen in New York City, was pretty routine. But the retread they gave the well-worn material in their pungent screenplay was first-rate, and as performed by the versatile Jane Fonda as the prostitute and a laconic Donald Sutherland cast as the detective,

Opposite, top: Murder My Sweet *and bottom:* The Big Sleep. *Below: Donald Sutherland as John Klute*

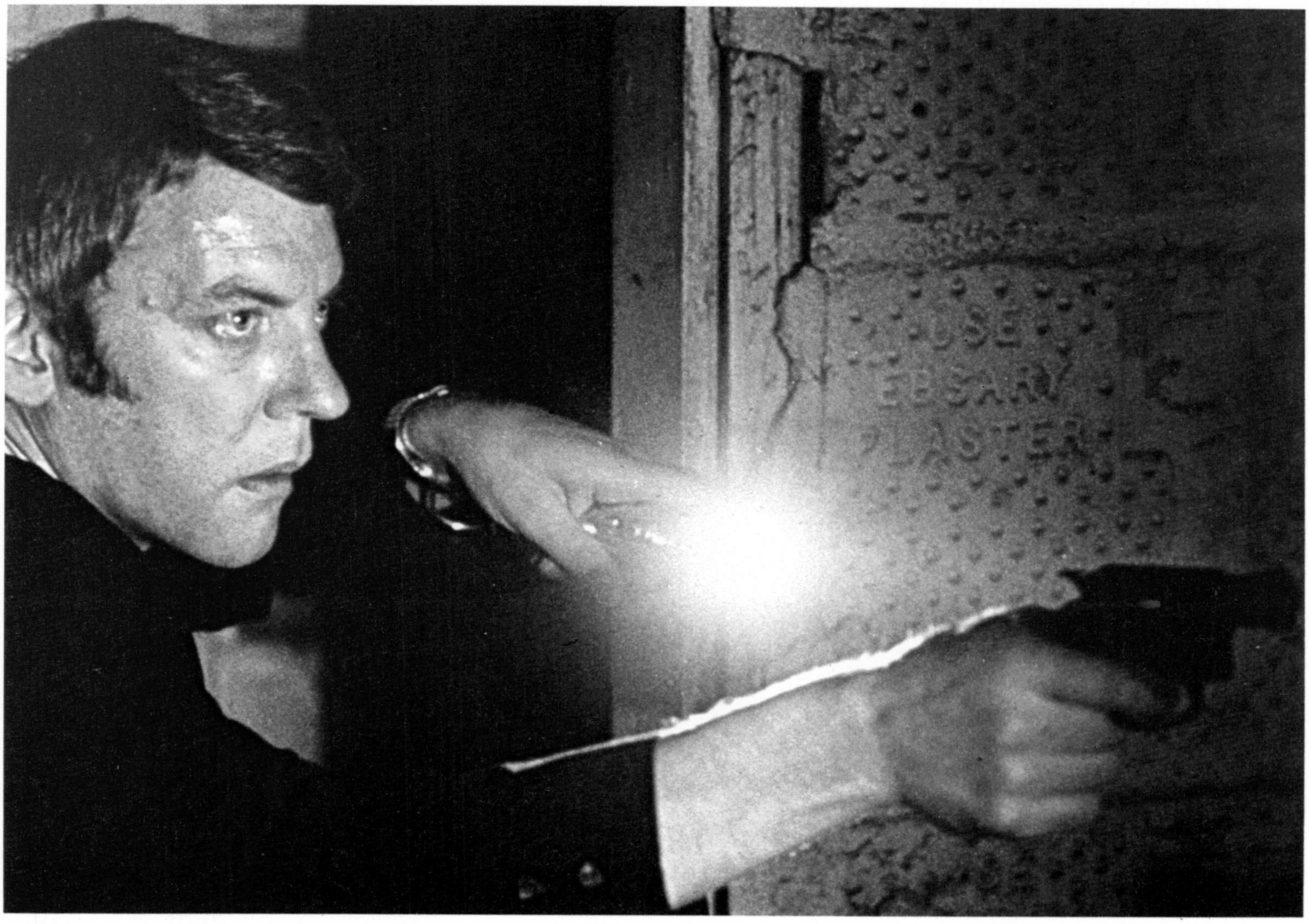

provided an impressive thriller that did not mince words in the telling of its rather sordid tale. The climax, with Sutherland rescuing Fonda from the sadistic clutches of the villain just in the nick of time, didn't quite ring true, but everything else in Alan J. Pakula's meticulous production (and direction) did. The atmospheric and genuinely scaring score was by Michael Small, and it was stunningly photographed by Gordon Willis. Charles Cioffi, Roy R. Schneider, Dorothy Tristan and Rita Gam were also featured.

While Jack Clayton was recreating the Twenties for *The Great Gatsby* on the East coast, Roman Polanski was turning the Los Angeles clock back to the Thirties for **Chinatown** (Paramount). A private-eye thriller in the manner of Dashiell Hammett or Raymond Chandler, this brilliant entertainment was one of the most highly praised and commercially successful releases of 1974. It drew Academy Award nominations in eleven categories. The Oscar for best screenplay was won by Robert Towne for a multi-layered story in which crimes and corruption were unpeeled like onion skins, with a murder on the outside and land-grabbing fraud at the core. Jack Nicholson (seen here) is a gumshoe suspecting and then protecting the victim's widow (Faye Dunaway), whose father is plotting control of LA's water supply. This villain (John Huston) also has a murky private life: he is the father of his daughter's child. Nicholson, who is disfigured most of the time by a slit nostril (administered by Polanski himself as one of the tycoon's goons), and Faye, who is killed in the violent finale, both scored strongly: he coolly humorous, she tautly distraught as the nasty tale unfolded. Perry Lopez, Diane Ladd, John Hillerman, Darrell Zwerling and Roy Jenson were also cast in the Robert Evans production, the misleading title of which had little to do with anything: the last scene just happened to occur in LA's Chinese district.

• A • WOMAN'S • PLACE •

Writing in his autobiography about **Casablanca** (1943), arguably Warner Bros.' most enduring achievement, Jack Warner recalled a conversation with the film's director Michael Curtiz, in which Curtiz remarked to him: 'Well, Jock, the scenario isn't the exact truth, but ve haff the facts to prove it.' Regardless of what was, or wasn't the truth, **Casablanca** captured the mood and the immediacy of a war-time situation involving political refugees from Nazi-occupied Europe and their desperate attempts to attain exit visas to Lisbon—and freedom. Set in Rick's Café-Americain, owned by Richard Blaine (Humphrey Bogart, left), a man who once fought with Spanish loyalists and smuggled arms to Ethiopia but now refuses to stick his neck out for anyone, its plot centred on the unexpected arrival at the café of Victor Laszlo (Paul Henreid) and his wife Isla (Ingrid Bergman, right), the only woman Rick has ever loved. Their affair, which began and ended in Paris shortly before the Nazi occupation, starts all over again, shines through the film's numerous and somewhat far-fetched sub-plots, and ends—as it did once before— unhappily, when Ilsa and her husband, having obtained the necessary exit visas, for which they had gone to Casablanca in the first place, board the plane leaving Rick to resolve his inner conflicts by again sticking his neck out and working on the side of peace. Based on an unproduced play called *Everybody Goes To Rick's* (by Murray Burnett and Joan Alison) which the studio purchased because of its exotic locale, the material, as originally worked over by Julius J. and Philip G. Epstein, amounted to little more than a heady concoction of melodramatic incidents with no discernible narrative thrust, and whose excitement relied on stock situations and two-dimensional characters. Howard Koch was called in to give the Epstein treatment its centre of gravity, and although he certainly succeeded, it was Michael Curtiz, bulldozing his way through the clichés, who was responsible for turning second-rate material into sublime screen entertainment. Nor can one underestimate Curtiz's superb cast (apart from the principals, there were fine performances from Claude Rains, S. Z. Sakall, Sydney Greenstreet, Conrad Veidt, and Peter Lorre) and the way in which their personalities melded together to turn, by some miraculous alchemy, lines such as 'Was that cannon fire, or is my heart pounding?' into cinematic gold. Musically, apart from the incomparable Dooley Wilson's *As Time Goes By* (by Herman Hupfeld), Max Steiner's score contributed immeasurably to the film's overall success: so did the brilliant chiaroscuro of Arthur Edeson's black-and-white photography. **Casablanca** went on

general release during the timely Casablanca Conference of Anglo-American leaders at the beginning of 1943, and benefited greatly from the resultant publicity. The three Academy Awards it won a few months later further helped to establish it as one of the year's biggest grossing films. Today its popularity has not diminished, and it remains one of the greatest films of its decade. And to think the studio originally wanted Ann Sheridan, Ronald Reagan and Dennis Morgan . . . The producer was Hal B. Wallis.

Double Indemnity (Paramount, 1944) had all the suspense of a hand-grenade with the pin out. The fact that it still grips after several viewings, hooking attention from first scene to last, gives it a claim to rank as one of the most brilliant examples of storytelling in movie history. Billy Wilder (whose usual partner, Charles Brackett, thought the story disgusting and refused to collaborate) worked with Raymond Chandler on the script. It is based on James Cain's short novel, resembling his *The Postman Always Rings Twice*, about an insurance salesman lured by a woman to murder her husband in such a way that they could collect on his accident policy. Their sex-charged plotting of the crime, the killing itself, the body's disposal, and the ever-increasing menace of the subsequent insurance investigation, had a cold-blooded fascination that no director but Wilder could command. He had to use much coaxing to make Fred MacMurray eschew his nice-guy persona for the woman-hungry murderer role; it was his best. Equally potent were Barbara Stanwyck, as the amoral wife, and Edward G. Robinson as the investigator, telling support came from Porter Hall, Jean Heather, Byron Barr, Richard Gaines, Fortunio Bonanova, and Tom Powers. The influence of Chandler was apparent in the trenchant dialogue and the seedy Los Angeles atmosphere of Joseph Sistrom's production. It had seven Academy nominations but the actual awards went to *Going My Way*; 40 years on, it has won the Oscars of time.

One of the great soap-operas of the forties, **Mildred Pierce** (1945) was turned down by both Bette Davis, who was first choice for the title role, and Barbara Stanwyck. It was producer Jerry

Below: Barbara Stanwyck, Fred MacMurray and Edward G. Robinson in Double Indemnity*; above: Jack Carson and Joan Crawford in* Mildred Pierce

Wald who thought of Joan Crawford, and his perspicacity resulted in a $5 million winner for Warner Bros. studios. It also resulted in a first-class, highly literate drama of a determined woman's rise from waitress to restaurateur, the motivation for success being her spoilt, indulged older daughter (Ann Blyth) on whom she lavishes (but does not receive in return) all the love she can. Echoing the star's own struggles, both private and professional, the part clearly had personal reverberations for Crawford (above, right) which she exploited to magnificent effect under Michael Curtiz's demanding direction.

An atmosphere of sexual tension that seldom emanated from the family-show MGM of the Forties was generated in **The Postman Always Rings Twice** (1946) by director Tay Garnett and his excellently cast stars, Lana Turner and John Garfield. Carey Wilson produced the James Cain shocker about husband murdered by wife and lover, following the success Paramount had with Cain's similar *Double Indemnity*, and rang the box-office bell. Script by Harry Ruskin and Niven Busch. Also cast: Cecil Kellaway, Hume Cronyn, Audrey Totter. Visconti had made an Italian version, in 1942.

Another quintessential 'woman's picture' and a four-handkerchief weepie that even attacked the sensibilities of hardened males, Universal's **Madame X** (1966), in its sixth (count 'em) screen incarnation, gave Lana Turner one of the very best roles of her career and, trouper that she was, she devoured it greedily. In a role previously played by Dorothy Donnelly (1915), Pauline Frederick (1920), Ruth Chatterton (1929), Gladys George (1937) and Madame Kyveli (1960, for Orestes Laskos' Greek version), Turner also starred as a married woman whose love affair with a wealthy playboy ends in his accidental death, her own 'disappearance' in a mock drowning episode, the murder of a blackmailer, and her standing trial and being defended by an attorney who is unaware that the woman whose life he is fighting for is his very own mother. It was melodramatic in 1909 when it first appeared as a play by Alexandra Bisson, but melodrama of the highest order and, in Ross Hunter's expensive production (which switched the locale from France to America), that's how it remained. Jean Holloway's screenplay made several other changes, most notably 'Madame X's' genuine attachment to rather than loathing of her politician husband, sympathetically played by John Forsythe. But in all essentials the script was true to the spirit of the original play. Ricardo Montalban was Miss Turner's lover, Keir Dullea her unsuspecting son, Burgess Meredith the blackmailer and, as Forsythe's mother, Constance Bennett acted in her last screen appearance before her death.

Top: John Garfield and Lana Turner in The Postman Always Rings Twice*; below: twenty years on, Turner in* Madame X

· THE · PERFECT · CRIME ·

MGM's **The Asphalt Jungle** (1950) might be called *Father Of The Crime*, the seminal thriller from which countless movies about big robbery plots have sprung (including three more MGM versions of its own W. R. Burnett original). John Huston's script (with Ben Maddow) and direction gave it a sinister urgency. There was also a whole gallery of vivid character portrayals by cast members Sterling Hayden, Anthony Caruso and Sam Jaffe (centre, left to right) and Louis Calhern, James Whitmore, Jean Hagen, Marc Lawrence, John McIntire, Teresa Celli, Dorothy Tree, Barry Kelley and last but not least an eye-catching new blonde, Marilyn Monroe. The Arthur Hornblow Jr production became a great and enduring success.

North by Northwest (1959) was Alfred Hitchcock's first at MGM and, say many aficionados, his best ever. The studio replaced CinemaScope with Paramount's big-screen process, VistaVision, just this once; the whole production was going to be made for Paramount at one time. The movie had Cary Grant and Eva Marie Saint whirling in the vortex of Ernest Lehman's devilishly clever script to its climax among the great stone faces of Mount Rushmore. To delight the audiences, thrilling Hitchcock touches abounded, and to delight the studio, so did hefty grosses in all cinemas. The cast also included: James Mason, Jessie Royce Landis, Leo G. Carroll, Philip Ober, Josephine Hutchinson, Martin Landau, Edward Platt, Adam Williams, Robert Ellenstein, Philip Coolidge.

Below: Cary Grant and Eva Marie Saint in North by Northwest

Cary Grant and Audrey Hepburn were teamed for the first time in **Charade** (Universal, 1964), a Hitchcock-influenced brew of mystery and suspense. Set in France, the film opened in the Alpine resort of Mégève where Hepburn, after a casual encounter with Grant, returns to Paris only to discover that her husband has been murdered and that a quartet of his World War II accomplices, believing that she knows the whereabouts of a quarter of a million dollars in gold, are out to get her. Grant follows her to Paris and offers to help. But can she trust him? And what about Walter Matthau, her informant, who advises her to find the gold as soon as possible and, for her own safety, to hand it over to him? Scenarist Peter Stone, working from a story he devised with Marc Behm, posed many questions in the course of the convoluted plot's eventual unravelling, and while not all of them were convincingly answered, the film's overall pace and many of its individual moments, as well as the exciting finale, more than compensated for the areas of narrative untidiness. The two central performances and the chemistry they engendered, helped the film garner many happy box-office returns. Stanley Donen's direction was a true marriage of style to content, Charles Lang Jr's Technicolor photography glowed, and Henry Mancini's score provided a first rate musical accompaniment to the action. Donen produced, and in subsidiary roles cast James Coburn and Ned Glass (as villains), Jacques Marin, Paul Bonifas and Dominique Minot.

Above: Grant with Audrey Hepburn in Charade, *and centre:* The Asphalt Jungle

porting cast that included Charles Durning (as a corrupt detective on the lookout for Redford), Ray Walston, Eileen Brennan, Harold Gould, John Hefferman and Dana Elcar. A Richard D. Zanuck–David Brown presentation, produced by Tony Bill and Julia Phillips, it grossed $68,450,000.

Howard Rodman and Dean Riesner provided producer-director Don Siegel and star Walter Matthau with a first-class screenplay for **Charley Varrick** (based on John Reese's novel *The Looters*). It told the unusual tale of a small-time bank robber who inadvertently finds that one of the New Mexico banks he has just knocked off to the tune of $750,000 was a receptacle for Mafia money. Matthau, fearful of the consequences, wants to return the fruits of the successful heist. His partner (Andy Robinson) does not. The excellence of the screenplay, combined with the conviction of the performances and Siegel's sure-footed direction—particularly in the wham-bang opening sequence featuring Matthau's getaway from the bank—added up to one of the tautest, most entertaining melodramas in several years. Joe Don Baker was effective as a Mafia hit man, and there was solid support from Felicia Farr, John Vernon, Sheree North, Norman Fell, Benson Fong, William Schallert and, in a brief appearance as Matthau's wife (who is killed in the getaway chase), the excellent Jacqueline Scott (Universal, 1973).

Left: Paul Newman shows two sides of a poker face, Robert Redford is his back-up in The Sting. *Below: Walter Matthau plays Charley Varrick*

The teaming of Paul Newman and Robert Redford proved to be box-office dynamite in **The Sting** (Universal), one of 1973's big grossers, as well as blockbuster entertainment which gave confirmed home-bodies everywhere the perfect excuse to abandon their TV sets for a couple of hours in order to see what all the fuss was about. And what they discovered was a well-constructed, beautifully written tale in which the magic Newman-Redford chemistry, so successfully tested in *Butch Cassidy and the Sundance Kid* (20th Century-Fox, 1969) proved miraculously infallible in the telling of a tale about a pair of smooth con artists in Twenties' Chicago who fleece a big-time racketeer at his own game. David S. Ward's rather convoluted (sometimes confusing) screenplay required close attention if some of its finer points were not to be missed, but even though certain details were easily lost or remained unexplained in the unfurling of the narrative, the gist of it remained comprehensible and made for compulsive viewing. Best scene was a poker game on board a train in which Newman successfully baits his adversary, Robert Shaw. The film's surprise ending, which many considered to be a con in itself, sent audiences home chuckling with pleasure; and, apart from the presence of its two superstars, was probably the main reason for keeping cash registers ringing wherever the film was shown. Other contributing factors to the film's success were the Scott Joplin tunes which Marvin Hamlisch scored so skilfully; Robert Surtees' 'rotogravure' photography, and the marvellous period detail reflected in Henry Bumstead's sets and Edith Head's costumes—not to mention a terrific sup-

· METAPHORS ·

Five Star Final (Warners, 1931) exposed the iniquities of a muck-raking, New York tabloid and the ruthless way it exploited people for its own circulation-building ends. Edward G. Robinson (right, centre) as a hard-bitten editor (with a streak of humanity) is asked by newspaper magnate Oscar Apfel to revive a 20-year-old unsolved murder case in an attempt to attract readers regardless of the pain the exercise will cause to the family involved. Unevenly directed by Mervyn LeRoy from Byron Morgan's screenplay (based on the play by Louis Weitzenkorn) the film's undeniable impact was mainly to be felt in the hard-hitting scenes that take place in the newspaper offices themselves. They compensated, in part, for the mawkish and banal moments between the victimized mother (Frances Starr) and her equally distraught husband (H. B. Warner). Completing the cast for producer Hal B. Wallis were Anthony Bushell, Ona Munson, Aline MacMahon (her debut at the studio). Boris Karloff, Evelyn Hall and George E. Stone. It was remade in 1936 as *Two Against the World.*

After their comedy success in *Boy Meets Girl*, James Cagney and Pat O'Brien teamed up for **Angels with Dirty Faces** (1937), a tough drama masquerading as social comment, and typical of Warner Bros.' belief that people are all victims of society; the more corrupt the society the more corrupt the victims. Cagney played Rocky Sullivan, a well-known criminal who, on returning to his old slum-infested neighbourhood finds himself something of a hero, a fact which pleases him as much as it disturbs the local parish priest (O'Brien) who worries that Rocky's presence will have an adverse influence on the young, impressionable lads, and thereby undermine his own authority over them. In the film's memorable final scene, with Cagney about to meet his maker via the electric chair, O'Brien begs him to become a coward and turn yellow, thus destroying the hero-worshipping boys' illusions about him. Vigorously directed by Michael Curtiz from an intensely earnest screenplay by John Wexley and Warren Duff (story by Rowland Brown), it showed off Cagney at his histrionic best. Also cast were Humphrey Bogart, Ann Sheridan, George Bancroft and Marilyn Knowlden. The associate producer was Sam Bischoff. (First National.)

First edition and last mile: above: Edward G. Robinson in Five Star Final*; below: James Cagney and Pat O'Brien (as priest) in* Angels with Dirty Faces

Stephen Kingsley's play, **Dead End**, was a big Broadway hit which belongs very much to the mid-1930s: a crime story with a strong moral streak. Samuel Goldwyn had always shunned gangster pictures, but he saw in **Dead End** a subject that had something more. Pausing only to ask the advice of William Wyler (who would eventually direct it), he bought the screen rights for the hitherto unheard-of sum of $165,000. With the help of Lillian Hellman's screenplay, Goldwyn preserved the spirit of the play but increased its box-office appeal by bringing in Sylvia Sidney and Humphrey Bogart. She plays Drina, the girl who dreams of a little house in the country where the snow falls 'clean and white'; he plays 'Baby Face' Martin, the gangster who has 'escaped' from the East River tenement which gives the film its title, but who is inexorably drawn back there. The real star, however, was Richard Day's awe-inspiring set. Juxtaposing the tenement with the elegance of Sutton Place, it summed up the movie's theme in the first loving pan across it by Gregg Toland's camera. Goldwyn, true to form, was upset by how dirty it looked. When reminded it was meant to be a slum, he snapped, 'This slum cost a lot of money! It should look better than an ordinary slum!' But even the set was quickly eclipsed in the public memory by the Dead End Kids, a bunch of young East Side hoodlums, ragged, rough and foul-mouthed, who were a casting director's dream and who went on to star in other films. Rather than a moral about crime being created by poverty, it is likely that audiences took from the film a sort of sneaking envy of the fun the Dead End Kids seemed to have. Joel McCrea, Wendy Barrie, Claire Trevor, Allen Jenkins and Marjorie Main were the other main members of an altogether terrific cast.

Originally entitled *Three-Time Loser*, **You Only Live Once** (Walter Wanger Productions) is the film in which German director Fritz Lang most perfectly merged his expressionist leanings with the dramatic storytelling that would become his Hollywood stock-in-trade. Eddie Taylor (Henry Fonda), a petty criminal, gets out of jail determined to go straight, but is framed for a bank robbery and ends up back inside. He grows more and more bitter, refusing even to see his sweetheart (Sylvia Sidney), and resisting the approaches of the sympathetic chaplain, Father Dolan (William Gargan). At the end, he busts out, shooting Father Dolan in the process, and heads for the Canadian border, where he dies in an ambush. Lang made the film with his usual perfectionism, taking an hour to get a frog to plop into a pool at just the right angle (the result is worth it). He balances social criticism (Eddie as a victim of circumstance) against an ever-growing sense of fate. He makes sure that the audience gets drawn into complicity by encouraging them to think Eddie guilty of the bank robbery (we see only the robber's outline, which looks just like him), builds up sympathy for him, then destroys it by the murder of the priest. At the end, aided by Leon Shamroy's wonderful camerawork and lighting, he has Eddie go to his death almost as a release from the sufferings of the world. As he peers into the mist, he seems to see Father Dolan and hear him say, 'The gates are opening, Eddie'. The next moment, he is dead. Graham Baker wrote the screenplay which was adapted from a story by Gene Towne, Walter Wanger himself produced and Alfred Neuman wrote the music.

Top: on the street in Dead End*; above: on the set of* You Only Live Once

You could count on the fingers of one hand the number of British films about Northern Ireland. Carol Reed's **Odd Man Out**, made for Two Cities Films (a subsidiary of the Rank Organization) in 1946 and released in Britain early the following year, is one of the first. Purely as a film, it is unlikely to be bettered. Reed was then at the height of his powers, and the screenplay, by R. C. Sherriff and F. L. Green, based on the latter's novel, gave him the perfect opportunity to make a tense, moody masterpiece. **Odd Man Out** is about a gunman from a (tactfully unnamed) illegal political organization on the run after a robbery has gone wrong in Belfast. Wounded and increasingly delirious, he wanders from one hiding place to another—an old air raid shelter, a genteel suburban villa, a busy pub, the studio of a crazy artist called Lukey

(Robert Newton), who wants to paint him as Christ. Finally, he staggers out and dies at the dock gates, in a starkly lit and beautifully photographed scene (Robert Krasker was behind the camera) that merges the best of French pre-war cinema with the best of Hollywood *film noir*. At the centre, however, is James Mason's performance as Johnny MacQueen. 'At last,' exclaimed one critic, 'a picture that's worthy of Mr Mason!' With the eyes of a hunted animal and a face sweating with fear, Mason (even if his accent is a little variable) gives one of his finest performances. Robert Newton, as usual, goes a bit too far, but Kathleen Ryan, Cyril Cusack, F. J. McCormick, William Hartnell and the veteran actor, W. G. Fay, as Father Tom, are memorable in a predominantly Irish cast. Carol Reed produced as well as directed, and the film won the British Film Academy Award as Best Film of 1947.

A film still largely underappreciated, RKO's **Out of the Past** (GB: **Build My Gallows High**, the title of the original novel) was one of the masterworks of *film noir*, a hard-boiled drama of double-crossing, back-sliding and revenge that was also a piercing emotional journey. Producer Warren Duff and director Jacques Tourneur gave Robert Mitchum his first starring role after both John Garfield and Dick Powell turned the picture down. Playing a gas station owner in a small mountain community whose love for pretty local girl Virginia Huston is doomed by an earlier liaison with 'black widow' Jane Greer, Robert Mitchum was to carve out the cynical, laconic, droopy-lidded screen persona on which he would play variations for the rest of his career. And almond-eyed Jane Greer passed directly into the *femme fatale* hall of fame with this one performance. Other important cast members were smiling rattlesnake Kirk Douglas, voluptuous and dangerous Rhonda Fleming and deaf-mute Dickie Moore, the most arrestingly symbolic character. Geoffrey Homes (a pseudonym for Daniel Mainwaring), working from his own novel, dealt out a rough, tough, thrill-packed hand with the best dialogue heard west of Chandler and the most alluringly diabolical characters south of Hammett. The 1947 picture was a major victory for director Tourneur, whose rich visual style added a crucial dimension and Nicholas Musuraca whose hypnotic cinematography was always in sync with the psychological zig-zags inherent in the plot. Executive producer Robert Sparks also cast Richard Webb, Steve Brodie, Paul Valentine and Ken Niles. 'A MAN ... trying to run away from his past. A WOMAN ... trying to escape her future! When they clash it's *WILDFIRE!*' For once, the studio hyperbole came close to the essence of a picture.

Over-the-shoulder shots: above: Robert Mitchum and Jane Greer in Out of the Past*; below: James Mason on the run in* Odd Man Out

Max Ophuls was a German director whose place in the history of cinema depends on a number of European films. However, he spent most of the 1940s in Hollywood, and it was there that he made **The Reckless Moment** for Columbia in 1949. It was a small film with a limited budget, but with an excellent screenplay by Henry Garson and Robert W. Soderberg, based on a story by Elizabeth Saxnay Holding. It is a particularly fine example of *film noir*, thanks to Ophuls' direction, to the marvellous central performances by James Mason and Joan Bennett, and to Burnett Guffey's cinematography. Set in the (then) small southern Californian coastal town of Balboa, it is about a family whose eldest daughter (Geraldine Brooks) becomes involved with an unscrupulous older man. An accident leads to the man's death, and Lucia Harper (Bennett) disposes of the body. She then finds herself being approached by a charming, almost apologetic blackmailer, called Martin Donnelly (Mason). The film's strength lies in two things: the sense of evil intruding on the ordinary world of the Harper family; and the charged ambiguity of the relationship that builds up between Bennett and Mason, two actors who Hollywood never really understood but who repay tenfold the attention Ophuls lavishes on them here. Mason is insistent about the money, but genuinely solicitous over Bennett's health ('You smoke too much,' he comments. 'It's bad for your health.') And she, to her horror, finds herself seeing in Mason an alternative to her almost permanently absent husband. Always tense in its action scenes, completely convincing in its quieter ones and disturbing throughout, **The Reckless Moment** is a veritable gem of a movie.

Above: James Mason and Joan Bennett in The Reckless Moment; *below: Joseph Cotten and Orson Welles in* The Third Man, *and inset: Lee Marvin and Spencer Tracy in* Bad Day at Black Rock

Carol Reed's moody post-war thriller, **The Third Man** (London Films), raised a lot of hopes for the British film industry. It was one of the first films to get financial help from the recently formed National Film Finance Corporation, and it benefited from the deal producer Alexander Korda did with David O. Selznick to ensure that it had American distribution. The same deal also ensured that three key members of the cast—Joseph Cotten, Alida Valli and Orson Welles—were American, rather overshadowing Trevor Howard as the nominal lead. **The Third Man**, scripted from his own unpublished short story by Graham Greene, won the Grand Prix at Cannes in 1949, making it the first British film to do so. The British Film Academy also voted it Best British Film of 1949, and Robert Krasker's black and white photography won the 1950 Oscar. Set in Vienna, **The Third Man** is about the black market dealings of the mysterious Harry Lime (Orson Welles), who pops up everywhere when least expected—a trick he pulls off by travelling exclusively by sewer. Howard is the hapless British intelligence officer who is set the task of tracking him down. The film's mood was faultless, thanks to Krasker's photography, to Reed's use of lighting but perhaps most of all to Anton Karas' zither music, which accompanies the whole film. Karas' *Harry Lime Theme* is unforgettable. So, too, is the moment when Lime is revealed as a kitten strolls into a doorway and brushes against his legs. All in all, one of the most memorable 93 minutes in the history of the British film.

Good days at Culver City when MGM made **Bad Day at Black Rock** (1954). Brooding silences, with intimations of an explosive climax at any moment, characterized Spencer Tracy's performance and the movie itself, keeping audiences in suspense and exhibitors out of the red. Lee Marvin (below, supine), Robert Ryan, John Ericson, Anne Francis, Dean Jagger, Walter Brennan and Ernest Borgnine performed tellingly for John Sturges in the Millard Kaufman drama, produced by Dore Schary in CinemaScope and Eastman Color.

The qualities evinced by James Dean (illustrated) in *East of Eden*—lonely, misunderstood and discontented—reached their fullest expression in his second film, **Rebel Without a Cause**, directed by Nicholas Ray for Warner Bros. in 1955, whose distillation of the period's fashions, slang and mores was as much sociology as it was entertainment. A hitherto neglected subject—the problems of post-war youth and the very real generation gap that existed between parents and their children—it burst forcefully on to the screen and consolidated Dean's stature as the country's most important new young actor since Brando, as well as affirming his status as a cult hero. It also gave erstwhile child-star Natalie Wood a chance to show that she was no longer just a pretty little girl, but an attractive young woman with talent. And, as Dean's hero-worshipping friend Plato, Sal Mineo made quite an impression too. Dean's parents, however (Jim Backus and Ann Doran), were treated (and played) as caricatures, which unbalanced the film slightly, though doubtless scenarist Stewart Stern deliberately intended the bias. Also featuring Corey Allen, William Hopper, Dennis Hopper, Rochelle Hudson and Edward Platt, **Rebel Without a Cause**, produced by David Weisbart in CinemaScope and Warner Color, was one of the year's big successes, and one of the decade's most powerfully expressed statements on contemporary youth.

SINGING & DANCING

Like everything else, the musical was something that Hollywood inherited—in this case from Broadway and the international world of the operetta. For obvious reasons, singing was a comparatively late addition to the film capital's repertoire of genres, though the silent screen saw a fair amount of dancing.

To start with, the links with the theatre were maintained: but, after a few years, this nod in the direction of realism became pretty perfunctory. Take *42nd Street* (1933), that classic backstage musical: the title song begins with Ruby Keeler doing a tap dance on top of a taxi which would have needed to be as big as a bus with a ballroom floor for a roof, and goes on to inhabit a set that fills a sound stage and would have been impossible in a theatre. By the early 1930s, the Hollywood musical had taken off on its own, occasionally borrowing ideas from Broadway, often stealing its directors, but mainly just using its songs and rewriting its plots.

It's easy to define a musical: it is a film with songs. Sometimes (as in the backstage musicals) there is a reason for the songs, sometimes they just happen. For no more obvious reason than the fact that it is an MGM musical, the Olympic weightlifting team, which happens to be sharing a transatlantic liner with Jane Russell and Marilyn Monroe in *Gentlemen Prefer Blondes* (1953), joins in a big dance routine. Occasionally, songs sort of grow out of the plot, as when Gene Kelly and Donald O'Connor and Debbie Reynolds wish each other *Good Morning* in *Singin' in the Rain* (1952), or Judy Garland demonstrates the day's work to James Mason in their Malibu living room in *A Star is Born* (1954).

In all the best musicals, however, the numbers don't contribute to the plot: they *are* the plot. In *Top Hat* (1935), Ginger hates Fred because his dancing in the room upstairs keeps her awake, so he dances her to sleep with a sandman shuffle. Fred loves Ginger, but Ginger thinks Fred is the husband of her friend, so she shuns him. When they talk, the sparks fly. However, when they dance *Cheek To Cheek*, the feathers on Ginger's dress may fly (look closely and you can see them coming off all over the place), but the breach is healed. So perfect a dancing team have got to be the ideal couple.

More than any other Hollywood genre, the musical belongs, not to the director (though Vincente Minnelli was its genius), nor the writer, the composer, the choreographer—important every one—nor even to the stars (witness the number of occasions a film would be developed for one star but would end up headed by another), but to the studio, to the entire production set-up, to the reservoir of skill, talent and commitment which made Hollywood what it was. It has been called the Dream Factory, as though the two words were self-contradictory. They weren't, and nothing proves it more completely than the musical. It was a team effort, put together with organization and hard work. The result frequently approached and sometimes achieved genius, and it was the stuff that dreams are made of.

MGM was the great studio for musicals, probably because it was the richest, the most lavish and the only one to get through the Depression without declaring a loss. In the 1930s, they had Nelson Eddy, Jeanette Macdonald and Eleanor Powell. They celebrated the master showman Florenz Ziegfeld in three films (*The Great Ziegfeld*, 1936; *Ziegfeld Girl* 1941; and *Ziegfeld Follies*, 1945) which surpassed the master in pure showmanship. Then they had Judy Garland, about whom nothing that is said is ever enough. They had Gene Kelly who, with *On the Town* (1949) and *Singin' in the Rain*, brought new life to the genre. They had *The Band Wagon*, felt by many to be the greatest musical of them all. They even did the best Presley pic, *Jailhouse Rock*, in 1957. So they get the lion's share of this chapter.

In the 1930s, though, Warner Bros. were the market leaders with their New Deal in Entertainment (the slogan of Roosevelt's administration which they adopted for the *42nd Street* publicity campaign). Warners started it all in 1927 with *The Jazz Singer*. And, with Busby Berkeley's spectacles of suppressed eroticism and unbridled extravagance, they turned out a string of films which still take the breath away. The late 1930s and early 1940s was 20th Century-Fox's musical heyday, from *Alexander's Ragtime Band* in 1938 through to *Stormy Weather* in 1943. They never left the field, though, returning in triumph with *The Sound of Music* in 1965, the most financially successful musical of all time. RKO had Fred and Ginger from *Flying Down to Rio* (1933) to *The Story of Vernon and Irene Castle* (1939). Paramount had its sights set elsewhere, but still found time for films like *Holiday Inn* (1942), which gave us *White Christmas*. And so on, through Universal and Columbia and Sam Goldwyn and even a few independents: with the right package and enough money, the dream could generally be conjured up.

One last point about the musicals in this chapter. Between 1933 and 1953, the relationship between the dancer and the camera goes through several changes. Busby Berkeley's dancers couldn't really dance, any more than he could choreograph. He had no real knowledge of the medium, and was known as 'the One-Two-Three-Kick Man'. What he did know about was cinema. In their skimpy costumes, Berkeley's girls moved gently or just lay around in geometrical patterns, and it was the camera that created the dance. Fred and Ginger danced much better—better than anyone before or since—and the camera simply recorded their numbers: most of their great routines are shot in a single take. But musicals reached their apogee at MGM in the late 1940s and early 1950s. At MGM, every thing moved: the camera and the dancer danced together. Look at the title number in *Singin' in the Rain*, where the excitement comes as much from the camera's little swoops and rushes as it does from Gene Kelly's brilliant dancing.

After that, the tradition of the musical went rather downhill. There were still big musicals like *My Fair Lady* (1964), *West Side Story* (1961) and *The Sound of Music* (1965), but they came from big stage shows. The Hollywood musical had gone back to its origins: with escalating costs and changes in public taste, only the big name of a Broadway hit could offer the chance of recouping the cost of a movie musical, though there were great movies in which songs were a lot more than just background noise, like *Nashville* and *Cabaret* (both 1972). The heyday of the Hollywood musical runs, perhaps not entirely coincidentally, from the birth of the talkies to the coming of age of television. A third of the films in this chapter are from MGM, as is only right; just nine were made after the 1950s, and four of those aren't really musicals. The success of *Grease* and *Fame* suggests that a rebirth is still possible. But, for the moment, the Hollywood musical is lying fallow. May it rest in anything but peace.

• THE • LION'S • • SHARE : MGM •

With its manhunt melodrama properly combined with its Rudolf Friml/Herbert Stothart score, the musical version of **Rose Marie** (1935) was better entertainment than the silent version had been. Jeanette MacDonald and Nelson Eddy trilled and boomed 'Indian Love Call', 'Song Of The Mounties' and 'Rose Marie, I Love You'—and that last sentiment was echoed by the public to the tune of paybox millions. New star material seemed likely in James Stewart as Jeanette's brother, but on this occasion another supporting actor, David Niven, was hardly noticed. Reginald Owen, Allan Jones Gilda Gray, Alan Mowbray, Una O'Connor, Robert Greig and Herman Bing were also cast. Hunt Stromberg, W. S. Van Dyke and Francis Goodrich and Albert Hackett produced, directed and scripted.

Metro Goldwyn Mayer's cinematic glorification of Broadway's legendary Florenz Ziegfeld began four years after the impresario's death at the age of 65 with **The Great Ziegfeld** (1936), and continued with *Ziegfeld Girl* (1941) and *Ziegfeld Follies* (1945). Though all three films traded in spectacle, the first was the best, the longest (180 minutes) and the most opulent. With a budget of over a million and a half dollars, and a cast that included William Powell as the great showman, Luise Rainer as his first wife, and Myrna Loy as his second wife, it was the classiest biographical picture to emerge from Hollywood, and one of the most successful in its recreation of the period in which Ziegfeld flourished. Its money-no-object approach mirrored Ziegfeld's own attitude towards show business entirely: and although for legal reasons, fiction melded with fact in scenarist William Anthony McGuire's efficient account of both Ziegfeld's private and professional life, what was never distorted was the essence of his subject's reach-for-the-stars approach to his work. Nor did the screenplay put a foot wrong in conveying the sheer daring of the man's creative imagination or his infallible eye for talent. Best of all, though, by utilizing the full resources of a major motion picture studio, the film was able to offer audiences a breathtakingly effective cinematic equivalent of a night out at the Follies. If Ziegfeld had had the resources of a film studio at his command, this, you were made to feel, was just the sort of movie he himself would have produced to honour his 40 years in the business. For, as convincing as most of the performances were (and for a Hollywood biopic they were exceptionally convincing), it was the musical numbers staged by Seymour Felix, in settings devised for them by Cedric Gibbons, that understandably attracted the crowds. And although none of these numbers could rival, in originality and ingenuity, the work being done by Busby Berkeley at Warner Bros., the sheer overwhelming size of them set a new standard in opulence that has never been surpassed. Most spectacular of all was the wedding-cake setting used for Irving Berlin's 'A Pretty Girl Is Like A Melody' (vocal by Dennis Morgan—billed as Stanley Morner—but with Allan Jones's voice on the sound track) in which scores of extras, in what is now a collector's item of super-opulent kitsch, sang and danced snippets from the classics as the camera worked its way round the mighty edifice until it reached Virginia Bruce at the top (opposite). The basic structure of the set was used again with certain variations for the title number of the Jeanette MacDonald/Nelson Eddy vehicle *Sweethearts* (MGM 1938) and the finale of *Till the Clouds Roll By* (MGM 1946). It made stunning use of an all-enveloping curtain, which appeared again in *Sweethearts*. In fact, imaginatively deployed curtains would soon become a feature of MGM's more elaborate production numbers, most effectively in the finales of *The Broadway Melody Of 1940, Lady Be Good* (1941) and *Babes On Broadway* (1942). Though nothing else in **The Great Ziegfeld** was quite as eye-catching as the Berlin number. Seymour Felix's staging of 'You Gotta Pull Strings', 'She's A Ziegfeld Follies Girl', 'You', and 'You Never Looked So Beautiful' (by Walter Donaldson and Harold Adamson) in a continuous sequence had as much pazazz as the camera could contain: as did 'A Circus Must Be Different In a Ziegfeld Show', devised by Harriet Hoctor (music by Con Conrad, lyrics by Herb Magidson). On a more modest scale there was Fanny Brice

Left: Jeanette MacDonald and Nelson Eddy in Rose Marie; *opposite:* The Great Ziegfeld

Below: Eleanor Powell in Born to Dance

Right: Judy Garland, the Cowardly Lion and The Tin Man in The Wizard of Oz

singing 'Yiddle On Your Fiddle' (by Irving Berlin). 'Queen Of The Jungle' (by Walter Donaldson and Harold Adamson), and part of 'My Man' (by Channing Pollock and Maurice Yvain). Luise Rainer, more at home in her dramatic moments, such as the famous phone call to Ziegfeld on reading he has remarried, was however charming in 'Won't You Come And Play With Me' and 'It's Delightful To Be Married' (adapted by Anna Held and Vincent Scotto from 'La Petite Tonkinoise' by Scotto and Henri Christine), the latter song cropping up again as part of George Pal's animated sequence in *Ziegfeld Follies*. There was a fairly good impression by Buddy Doyle of Eddie Cantor (in long shot) singing 'If You Knew Susie' (by Buddy De Sylva and Joseph Meyer) and a fair to middling one of Will Rogers by A. A. Trimble. Ray Bolger featured prominently in one of the star turns on the New Amsterdam Roof: Frank Morgan was delightfully (and predictably) vague as a friendly rival of Zeigfeld's, and Nat Pendleton perfect casting as strongman Sandow, Ziegfeld's first major show-biz attraction. Completing the cast were Ernest Cossart, Joseph Cawthorn, Paul Irving, Herman Bing, Charles Judels and Raymond Walburn. It was produced by Hunt Stromberg and directed with workmanlike efficiency by Robert Z. Leonard. The classical music interpolated in the *A Pretty Girl Is Like A Melody* number included snippets from Dvorak's *Humoresque No. 7 in G Flat; One Fine Day* from Puccini's *Madame Butterfly;* Liszt's *Liebestraum*; Johann Strauss II's *The Blue Danube Waltz*; *On With The Motley* from Leoncavallo's *Pagliacci*; and *Rhapsody In Blue* by George Gershwin.

They could have called it 'The Broadway Melody of 1937' but in deference to Eleanor Powell, each one of whose taps was worth its weight in silver dollars, they named it **Born to Dance** (1936). And it mattered not one iota that Miss Powell found herself understudying Virginia Bruce (who played an impossibly difficult musical comedy star) because, just like little Ruby Keeler in *42nd Street* (Warner Bros. 1933) she stepped in at the last moment and, well, you know the rest. Nor did it matter a jot that Miss Bruce featured in Sid Silvers' and Jack McGowan's screenplay (story by McGowan, Silvers and Buddy De Sylva) as a singer, while there could be no mistaking the fact that Miss Powell's talents lay in other directions. What counted in **Born to Dance** wasn't its thimbleful of plot (which also involved sailors on shore leave) but the splendour of Cole Porter's tip-top score and the razz-a-matazz of its staging (by Dave Gould). Particularly splashy was the all-out 'Swingin' The Jinx Away' finale, set on board a typical musical comedy battleship and involving the services of literally scores of dance extras as well as Buddy Ebsen, Frances Langford and, of course, Miss Powell (left), whose spectacular entrance down a long spiral stairway left no one in any doubt as to who was the star of the show. Other musical highlights in this nautical farrago were Miss Bruce's rendering of 'I've Got You Under My Skin'; Powell tapping her way through the sound barrier with 'Rap-Rap-Tap On Wood'; Reginald Gardiner conducting an invisible orchestra in Central Park in a version of Ponchielli's 'Dance Of The Hours' which miraculously turns into 'Easy To Love'; and a deliciously camp item called 'Love Me, Love My Pekinese' sung by Miss Bruce to a ship-load of admiring sailors. Completing the score were the opening number *Rolling Home*, *Hey Babe*, *Hey*, and *Entrance Of Lucy James*. James Stewart received second billing and though clearly no asset to musical comedy, got by on his charm and good looks. Also cast were Alan Dinehart, Una Merkel, Raymold Walburn, Juanita Quigley and the dance team of Georges and Jaina. It was zestfully directed by Roy Del Ruth and the producer was Jack Cummings.

The Wizard of Oz was an enchanting entertainment that really lived up to the blurb—'for children of all ages'. Today, it still seems as fresh as it was in 1939, when it became an instant movie classic and made an international star of 17-year-old Judy Garland. Although Mervyn LeRoy's production was beset with problems in every department—not least that of the screenplay which went through numerous versions—the finished product was superb, more than compensating for the many difficulties encountered in its gruelling five-month shooting schedule, and the many months of pre-production preparation. In the end everything worked—from the final screenplay adapted from L. Frank Baum's novel and credited to Noel Langley, Florence Ryerson and Edgar Allan Woolf—to the songs, by Harold Arlen and E. Y. Harburg, giving plenty of opportunity for excitement, spectacle, tenderness and comedy. Four noted directors were involved in the production: Richard Thorpe was fired after 12 days and his footage scrapped because it lacked fairy-tale feeling. George Cukor directed three days of tests in which he got rid of Judy's blonde wig and 'cute' doll-face make-up (a hang-over, perhaps, from the studio's unsuccessful attempt to obtain Shirley Temple), which made the point that restoring Dorothy's down-to-earth ingenuousness was the way to enhance the fairy-tale quality of her Technicolored adventure in the Land of Oz. Victor Fleming, who received sole director credit, spent four months getting these sequences on film before having to leave to take over *Gone with the Wind*. Fleming drew unsurpassed performances from Ray Bolger as the Scarecrow, Bert Lahr as the Cowardly Lion, Jack Haley (replacing Buddy Ebsen who fell ill with aluminium poisoning) as the Tin Man (the last two illustrated, with Garland), and Margaret Hamilton as the Wicked Witch. Choreographer Bobby Connolly was in charge of the musical numbers and the daunting task of teaching 150 midget-Munchkins to sing and dance. (In all, 9,200 actors were employed on the film, and there were

3,210 costume designs, 8,428 separate make-ups and 68 sets!) Though it was a brilliant idea to open the film in black and white for the Kansas scenes, directed by King Vidor in ten days after Fleming departed, and then going into colour as Dorothy (Garland) enters the Land of Oz, it was not the eye-catching colour photography or Connolly's elaborately staged musical numbers that lingered in the memory, but Vidor's staging of Judy's simple and tender singing of 'Over The Rainbow' in her own backyard. Incredible as it now seems, anti-LeRoy politicking after the first sneak preview nearly succeeded in getting this classic sequence cut out of the picture. Billie Burke (dubbed by Lorraine Bridges) was cast as Glinda the Good Witch, and Frank Morgan played the Wonderful Wizard, with Charles Grapewin as Uncle Henry, Clara Blandick as Auntie Em, and Pat Walshe as Chief of the Wicked Witch's Winged Monkeys. Other songs: *Come Out, Come Out Wherever You are* (Burke); *It Really Was No Miracle* (Garland); *Ding Dong The Witch Is Dead* (Garland, Burke, Munchkins); *We Welcome You To Munchkinland* (Munchkins); *Follow The Yellow Brick Road* (Garland, Munchkins); *We're Off To See The Wizard* (Garland, Bolger, Lahr, Haley); *If I Only Had A Brain (A Heart, The Nerve)* (Bolger, Lahr, Haley); *Lions And Tigers And Bears* (Lahr); *You're Out Of The Woods* (chorus); *The Merry Old Land Of Oz* (chorus); *If I Were King Of The Forest* (Lahr); *Optimistic Voices* (chorus on soundtrack).

MGM pulled out all the stops for **Ziegfeld Girl**, an eye-filling spectacle that traced the lives and loves of three Ziegfeld girls: vaudeville singer Judy Garland

(left), elevator girl Lana Turner (right), and wife of a penniless violinist, Hedy Lamarr (centre). Garland makes it; Turner doesn't; and Lamarr swops her place in the chorus for married bliss. With Busby Berkeley in charge of the production numbers, Cedric Gibbons the sumptuous sets and Adrian the mind-boggling costumes, the visual aspect of the film was, in every respect, splendiferous. Where it let itself down was in its soap-opera plot (by William Anthony McGuire, screenplay by Marguerite Roberts and Sonya Levien), an endless parade of sob-story clichés that held not a single surprise. Viewed today through the jaundiced eyes of the Eighties, the film emerges as a camp wallow from start to finish; a highly-charged dose of Forties' sentimentality that also happens to be quite preposterously entertaining. All the same, apart from Busby Berkeley's brilliantly inventive staging of a Spanish dance by Antonio and Rosario, where the lighting and the camera movements create an excitement equal to that provided by the performers, the two big set pieces—'Minnie From Trinidad' by Roger Edens (performed by Garland) and 'You Stepped Out Of A Dream' (sung by Tony Martin) by Gus Kahn and Nacio Herb Brown relied on opulence rather than on invention for their effects. Pandro S. Berman's production borrowed several sequences from *The Great Ziegfeld* (MGM, 1936), including the famous 'wedding cake set' but, instead of Virginia Bruce being the cherry on top of the edifice, part of the set was reconstructed to allow Judy Garland to take her place which, in a skilful piece of editing, she did most tellingly. The men in **Ziegfeld Girl** (1941) were James Stewart (top-billed) as Miss Turner's truckdriver sweetheart, Tony Martin, who has a brief dalliance with the beauteous Hedy Lamarr, together with Jackie Cooper, Ian Hunter, Charles Winninger (as Mr Gallagher), Al Shean (as himself), Edward Everett Horton, Philip Dorn, Paul Kelly and Dan Dailey. The cast was completed by Eve Arden, Felix Bressart and Rose Hobart. It was directed very stylishly by Robert Z. Leonard. Other songs and musical numbers included: *Laugh? I Thought I'd Split My Sides* (Garland, Winninger) Roger Edens; *Caribbean Love Song* (Martin) Edens, Ralph Freed; *I'm Always Chasing Rainbows* (Garland) Joseph McCarthy, Harry Carroll; *Whispering* (unidentified male vocal trio) John Schonberger, Richard Coburn, Vincent Rose; *Mr Gallagher And Mr Shean* (Winninger, Shean) Ed Gallagher and Al Shean; *You Never Looked So Beautiful Before* (Garland, chorus) Walter Donaldson, Harold Adamson.

Young hopefuls: Judy Garland, Hedy Lamarr and Lana Turner (left to right) in Ziegfeld Girl.

Fred Astaire and Judy Garland as 'A Couple Of Swells', a classic number from a classic musical, **Easter Parade** (1948). Spangled with Technicolor and 17 Irving Berlin Songs, showered with press praise, the Arthur Freed production stepped out into immediate box-office success and lasting fame. Astaire had announced his retirement two years before, but started another 20 years of stardom by answering MGM's SOS when Gene Kelly broke an ankle on the eve of production. Judy was at her peak and Ann Miller displayed a vivid dancing personality opposite Peter Lawford; Jules Munshin, Clinton Sundberg and Jeni Le Gon shone in support. Sidney Sheldon joined Frances Goodrich and Albert Hackett to script their original story, directed by Charles Walters. Robert Alton handled the musical numbers, scoring of which won Oscars for Roger Edens and Johnny Green.

On the Town (1949) started life as a Jerome Robbins ballet called *Fancy Free*. The material was reworked by composer Leonard Bernstein with a book and lyrics by Betty Comden and Adolph Green, and surfaced as a hit Broadway musical in 1944. Producer Arthur Freed prevailed on Louis B. Mayer to purchase the property—which he reluctantly did while, at the same time, condemning the show as 'smutty' and 'Communistic' because of a scene in it in which a black girl danced with a white man. Five years later, Freed, now securely entrenched as the studio's top producer of musicals, was finally given the green light by Mayer to proceed with the project. The result was the freshest, most invigorating and innovative screen musical of the decade, and the perfect vehicle for Gene Kelly who not only starred in it, but directed and choreographed it together with Stanley Donen. The story of **On the Town** was not nearly as innovative as its production. Three sailors disembark from their battleship in the Brooklyn Navy Yard at six o'clock one morning and spend the next 24 hours in search of women and fun. Kelly falls in love with a poster of the subway's Miss Turnstiles (Vera-Ellen, illustrated with Kelly opposite page) and spends half the film searching for its real-life model whom he finally tracks down at Symphonic Hall where she is receiving ballet instruction from a Maria Ouspenskaya-type ballet mistress (Florence Bates). Sinatra, again cast as the timid butter-wouldn't-melt-in-the-mouth innocent, is chased with relentless zeal by a lady cab driver called Brunnhilde Esterhazy (Betty Garrett), while the third (Jules Munshin) makes a hit with an anthropologist (Ann Miller) he happens to meet at the Anthropological Museum. Which more or less took care of the story, except that Kelly and Donen invested it with so much that was new and exciting—from the expressive 'Miss Turnstiles' Ballet (Bernstein) to the scintillating sequence atop the Empire State building where the three couples rendezvous—that they changed the entire concept of the film musical, opening it out (some of it was actually filmed on location in New York and its environs) and relying on the dance for its chief mode of musical expression. The underlying feeling of the film was essentially balletic, and even when its cast were standing still (which wasn't very often) you felt they were about to take off any second. In fact, so concerned was Kelly that **On the Town** should retain its balletic flavour, that in the 'Day In New York' ballet (Bernstein) he substituted four trained ballet dancers (Alex Romero, Gene Scott, Carol Haney and Marie Grosscup) for Sinatra, Munshin, Betty Garrett and Ann Miller. Agnes de Mille had done this six years earlier on stage in

Not quite cheek to cheek: below: Fred Astaire and Judy Garland in Easter Parade*; opposite: Vera-Ellen and Gene Kelly, and inset: Frank Sinatra, Betty Garrett, Jules Munshin, Ann Miller, Kelly and Vera-Ellen in* On the Town

the Dream ballet for *Oklahoma!*, but it had never been attempted on the screen before. The less overtly balletic numbers were equally successful, such as Roger Edens, Betty Comden and Adolph Green's 'Prehistoric Man', danced by Miller in the anthropology museum supported by the rest of the principals; and the rousing 'New York, New York' (by Leonard Bernstein, Comden and Green) exuberantly performed by Kelly, Sinatra and Munshin. Completing the cast were Alice Pearce as ugly-duckling Lucy Schmeeler, George Meader, Bea Benedaret, Hans Conried and, briefly, singer Bern Hoffman. It was filmed in Technicolor. The inset picture shows (from left) Sinatra, Garrett, Munshin, Miller, Kelly and Vera-Ellen. Other songs and musical numbers: *I Feel Like I'm Not Out Of Bed Yet* (Hoffman); *Come Up To My Place* (Sinatra, Garrett) Berbstein, Comden, Green; *Miss Turnstiles* (Vera-Ellen) Bernstein; *Main Street* (Kelly, Vera-Ellen); *You're Awful* (Sinatra, Garret); *On The Town* (Kelly, Sinatra, Munshin, Miller, Garrett, Vera-Ellen); *You Can Count On Me* (Kelly, Sinatra, Munshin, Miller, Garrett, Pearce); *Pearl Of The Persian Sea; That's All There Is, Folks* Edens, Comden, Green. It wasn't until the last twenty minutes or so that the high standard the film set for itself flagged and became bogged down in plot. And if, while watching the movie today, a slight feeling of *déjà vu* insinuates itself, it is because such films as *Hit the Deck* (MGM, 1955), *Skirts Ahoy* (MGM, 1952), *It's Always Fair Weather* (MGM, 1955), *All*

Ashore (Columbia, 1953), *So this is Paris* (Universal International, 1955), and *Three Sailors and a Girl* (Warner Bros, 1953), all of which contained similar ingredients to **On the Town**, have blunted one's appetite for this kind of yarn. Also, it is to be regretted that most of Leonard Bernstein's original Broadway score was jettisoned in favour of a more 'commercial' one by Roger Edens, a particularly unfortunate loss being *Lonely Town*, one of Bernstein's most poignant songs. All the same, **On the Town**, which cost $2,111,250 to make (and grossed over $4,500,000 on its initial release) pushed the Hollywood musical out of its claustrophobic confines in search of new ideas, and was a landmark of its time. Edens, Conrad Salinger and Lennie Hayton scored it, it was photographed by Harold Rosson, costumed by Helen Rose and designed by Cedric Gibbons and Jack Martin Smith.

Ethel Merman belted it out on stage for 1,159 performances; Judy Garland was signed for the screen version, and Betty Hutton finally got to play it. The role was Annie Oakley, the show was Irving Berlin's **Annie Get your Gun**, which George Sidney directed (replacing Busby Berkeley and Charles Walters) to give MGM its top money-making musical of 1950. Sidney Sheldon's adaptation and screenplay from Herbert and Dorothy Fields' original book stuck as closely to the Broadway version of the show as was considered decent by Hollywood's meddlesome standards—and although the score lost a few numbers between Times Square and Culver City (most notably *Moonshine Lullaby* and *Who Do You Love, I Hope*) the spirit of the piece was left intact. The simple story of an unorthodox love affair between two prize sharpshooters who are attached to different Wild West shows, the film co-starred Howard Keel in the role played on stage by Ray Middleton, with Louis Calhern (who replaced Frank Morgan after the latter's death) as Buffalo Bill, J. Carrol Naish as Sitting Bull, and Edward Arnold as Pawnee Bill. Keenan Wynn, Benay Venuta and Clinton Sundberg completed the cast. It was photographed in Technicolor, and was another triumph for producer Arthur Freed, and for Robert Alton, whose staging of the musical numbers (Hutton in 'I'm An Indian Too', (seen left) did Berlin's magnificent score proud. All the performances were spot-on, especially Hutton's, which, after a slightly frenetic start, settled down to become the highwater mark of her career. The musical director was Adolph Deutsch. Songs and musical numbers: *Colonel Buffalo Bill* (chorus); *I've Got The Sun In The Morning* (Hutton); *You Can't Get A Man With A Gun* (Hutton); *They Say That Falling In Love Is Wonderful* (Hutton, Keel); *My Defences Are Down* (Keel); *There's No Business Like Show Business* (Hutton, Keel, Wynn, Calhern); *Doin' What Comes Naturally* (Hutton and children); *The Girl That I Marry* (Keel); *Anything You Can Do* (Hutton, Keel).

Singin' in the Rain (MGM, 1952) was the story of a matinée idol called Don Lockwood (Gene Kelly) and his romance with chorus girl Kathy Selden (Debbie Reynolds). One of the best, and best written story-lines (by Betty Comden and Adolph Green) to grace a Hollywood musical, it was the perfect subject on which to hang the Arthur Freed/Nacio Herb Brown songs that accompanied it, and a marvellous opportunity to take a light-hearted and often satirical look at the early days of talking pictures. With the exception of two numbers—'Fit As A Fiddle' (by Freed, Al Hoffman and Al Goodhart) and 'Moses Supposes' (the latter written especially for the film by Roger Edens, Comden and Green)—all the Freed/Brown numbers featured in **Singin' in the Rain** were from earlier MGM movies: *All I Do Is Dream Of You* sung by Debbie Reynolds (after popping out of an enormous cake at a typical Hollywood party) was first heard in *Sadie*

Bottom left: Betty Hutton in Annie Get Your Gun*; above: Gene Kelly and Cyd Charisse in 'The Broadway Ballet'; and opposite: Kelly in the title number of* Singin' in the Rain

McKee (1934); *Should I?* was featured in *Lord Byron of Broadway* (1929); *Singin' In The Rain* came from *Hollywood Revue of 1929*; *I've Got A Feelin You're Foolin'*, *You Are My Lucky Star* and *Broadway Rhythm*, all from *Broadway Melody of 1936* (1935); *The Wedding Of The Painted Doll* from *Broadway Melody* (1929); *You Were Meant For Me* from *Broadway Melody* (1929); *Would You* from *San Francisco* (1936); *Good Morning* from *Babes in Arms* (1939), *Beautiful Girl* (sung here with flair by Jimmy Thompson) from *Going Hollywood* (1933), and *Broadway Melody* from *Broadway Melody* (1929). Just as most of its music had featured prominently in past films, so everything else in **Singin' in the Rain** drew its inspiration from the movies. In fact most of the film was a compendium of borrowings drawn from a variety of real-life sources and personalities. The scene on the sound stage, for example, with dumb blonde Jean Hagen, in a *tour-de-force* performance, desperately trying to 'speak into the bush' where the microphone has been hidden, had its origins in reality. Douglas Shearer, head of MGM's sound department, was consulted regularly about the hazards of early sound recording, and most of the tribulations suffered by the artists and technicians in **Singin' in the Rain's** reconstruction of those times, actually happened. Roscoe Dexter (Douglas Fowley) the director in that particular scene, was modelled on Busby Berkeley, while R. F. Simpson, the studio boss (Millard Mitchell), was inspired by producer Arthur Freed. Dora Bailey the columnist (played by Madge Blake) was modelled on Louella Parsons,

Kelly himself on a composite of several matinée idols (particularly Fairbanks, in the 'Duelling Cavalier' sequences) and Cyd Charisse, in the 'Broadway Ballet', on Louise Brooks. Musically, the ballet, choreographed by Kelly, was the film's most ambitious sequence, also drawing its inspiration from the movies. Entirely new, however, was what Kelly calls the 'Crazy Veil' sequence in which Cyd Charisse danced with a soft, light piece of voile, which required the use of three aeroplane motors to control the veil's billowing movement.

Choreographically, it was Kelly at his most lyrical, and a highspot in a film crowded with them. In fact, **Singin' in the Rain**, directed and choreographed by Kelly and Stanley Donen, remains an undoubted masterpiece and the finest, most durable musical ever to have come out of Hollywood. If the test of a great musical is that you can see it over and over again without longing for the dialogue to end and the musical numbers to begin, then **Singin' in the Rain** passes *cum laude*. And it is more popular in today's nostalgia-addicted world than it was on its initial release. But even to those not seduced by nostalgia, it remains an invigorating musical, perfect in its reconstruction of a world gone forever, and unforgettable if only for Kelly's joyous dancing in the title number as he abandons himself to a Californian cloudburst, kicks and stamps in a gutterful of water, and climbs halfway up a lamp-post, arms outstretched, and water pouring on to his face, defying adversity. The number, 'an irrepressible ode to optimism' as it has been described by Comden and Green, was the apotheosis of his art, and the climax of an adventurous career. Though the rest of the film never quite equalled the magic of those five glorious minutes, every other number was still head and shoulders above most of the musicals of the Fifties. Donald O'Connor has never been as good again, most notably in his justly celebrated 'Make 'Em Laugh' routine, in which he danced, sang, and clowned as if his artistic life depended on the success of it. Every trick in his repertoire was aired afresh and the cumulative effect was devastating in its virtuosity. As for Debbie Reynolds, her dancing in the buoyant 'Good Morning' never for an instant betrayed her lack of experience, and she was a most sympathetic partner for Kelly in the lyrical 'You Were Meant For Me' into which Kelly attempted to inject the perfect romantic atmosphere on a sound stage through the auspices of five hundred kilowatts of stardust and a soft, summer breeze. It was the third time he had used this 'make-believe' device—first with Kathryn Grayson in *Anchors Aweigh* (MGM, 1945), and next in *Summer Stock* (MGM, 1950) where he wooed Judy Garland. The producer was Arthur Freed. Harold Rosson photographed it (in Technicolor), Cedric Gibbons and Randall Duell were the art directors. Walter Plunkett created the costumes, Lennie Hayton was the muscial director; Conrad Salinger, Wally Heglin and Skip Martin orchestrated the numbers, and the cast was completed by Rita Moreno, King Donovan, Kathleen Freeman and Mae Clark.

As good as *Julias Caesar*, MGM's other artistic triumph of 1953, in its very different way, **The Band Wagon** jumped close to the top of the Arthur Freed/ Vincente Minnelli hit list, starring Fred Astaire, Nanette Fabray and Jack Buchanan (below in the hilarious 'Triplets' number which had been done before in one of Buchanan's Broadway shows,

Below: hilarity in The Band Wagon*; opposite: two lively moments from* Seven Brides for Seven Brothers

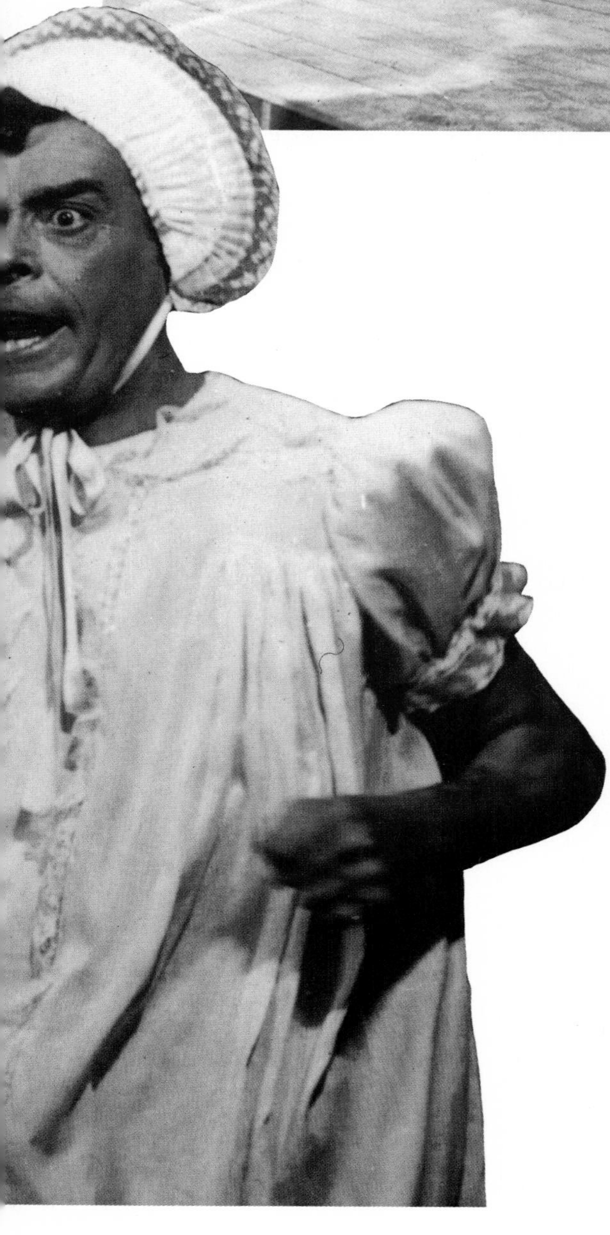

'Between the Devil' in 1937), Cyd Charisse, Oscar Levant and James Mitchell. They had a witty Betty Comden/Adolph Green script to work on, and great Schwartz/Dietz songs from the Thirties like *Louisiana Hayride*, *I Guess I'll Have To Change My Plan*, *Dancing In The Dark*, *A Shine On Your Shoes*, *By Myself*, *Something To Remember You By*, *I Love Louisa*, and *You And The Night And The Music*, topped by a new audience-rouser, *That's Entertainment*.

Howard Keel could hardly believe it when Jane Powell tamed his backwoods brothers, Marc Platt, Matt Mattox, Jacques d'Amboise, Tommy Rall, Jeff Richards and Russ Tamblyn in **Seven Brides for Seven Brothers**. Neither could MGM when the movie became 1954's most sensational hit—and it was still getting bookings around the world twenty years later. The unusually strong story concerned the seven Pontipec brothers, all of whom lead a rough lonely life on their farm in Oregon, and their successful (and unorthodox) hunt for wives. Jack Cummings produced it on the back lot, so to speak, while more expensive musicals with stage-famous titles were being made front and centre. It did for the screen what 'Oklahoma' had done for the theatre; created a new style of musical, roaring with vitality, prancing with open-air freshness. Credit Stanley Donen's direction, Michael Kidd's choreography, the Gene de Paul/Johnny Mercer songs (*When You're In Love*, *Wonderful Day*, *Bless Yore Beautiful Hide*, *Spring*, *Lonesome Polecat*, etc.) and the Albert Hackett/Frances Goodrich/Dorothy Kingsley script from Stephen Vincent Benet's *Sobbin' Women*. It was in AnscoColor and CinemaScope.

Elvis Presley, after a couple of milder movies, sulked volcanically through a melodramatic role in **Jailhouse Rock** (1957) with frequent intervals to let the music rock and the pelvis roll. Adolescents of all ages gave it a frenzied welcome. The title song sold two million discs in its first fortnight of release and the movie soon brought in twice that many dollars in rentals. Richard Thorpe directed Guy Trosper's screenplay, from a story by Ned Young; Pandro Berman produced; Judy Tyler, Mickey Shaughnessy, Dean Jones and Jennifer Holden were featured.

Another fair lady from the team of Alan Jay Lerner and Frederick Loewe, **Gigi** (1958) was the last of the great MGM musicals and it justly deserved its eight Academy Awards. The delightful story of a young girl reared by her grandmother and her great-aunt to follow the family tradition by becoming a courtesan, it starred Leslie Caron (above, giving the performance of her career) as Gigi, with Louis Jourdan as the handsome, outrageously eligible Gaston Lachaille who scandalizes Gigi's family by actually proposing marriage to her, Maurice Chevalier as his wordly grandfather Honoré, and Hermione Gingold and Isabel Jeans as Gigi's grandmother and great-aunt respectively. Set in *fin de siècle* Paris, it was brilliantly costumed by Cecil Beaton, directed by Vincente Minnelli and scripted by Alan Jay Lerner from the novel by Colette with grace and elegance. In fact, **Gigi** was a stylish triumph from start to finish which sadly—but gloriously—marked the end of an era. (Its producer Arthur Freed would make only one more musical, *Bells are Ringing*, MGM 1960.) If **Gigi** was one of Freed's finest achievements, it also showed Minnelli on top of

Energy and elegance: left: Elvis in Jailhouse Rock*; above and opposite: Louis Jourdan and Leslie Caron in* Gigi

his form. For sheer sustained visual opulence and the brilliant use it made of colour, the film ranks with his work on *Meet Me in St Louis* (MGM, 1944) and *An American in Paris* (MGM, 1951). Musically, too, it was perfection; the highlight of its ravishing and extraordinarily durable score being whatever number you may care to choose: be it the rousing 'The Night They Invented Champagne' (Caron, Jourdan, Gingold); the incomparable 'Gigi' (Jourdan); the tender 'Say A Prayer For Me Tonight' (Caron); Chevalier's jaunty ode to old age 'I'm Glad I'm Not Young Anymore'; or, perhaps best of all, the touching 'I Remember It Well', magnificently performed by Chevalier and Gingold on the terrace of a Deauville Hotel against a calculatedly romantic sunset. The richly textured orchestrations throughout were by Conrad Salinger, with André Previn in charge of the musical direction. Leslie Caron's vocals were dubbed by Betty Wand, and the cast was completed by Eva Gabor, Jacques Bergerac and John Abbott. It was magnificently photographed in Metrocolor and CinemaScope by Joseph Ruttenberg. Other songs: *Thank Heaven For Little Girls* (Chevalier); *It's A Bore* (Jourdan, Chevalier); *The Parisians* (Caron); *Waltz At Maxim's (She's Not Thinking Of Me)* (Jourdan); *Gossip* (chorus).

Wow! or words to that effect were elicited from practically everybody when Gene Anthony Ray and Carol Massenburg went into their dance in **Fame** (1981). They, and what looked like hundreds of other young dancers, singers, musicians and—not least—actors, performed with an elan unsurpassed even in the Rooney–Garland heyday. They played pupils at New York's real High School of the Performing Arts, director Alan Parker focusing on eight of them (Ray, Maureen Teefy, Paul McCrane, Irene Cara, Barry Miller, Lee Curreri, Laura Dean, Antonia Franceschi) for interwoven stories of success, failure and love. A small miracle was the capture of Manhattan's atmosphere, in all its tawdry confusion and exhilarating glamour, by a largely British team: Parker, producer Alan Marshall, photography director Michael Seresin, designer Geoffrey Kirkland, editor Gerry Hambling and cameraman John Stanier. Writer Christopher Gore and co-producer David De Silva headed their brilliant collaborators; composer Michael Gore won two Oscars, for best original score and best song, *Fame* with lyrics by Dean Pitchford. A *Fame* series for TV ensued.

• A • NEW • DEAL • IN • ENTERTAINMENT : • WARNER • BROS •

It is of no consequence at all that **The Jazz Singer** (1927) is really a rather wretched drama about a rabbi's son, played by Al Jolson, whose love of show-business causes a rift between him and his orthodox father: a rift which is finally resolved on the old man's death-bed on the eve of the Jewish Day of Atonement. The eye-rolling, breast-beating, hair-tugging style of acting indulged in by Warner Oland (as the rabbi) and Eugenie Besserer as his wife, a woman torn between the love of a husband and the love of a son, gives the film a ludicrous aspect today which, again, is of little consequence. What is really important about **The Jazz Singer** is that it was the first motion picture in which spoken dialogue was heard. True, the words uttered by Jolson were improvised (contrast their freshness with some of the film's silent titles, a typical example being 'God made her a woman and love made her a mother') and although the words he spoke numbered only 281, plus a few astonished ad libs from Miss Besserer, they revitalized the film business and helped to turn Warner Bros. into one of the top three studios in the industry. Apart from its revolutionary aspect, **The Jazz Singer** gave a wide audience a chance to see and experience Jolson performing as he must have done in those legendary Winter Garden concerts in New York. After watching and listening to him unleashing his magic on the film's musical numbers, it was not difficult to understand why he was called the greatest entertainer in the world. Others in this epoch-making production were May McAvoy, (in Jolson's arms), the celebrated cantor Joseph Rosenblatt, Otto Lederer and William Demarest. **The Jazz Singer** was photographed by Hal Mohr and directed by Alan Crosland. It was written by Alfred A. Cohn from a story and play by Samson Raphaelson. Songs included: *Blue Skies* (by Irving Berlin); *Mother I Still Have You* (by Al Jolson and Louis Silvers); *My Mammy* (by Sam Lewis, Joe Young and Walter Donaldson); and *Toot Toot Tootsie Goodbye* (by Gus Kahn, Ernie Erdman and Dan Russo).

Just as *Broadway Melody* (MGM 1929) created a vogue for the backstage musical before familiarity with the genre began to breed contempt, so **42nd Street**—another behind-the-scenes saga—single-

Right: The Jazz Singer; *facing page:* Fame

handedly revitalized a dying, if not already dead, institution. The movie offered Depression-weary audiences, via its dance director, Busby Berkeley, an entertainment that managed to be simultaneously hard-hitting and escapist. Freshness was the keynote to **42nd Street**, and it was apparent in every aspect of Darryl F. Zanuck's production, from his casting of newcomers Dick Powell and Ruby Keeler as the young hero and heroine, to his choice of composers Al Dubin and Harry Warren. His most far-reaching decision of all, however, was to sign Berkeley (on Mervyn LeRoy's advice) to breathe life into the production numbers. 'Young And Healthy', for example, apart from Sol Polito's brilliant black and white photography (soon to become a feature of Berkeley's musicals in the same way that Van Nest Polglase's white sets were a fixture of the Astaire-Rogers musicals at RKO), offered viewers a kaleidoscope of pulchritude as its participants grouped themselves into interesting formations, and demonstrated just how effective a few lengths of ribbon could be when imaginatively deployed. More innovative was 'Shuffle Off To Buffalo', set on a Pullman carriage that jack-knifed open to reveal a trainload of women preparing for bed as Ginger Rogers and Una Merkel cynically warn a honeymoon couple (Keeler and Clarence Nordstrom) to be wary of marriage ('When she knows as much as we know, She'll be on her way to Reno' runs one of the couplets). The number showed Berkeley at his inventive best, and proved that he did not have to rely on spectacle alone to achieve some of his most memorable effects. Spectacle, however, dominated the grand **42nd Street** finale, a rousing, gloriously costumed, stunning paean to Broadway and its denizens. The fact that Ruby Keeler (illustrated), in this her first of nine films for the studio, couldn't sing, and wasn't a particularly good dancer, somehow didn't seem to matter. On the contrary, if she was able to become a star, so could every other kid like her in America—and audiences, pummelled into despair by the Depression, went home with hope in their hearts. A milestone in Hollywood's history, **42nd Street** was scripted by Rian James and James Seymour (from a story by Bradford Ropes), and contained the immortal line—uttered by a desperate Warner Baxter to an unflappable Ruby Keeler as she is about to go on stage in place of the show's ailing leading lady, 'Sawyer, you're going out a youngster, but you've got to come back a star!' Dick Powell played Ruby's sweetheart, Bebe Daniels the leading lady she replaces. Other well-

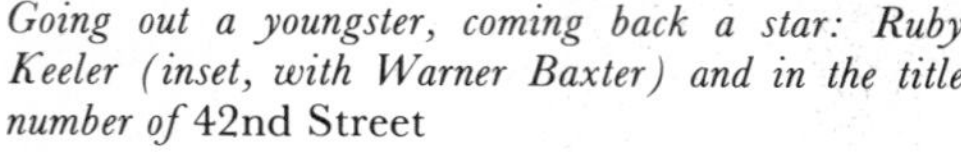

Going out a youngster, coming back a star: Ruby Keeler (inset, with Warner Baxter) and in the title number of 42nd Street

Below: Gold Diggers of 1933; *opposite:* Yankee Doodle Dandy

known Warner regulars in the cast were: George Brent, Guy Kibbee, Ned Sparks, Allen Jenkins and, briefly, Al Dubin and Harry Warren who, apart from the numbers already mentioned, wrote two other songs for the show: *It Must Be June*, and the durable *You're Getting To Be A Habit With Me*. Composer Harry Akst also had a small part, and the movie was directed by Lloyd Bacon.

The success of *42nd Street* left the studio in no doubt as to the kind of musical escapism Depression-torn audiences wanted. Its follow up, **Gold Diggers of 1933**, loosely based on Avery Hopwood's play, was an even more elaborate piece of escapism which consolidated the reputation of its dance director Busby Berkeley who, in the film's three major production numbers, revealed himself to be the enviable possessor of the most fertile imagination in his particular field. Boasting no fewer than three love stories for the price of one (Warren William and Joan Blondell, Guy Kibbee and Aline MacMahon—a teaming the studio would return to on several more occasions—and Dick Powell and Ruby Keeler—ditto) the Erwin Gelsey/James Seymour screenplay (with dialogue by David Boehm and Ben Markson) traversed familiar backstage territory, this time focusing on the efforts of songwriter Powell to raise $15,000 to stage a show he has written. Directed by Mervyn LeRoy with a pace and attack rare in musicals, and with a top-notch score by Al Dubin and Harry Warren, **Gold Diggers of 1933** opened with the prophetic *We're In The Money* (sung by Ginger Rogers). Though the film's production costs were twenty times the amount songwriter Powell needed for *his* show, it grossed a fortune. Robert Lord supervised the production. Other songs included; *I've Got To Sing A Torch Song*, *Pettin' In The Park*, *The Shadow Waltz* and *My Forgotten Man*.

Though a great deal of **Yankee Doodle Dandy** (1942) was unadulterated corn, its heart was in the right place, and its timely appearance assured it enormous success. A routine biopic of the great showman George M. Cohan, its strongest selling point (apart from the perennial Cohan songs themselves) was James Cagney's truly mesmeric portrayal (right) of the versatile pint-sized entertainer. Director Michael Curtiz, working from a screenplay by Robert Buckner and Edmund Joseph, realized exactly what was needed to make flag-waving material of this kind of work, and directed it all with a patriotic zeal which would have warmed its subject's heart. All the other creative contributions were top-notch too, from James Wong Howe's photography to Milo Anderson's costumes. Nor were there any blemishes in a cast that included Joan Leslie (as Mrs Cohan), Walter Huston, Richard Whorf, George Tobias, Irene Manning, Rosemary De Camp, Jeanne Cagney, S. Z. Sakall, Frances Langford and Eddie Foy Jr, (playing Eddie Foy Sr) who appeared with Cagney in a memorable scene where the two of them rib each other most endearingly. Songs included: *Give My Regards To Broadway*, *I Was Born In Virginia*, *Mary's A Grand Old Name*, *So Long Mary*, and *Yankee Doodle Boy*. The producers were Jack Warner and Hal B. Wallis, with William Cagney as associate producer. The box-office gross was $4,800,000.

The 1937 version of **A Star is Born** (Selznick International) was conceived by Dorothy Parker, Alan Campbell, Robert Carson and William Wellman, and inspired by Adela Rogers St. John's *What Price Hollywood?* Moss Hart's screenplay for his and director George Cukor's 1954 version of the same subject, also called **A Star is Born**, was as brilliant an evocation of Hollywood as the screen had seen, and it materialized into the best 'behind-the-scenes' musical ever made. From its dazzling opening at a Hollywood première, where James Mason's drunken Norman Maine first meets Judy Garland's Esther Blodgett, to the poignant final moments where Mason commits suicide, the film never faltered. And as the band singer whose career ascends in direct ratio to the decline of her alcoholic actor husband, Judy Garland (below) gave the performance of her career. Garland's vulnerability, sense of humour, intensity and sheer musicality—this time brought to bear on a superb score by Harold Arlen and Ira Gershwin—merged, on this occasion, in one overwhelming explosion of talent. James Mason was equally accomplished as the tormented husband who, on realizing that his problems are about to truncate his wife's career, decides to destroy himself rather than the woman he loves. The film's big scenes were shared equally between the two stars, and neither of them missed a trick. Also featured were Jack Carson, appropriately loathsome as Libby, the studio's long-suffering, resentful PR man, Charles Bickford, who played studio boss Oliver Niles with grim-faced authority, and Tom Noonan in the thankless role of Danny McGuire, Garland's best friend. Regrettably, approximately 37 minutes of film were edited out of the final release print (including the number *Lose That Long Face*), thus creating gaps in

Below: A Star is Born, *Judy Garland; and opposite: a lady is made: Wilfrid Hyde-White, Audrey Hepburn and Rex Harrison in* My Fair Lady

some of the narrative. Nonetheless, George Cukor's **A Star is Born** remains the definitive version of a classic story. The film was produced by Sid Luft, in Technicolor and CinemaScope, for Transcona Enterprises. The really spectacular 18-minute long 'Born In A Trunk' sequence was choreographed by Richard Barstow to music by Roger Edens and lyrics by Leonard Gershe. Songs included: *Gotta Have Me Go With You, The Man That Got Away, It's A New World,* and *Somewhere There's A Someone.* The film was remade for a fourth time in 1977 with Barbra Streisand and Kris Kristofferson. And, in 1983, a restored, 175-minute version of 1954, using stills and dialogue, but restoring *Lose That Long Face* and the scene illustrated left, was given limited release in Britain and the US.

Controversy raged over the casting of Audrey Hepburn (below) in place of Julie Andrews for the 1964 film of Lerner and Loewe's Broadway blockbuster **My Fair Lady** (based on Shaw's *Pygmalion*); and, had Cary Grant accepted the role of Higgins when Jack Warner originally offered it to him, Warner's life might decidedly not have been worth living. But Grant had the good sense to refuse, emphatically telling Warner that if Rex Harrison wasn't cast, he wouldn't even bother to see the film, thus making way for one of the greatest performances in the history of the screen musical. On the other hand, Audrey Hepburn's early scenes as Eliza Doolittle were quite simply inadequate. Her ravishing good looks saved the day in the second half, though by no stretch of the imagination would her idiosyncratic speech rhythms have fooled Theodore Bikel's Zoltan Karpathy for an instant. Still, under director George Cukor's tasteful scrutiny, the show weathered this major piece of miscasting and emerged

The people were beautiful ... bottom: Santana; and below: the crowd at Woodstock

triumphant, with Cecil Beaton's costumes and sets and Hermes Pan's choreography all contributing to its success. Other pleasures were Stanley Holloway as Doolittle (James Cagney was offered the role, but turned it down). Wilfrid Hyde-White as Pickering, Gladys Cooper as Mrs Higgins, Isobel Elsom as Mrs Eynsford Hill, and Jeremy Brett as her son Freddy. Mona Washbourne and John Holland were also cast. Produced in Super Panavision and Technicolor by Jack Warner and with a screenplay by Alan Jay Lerner, the $17 million production (of which $1 million went on Miss Hepburn's salary and $5,500,000 on the rights alone) returned a profit of $12 million. Songs included: *I'm Getting Married In The Morning, All I Want Is A Room Somewhere, Why Can't The English Teach Their Children How To Speak?, Show Me, The Rain In Spain, Ascot Gavotte, I Could Have Danced All Night,* and *Just You Wait Henry Higgins.*

An account of the already legendary rock festival that took place over a period of three days on a 600 acre farm near Bethal, N.Y. in August 1969, **Woodstock** (1970) was a definitive documentation of an era and its music. Half a million people flocked to the event, one of the best of its kind ever staged, including the director/cameraman Michael Wadleigh, who, with twelve other cameramen, recorded the occasion (on 16mm) for posterity, concentrating as much on the enthusiastic young audience as on the rock stars who comprised the once-in-a-lifetime line-up, most notably Richie Havens, Joan Baez, Crosby, Stills, Nash and Young, The Who, John Sebastian, Joe Cocker, Sha-Na-Na, Country Joe and the Fish, Arlo Guthrie, Santana, Sly and the Family Stone, Ten Years After, and the late Jimi Hendrix. In all, Wadleigh shot 315,000 feet of film (approximately 120 hours) which he, the producer Bob Maurice and a team of superbly creative editors, using a split-screen technique, finally managed to reduce to 184 minutes. The associate producer was P. Dale Bell. The bottom line of **Woodstock's** balance sheet totalled an impressive $13,500,000 in box-office receipts, making it one of Warner Bros.' most successful films of the year. Musical items by the stars included: *Long Time Gone, Wooden Ships, Going Up The Country, Joe Hill, Swing Low Sweet Chariot, Summertime Blues, At The Hop, With A Little Help From My Friends, Coming into Los Angeles, Dance To The Music, Star-Spangled Banner,* and *Purple Haze.*

· SOUNDS · OF · THE · CENTURY : 20TH · CENTURY-FOX ·

Above: Alexander's Ragtime Band, *with Alice Faye; below:* Down Argentine Way, *with Carmen Miranda*

Alexander's Ragtime Band (1938) was a magnificent musical cavalcade whose catalogue of 23 Irving Berlin compositions made it one of the best and most durable musicals produced by 20th Century-Fox in the thirties. With such evergreens as 'Now It Can Be Told', 'Blue Skies', 'A Pretty Girl Is Like A Melody', 'Say It With Music' and 'Heat Wave', thrillingly sung in contrasting styles by leading lady Alice Faye and co-star Ethel Merman—the sheer range and variety of Berlin's prodigious output was amply demonstrated. Though plot-wise it was little more than an on-off-and-on-again love affair between a band leader played by Tyrone Power, and a singer Alice Faye, the film effectively reflected the changes in popular music between 1915 and 1938, even though the protagonists hardly aged a day in 23 years! Kathryn Scola and Lamar Trotti's screenplay, with its numerous cues for songs, found employment for Don Ameche (who loves Miss Faye but loses her to the good-looking Tyrone Power), as well as Jack Haley, Jean Hersholt, Dixie Dunbar, Chick Chandler, Helen Westley, John Carradine, Wally Vernon, Ruth Terry, and Douglas Fowley. It was produced by Darryl F. Zanuck, with Harry Joe Brown as his associate, and directed efficiently but with little sense of period, by Henry King. Other songs: *Alexander's Rag-Time Band* (Faye); *Rag-Time Violin*; *Everybody's Doing It* (Faye, Dunbar, Vernon); *This Is The Life* (Vernon); *Oh How I Hate To Get Up In The Morning* (Haley); *We're On Our Way To France*; *Pack Up Your Sins And Go To The Devil* (Merman); *What'll I Do?*; *Remember* (Faye); *Everybody Step* (Merman); *All Alone* (Faye); *Gypsy In Me*; *Easter Parade* (Ameche); *My Walking Stick* (Merman); *International Rag* (Faye, Chandler, Vernon); *When The Midnight Choo-Choo Leaves For Alabam* (Faye); *For Your Country And My Country*; *I Can Always Find A Little Sunshine At The YMCA*.

While an appendectomy prevented Betty Grable from playing the lead in Paramount's *Man about Town* (1939), ironically, it was an appendectomy that clinched her star-billing in **Down Argentine Way** (1940). This time it was Alice Faye who was rushed to hospital, with Betty being summoned from Broadway by producer Darryl F. Zanuck to take her place. And, although it made a star of her, a Brazilian bombshell called Carmen Miranda was the real hit. She sang three songs (including the catchy 'South American Way' by Al Dubin and Jimmy McHugh) and took the country by storm. For the rest, it was a brightly Technicolored concoction, all about an American heiress (Grable) who falls in love with an Argentinian horse-breeder (Don Ameche). Betty's legs looked a treat. The Nicholas Brothers and Thomas and Catherine Dowling featured as speciality items, with J. Carrol Naish, Henry Stephenson, Katherine Aldridge, Leonid Kinskey, Chris Pin Martin and Robert Conway in support. The musical numbers were staged by Nick Castle and Geneva Sawyer, 'Down Argentine Way' being the choreographic hit of the show. Another was the Greenwood/Kinskey ditty, 'Sing To Your Senorita' (both numbers by Mack Gordon and Harry Warren). The director was Irving Cummings. Other songs: *Two Dreams Met*; *Nenita* (Gordon, Warren): *Mama Yo Quiero* (Al Stillman, Jaraca and Vincente Paiva); *Doin' The Conga* (Gene Rose); *Bambu*.

If *Stage Door Canteen* utilized some of the world's most talented white performers, **Stormy Weather** (1943) rounded up the country's top black artists in a non-stop explosion of song and dance items—loosely threaded together by the merest wisp of a plot involving a tenuous romance between Lena Horne and Bill Robinson. The film spanned a quarter of a century (from 1911 to 1936) in the evolution of black music, and used a revue format to present a series of songs, dances and sketches characteristic of the periods touched upon. Apart from Miss Horne and Mr Robinson, the all-black cast included Cab Calloway and His Orchestra, Fats Waller, The Nicholas Brothers, Katherine Dunham and her dancers, Dooley Wilson (who, unfortunately, wasn't given a song), Ernest Whitman, The Tramp Band, The Shadracks, Ada Brown, and Babe Wallace. The musical numbers were staged by Clarence Robinson, the most elaborate being the title number (by Harold Arlen and Ten Koehler), thrillingly sung by Miss Horne (illustrated) and danced by Katherine Dunham and her troupe. The screenplay was by Frederick Jackson and Ted Koehler, adapted by H. S. Kraft from a story by Jerry Horwin and Seymour B. Robinson. It was directed by Andrew Stone and produced by William Le Baron. Other songs and musical numbers included; *There's No Two Ways About Love* (Robinson, Horne, Calloway) Ted Koehler, James P. Johnson, Irving Mills; *Ain't Misbehavin'* (Waller) Andy Razaf, Fats Waller, Harry Brooks; *Dat, Dot, Dah* (Wallace, The Tramp Band) Cyril J. Mockridge; *I Can't Give You Anything But Love Baby* (Horne, Robinson) Dorothy Fields, Jimmy McHugh; *That Ain't Right* (Brown, Waller) Nat King Cole, Irving Mills; *Diga, Diga, Doo* (Horne, chorus) Fields, McHugh; *I Lost My Sugar In Salt Lake City* (Mae E. Johnson) Johnny Lange, Leon René; *Geechy Joe* (Calloway) Jack Palmer, Andy Gibson, Calloway; *Jumpin' Jive* (Nicholas Brothers) Calloway, Frank Froeba, Palmer; *My, My, Ain't That Something* (Robinson, Finale, Nicholas Brothers, Horne, Calloway) Pinky Tomlin, Harry Tobias; *Rang Tang Tang* (Robinson, children) Cyril J. Mockridge; *At A Georgia Camp Meeting* Kerry Mills; *De Camptown Races* Stephen Foster; *Linda Brown* Al Cowans; *Nobody's Sweetheart* (Whitman) Gus Kahn, Ernie Erdman, Elmer Schoebel, Billy Meyers; *Rhythm Cocktail* (Robinson, Calloway) Calloway.

The screenplay fashioned by Charles Lederer for 20th Century-Fox's 1953 version of Joseph Fields and Anita Loos' smash musical comedy **Gentlemen Prefer Blondes** (from Loos' celebrated novel) was spot-on for three-quarters of its playing time, but deteriorated sadly towards the end. A pity, for until its decline and fall, this lavishly produced (by Sol C. Siegel) yarn about a couple of big girls from Little Rock was smashing entertainment. Fortunately, its two stars, Marilyn Monroe as Lorelei Lee (in the role created on Broadway by Carol Channing) and Jane Russell as Dorothy, both giving their best performances to date, never for an instant faltered. And in the witty dance sequences created for them by choreographer Jack Cole, they were sensational—particularly Monroe, who benefited greatly from Cole's really classy staging of the film's best song, 'Diamonds Are A Girl's Best Friend' (by Jule Styne and Leo Robin, who wrote the original Broadway score). Russell was at her best in Hoagy Carmichael/Harold Adamson's 'Ain't There Anyone Here for Love', staged by Cole in a ship's gymnasium, and featuring a couple of dozen of the world's most beautifully built men. Together the girls did 'Bye Bye Baby', and the stunning opening number, 'A (Two) Little Girl(s) From Little Rock' (the two remaining Styne/Robin songs held over from the stage production), as well as another Carmichael/Adamson contribution called 'When Love Goes Wrong'. On each occasion they ignited the screen with their particular brands of sex appeal, their combustible presences enriching the studio coffers by over $5 million. Charles Coburn was delightful as a diamond millionaire Monroe temporarily sets her sights on, Tommy Noonan (as Monroe's fiancé) gave his usual interpretation of a 'nebbish', Elliot Reid played a private detective hired by Noonan's millionaire father (Taylor Holmes) to see that his son and Monroe remain apart, and young George Winslow as a precocious six-year-

Far left: Lena Horne in Stormy Weather*; above and top right: Marilyn Monroe and Jane Russell in* Gentlemen Prefer Blondes

old called Henry Spofford III, gave the best supporting performance of all. The direction was by Howard Hawks.

Yul Brynner's justly celebrated performance as the King of Siam in Rodgers and Hammerstein's long-running Broadway smash was dynamically captured in the screen version of **The King and I** (1956), lavishly produced by Charles Brackett. Though Gertrude Lawrence was not on hand to repeat her performance as Anna, the school teacher who, with a son of her own, journeys from England to Siam to undertake the education of the King's children, Deborah Kerr was, and, happily—with her vocals dubbed by Marni Nixon—proved to be more than a match for the dominating Brynner (illustrated right). It was a performance full of warmth and tenderness and, although her role in *From Here To Eternity* (Columbia, 1953) was showier, it was one of the best things she has ever done. Under the direction of Alfred Newman and Ken Darby, Rodgers' marvellous score had never sounded so good, nor had choreographer Jerome Robbins' set-piece, 'The Little House Of Uncle Thomas', ever looked as good. And although four numbers—*My Lord And Master*, *Shall I Tell You What I Think Of You*, *Western People Funny* and *I Have Dreamed*—were excised for the film, it did not prevent the celluloid version of the show from achieving the rare distinction of being even more satisfying than the original stage presentation. Rita Moreno was cast as the King's slave Tuptim, and Carlos Rivas as her lover Lun Tha, with other roles under Walter Lang's stylish direction going to Martin Benson, Terry Saunders, Rex Thompson (as Kerr's young son), Alan Mowbray, Patrick Adiarte, and, in the 'Uncle Thomas' ballet, Yuriko, Marion Jim, Robert Banas and Dusty Worrall. It was photographed in CinemaScope 55 and Eastmancolor by Leon Shamroy; the superb costumes were by Irene Sharaff, the sets by Walter M. Scott and Paul S. Fox, and the art direction by Lyle Wheeler and John De Cuir. The screenplay, based on Oscar Hammerstein II's book which, in turn, was based on Anna Leonowens' book *Anna And The King Of Siam*, was by Ernest Lehman. Other songs and musical numbers: *I Whistle A Happy Tune* (Kerr); *Hello Young Lovers* (Kerr); *March Of The Siamese Children; A Puzzlement* (Brynner); *Getting To Know You* (Kerr, children); *We Kiss In A Shadow* (Moreno, Rivas); *Something Wonderful* (Saunders); *Song Of The King* (Brynner); *Shall We Dance* (Brynner, Kerr).

Family gathering: Yul Brynner and brood in The King and I

Jayne Mansfield of limited talent and squeaky voice fame, made her first starring appearance in **The Girl Can't Help It** (1957), a spoof, with intermittent moments of fun, on the rock craze. Borrowing quite heavily from Garson Kanin's plot of *Born Yesterday* (first seen as a Broadway play, then as a Columbia film in 1950), Frank Tashlin and Herbert Baker's screenplay was all about an agent's attempts to groom a gangster's moll (Mansfield) for stardom, with the accent throughout being on Miss M.'s highly vital statistics. Tom Ewell (pictured above with Miss M.) was top-billed as the agent and Edmond O'Brien was cast as the gangster; with other parts going to Henry Jones, John Emery and Juanita Moore. Musically, there was a full programme and, on numerous occasions, performers such as Julie London, Ray Anthony, Fats Domino, The Platters, The Treniers, Little Richard, Gene Vincent, The Chuckles, Eddie Fontaine, Abbey Lincoln, Johnny Olen, Nino Tempo and Eddie Cochran, came to the rescue of the leading players when the script simply ground to a halt. It was produced and directed by Tashlin, and photographed in CinemaScope and Eastmancolor. Songs included: *Rock Around The Rockpile*, *The Girl Can't Help It*, *She's Got It*, *Ready Teddy* John Marascalco, Robert A. Blackwell; *Be-Bop-A-Lu-La* Vincent, Sheriff Tom Davis; *Cool It Baby*, *Everytime*, *Big Band Boogie*, *20 Flight Rock*, *Spread The Word*, *Blue Monday* Domino, Dave Bartholomew; *The Great Pretender* Buck Ram; *Cry Me A River* Arthur Hamilton.

Though Rodgers and Hammerstein's monumentally successful **The Sound of Music** (1965)—which has grossed over $80 million to date—was a decided improvement on the long-running Broadway hit from whence it came, the mawkish sentimentality it oozed from every frame of its 174-minute running time made it difficult to enjoy without the uneasy feeling that one's emotions were being mercilessly manipulated. Yet, as a piece of old-fashioned popular entertainment with both eyes firmly on the box-office cash registers of the world, it was a shrewdly professional piece of work, stunningly presented, and crafted with awesome expertise. It also starred Julie Andrews (below) who, alone in a cast that included an unsympathetic and rather wooden Christopher Plummer, as well as Eleanor Parker (as the Baroness), Richard Haydn (as Max Detweiler), Peggy Wood (as Mother Abbess) and Charmian Carr (as Liesl), managed to wade through the molasses of Ernest Lehman's screenplay (from the book by Howard Lindsay and Russel Crouse) while keeping her head above it all. She played Maria, the postulant nun who forsakes the abbey for a position as governess to the seven children (illustrated) of martinet widower Captain Von Trapp (Plummer), and remains on in his household (after the obligatory setbacks) to become his wife. It was Andrews' extraordinarily assured and appealing central performance—coupled with some magnificent Todd-AO and Color-by-De Luxe aerial views of Salzburg (the story's setting), photographed by Ted McCord, that were largely responsible for the film's enormous success. Marc Breaux and Dee Dee Wood choreographed the simple but effective dance routines, Boris Leven, the art director, made excellent use of Salzburg's architectural landmarks, and the production and direction were by Robert Wise. Completing the cast: Heather Menzies, Nicolas Hammond, Duane Chase, Angela Cartwright, Debbie Turner, Kym Karath, Anna Lee, Portia Nelson, Ben Wright, Daniel Truhitte, Norma Varden, Gil Stuart, Marni Nixon, and Evadne Baker. Christopher Plummer's vocals were dubbed by Bill Lee. Songs and musical numbers: *The Sound Of Music* (Andrews); *Praeludium* (nun's chorus); *Morning Hymn And Alleluia* (nun's chorus); *Maria* (Lee, Nixon, Nelson, Baker); *I Have Confidence In Me* (Andrews); *Sixteen Going On Seventeen* (Carr, Truhitte); *Climb Every Mountain* (Wood); *Lonely Goatherd* (Andrews, Baird Marionettes); *Do-Re-Mi* (Andrews, children); *Something Good* (Andrews, Plummer); *Edelweiss* (Plummer, Andrews, children); *So Long, Farewell* (children); *Processional* (orchestra); *My Favourite Things* (Andrews).

Top left: Jayne Mansfield and Tom Ewell in The Girl Can't Help It*; below:* The Sound of Music *(Julie Andrews standing by wall)*

· THE · PEAK · OF · PERFECTION : · PARAMOUNT ·

With **Applause**, filmed at the Astoria Studios in New York in 1929, 29-year-old torch singer Helen Morgan was given the finest screen role of her career, and director Rouben Mamoulian a chance to turn his considerable talents to talking pictures. The result was an unqualified artistic success for both of them. The story of an ageing Broadway burlesque queen called Kitty Darling, it showed Morgan sharing a squalid, drunken existence with Hitch, an unscrupulous comedian, and the effect her 17-year-old daughter, April, has on her when she arrives from a convent to take up residence in the big city. April's appearance makes Morgan decide to marry the no-good Hitch out of a sense of propriety, but the marriage is a disaster and in no time at all Hitch is making passes at April who rejects them and, instead, becomes engaged to a sailor. Distressed, however, at her mother's rapid decline, April decides to give up the sailor in order to look after her. But Morgan takes poison rather than allow her daughter to ruin her happiness by becoming her 'meal ticket'. Showing tremendous cinematic flair, Mamoulian contrasted the relentlessly sordid aspects of his story (from the novel by Beth Brown) with lengthy passages depicting a more serene existence at the convent and, in both milieus, allowed his camera to move with more fluidity than was customary for early talking pictures. His use of sound was equally innovative, and instead of using only one microphone he insisted, for certain scenes, on two, the sound from both being mixed together later. Because of the uncompromisingly unglamorous view it took of its subject, **Applause** was not the box-office success Mamoulian and his producers Jesse L. Lasky and Walter Wanger had hoped for, yet it remains one of the most striking of all the early talkies—and the apogee of its star's up-and-down career. Certainly she did nothing finer, and the four songs she sings in the film are superbly rendered. Joan Peers co-starred as her daughter, and was splendid; but Fuller Mellish Jr's performance as Hitch was unfortunately not up to their high standard, being melodramatic and overstated. The scenario and dialogue were by Garrett Fort and the cameraman was George Folsey. The rest of the cast included Henry Wadsworth, Jack Cameron and Dorothy Cummings. Songs included: *What Wouldn't I Do For That Man* E. Y. Harburg, Jay Gorney; *Yaka Hula Hickey Dula* E. Ray Goetz, Joe Young, Pete Wendling; *Give Your Little Baby Lots Of Lovin'* Dolly Morse, Joe Burke; *I've Got A Feelin' I'm Fallin'* Billy Rose, Harry Link, Fats Waller (all sung by Helen Morgan); *Pretty Baby* Gus Kahn, Egbert Van Alstyne, Tony Jackson; *Turkey Trot* Robin Hood Bowers, Edgar Smith; *Waiting For The Robert E. Lee* Lewis F. Muir, L. Wolfe Gilbert; *Doin' The New Racoon* Dolly Morse, Joe Burke.

Below: arms and the woman: Helen Morgan as Kitty Darling in Applause

Floorshows and flick-knives: below: Holiday Inn; *bottom:* King Creole

Holiday Inn (1942) was a bumper musical package that paired Bing Crosby and Fred Astaire for the first time. They played a song-and-dance team which splits up when Crosby decides to take to the country and lead a life of moderate relaxation—working only on public holidays. In fact, he opens a Holiday Inn on New Year's Eve dedicated to that very proposition—and for eight days a year, entertains the public there. A romantic sub-plot involving Marjorie Reynolds (whose singing voice was dubbed by Martha Mears) and Virginia Dale slid easily into the general scheme of things, without in any way proving an encumbrance to the generous musical programme provided by Irving Berlin—who also thought up the story which Elmer Rice adapted and Claude Binyon scripted. Each of the eight public holidays celebrated in the film had an accompanying song (July 4 had two), the most famous of all being the staggeringly successful, timelessly popular 'White Christmas', introduced, of course, by Crosby, whose Decca recording went on to sell over 25 million copies. In addition Crosby had nine other songs, and did a duet with Astaire who, in turn, took the floor no fewer than six times—most memorably in a routine involving firecrackers called 'Let's Say It With Fire-Crackers'. The rest of the cast included Walter Abel, Louise Beavers, Marek Windheim, Irving Bacon, Jacques Vanaire, Harry Barris and Bob Crosby's Bob Cats. Danny Dare staged the musical numbers and it was produced and directed by Mark Sandrich. **Holiday Inn** received unanimously favourable reviews, grossed a fortune and even had a chain of motels named after it. (Illustration shows Crosby and Marjorie Reynolds, both in blackface, singing 'Abraham, Abraham' in the 'Lincoln's Birthday' sequence). Other songs and musical numbers: *I'll Capture Your Heart Singing* (Crosby, Astaire, Dale); *Lazy* (Crosby); *You're Easy To Dance With* (Astaire, Dale, Reynolds); *Happy Holiday* (Crosby, Reynolds); *Holiday Inn* (Crosby, Reynolds); *Let's Start The New Year Right* (Crosby); *Be Careful, It's My Heart* (Crosby, Astaire, Reynolds); *I Can't Tell A Lie* (Astaire, Reynolds, Bob Cats); *Easter Parade* (Crosby); *Song Of Freedom* (Crosby); *Plenty To Be Thankful For* (Crosby).

Elvis Presley (right), playing 'a hustler out to make a fast buck', actually gave something resembling a performance in **King Creole** (1958), a melodrama set in New Orleans and based on Harold Robbins' novel *A Stone For Danny Fisher*. Scripted by Herbert Baker and Michael V. Gazzo as a Presley show piece, it allowed room for several numbers (including the popular title song by Jerry Lieber and Mike Stoller) as well as 'Hard Headed Woman' (by Claude DeMetrius), at appropriate points in a story which saw Presley's rise from earnest bus boy-cum-musician to Bourbon Street nightclub singer in the company of several decidedly unsavoury heavies—including Walter Matthau and Vic Morrow. Also cast: Carolyn Jones giving the best performance in the film as Matthau's ex-girlfriend for whom Presley falls, Dean Jagger as Presley's ineffectual father and Jan Shephard as his sister, as well as Paul Stewart and Dolores Hart. Michael Curtiz' direction successfully captured the essentially seedy atmosphere of the film's milieu and managed to extend Presley's hitherto limited range as an actor. Hal Wallis produced. Other songs: *Dixieland Rock* Schroeder, Frank; *As Long As I Have You*; *Crawfish* Fred Wise, Ben Weisman; *Don't Ask Me Why*; *New Orleans* Sid Tepper, Roy C. Bennett; *Lover Doll* Sid Wayne, Abner Silver; *Trouble*; *Steadfast, Loyal And True* Jerry Lieber, Mike Stoller; *Young Dreams* Schroeder, Kalmanoff.

Robert Altman's **Nashville** (1975) wove a rich tissue of narrative and musical strands as it traced the overlapping lives of 24 people in the Tennessee capital of country-and-western during the campaign of a Presidential candidate, whose assassination brings the film to a dramatic end. In spite of the dangers inherent in such an undertaking, it was a triumph for its director and his familiar repertory company of actors, many of whom them-

Summer days, summer nights: below: Nashville*; bottom:* Grease

boy Song)*; *My Idaho Home*; *Dues* Blakely; *I Never Get Enough* Baskin, Ben Raleigh; *Rose's Cafe* Allan Nicholls; *Old Man Mississippi* Juan Grizzle; *My Baby's Cookin' In Another Man's Pan* Jonnie Barnett; *One, I Love You* Baskin; *I'm Easy*; *Honey*; *It Don't Worry Me* Keith Carradine; *Since You've Gone* Gary Busey; *Trouble In The USA* Arlene Barnett.

selves wrote the songs they sang. The film, by its very nature, boasted no star roles but, out of a huge cast, particularly noteworthy were Ronee Blakely as a singer on the verge of a breakdown, Gwen Welles as a starlet reduced to stripping at stag suppers, Shelley Duvall as a spaced-out groupie, Keith Carradine as a heartless Don Juan, Lily Tomlin as the mother of deaf-mute children, and Henry Gibson as the *éminence grise* of country-and-western. Also to be seen were Ned Beatty, Karen Black, Allen Nichols (above, left), Barbara Harris (above, right), Michael Murphy, Keenan Wynn and, as Opal from the BBC, Geraldine Chaplin. It was scripted by Joan Tewkesbury (though, reportedly, everyone involved had a hand) and produced, in Panavision, by Altman, with Martin Starger and Jerry Weintraub as executive producers. Songs and musical numbers: *200 Years* Richard Baskin, Henry Gibson; *Yes, I Do* Baskin, Lily Tomlin; *Down To The River* Ronee Blakely; *Let Me Be The One* Baskin; *Sing A Song* Joe Raposo; *The Heart Of A Gentle Woman* Dave Peel; *Bluebird* Blakely; *The Day I Looked Jesus In The Eye* Baskin, Robert Altman; *Memphis*; *Rolling Stone*; *I Don't Know If I Found It In You* Karen Black; *For The Sake Of The Children* Baskin, Richard Reicheg; *Keep A' Goin'* Baskin, Gibson; *Swing Low Sweet Chariot* (arr. Millie Clements); *Tapedeck In His Tractor (The Cow-*

John Travolta consolidated his *Saturday Night Fever* (Paramount, 1977) success the following year with **Grease**, a Robert Stigwood/Allan Carr production of the long-running Broadway hit. Adapted by Carr from Jim Jacobs and Warren Casey's Fifties-style book (screenplay by Bronte Woodard), it was designed specifically as a mammoth showcase for the good looks and sex appeal of its super-star lead and, as such, was a triumphant success. Though contemporary in its language and in its approach to its subject (high school romance), the film tapped a decided vein of nostalgia by virtue of its Fifties setting, and the casting of such stalwarts as Eve Arden, Joan Blondell, Edd Byrnes, Sid Caesar, Alice Ghostley and Dody Goodman. Frankie Avalon was also in it (as part of a dream sequence) and there was a nostalgia about his appearance. All about how Travolta's summer romance with co-star Olivia Newton-John (pictured here together) sours when they find themselves attending the same high school, its infectious high spirits were the results of Particia Birch's jet-propelled choreography, Woodard's racy (if somewhat loosely constructed) screenplay, an instantly accessible score by Jim Jacobs and Warren Casey (augmented by Barry Gibb, John Farrar, Louis St Louis and Scott J. Simon), and the attractive performances from a cast whose younger members included the marvellous Stockard Channing, Jeff Conaway, Barry Pearl, Michael Tucci, Kelly Ward and Didi Conn. It was stunningly photographed in Panavision and Metrocolor by Bill Butler. Songs and musical numbers: *Grease*, *Summer Nights*, *Hopelessly Devoted To You*, *You're The One That I Want*, *Sandy*, *Beauty School Dropout*, *Look At Me I'm Sandra Dee*, *Greased Lightnin'*, *It's Raining On Prom Night*, *Alone At A Drive-In Movie*, *Blue Moon*, *Rock 'n' Roll Is Here To Stay*, *Those Magic Changes*, *Hound Dog*, *Born To Hand-Jive*, *Tears On My Pillow*, *Mooning*, *Freddy My Love*, *Rock 'n' Roll Party Queen*, *There Are Worse Things I Could Do*, *We Go Together*, *Love Is A Many Splendoured Thing*.

• ON • TOP • OF • THE • WORLD : UNIVERSAL • AND • RKO •

Though Fred Astaire admitted in his autobiography that he disliked top hat, white tie and tails, you'd never have known it from his classic title song tribute to all three (below) in **Top Hat** (RKO, 1935)—the first Astaire–Rogers musical in which the team had top billing, and usually regarded as the best of the series. In fact **Top Hat**, with its cunningly contrived, soufflé-light plot and a score by Irving Berlin that must surely rank as one of the finest ever written for a film, comes as near to perfection as could decently be expected. Plotwise, the movie takes the mistaken identity theme to the enth degree, Astaire being the chief victim of the farcical situations that occur when Miss Rogers, with whom he has fallen in love, believes him to be the husband of a friend of hers. The deception persists throughout most of the film's 101-minute running time, but in such skilful counterpoint to the score, and with its numerous variations on its single theme spiralling off into the realms of the sublimely absurd, that it is impossible not to surrender completely to the delightful idiocy of it all. And Astaire demonstrated again that he was simply incapable of a graceless movement. Miss Rogers, who was in three out of the five routines, again proved herself to be, if not quite the equal of her miraculous partner, an excellent dancing co-star just the same. The slightly common quality which emanated from her was what was needed to humanize the duo and, artistically as well as temperamentally, the combination proved infallible. The cast was completed by Edward Everett Horton (as Fred's manager), Helen Broderick (as Horton's wife, whom Rogers believes has married Astaire). Erik Rhodes, Eric Blore, Leonard Mudie, Lucille Ball (as a clerk in a flower shop), Edgar Norton and Gina Corrado. It was written by Dwight Taylor and Allan Scott and adapted from a play by Alexander Farago and Aladar Laszlo by Karl Noti. Hermes Pan was the dance director, Pandro S. Berman the producer, and it was directed, once again, by Mark Sandrich. Other musical numbers: *No Strings* (Astaire); *Isn't This A Lovely Day* (Astaire, Rogers); *The Piccolino*, the latter providing the film with its 'big finish' but in which the dancing sequence for Fred and Ginger needed, perhaps, to be a little longer than it was.

Below left: Fred, with the boys in Top Hat*; here: with Ginger in* Follow the Fleet

A year after *Top Hat* came **Follow the Fleet** (RKO) and it was apparent the fabulous team of Fred Astaire, Ginger Rogers and Irving Berlin could do no wrong. Refurbished from a 1922 play by Hubert Osborne called *Shore Leave* which, in turn, provided the inspiration for the 1927 Broadway musical *Hit The Deck* (filmed by RKO in 1930), its adapters Dwight Taylor and Allan Scott concentrated the serious love interest (as also in RKO's *Roberta*, 1934) on its two co-stars, leaving Astaire and Rogers free to entertain the customers. Which they did stupendously. He played an ex-dancer turned sailor; she was a former partner of his, now singing for her supper in a San Francisco dancehall. They meet up at a dance contest and join forces to put on a fund-raising show for the restoration of a schooner. The plot was no masterpiece, but it was innovative in that it dispensed with the hitherto obligatory comedians (Blore, Pangborn, Everett Horton *et al*) who usually tagged along on such occasions. It allowed Ginger Rogers to do a solo tap dance (her first and last in an Astaire/Rogers musical), and, for the first time in six movies took Astaire out of formal attire and put him into something more relaxed than top hat, white tie and tails—except for one extremely formal number, the famous 'Let's Face The Music And Dance' (above) first sung by Astaire, then danced by him and Rogers as the finale to their fund-raising effort. The rest of the numbers showed the team in a much more casual mood than audiences had become used to, and the results were enchanting. Then, of course, there was Berlin's seductive score. By alternating his more zingy numbers—such as 'Let Yourself Go' and 'I'm Putting All My Eggs In One Basket' with such sombre ballads as 'Get Thee Behind Me Satan' and 'But Where Are You?' both sung by a lovelorn Harriet Hilliard, Berlin created a perfectly balanced musical programme. Randolph Scott appeared as Miss Hilliard's love interest, and the man for whom the schooner is being salvaged; with Astrid

Allwyn, Ray Mayer, Harry Beresford, Addison Randall and Russell Hicks in support. And if you look closely you'll catch glimpses of Betty Grable, Lucille Ball and Tony Martin. The film was produced by Pandro S. Berman, choreographed by Hermes Pan, and directed by Mark Sandrich.

Apart from Helen Westley (as Parthenia Hawks) and Queenie Smith (as Ellie) all the principal performers in director James Whale's memorable screen version of Edna Ferber, Jerome Kern and Oscar Hammerstein II's **Show Boat** (Universal, 1936) had appeared in various stage productions of the classic musical, and their total familiarity with (and commitment to) their roles was very much in evidence throughout. Irene Dunne (below) played Magnolia Hawks, with Allan Jones as her Ravenal, and Charles Winninger Cap'n Andy, with Paul Robeson quite magnificent as Joe, and Helen Morgan ditto as the mulatto Julie. Donald Cook played Morgan's husband Steve, with other roles going to Hattie McDaniel as Joe's wife Queenie, Francis X. Mahoney as Rubberface and Charles Middleton as Sheriff Mahoney, An extremely faithful adaptation (by Hammerstein himself) of the original 1927 Broadway presentation, plus the addition of three new Kern/Hammerstein songs—'I Have The Room Above Her' (sung by Jones and Miss Dunne); 'Ah Still Suits Me' (sung by Paul Robeson), and 'Gallavantin Around' (sung by Miss Dunne in blackface)—the film only falters in its modern section towards the end in which several plot points were arbitrarily and unconvincingly resolved. For the rest Whale's **Show Boat** with its brilliant camerawork by John J. Mescall, the vigorous staging of its musical numbers by LeRoy Prinz, and the visual splendour of its art direction (by Charles D. Hall) offered a most satisfactory version of a masterpiece. The producer was Carl Laemmle Jr. It was remade by MGM in 1951. Other songs: *Cotton Blossom, Cap'n Andy's Ballyhoo, Where's The Mate For Me?, Make Believe, Ol' Man River, Can't Help Lovin' Dat Man, Mis'ry's Comin' Around* and *You Are Love, Bill.*

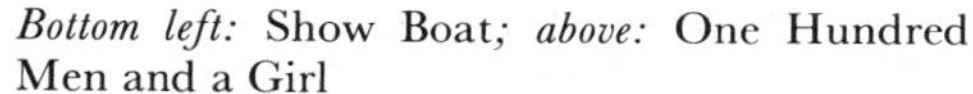

Bottom left: Show Boat; *above:* One Hundred Men and a Girl

A big hit for Universal in 1937, **One Hundred Men and a Girl** owed its success to a combination of its delightful story, and the spontaneous vitality and fresh charm of Deanna Durbin (above). The young soprano appeared as a girl determined to enlist eminent conductor Leopold Stokowski's aid in launching an orchestra which would give work to one hundred unemployed musicians, one of whom is her father (Adolphe Menjou, being hugged). She marches the lot into the home of the unsuspecting maestro who capitulates by conducting Liszt's *Hungarian Rhapsody No 2* from the top of his staircase. It was a fairytale from start to finish, and audiences loved it. There were opportunities, too, for Deanna to break into song, and if her rendition of 'The Drinking Song' from Verdi's *La Traviata* was a shade uncertain, nobody minded. The cast also featured Eugene Pallette, Mischa Auer (right) and Alice Brady, and the screenplay was by Bruce Manning, Charles Kenyon, Hans Kraly and James Mulhauser. It was produced by Charles R. Rogers and Joe Pasternak, and directed with a light and confident touch by Henry Koster. Other songs and music included the hit *It's Raining Sunbeams* by Sam Coslow and Frederick Hollander as well as *A Heart That's Free* Alfred G. Robyn, Thomas T. Railey; *Alleluia* Mozart (from Exultate, Jubilate K165); excerpts from *Lohengrin* Wagner and Tschaikovsky's *Fifth Symphony.* After the film's release, Miss Durbin's salary was doubled to $3,000 a week, with a $10,000 bonus for each subsequent film.

· OCCASIONAL · · MELODIES : · GOLDWYN AND · · THE · REST ·

Adapted by Hugh Herbert from a story by Ben Hecht, **The Great Gabbo** (James Cruze Productions, 1929) gave the celebrated Austrian actor-director Erich von Stroheim (seen below) a heaven-sent opportunity to chew up the scenery—which he did to stunning effect. He played Gabbo, a ventriloquist whose unbridled egotism results in his losing the one girl he loves (Betty Compson), his sanity and, finally, his dummy and soul-mate Otto, whom he smashes up in an outburst of jealous rage. Dramatic stuff, directed a trifle crudely by James Cruze (real-life husband of Miss Compson), and vigorously performed by a cast that included Donald Douglas and Marjorie 'Babe' Kane. The choreography was by Maurice Kusell, and the songs by Paul Titsworth, Lynn Cowan, Donald McNamee and King Zany. These were: *The New Step*, *I'm In Love With You*, *I'm Laughing*, *Ickey*, *Every Now And Then*, *The Web Of Love*, *The Ga-Ga Bird*.

Samuel Goldwyn abandoned the idea of adapting Bernard Shaw's play *Androcles And The Lion* as a vehicle for Eddie Cantor and turned, instead, to Broadway's George S. Kaufman and Robert E. Sherwood for a script that would suit his money-making star's unique qualities. The association was not a happy one, however, and ended in court after Goldwyn refused to pay the two writers, claiming that they had supplied him with no more than an unworkable first draft. Three gag-writers (Arthur Sheekman, George Oppenheimer and Nat Perrin) were then engaged to pep up the original Kaufman/Sherwood story, after which William Anthony McGuire was called in to structure it all into a workable motion-picture. The result was **Roman Scandals** 1933, a quintessential Cantor musical. In it, Cantor (above) plays a delivery boy in a mid-west town, who dreams he is a food-tasting slave to an evil Emperor in Ancient Rome, where most of the film is then set. It even contrived a scene which allowed Cantor to go into blackface. The number—an elaborate affair complete with revolving mirrored doors, was the film's musical highspot—and, although the philosophy it expressed, as well as the degrading use it made of the black women in it, may strike contemporary viewers as singularly distasteful, there can be no denying the brilliance of Busby Berkeley's staging. Less successful was the rather disorganized slave-market sequence in which Berkeley's chorines were nude except for long blonde wigs. The number was shot at night, and on a closed set. Though the film was primarily a vehicle for its star, it also gave torch singer Ruth Etting a chance to sing a Dubin/Warren ballad called 'No More Love'; which she did most touchingly. Gloria Stuart and David Manners were the young lovers whose romance Cantor helps promote, Veree Teesdale the Empress Agrippa, and Edward Arnold the spouse she is constantly trying to poison. Greg Toland photographed it, and the director was Frank Tuttle. There was another Dubin/Warren song, *Build A Little Home*, and *Put A Tax On Love* by L. Wolfe Gilbert and Harry Warren; both were sung by Cantor.

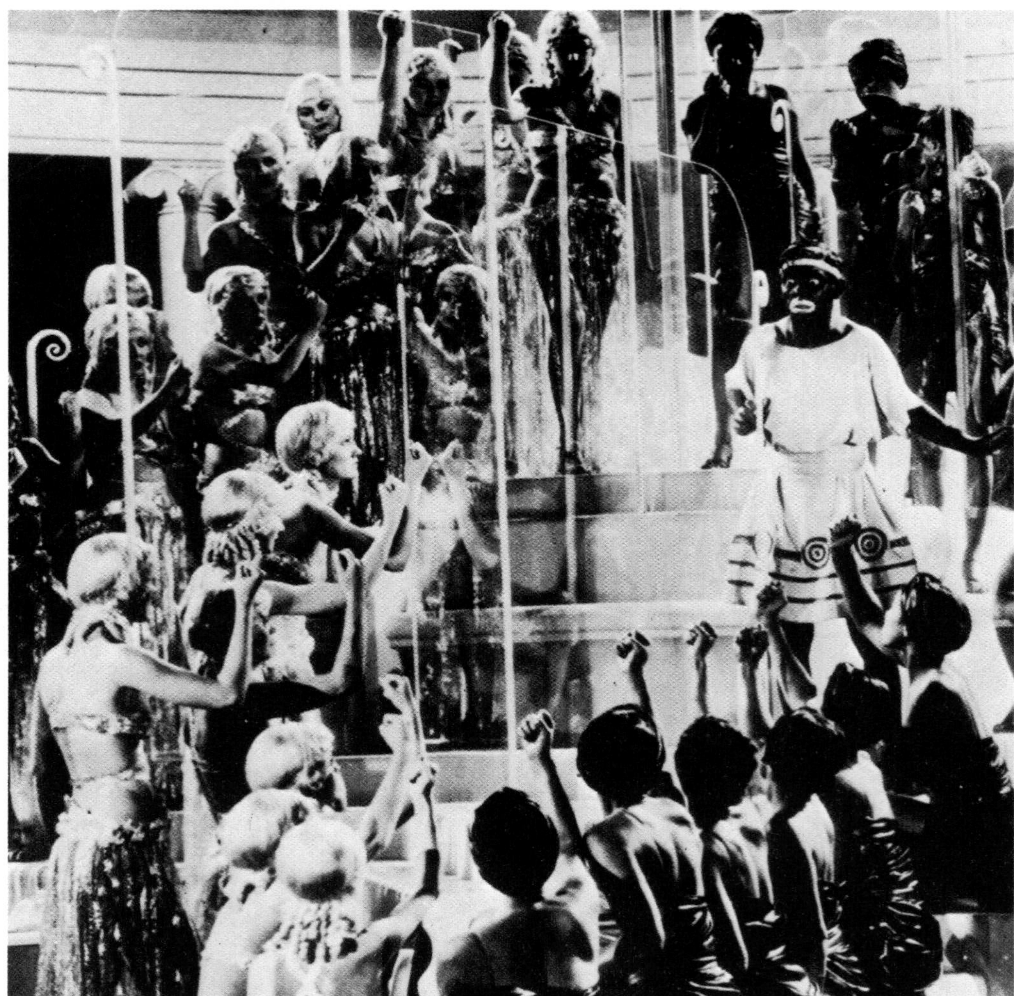

Above: Eddie Cantor in Roman Scandals; *bottom left: Eric von Stroheim in* The Great Gabbo

Cover Girl (Columbia, 1944), written by Virginia Van Upp, and adapted by Marion Parsonnet and Paul Gangelin from a play by Erwin Gelsey, was the conventional story of a Brooklyn night-club dancer, Rita Hayworth, who deserts her lover Gene Kelly (together, opposite) and becomes a cover girl. But she soon learns that money and fame are no substitute for love, and returns to the man she cares for. The story was told against a series of flashbacks, set at the turn of the century, in which Hayworth's grandmother (also played by Hayworth) is shown to have followed exactly the same course. Lee Bowman and Otto Kruger were the two wealthy men who lured Hayworth away from Kelly; Phil Silvers was Kelly's faithful side-kick, while Eve Arden was cast as a wise cracking, high-powered executive on the look-out for the ideal cover girl. Apart from its hackneyed plot, the film groaned under the weight of much that was trite and unoriginal, not least of which was the main production number (staged by Seymour Felix) glorifying the American cover girl through giant 'blow-ups' of the country's most famous magazines. (MGM would do it better in *Easter Parade* 1947, to the accompaniment of Irving Berlin's 'The Girl On the Magazine Cover'). Yet, for all its blemishes, **Cover Girl** was important in that it marked Kelly's transition from hoofer to dancer, his famous 'alter ego' sequence being remarkably advanced for its time. The dance began in a mood of tranquillity, with Kelly walking alone one night and seeing his reflection in a window. The reflection turns to flesh and blood, steps down from the window and then begins to dance with him. The rest of the numbers—all but one by Jerome Kern and Ira Gershwin—were far less innovative, the two best staged being the haunting 'Long Ago and Far Away', sung by Kelly and Hayworth (the latter dubbed by Martha Mears). **Cover Girl** was produced (in Technicolor) by Arthur Schwartz, choreographed, by Felix, Val Raset and Kelly, and also featured Jinx Falkenburg, Leslie Brooks, Jess Barker, Curt Bois, Ed Brophy, Thurston Hall and The Cover Girls. Other songs and musical numbers: *Put Me To The Test* (Kelly, Hayworth); *Sure Thing* (Hayworth); *That's The Best Of All*; *The Show Must Go On* (Hayworth, chorus); *Who's Complaining?* (Silvers) Kern, Gershwin; *Poor John* (Hayworth) Fred W. Leigh, Harry E. Pether.

Below: Kelly and Rita Hayworth in Cover Girl; *bottom: Brando, Jean Simmons, Sinatra and Vivian Blaine in* Guys and Dolls

Samuel Goldwyn's penultimate film, in 1955, was an expensive recreation of the Jo Swerling/Abe Burrows/Frank Loesser masterpiece **Guys and Dolls**. Having paid $1 million for the rights from Broadway producers Feuer and Martin, Goldwyn then spent a further $4,500,000 on his production, a hefty chunk of which went on the casting of Marlon Brando (left) as Sky Masterson (the role was originally offered to Gene Kelly but MGM, to whom Kelly was still under contract, refused to release him) and Frank Sinatra (centre right) as Nathan Detroit. Jean Simmons (centre left) was cast as missionary Sarah Brown, Vivian Blaine (right, repeating the role she created on stage) was Miss Adelaide, with Stubby Kaye, B. S. Pully and Johnny Silver (also recruits from the original stage production) as Nicely Nicely Johnson, Big Jule and Benny Southstreet. Joseph L. Mankiewicz, who had never directed a musical before, was handed the choice directorial assignment, and also provided a screenplay based on Swerling and Burrows' book which, in turn, was culled from Damon Runyon's short story *The Idylls Of Sarah Brown*. The result was a show which, while totally failing to capture the convivial intimacy of the stage presentation was, nonetheless, full of good things—the best being Michael Kidd's spirited, high-octane choreography, seen at its best in the opening sequence and in 'The Crap Game Dance' performed in a sewer. Sinatra sauntered through the role of Nathan with the air of a lovable heel, and although he only had one solo—'Adelaide', specially written for the film by Loesser—was vocally at the peak of his powers. Vivian Blaine was delightful as his showgirl fiancée of 14 years' standing, though the most authentically Runyonesque performance of all came from Stubby Kaye, Brando as gambler Masterson, and Simmons as the missionary lady he falls for after a romantic stint in Havana (undertaken, initially, as a bet with Sinatra), were both better than expected; Brando, using his own singing voice, was particularly effective in 'Luck Be A Lady'. Two of the stage show's songs—*A Bushel And A Peck*, and the melodious *I've Never Been In Love Before* were replaced by 'Pet Me Poppa' and 'A Woman In Love'—good songs both of them, but no improvements on the originals. **Guys And Dolls** ran 158 minutes, was filmed in CinemaScope and Eastmancolor, and was released by MGM. Apart from the 1955 Goldwyn Girls, the cast also included Sheldon Leonard, Dan Dayton, Johnny Silver, George E. Stone, Kay Kuter, Regis Toomey, Kathryn

Givney, Veda Ann Borg, Alan Hokanson and Joe McTurk. Other songs and musical numbers: *Fugue For Tin Horns* (Sinatra, Silver, Dayton); *Follow The Fold* (Simmons, Kuter, group); *The Oldest Established* (Sinatra, Silver, Kaye, ensemble); *I'll Know* (Brando, Simmons); *Adelaide's Lament* (Blaine); *A Woman In Love* (Brando, Simmons, Ruben De Fuentes, trio, Renee Renor); *If I Were A Bell* (Simmons, Brando); *Take Back Your Mink* (Blaine, girls); *Sue Me* (Sinatra, Blaine); *Sit Down You're Rockin' The Boat* (Kaye, Givney, Hokanson, Simmons); *Guys And Dolls* (Sinatra, Silver, Kaye); *Pet Me Poppa* (Blaine, girls).

Twelve years after it first took Broadway by storm, Rodgers and Hammerstein's **Oklahoma!** reached the screen in 1955 in a new process known as Todd-AO. The show itself was far better than the process it launched in which the colour varied from scene to scene and some of the images appeared decidedly distorted. Despite the shedding of one of the stage version's songs, this watershed musical transferred triumphantly to celluloid and was almost as entertaining, if not quite as magical, as it was when it first opened. Gordon MacRae (seen below right) was Curly, Shirley Jones (left) was Laurey, the girl he loves, Charlotte Greenwood was Aunt Eller and, as Will Parker and his girl Ado Annie, Gene Nelson and Gloria Grahame couldn't have been improved upon. Rod Steiger was a suitably unlikeable Jud Fry, and the cast was completed by Eddie Albert (as Ali Hakim), James Whitmore, Barbara Lawrence, Jay C. Flippen, Roy Barcroft and, substituting for MacRae and Jones in the 'Out Of My Dreams' ballet—dancers James Mitchell and Bambi Lynn. Greatly contributing to the richness of sound that was a feature of the new Todd-AO process, was Robert Russell Bennett's orchestration and the marvellous orchestral playing under the direction of Jay Blackton and Adolph Deutsch. Agnes De Mille (who helped create the show on Broadway) was again responsible for the choreography and, in numbers such as 'The Farmer And The Cowman' and 'Everything's Up To Date In Kansas City' (dynamically danced by Nelson) revealed just why she was such a major force among contemporary American choreographers. The screenplay, based on Oscar Hammerstein II's original book, was by Sonya Levien and William Ludwig, and if today it seems unavoidably dated—the corn indeed being 'as high as an elephant's eye'—25 years ago it sounded just fine. Other songs and musical numbers: *Oh What A Beautiful Morning* (MacRae); *Surrey With The Fringe On Top* (MacRae, Jones, Nelson); *I Can't Say No* (Grahame); *Many A New Day* (Jones and chorus); *People Will Say We're In Love* (MacRae, Jones); *Poor Jud Is Dead* (Steiger, MacRae); *All Or Nothin'* (Nelson, Grahame); *Oklahoma!* (MacRae, Jones, Nelson, Greenwood and company).

Above: rumbling in West Side Story*; below: ranching (Shirley Jones, Gordon MacRae) in* Oklahoma!

Although the sight of the aggressively masculine Jets and their equally macho enemies, the Sharks, donning balletic poses as they sauntered down a grimly realistic West Side back street in New York was initially a jolt to the system, there was no denying the power and impact of producer Robert Wise's 1961 Panavision adaptation of the Arthur

Laurents/Leonard Bernstein/Stephen Sondheim Broadway hit **West Side Story** (United Artists/Mirisch). A contemporary reworking of the Romeo and Juliet tragedy concerning the doomed love of a white boy for a pretty Puerto Rican girl, it was originally conceived by Jerome Robbins with the emphasis on dance—an emphasis which prevailed in the screen version since Robbins, who received a co-director credit with Robert Wise, was also its choreographer. The most galvanic, award-laden movie musical to emerge in the Sixties, **West Side Story** was a brilliant fusion of talents, the only element in it which has since dated being Laurents' book (adapted for the screen by Ernest Lehman) with its rather quaint-sounding street-gang lingo. For the rest, the film, like the stage show, was magnificent entertainment. Natalie Wood received top billing as Maria and was enchanting, though her co-star Richard Beymer, cast as Tony, was critically lambasted (unfairly) for giving what was considered an underpowered performance in a dynamic cast that included Rita Moreno as Anita, George Chakiris as Rita Moreno's Puerto Rican lover Bernardo and Russ Tamblyn as Riff. Also: Tucker Smith (Ice), Tony Mordente (Action), David Winters (A-rab), Eliot Feld (Baby John), Burt Michaels (Snowboy), Sue Oakes (Anybody's) and Carole D'Andrea, Jose de Vega and Simon Oakland. The musical directors were Johnny Green and Saul Chaplin, with Sid Ramin and Irwin Kostal in charge of the orchestrations. Boris Leven was the art director and it was stunningly photographed, in Technicolor and Panavision 70 by Daniel Fapp. Marni Nixon dubbed the vocals for Wood, Jim Bryant for Beymer and Betty Wand for Moreno. Songs and musical numbers: *Prologue* (orchestra); *Jet Song* (Tamblyn, Jets); *Something's Coming* (Beymer); *Dance At The Gym* (orchestra and ensemble); *Maria* (Beymer); *America* (Chakiris, Moreno, chorus); *Tonight* (Beymer, Wood); *Gee Officer Krupke* (Tamblyn, Jets); *I Feel Pretty* (Wood); *One Hand, One Heart* (Wood, Beymer); *Quintet* (Wood, Beymer, Chakiris and Sharks, Moreno, Tamblyn and Jets); *Rumble* (orchestra); *Cool* (Smith, Jets); *A Boy Like That* (Moreno, Wood); *I Have A Love* (Wood, Moreno); *Somewhere* (Wood, Beymer); *Roof Dance* (Wood).

Resisting the tendency to 'open out' the musical numbers as he had done in *Sweet Charity* (Universal, 1969) Bob Fosse, in his *tour de force* **Cabaret** (Allied Artists, 1972), went to the other extreme in the film version, and confined almost all of them to the small stage of a smoky, crowded cabaret in Berlin just before the outbreak of hostilities in the late Thirties. It was part of a radical re-assessment of the Joe Masteroff/John Kander/Fred Ebb stage show on which it was based and, like everything else in the movie, was a distinct improvement on its Broadway counterpart. All the songs (several were specially written for the film by its composers Kander and Ebb) commented on the action as opposed to being integrated into it; the screenplay, by Jay Presson Allen and Hugh Wheeler (the latter billed as 'research consultant') based on John van Druten's play *I Am A Camera* and Christopher Isherwood's *Goodbye To Berlin*, was much sounder in both content and construction than Masteroff's book for the stage show; and, with Liza Minnelli (illustrated) cast as Sally Bowles (a fifth rate American singer eking out a living in a decadent, sexually ambiguous *milieu*) the central character sprang vividly and memorably to life. The fact that the hugely talented Miss Minnelli was called upon to play a performer of no conspicuous ability whatsoever—and got away with it without throwing the entire plotline off balance, was a remarkable testament to her unique qualities as an actress and as a star 'presence'. She shared the majority of the songs with Joel Grey, who repeated his mesmeric stage performance as the cabaret's cynical MC—the most effectively staged (by Fosse) of these being 'Money, Money' and 'Mein Herr', both written specially for the film. Other musical highlights were an explosive performance of the title number by Minnelli and, from Grey, 'Wilkommen', the lascivious 'Two Ladies' about the attractions of a *ménage à trois*, and the nauseating, sinister, anti-semitic but compelling 'If You Could See Her' danced with an organza-clad chimpanzee. Michael York co-starred as the young bisexual writer from Britain who fetches up in digs with Minnelli in Berlin, and through whose eyes the era is witnessed; Helmut Griem was the wealthy, irresponsible playboy with whom they both have affairs, and Marisa Berenson and Fritz Wepper a young Jewish department-store heiress and her sweetheart. It was dazzlingly photographed (in Technicolor) by Geoffrey Unsworth, with Ralph Burns in charge of the musical direction and orchestrations. Cy Feuer was responsible for the production. Other songs and musical numbers: *Maybe This Time* (Minnelli); *Sitting Pretty* (orchestra); *Tiller Girls* (Grey, girls); *Heiraten* (Greta Keller—voice only); *Tomorrow Belongs To Me* (boys' chorus).

A star is born, Mark II: Liza Minnelli, as Sally Bowles in Cabaret

FEAR & FANTASY

Towards the end of 1895, in the very early days of moving pictures, the cinema's main function in life seemed to be to record reality. Not that reality was necessarily dull or reassuring: audiences allegedly fled from the first film show because they thought the train they saw coming towards them on the screen was going to continue on outwards and crush them. But, once film watchers got used to this change in the scheme of things, they were fed on a diet of domestic scenes, pictures of street life, simple jokes and records of public events. They weren't always true—a record of the Coronation of Edward VII was 're-enacted' in the filmmaker's back garden—but they were, apparently, real.

One early filmmaker, however, recognized the new medium's potential for offering other, less pedestrian forms of entertainment. His name was George Méliès and he was a music hall proprietor. Méliès realized that the 'reality' which the camera endowed on objects could be used to trick audiences, and he developed certain techniques to enhance this manipulation. On stage, fantasy scenes required enormous expense and, even so, the wires still showed. On film, the illusion was far more convincing, and the audience didn't have to sit through slow and noisy scene changes.

Since Méliès, these techniques have obviously progressed and multiplied. There has been the extraordinary model work of Willis O'Brien (who set Kong in motion) and his successor, Ray Harryhausen. There have been the make-up skills of Jack Pierce, who constructed Boris Karloff's monster in *Frankenstein* (1932) and there are the computer-aided special visual effects of the modern space epic. Between them, they have made the unreal seem tangibly real and, in the case of the *Star Wars* saga, have made the fantastic seem almost everyday.

But the cinema has another related capability which it shares with no other art form (except, of course, television), and that is to frighten. Not only can we be drawn further and further into some horribly realistic nightmare world, as we are in *The Innocents* (1961) or *The Haunting* (1963), *Psycho* (1960) or *The Birds* (1963); we can also be treated to shock effects by the simple cinematic device of the cut. As we follow the crew through the corridors of the spacecraft Nostromo in *Alien* (1979), our apprehension is heightened by the almost certain knowledge that, before too long, there will be a shock cut to H. R. Giger's hideous little creature.

The last little shock in *Carrie* (1976) would be impossible in any medium but motion pictures. The fact that the shock is later revealed to be part of a dream does nothing to lessen its impact. In fact, it provides a kind of key to the whole fascination of the cinema of fear and fantasy. René Clair, the distinguished French director who was part of the avant garde movement of the 1920s, explained some of the thinking behind his early films when he said that 'the moviegoer is like a dreamer in a sleep'. The cinema can effortlessly follow the logic of dreams, and it is just as likely to do so through the landscape of nightmare.

The cinema of fear and the cinema of fantasy are not, of course, the same: *Snow White and the Seven Dwarfs* (1937) and *Halloween* (1978) are scarely aimed at the same audience. The split only began to be noticeable around World War II; since then, the gulf between the two has steadily

widened. Lon Chaney's *Phantom of the Opera* (1925) and Willis O'Brien's giant ape, although they undoubtedly *did* frighten contemporary audiences, had about them the gentler feel of fantasy. It was when the fantasy film moved decisively into the lower end of the budget bracket, as it did with Universal International's creature features of the 1950s, that scaring audiences out of their wits became more important than stimulating their imagination. Looking back, of course, a film like Universal's 1935 *The Bride of Frankenstein* now seems wistful, almost poetic, rather than the shocker that was intended by the studio. But tastes change, and the thresholds of what is permissible get lowered all the time. Nowadays, there is no need to invoke the undead, the extra-terrestrial or things from the deep to make your audience gasp: all you need is a good, sharp bread knife. This chapter includes only one true 'splatter' movie—the genre's classic, *Halloween*—but the spread of guts and gore can be seen in films like *Alien, The Omen* (1976) and *Blade Runner* (1982). It is, as they say in the trade, what today's kids want.

In recent years, however, the fantasy film has been brought back in from the cold by a generation of filmmakers who grew up on the gentler fare of the 1950s. Before *Star Wars* (1977), no one would have believed that a film that cost that much money could ever have succeeded with so gentle and unviolent a foray into the dreamworld. Since its box-office triumph, fantasies have grown gentler, with the cute and rubbery *E.T.* (1982) and the cuddly Ewoks of *Star Wars'* successor, *Return of the Jedi* (1983). However, the tide of splatter has, for all that, not been stemmed.

On the whole, the recent films are an exception. Science fiction and horror films have come from the lower end of the market. They have rarely had stars in them, and they have been cheaply made. What invariably strikes one looking at the science fiction pulps of the 1950s was how rarely the execution of the sets and the special effects measured up to the imagination of the plots. Maybe that is why they settled into the youth market, which will put up with a lot providing things keep moving. And things of all shapes and sizes moved a great deal through the cinematic fantasyland of the 1950s.

A psychologist has suggested a remarkably plausible reason for this bond between adolescents and horror movies. The great horror legends like Dracula, the werewolf and Dr Jekyll and Mr Hyde are about people whose bodies are undergoing changes they can't control and in most cases don't really understand. The adolescent, having just gone through puberty, is experiencing much the same thing, with the body passing on instructions to the brain that the brain hasn't yet learned to deal with. The fact that the beast nearly always pursues the beauty tells us something about horror movies, too. No one could seriously challenge the claim that vampire movies are full of sexual imagery. Bram Stroker's original novel, Dracula (1897), for instance, put its repressed Victorian heroine in touch with a temptation she couldn't refuse, certainly not in favour of the rather dreary young man to whom she had previously been attached. The overall fascination of horror movies comes from a similar motive. We are all simultaneously drawn to and terrified of the unknown. The safe world in which we live is certainly more reassuring and more comfortable, but sometimes we want excitement. Horror movies fulfil that need at minimum risk—whatever warnings the publicity campaigns may give.

· FROM · BEYOND · THE · GRAVE ·

The Monster (MGM, 1925) is a title that might have served for four out of five Lon Chaney movies. No villainy was too vile for Lon, no disguise too grotesque. Unusually, he wore very little make-up as this particular monster (looking, in fact, remarkably like his future successor in monstership, Boris Karloff). He played an insane surgeon who abducted passing motorists for experiments in bringing the dead back to life. Gertrude Olmstead, Hallam Cooley and Johnny Arthur were featured, and Roland West directed the Willard Mack/Albert Kenyon script, from a play by Crane Wilbur.

Advertized as 'the story of the strangest passion the world has ever known' Universal's **Dracula**, based on Bram Stoker's classic horror story (and a successful stage play by Hamilton Deane and John Balderston), was an immediate hit with audiences. It was also the studio's biggest moneymaker of 1931, and it set a trend of horror films which Universal would exploit with varying degrees of success for the remainder of the decade. Though director Tod Browning originally sought Lon Chaney for the central role of the Transylvanian Count, Chaney demurred—then died. Thus it became possible for the Hungarian-born Bela Lugosi, who had opened the play on Broadway in 1927, to recreate his mesmeric performance on film. It is doubtful if the movie would have been the great success it was without Lugosi especially as much of the horror in Garrett Fort's

Left: Lon Chaney and Walter James in The Monster; *below: Bela Lugosi in a scene from* Dracula

screenplay took place off screen. But with Bela Lugosi dominating the proceedings so completely and allowing such an overwhelming miasma of evil to seep through the tale, it hardly mattered that the film's visual content was rather tame. Dwight Frye played Renfield, the English real-estate agent who travels to Transylvania to discuss the sale of the Castle Dracula with its aristocratic and outwardly gracious owner; Helen Chandler and Frances Dade were Minna Seward and her friend Lucy Watson, Edward Van Sloan was vampire fighter Professor Von Helsing, and David Manners played Minna's sweetheart John Harker. Other roles went to Michael Visaroff (as the innkeeper), Herbert Bunston, Charles Gerrard and Joan Standing. The sparingly used background music was from Tchaikovsky's *Swan Lake*. In 1922 the German director Murnau filmed a version under the title *Nosferatu* (with Max Schreck); it was remade in 1958 by Hammer Films with Christopher Lee and it was filmed yet again by universal in 1979, with Frank Langella as Dracula.

Take *Jane Eyre*, transpose it to the West Indies, mix in a healthy dose of voodoo mysticism and a soupçon of scientific scepticism and you have the recipe for **I Walked with a Zombie** (RKO, 1943). Frances Dee (below centre), a trained nurse, is brought to the tropics by Tom Conway (below right) to tend his wife, who walks and breathes but cannot speak or think. Amid the barbaric rhythm of voodoo drums, Dee learns the truth—her patient is a zombie, one who is dead but has been brought back to life by native sorcerers. The most amazing thing about this outrageous *pot-pourri* was that it worked. Jacques Tourneur's direction, Curt Siodmak and Ardel Wray's screenplay (based on a story by Inez Wallace), the photography of J. Roy Hunt and art direction of Albert D'Agostino and Walter Keller, combined to create the most challenging and poetic of the Val Lewton-produced horror pictures. Also cast: James Ellison, Edith Barrett, James Bell, Christine Gordon (below left, the zombie) and Theresa Harris.

In those late-night conversations when people talk about their favourite ghost stories, Jack Clayton's film version of Henry James' *The Turn Of The Screw*, **The Innocents** (produced by Achilles Productions for 20th Century-Fox, 1961) crops up again and again. A Victorian governess (Deborah Kerr) faces up to the ghosts of a large old house, conjured up by her two difficult young charges. She also faces up to her own repressed sexuality—an 'explanation' for the ghosts which rather divided the critics. What made **The Innocents** such a genuinely spine-chilling experience, however, was the very ordinariness of the manifestations. The first time Miss Giddens (Kerr) sees Peter Quint (Peter Wyngarde), for example, she is in the garden on a bright summer's day, picking flowers. Suddenly, all the sounds of summer fade away leaving only a slight buzzing. She glances up, and there is Quint looking down at her from the top of a tower. All the performances were excellent, especially Martin Stephens and Pamela Franklin as the children. The real quality of the film, however, lay in Clayton's direction and Freddie Francis' black and white CinemaScope photography.

Top left: Bela Lugosi in Dracula*; below: Christine Gordon, Frances Dee, and Tom Conway in* I Walked with a Zombie*; facing: Megs Jenkins, Pamela Franklin and Deborah Kerr in* The Innocents, *and inset: Julie Harris in* The Haunting

Michael Winner attempted a kind of prequel, *The Nightcomers*, in 1971, with Marlon Brando as the still-living Peter Quint. It was not a success.

The Haunting, an MGM British thriller, eschewed the clutching hands and shrouded corpses of the haunted-house school; producer-director Robert Wise got his effects with atmospheric touches, strange sounds, and the fear reactions of Julie Harris. Also cast: Richard Johnson, Claire Bloom, Russ Tamblyn, Fay Compton, Rosalie Crutchley, Lois Maxwell, Valentine Dyall and Diane Clare. Nelson Gidding's script was based on a Shirley Jackson novel. (1963).

Standing in the shadows: Christopher Lee in Dracula, Prince of Darkness

Marking Christopher Lee's return to the role after an eight-year sabbatical, **Dracula, Prince of Darkness** (1965) was the most lavish of all Hammer's horror films. Unfairly attacked for a gory resuscitation scene—the hapless victim is strung up by a chain winch over a coffin containing the dust of Dracula and bled to death, thus reviving the Count—it is probably the peak of the studio's pictorially lush and brilliantly coloured vampire tales. The story is much as before—a group of travellers in the Carpathians falls prey to or narrowly escapes vampirization—but director Terence Fisher's genius for conjuring up a simultaneous sense of menace and awe was never better demonstrated. He has Michael Reed's (Techniscope, Technicolor) camera prowl the castle and track its victims with all the stealth and elegance of Dracula himself. Lee is on top form, proving as usual that evil can be more attractive and sophisticated than the forces of good. Andrew Keir gives him a good run for his money, though, as a no-nonsense Friar. He then, as propriety requires, dispatches him to eternity once more, this time via a disintegrating ice flow which casts him into running water (as fatal to vampires as sunlight and crosses). The terror of Transylvania rematerialized, however, in the form of Christopher Lee in at least ten more films, though none approached the brilliance of this one. The producer was Anthony Nelson-Keys, the screenplay was by John Sansom, and Barbara Steele gave one of her most sensuously evil performances as a tourist who becomes an early victim.

• THINGS • AREN'T • WHAT • THEY • USED • TO • BE •

After the impact made ten months earlier by Bela Lugosi as Dracula, it was Boris Karloff's turn to create cinema history in the horror genre—which he indisputably did with **Frankenstein** (Universal, 1932). He would play the monster twice more (in 1935 and 1939) and, to this day, the character remains as welded to his name as Dracula to Lugosi's. Though the technical preparations that went into the creation of the monster caused Karloff (see below) hours of discomfort on the set (he was made 18 inches taller, 65 pounds heavier, and had his legs stiffened by steel struts), it was worth it in the end with the finished product resulting in one of the most memorable screen images of the Thirties. Make-up wizard Jack Pierce was responsible for that image, his major achievement resting in the way the creature managed to arouse both revulsion and sympathy at the same time. Though Karloff's performance remains the memorable one, he was in fact only billed fourth to Colin Clive (as his creator Dr Frankenstein), Mae Clark as Frankenstein's pretty fiancée, and John Boles as a friend who tries to dissuade the doctor from continuing his dangerous experiments. Also cast: Edward Van Sloan, Dwight Frye, Frederick Kerr, Lionel Belmore and Marilyn Harris. It was chillingly directed by James Whale, the two most memorable sequences being the monster's 'birth', and the one near the end of the film in which Karloff, after innocently throwing a little girl into a lake, realizes what he has done. It was written by Garrett Fort and Francis Edwards Faragoh, and adapted from a play by Peggy Webling which, in turn, was adapted from the classic gothic novel by Mary Shelley. The most radical change from the original lay in giving the screen monster a brain that once belonged to a criminal. Edison had made a version of the famous story in 1910 with Charles Ogle; in 1957 Hammer Films starred Peter Cushing in *The Curse of Frankenstein.*

Below: Boris Karloff breaks free in Frankenstein. *True love ways: King Kong and Fay Wray*

From primordial jungle to last stand atop the Empire State Building came **King Kong** (RKO), the simian superstar of one of the most original motion pictures ever made. Known at various times in its production history as *The Beast, The Eighth Wonder* and *Kong* before the final title was determined, the picture began principal photography in August 1932 but was not released until March 1933, the Depression's darkest hour. This was, in truth, Merian C. Cooper's film. He conceived the idea, and co-directed and co-produced (with Ernest B. Schoedsack). Cooper's own love of adventure and his Barnum-like abilities were captured in the character of Carl Denham, the entrepreneur who leads the expedition to Kong's island. Robert Armstrong played the part—by far the best role and performance of his career. David O. Selznick had little to do with the picture, but when he and B. B. Kahane saw how it was developing, they squeezed other budgets to provide extra funds for its completion. The final cost was $300,000 over the original budget. Technically, **King Kong** was a stupendous feat of special effects wizardry. Chief technician Willis O'Brien's staff, including E. B. Gibson, Marcel Delgado, Fred Reese, Orville Goldner, Carroll Sheppird, Mario Larrinaga and Byron L. Crabbe, breathed life into the 50-foot ape and the other prehistoric monsters that roam through his island. Their work set a standard of excellence against which all future 'trick' pictures would be measured. On the narrative level, James Ashmore Creelman and Ruth Rose completed the screenplay from Cooper and Edgar Wallace's original story. Among the script's inspired action elements were battles between Kong and various gigantic beasts, his rampage through the streets of New York and his final, futile attempts to swat the killer airplanes that riddle his body with machine-gun bullets. The story also provided a classic role for Fay Wray, as the beauty whose charms emasculate the beast. Her immortal screams, mixed with the ape's thunderous growls (sound effects by Murray Spivack) nearly blew the tops off theatres in 1933. One must not forget Max Steiner's score—it remains one of the most dynamic in the history of film music. Before its release, MGM offered to buy **King Kong** for $400,000 more than its negative cost ($672,000). RKO wisely refused to sell, and the film earned $1,761,000 in film rentals, despite the Depression. Periodic re-issues also proved very successful. Dino De Laurentiis acquired the rights and produced a much publicized, stratospherically-budgeted, up-dated, and very poor version in 1976, with Jeff Bridges and Jessica Lange, released by Paramount.

The original ending showing the death of Boris Karloff (below), alias Frankenstein's monster, was sensibly shelved by Universal when Carl Laemmle Jr realized what a hot property he had in the monster, and he commissioned a sequel to *Frankenstein* (1931) from John Balderston and William Hurlbut. The result was **The Bride of Frankenstein**, 1935, in which the monster (more human than in the earlier film) having, it seemed, escaped the flames that devoured the old mill at the end of *Frankenstein*, suffers further humiliations when a certain Dr Praetorius (Ernest Thesiger), who the monster meets in a cemetery, decides that what the creature needs is a she-monster to keep him company. Trouble is, when Praetorius, together with Frankenstein (Colin Clive), succeeds in creating such a companion (Elsa Lanchester, see below), she takes just one look at her 'mate' and rejects him. The denouement had everyone, except Frankenstein, being blown to bits. Again directed by James Whale (whose final excursion into horror this would be), and with a full-bodied musical score by Franz Waxman to help it along, it emerged as even more outrageous in its baroque excesses than its predecessor. John Mescall's camerawork was especially striking throughout, and nowhere better than in the sequence showing the 'birth' of the she-monster. Valerie Hobson appeared as Mrs Frankenstein, with other roles going to O. P. Heggie (as a blind hermit who provides the monster with hospitality), Dwight Frye, Ted Bollings, E. E. Clive and John Carradine. Elsa Lanchester, in addition to her role, appeared in a prologue as Mary Shelley, author of the original novel from which the central characters were once again drawn.

Opposite: the finale of King Kong*; here: the monster (Boris Karloff) meets his bride (Elsa Lanchester)*

Horror addicts were well-supplied with grotesqueries in **Tarantula** (1955, Universal), a modest but enjoyable piece of sci-fi which showed what happens when a nutritional formula designed to feed the world's increasing population goes wrong, and a tarantula is injected with the as yet unstabilized contents. The insect grows to enormous proportions and begins to feed off cattle and humans; and it takes the Air Force and few napalm bombs finally to destroy it, but not before a creepy time was had by all. John Agar was the top star, playing a young doctor, Mara Corday co-starred as a science student stationed near Desert Rock, Arizona, Leo G. Carroll was her employer, with other parts in Robert M. Fresco and Martin Berkeley's screenplay (story by director Jack Arnold and Fresco) going to Nestor Paiva as a sheriff, Ross Elliott as a local editor and Hank Patterson as a hotel clerk. The pilot who finally blasts the spider was played by an already typecast Clint Eastwood, in an early bit-part. William Alland produced; the excellent make-up was by Bud Westmore.

Universal-International presents
TARANTULA!
STARRING
JOHN AGAR
MARA CORDAY
LEO G. CARROLL
with NESTOR PAIVA · ROSS ELLIOTT

The plot of Alfred Hitchcock's **The Birds** (Universal, 1963) was pretty feeble, with many more narrative threads remaining untied than was usual for the 'master of suspense'. What one remembers most about the film is hardly Tippi Hedren's romance with attorney Rod Taylor (seen above) or Jessica Tandy, Taylor's mother, fearing loneliness and turning ultra-possessive; or even pretty Suzanne Pleshette and the role she played of a schoolteacher and Taylor's ex-girlfriend. As was so often the case with Hitchcock, the film's *raison d'être* lay not in its plot but in its eerie subtext—and in the notion of an entire community being threatened by a plague of birds. The film's underlying emotion, enhanced by the clever use of electronic sounds in place of more conventional background music, was menace, and in this respect Hitchcock certainly delivered the goods. Even when nothing happened you felt it was about to. Though much of the back-projection was obvious and the special effects transparent, the overall atmosphere created through the low-key direction gave the film its reputation as one of the most purely cinematic of the entire Hitchcock *oeuvre*—the great fire sequence (which featured a really remarkable long shot of Bodega Bay, the story's setting) being the film's most memorable set-piece. The cast also included Veronica Cartwright, Ethel Griffies, Charles McGraw and Ruth

McDevitt. Hitchcock produced, Evan Hunter wrote the screenplay from a story by Daphne Du Maurier, it was photographed by Robert Burke in Technicolor, and designed by Robert Boyle. The bird trainer in charge of all the anti-social behaviour was Ray Berwick.

With **Alien** (20th Century-Fox), the space craze of the late 1970s turned adult. Dan O'Bannon's story, which is, in effect, a serious version of his jokey, post-graduate film *Dark Star* (1974), is set on board a commercial spacecraft, the *Nostromo*. After a visit to a strange, deserted planet, one of the crew members, Kane (John Hurt), becomes host to a hideous creature which incubates inside him, then bursts out to terrorize the ship. Ripley (Sigourney Weaver) manages to escape into a shuttle, leaving the ship (whose remaining crew are all dead) to explode. But to her horror, she finds the alien aboard the shuttle with her.... Directed by former commercials wizard Ridley Scott, whose second feature it was, **Alien**'s enormous box-office success was probably mostly due to its nastier effects. The creature bursting out of Hurt is a moment of spectacular unpleasantness, as is the moment when one of the crew, Ash (Ian Holm), has his head ripped off to reveal he is a robot, then proceeds to extrude milky liquid all over the floor. Its real distinction, however, comes from its design, masterminded by the great illustrator, H. R. Giger. The ship is a superior piece of space hardware, but the dead planet on which the crew first gets contaminated is a truly brilliant piece of work—huge, eerie and vaguely organic. The creature itself is like the sort of nightmare you get after eating cheese. As one of the *Nostromo*'s crew remarks, 'It's got a great defence mechanism: you daren't kill it!' Tom Skerritt captained the craft, and Veronica Cartwright, Harry Dean Stanton and Yaphet Kotto made up the rest of the crew. Gordon Carroll, David Giler and Walter Hill produced, with Ronald Shusett as executive producer. **Alien** won an Oscar for special effects and a British Academy Award for Art Direction.

Before, during and after the attack: bottom left: Tarantula*; top left: Tippi Hedren and Rod Taylor in Hitchcock's* The Birds, *and above: Sigourney Weaver finds she is alone—except for the Alien lurking in a dark corner*

• TWISTED • SOULS •

Though Irving Thalberg left Universal in February 1923, before the release of **The Hunchback of Notre Dame**, the project had been his brainchild from the start, and it was his unbridled enthusiasm for it that persuaded Carl Laemmle to spend a great deal more money on it than was normal for the studio, and to release it as a 'roadshow' attraction. The finished film more than justified the expenditure. **Hunchback** remains a classic piece of silent film-making, in which Lon Chaney as Quasimodo, the bellringer of Notre Dame, gave one of the great performances in cinema history. An expert with make-up, Chaney excelled himself on this memorable occasion. At the cost of his physical comfort he masochistically attached a 70-pound rubber lump to his back, wore a leather harness that made it impossible for him to stand up straight, and donned a rubber suit covered with animal hair. Then, to disguise his facial features, he stuffed mortician's wax into his mouth, puttied his cheeks, matted his hair, and gave himself a grotesque, bulging false eye. For three arduous months he worked in this fashion, and if his suffering seems so heartfelt on screen, much of it was genuine! Perley Poore Sheehan's adaptation of the novel underplayed Victor Hugo's attack on the priesthood, altered the plot-line in such a way as to make the archdeacon of Paris' brother, Jehan, the real villain of the piece and, in order to ensure a happy ending, reunited Esmeralda with Captain Phoebus after Quasimodo's death. Under Wallace Worsley's stirring direction, press

and public alike were pleased with the changes, and the film, which established Chaney (above) as a major Hollywood star, was an immediate hit. Originally twelve reels in length, its running time was shortened after its initial roadshow release, one of the casualties of the cuts being Ernest Torrence, whose role as the beggar chieftain Clopin, considered by many to be as fine as Chaney's, was greatly truncated. Patsy Ruth Miller (above) was Esmeralda, Norman Kerry was Phoebus, Tully Marshall appeared as Louis XI, and Nigel de Brulier was Dom Claude the archdeacon. Also cast: Kate Lester, Gladys Brockwell, Brandon Hurst (as Jehan) and Raymond Hatton. Contributing immeasurably to the film's success were the spectacular sets most notably Notre Dame Cathedral which, like the Casino in *Foolish Wives* (1922), was constructed at Universal City. Edward T. Lowe provided the scenario and, assisting director Worsley to control the 2,000 extras employed in the crowd scenes, was a relative newcomer called William Wyler. The story had been filmed three times before, in the years 1906, 1911, and 1917; and would be filmed on two further occasions: by RKO in 1939 with Charles Laughton as its Quasimodo, and by Allied Artists in 1957 with Anthony Quinn.

One of the greatest of all horror films, and certainly the pinnacle of the genre in the silent era, **The Phantom of the Opera** (1925) gave man-of-a-thousand-faces Lon Chaney, then on loan to Universal from MGM, the chance to shatter audiences with his most grotesque face yet—that of Erik, the phantom of the title. Erik's menacing existence in the elaborate catacombs and dungeons beneath the Paris Opera terrified audiences almost as much as it terrified pretty Mary Philbin a young understudy at the Opera who, in one of the most effective moments in the film, rips off the phantom's mask to reveal a sight so hideous that, at each performance, several of the more faint-hearted patrons had to be revived afterwards with smelling salts!

Because of Chaney's extraordinary make-up, painfully achieved by distending his nostrils with a wire clip, filling out his cheeks with celluloid discs and dilating his eyes with drops, the studio took special care to withhold photographs of this monstrous apparition in order not to diminish the impact of the moment when it finally arrived. The actual set of the Opera House was constructed at Universal City and was an exact replica of the Paris Opera, containing five tiers of balconies, and seating 3,000 extras. Norman Kerry played Raoul, Miss Philbin's fiancé, and Arthur Edmund Carewe was Ledoux of the secret police, with other roles going to Snitz Edwards, Mary Fabian, Gibson Gowland, John Sainpolis, Virginia Pearson, Edith Yorke, Cesare Gravina, John Miljan and Chester Conklin. It was marvellously directed by a temperamental Rupert Julian, whose disagreements with Chaney over the latter's approach to the role led, ultimately, to Edward Sedgwick being called in to reshoot the spectacular chase finale, and to supervise the editing. It was adapted from Gaston Leroux's 1910 novel by Raymond L. Schrock and Elliott J. Clawson (with Tom Reed supplying the titles), and the outstanding and atmospheric set designs were by Charles D. Hall. This version was reissued in 1930 with several changes: talking sequences for Mary Philbin and Norman Kerry were added; extant scenes from the opera *Faust* had arias dubbed in; John Miljan's part was deleted, scenes featuring John Sainpolis were deleted, and new scenes were filmed and inserted in their place with Edward Martindel. It was remade in 1943 and later, by Hammer, in 1962. (Jewel).

The studio's last release of the Thirties was also one of the biggest and best films in RKO history. Victor Hugo's **The Hunchback of Notre Dame** (1939), as adapted by Bruno Frank and scripted by Sonya Levien, painted the world of King Louis XI in broad strokes, emphasizing the contrast between rich and poor, freedom and repression, and medievalism and enlightenment that marked the era. Producer Pandro S. Berman and director William Dieterle spurned any romantic or soft-headed approach to the material; indeed, the realism bordered on a grotesquerie at times, especially in its ugly portrayal of human nature, its unrelieved depiction of torture and suffering, and its incredibly misshapen Quasimodo (Charles Laughton, illustrated). Few pictures from this period would have dared show men being boiled alive by scalding oil, much less the appalling pillory scene in which the hunchback is whipped unmercifully, his hump exposed for all to see. Charles Laughton's superlative performance as the doomed outcast who falls in love with a gypsy girl (Maureen O'Hara) and twice saves her from death, overshadowed the other first-rate performances of Cedric Hardwicke, Thomas Mitchell and those two Hollywood newcomers Miss O'Hara and Edmond O'Brien.

Laughton—almost impossible to recognize under the heavy distortion of his make-up—still managed to convey Quasimodo's natural humanity. Though by no means a cheerful divertissement for the world's moviegoers to sample, **The Hunchback** pulsed with passion and vigour (abetted by Alfred Newman's bravura score) and audiences responded in kind to its gripping theatricality. Costing $1,826,000 to make, this spectacular brought in $3,155,000 in film rentals. It opened at about the same time as *Gone with the Wind* and was overshadowed by the more famous and profitable Selznick/MGM blockbuster; still, despite that fact, **The Hunchback of Notre Dame** provided a suitable finale to the best production year the studio would ever have.

The gigantic cast also included Alan Marshal, Walter Hampden, Harry Davenport, Katharine Alexander, George Zucco, Fritz Leiber, Etienne Girardot, Helene Whitney, Minna Gombell, Arthur Hohl, George Tobias, Rod La Rocque and Spencer Charters.

Two hunchbacks and a phantom: left: Lon Chaney in The Phantom of the Opera *(bottom) and (top, with Patsy Ruth Miller) in* The Hunchback of Notre Dame*; right: Charles Laughton in the 1939 remake of* The Hunchback

· LITTLE · DEVILS ·

Little Tina Rona (Patty McCormack, seen right), was more than just precocious. When, for example, she lost a writing award at school to a classmate, she took her revenge by cold bloodedly murdering him during a picnic. And anyone who disagreed that it was simply an accident was bumped off too. Based on the play by Maxwell Anderson and with a screenplay by John Lee Mahin, **The Bad Seed** (1956) was a chilling study of evil and, like evil itself, totally mesmeric. The film's climax, in which the child's mother (Nancy Kelly), realizing that the monster she has spawned must, herself, die, was cleverly handled by Mervyn LeRoy, the director, who, in the film's closing credits, sweetened the pill somewhat by allowing his cast, as if in a stage production, to take a 'screen call', with young Patty being put across her mother's knee and soundly spanked. In the Broadway production, the child remains unpunished for her sins, an ending which the Johnston office (Eric Johnston succeeded censor Will Hays in 1945) would not tolerate in the screen version. The cast of the Mervyn LeRoy production for Warner Bros. also featured Eileen Heckart and Henry Jones (who, like Nancy Kelly and Patty McCormack, had played their roles on Broadway) as well as William Hopper, Paul Fix and Jesse White.

Village of the Damned (1960) a really sinister horror movie, emerged from MGM British to intrigue big audiences after director Wolf Rilla, producer Ronald Kinnoch and writers Stirling Silliphant, George Barclay and Rilla had worked on John Wyndham's novel *The Midwich Cuckoos*. George Sanders and Barbara Shelley play the parents of Martin Stephens, whose strange manner and supernatural intelligence were shared by other children born at the same time. Also cast: Michael Gwynn, Laurence Naismith, Richard Warner, Thomas Heathcote, John Phillips, Richard Vernon, Rosamund Greenwood, Bernard Archard, Peter Vaughan.

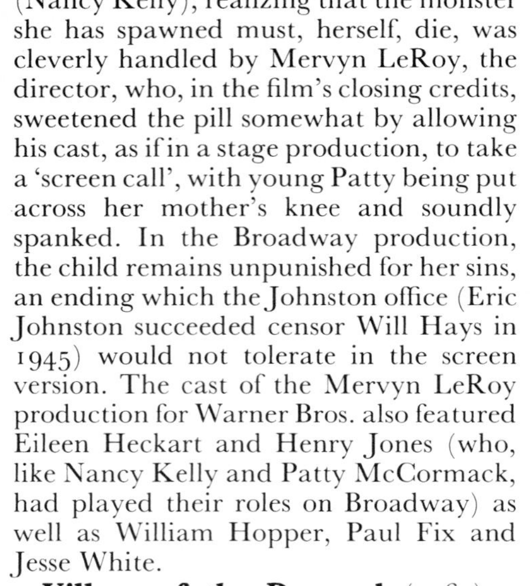

An evil spirit uncovered by Father Merrin (Max von Sydow, below centre) during an archaeological dig in Iraq finds its way to Georgetown, USA and into the soul of little Regan MacNeil (Linda Blair) with devastating consequences—as millions of cinemagoers from Iraq to Georgetown discovered in **The Exorcist** (1973). Produced and adapted by William Peter Blatty from his best-seller, and directed with considerable flair for the truly horrendous by William Friedkin, it contained scenes alternately hair-raising and stomach churning hitherto new to the America cinema. What made it all so nauseatingly special was the genuine sense of evil that permeated it. From the moment the possessed Regan urinates on to her mother's carpet to the graphic scenes in which she gibbers obscenely, spewing pints of green slime from her mouth, audiences were left in no doubt that they were privy to something truly diabolical, with the final exorcism itself quite shattering in its impact. A box-office smash to the tune of $82,200,000 (the biggest grosser in the history of Warner Bros. to that date and one of the highest grossing films of all time), it also featured Ellen Burstyn as Miss Blair's filmstar mother, Jason Miller (on the left), Jack MacGowran and Lee J. Cobb. Dick Smith did the make-up and deserved a bow all of his own.

Top right: Patty McCormack in The Bad Seed; *above: devastation hits the* Village of the Damned, *and below: Jason Miller, Max von Sydow and (under the covers) Linda Blair in* The Exorcist

'For everything holy, there is something unholy. That is the essence of temptation,' intones a monk in **The Omen** (20th Century-Fox, 1976). Judging by the number of unholy movies that were made in the mid-1970s, the world must be a holier place than it generally seems. Coming in the wake of *The Exorcist*, **The Omen** has itself spawned a pair of successors, *Damien, Omen II* (1978) and *The Final Conflict* (1981). But Richard Donner's film, from a script by David Seltzer and photographed by Gilbert Taylor in Panavision, is still the model for the modern 'demonic kid' story. The child of the US Ambassador to Rome (Gregory Peck) dies shortly after birth and, without telling his wife (Lee Remick), Peck agrees to another child being substituted. The child, Damien, played by the angelic Harvey Stephens, is not as sweet as he seems, and manages to dispose of anyone who tries to tell his secret. Even Peck gets shot by the police as he attempts to carry out the necessary ritual slaying in a church. Damien is then adopted by an old family friend, the President of the United States, and the demonic masterplan takes a step nearer the sequel. Of course, Peck and Remick are slow to accept that their kid is the Devil—a reluctance reinforced by the fact that everyone who tries to warn them, especially Patrick Troughton's Father Brennan, seems to be nuts. Damien's methods of dealing with the opposition are ingeniously nasty, and the whole film has a superior veneer of tension and terror. Mace Neufeld and Harvey Bernhard produced, Jerry Goldsmith composed the religiose score, forever slipping into *missae solemnae*, and David Warner, Billie Whitelaw and Leo McKern (as an archaeologist who seemed to have strayed in from *The Exorcist*) completed the cast.

Above: the angelic Harvey Stephens in The Omen*; below: Sissy Spacek and William Katt about to be doused in* Carrie

Brian de Palma's **Carrie** (United Artists, 1976) is a shocker which received the sort of release rarely accorded to a horror movie. Built around a frighteningly intense performance by Sissy Spacek as Carrie White, a young girl coming late and awkwardly into womanhood, **Carrie** builds irresistibly towards a climax that is scary, bloody and brilliantly choreographed, then caps it with one of the genre's great shock effects. In addition to being pubescent, Carrie is also psychic: she can move objects by telekinesis. Mocked by her fellow students because of her gaucheness and her fundamentalist mother (Piper Laurie), Carrie is set up for humilitation via a date with football hero Tommy Ross (William Katt) at the prom. When the trap is sprung—a bucket of pig's blood is tipped over her at her moment of triumph—Carrie unleashes her full fury on the hall, goes home to deal with her mother, and finally incinerates herself in the family home. **Carrie** is nasty, bloody, violent and extremely effective—a combination which accounted for its success at the box office on its first release and at any number of revivals. The script, by Lawrence D. Cohen, was from a novel by Stephen King, whose exercises in Gothic horror rarely translate so well to the screen. Paul Monash produced for Red Bank Films, and Amy Irving, John Travolta and Nancy Allen headed a cast of young Hollywood hopefuls who would soon go on to bigger—though not necessarily better—things.

• MORE • OR • LESS • • HUMAN •

One of Warner Bros.' more successful horror films, **The Mystery of the Wax Museum** (1933), directed by Michael Curtiz, and starring Lionel Atwill as the mentally and physically scarred owner of a wax museum, was genuinely horrific. The destruction by fire of the museum, with the slowly melting wax figures distorting the grotesque forms, as well as the gruesome climax in which an agonized Fay Wray literally crumbles Atwill's face to reveal how hideously disfigured it is, were as terrifying as anything conceived by that archdeacon of terror, James Whale, down the road at Universal. Written by Don Mullaly and Carl Erickson from a story by Charles Belden and filmed in eerie Technicolor by Ray Rennahan, the film also featured Glenda Farrell, with Frank McHugh, Allen Vincent and Gavin Gordon in support. Henry Blanke supervised the production.

Above: the end comes for Lionel Atwill in The Mystery of the Wax Museum, *and below: threatens Dorothy McGuire in* The Spiral Staircase. *Right: Joan Crawford in* Sudden Fear

Based on Ethel Lina White's novel *Some Must Watch*, **The Spiral Staircase** (1946) was a superb thriller in the Hitchcockian tradition. Dorothy McGuire played the movie's central figure, a mute companion-servant to bedridden Ethel Barrymore. McGuire suspects that one of her employer's sons is a maniac who has been murdering young girls who don't measure up to his ideas of physical perfection. Unaware that she is making a hideous mistake, the girl locks up her suspect (Gordon Oliver), only to discover that he is innocent while the real madman (George Brent) is closing in for the kill. Director Robert Siodmak, cinematographer Nicholas Musuraca, special effects expert Vernon L. Walker, art directors Albert S. D'Agostino and Jack Okey, and soundmen John L. Cass and Terry Kellum pulled out all the stops to make this a traumatic knockout, a film that was as intimidating and nightmarish as the Gothic mansion where the bulk of the action took place. Miss McGuire delivered a dexterous performance; she received firm support from Barrymore, Brent, Oliver, Kent Smith, Rhonda Fleming, Elsa Lanchester, Sara Allgood, Rhys Williams and James Bell. Dore Schary produced and Mel Dinelli wrote the tightly constructed screenplay. Note: **The Spiral Staircase** was the first fruit of a unique co-production venture between RKO and David O. Selznick's Vanguard Films. In this instance, Selznick furnished the basic novel, the screenplay and the services of Schary, Siodmak, McGuire and Barrymore, while RKO added all the remaining elements and profits were split fifty-fifty. RKO's share of the earnings came to $885,000.

In **Sudden Fear** (1952), Joan Crawford (right) portrayed a playwright and heiress. Jack Palance, an actor she fires but later marries, brings her perfect happiness until she discovers that he and a scheming blonde (Gloria Grahame) are plotting to kill her. Initial terror is replaced by Crawford's determination to thwart the plot, and she uses her dramatist's skill to design a scenario whereby the culprits will be caught in their own net. But her knowledge of the human equation proves faulty; by the time she discovers her own inability to carry through a key part of her plan, it is too late for anything except the most desperate sort of temporizing. It took too long for director David Miller to begin shoving his star toward the buzz saw, but once the suspense hooks took hold, they kept their grip through to the picture's rather contrived conclusion. Lenore Coffee and Robert Smith's screenplay (story Edna Sherry) also gave additional roles to Bruce Bennett, Virginia Huston and Touch Connors. Joseph Kaufman produced for his own independent company, with RKO distributing. Songs included: *Afraid* Elmer Bernstein, Jack Brooks; *Sudden Fear* Irving Taylor, Arthur Altman.

"'PSYCHO' SOCKO" was the headline studding *Variety*'s pages of box-office reports in 1960 when Alfred Hitchcock's most outrageous shocker broke out. For, although many of the critics were strangely cool, the public took to **Psycho** immediately and shot it up to the fifth biggest American gross (over $11 million) Paramount had ever reaped. Critical reassessment since then has placed it high in the Hitchcock canon, recognizing the sheer technical brilliance that unnerved audiences pleasurably and made them believe a totally incredible story about a motel owner (Anthony Perkins) switching identities with his dead mother and murdering a guest (Janet Leigh) who was absconding with her firm's money. Scenes of the ferocious stabbing in a shower—said by some to have been devised by Saul Bass, not Hitch—and the later killing of an investigator (Martin Balsam) are still regarded as classics in the genre. John Gavin, Vera Miles, John McIntire, Frank Albertson, Simon Oakland, Pat Hitchcock, Vaughn Taylor and Lurene Tuttle were also in the screenplay, which Joseph Stefano wrote from a story by Robert Bloch, and Bernard Herrmann's music score was a thriller in itself. 'No admission after the film has started' was a clever advertising gimmick that paid off. Three years after Hitchcock's death in 1980, Universal made a successful sequel, called inevitably *Psycho II*, again with Perkins and Miles.

A film student at the University of Southern California in the wake of George Lucas and Steven Spielberg, John Carpenter started off with two small budget movies, *Dark Star* (1974) and *Assault on Precinct 13* (1976), which had something of a cult following. With **Halloween** (Falcon International, 1978) he aimed at the youth/drive-in market and hit the target dead centre. His tale of a homicidal maniac loose in the small Illinois town of Haddonfield changed the course of modern horror movies, replacing Gothic extravagance with an expertly engineered string of shock effects created by cameras tracking the teenage victims amid a sea of darkness in which any number of nasty sharp things lurk. The film has spawned many imitators—as well as two sequels, *Halloween II* (1981) and *Halloween III: Season of the Witch* (1983), which Carpenter contented himself with producing—in which high school kids on dates are attacked by knife-wielding maniacs. But none has quite equalled the original for pure suspense and, in so far as such a thing is possible, tasteful blood-spilling. Carpenter, working from his own script and writing his own musical score, plays the game with such skill that, even when you know you are being wound up by sheer technique, you are content to sit forward and be gripped. This was also the film that made a star of Jamie Lee Curtis, Janet Leigh's daughter; and to complete the echoes of *Psycho*, Donald Pleasence plays a psychiatrist called Sam Loomis, the name of Miss Leigh's distraught boyfriend in the Hitchcock classic. Dean Cundey was responsible for the moody cinematography.

Like mother, like daughter: left: Janet Leigh (and Tony Perkins) in Psycho*; below: Jamie Lee Curtis in* Halloween

· KEEP · WATCHING · · THE · SKIES ·

If the stream of science-fiction features which bleeped and oozed their way into the world's cinemas in the 1950s produced one true classic, it was Fox's 1951 **The Day the Earth Stood Still**. Directed by master craftsman Robert Wise, with a screenplay by Edmund H. North based on Harry Bates' story, *Farewell To The Master*, and with music by Bernard Herrmann, special effects by Fred Sersen and photographed by Leo Tover, it tells of a tall, thin extraterrestrial called Klaatu (played by tall, thin Englishman Michael Rennie) who brings his flying saucer and accompanying massive robot to Washington to halt the world on the brink of its nuclear madness. The world at large is unwilling to listen, but Klaatu does get through to Patricia Neal and Billy Gray, a mother and son, in whose house, disguised as a Mr Carpenter, he takes a room to learn about the ways of earthlings. He also recruits a brilliant scientist (Sam Jaffe) to his cause, by the simple device of effortlessly solving the problem on which Jaffe has spent his life working. To make the world's leaders take note, Klaatu stops the planet's electrical power for 24 hours (hence the title), then blasts off again with the warning, 'The decision rests with you!' Klaatu's spaceship is a marvel of design (by Lyle Wheeler and Addison Hehr), and the scene of its landing—an overhead shot complete with shadow—is well ahead of most contemporary special effects. The codewords, should the occasion ever arise, are 'Klaatu verada nicto', which will make robots do your bidding.

Without so much as a by your leave to Shakespeare's agent, **Forbidden Planet** (MGM, 1936) pinched the whole plot of *The Tempest* and turned it into a sci-fi epic starring Robby the Robot. And what's more, it credited Irving Block and Allen Adler for the basis of Cyril Hume's script. Blow, blow, thou winter wind, thou art not so unkind as Nicholas Nayfack's ingratitude. Especially as his production was a spectacular hit, winning plaudits for Walter Pidgeon, Anne Francis, Leslie Nielsen, Warren Stevens, Jack Kelly, Richard Anderson, Jimmy Thompson, Earl Holliman, Robert Dix, James Drury, and director Fred Wilcox.

Few films have overcome the handicap of their title more completely than Don Siegel's horror masterpiece **Invasion of the Body Snatchers** (1956, Allied Artists). Based on a story by veteran SF writer Jack Finney (screenplay by Daniel Mainwaring), the film is about a town taken over by aliens. They arrive in pods, wait for their victims to fall asleep, then take over their bodies. The people look just the same, but behave like zombies. It is the old vampire theme, but with political overtones. The conformist utopia which the pod's leader outlines to town doctor Kevin McCarthy sounds

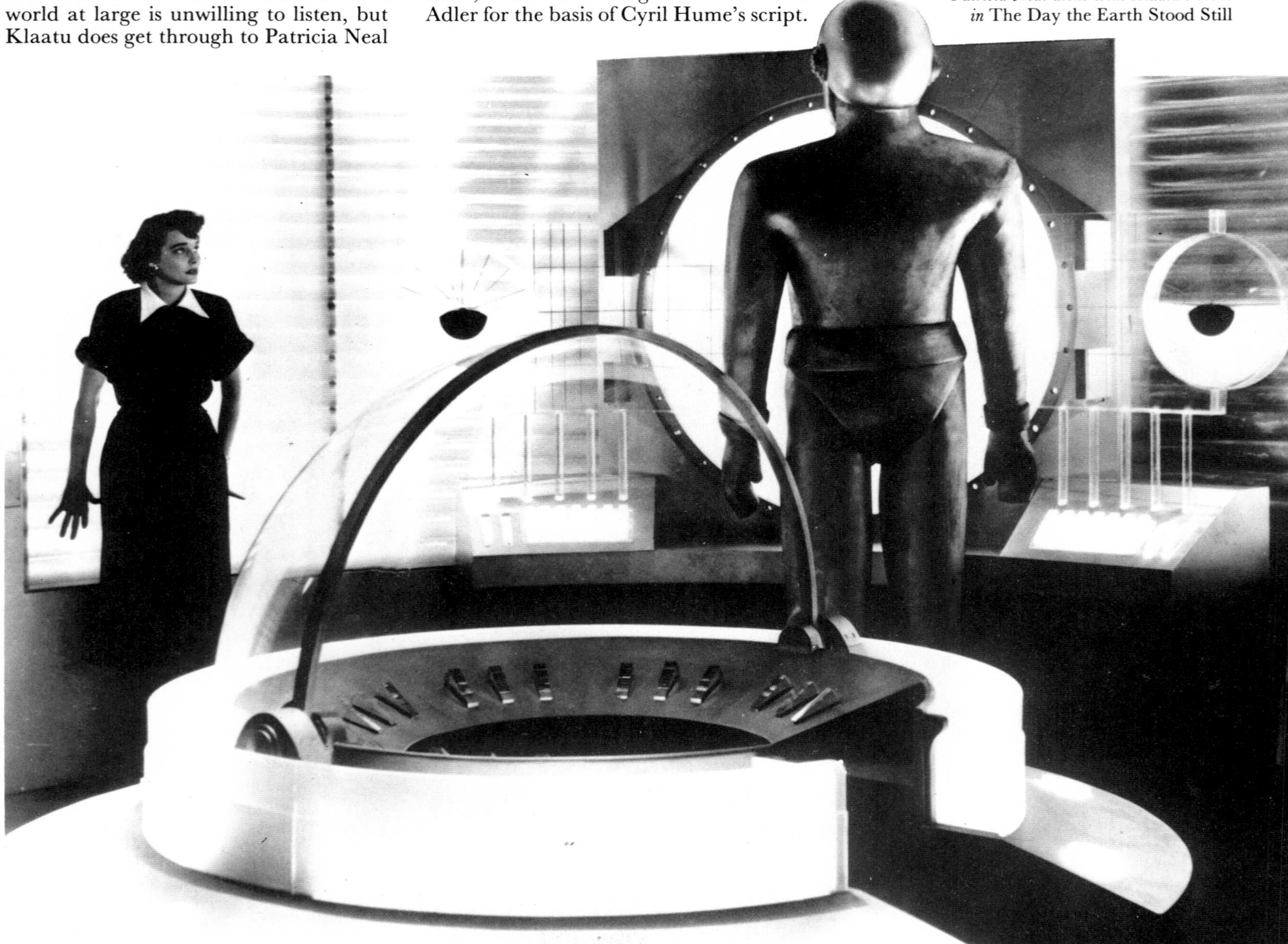

Patricia Neal alone with Klaatu's robot in The Day the Earth Stood Still

like a 1950s American reds-under-the-bed version of Communism. But director Siegel evidently intended the warning to be broader: 'Many of my associates are pods, people who simply exist, breathe and sleep.' The original idea for the film came from producer Walter Wanger, but the studio insisted on an ending which suggested that the authorities had the matter in hand. Siegel had wanted to end it with the hero pointing his finger at the audience and screaming, 'You're next!' Dana Wynter, as the doctor's girlfriend who gets turned into a pod, King Donovan, Carolyn Jones and Larry Gates

Above: Kevin McCarthy and Dana Wynter flee the pod people in Invasion of the Body Snatchers*; left: strangers in paradise—Jack Kelly and Anne Francis in* Forbidden Planet

made up the excellent, low-key cast. The pods were designed (for under $15,000) by Ted Haworth, and the photography, in black and white Superscope, was by Ellsworth Fredericks. The film was remade, impressively, with the Siegel ending by Philip Kaufman in 1978.

2001: A Space Odyssey (MGM, 1968) illustrated overleaf, science-fiction without death-rays or monsters, is a great film achievement. It was produced in Cinerama—and deep secrecy in Britain. After an expandable prologue resembling a preview of *Planet of the Apes*, Stanley Kubrick's film took an increasingly strong grip until its hero (Keir Dullea) was hurtled into the unknown regions of outer space. The final scenes were so stunningly bizarre that people's reactions ranged from exaltation to baffled anger. The talk it created had a cumulative effect on the box office: initial doubts that its cost would be recouped changed to estimates of $50 million in rentals, and by 1978 it was still drawing big cinema crowds. Kubrick's direction and special effects (which won an Academy Award) and, with Arthur C. Clarke, script were enhanced by a soundtrack which surprisingly featured *The Blue Danube* and a bit of Richard Strauss' *Thus Spake Zarathustra*; the latter became a kind of theme tune for real space flights. Also cast: Gary Lockwood as co-hero, a super-computer named Hal as villain (with Douglas Rain's voice), William Sylvester, Daniel Richter, Leonard Rossiter, Margaret Tyzack, Robert Beatty, Sean Sullivan.

The history of modern Hollywood can be divided up into two periods: before **Star Wars** and after it. Though it was not the first of the massive modern blockbusters—*Jaws* beat it on that count—George Lucas' space epic finally broke the association between science-fiction and low budgets, and smashed box-office records all over the world. Lucas had achieved a degree of independence from the normal constraints of Hollywood with his teenagers' nostalgia movie, *American Graffiti* (1973). From there, he was able to build his dream world and launch it in 1977 with proper dignity in **Star Wars**, which Gary Kurtz produced, via Lucasfilm, for 20th Century-Fox. That huge title that rolled up the screen, like the titles for the cheap serials of the 1950s which Lucas had loved as a youngster and from which, indeed, he took his inspiration, began with the words, 'In a galaxy far, far away...'

The screenplay, also Lucas', told of Luke Skywalker and Princess Leia, Han Solo and Obi-Wan Kenobi, the evil Darth Vader and his Death Star, and the lovable robots—or androids, as they would insist—See-Threepio and Artoo-Deetoo. It is a measure of the film's extraordinary success that these names, which would have seemed outlandish in 1976, were part of every child's vocabulary after the release of **Star Wars**, not least because of the massive and extremely successful franchise marketing campaign, which filled the shops with toy-size replicas. The story of **Star Wars** was, in a word, fun, involving Luke Skywalker (Mark Hamill) and his attempts to rescue Leia (Carrie Fisher) from the Death Star. Along the way we have the incidental joys of the bar on Tatooine, with its misshapen creatures from many galaxies and, as a climax, the assault on the Death Star by Skywalker, Solo (Harrison Ford) and the Rebel forces. Alec Guinness, by taking a small percentage of the profits as part of his salary, made more money as Obi-Wan Kenobi than in the rest of his films put together. At the time of the film's first release Lucas revealed that this was, in fact, the fourth episode in the saga, and that there would be nine in all. To date, we have had No. 5, *The Empire Strikes Back* (1980) and No. 6, *Return of the Jedi* (1983), each more successful than the last. **Star Wars**, at 121 minutes, got ten Oscar nominations and came away with six: Art direction (John Barry), Costume design (John Mollo), Editing (Lucas' wife, Marcia), Original score (John Williams), Visual effects and Sound.

Close Encounters of the Third Kind (Columbia, 1977), although it was a phenomenally successful film, never quite hit the box-office jackpot of director Steven Spielberg's earlier film, *Jaws*, or of George Lucas' space epic, *Star Wars*, which came out some six months earlier. This is a pity, because it is in most respects far superior to either of them. As an adventure story it has far more to it than the deft handling of suspense that characterized *Jaws*, and as a science-fiction saga it provoked awe rather than amusement. Like *Jaws*, it had its everyman figure at the centre of the plot in electric linesman

Above left: spaced out in 2001: A Space Odyssey*; left: the adorable androids from* Star Wars*; above: watching the skies for* Close Encounters of the Third Kind

Roy Neary (Richard Dreyfuss), who is one of the first to spot the UFOs. Like *Star Wars*, it harks back to the films of the 1950s. In this case it recalls the films in which American small towns are threatened by creatures from outer space. *The Thing* duly ended with the warning, 'Watch the skies!' In **Close Encounters**, people are forever watching the skies, but when the UFO finally comes during a long, long sequence which has yet to be surpassed in the special effects' sagas which have flooded out of Hollywood ever since, the aliens bring peace and understanding, not destruction. The US Army is on hand to communicate with them, not nuke them. It was, perhaps, a utopian vision, and one which Spielberg went on to sentimentalize in *E.T.* (1982), whose success proved that that was what the public wanted anyway. **Close Encounters** was shot under conditions of great secrecy in a hangar in Mobile, Alabama, so that its effects should not be known before its release. Producers Julia and Michael Phillips also had problems with the studio, (Columbia, later joined by the British company, EMI) when the promised budget of $11 million proved, as everyone must have known it would, inadequate. But the film's enormous success caused all conflict to vanish. Cinematographer Vilmos Zsigmond won a richly deserved Oscar (though the film boasted top lighting cameramen like William Fraker, Douglas Slocombe, Lazslo Lovacs and John Alonzo for additional scenes). A 'Special Edition' with extra footage was released in 1980. Teri Garr played Neary's wife, who is only just so long-suffering, and Melinda Dillon another UFO-watcher whose little son (Cary Guffey) takes a trip with the extra-terrestrials. French director François Truffaut played a scientist on the same trail as Neary.

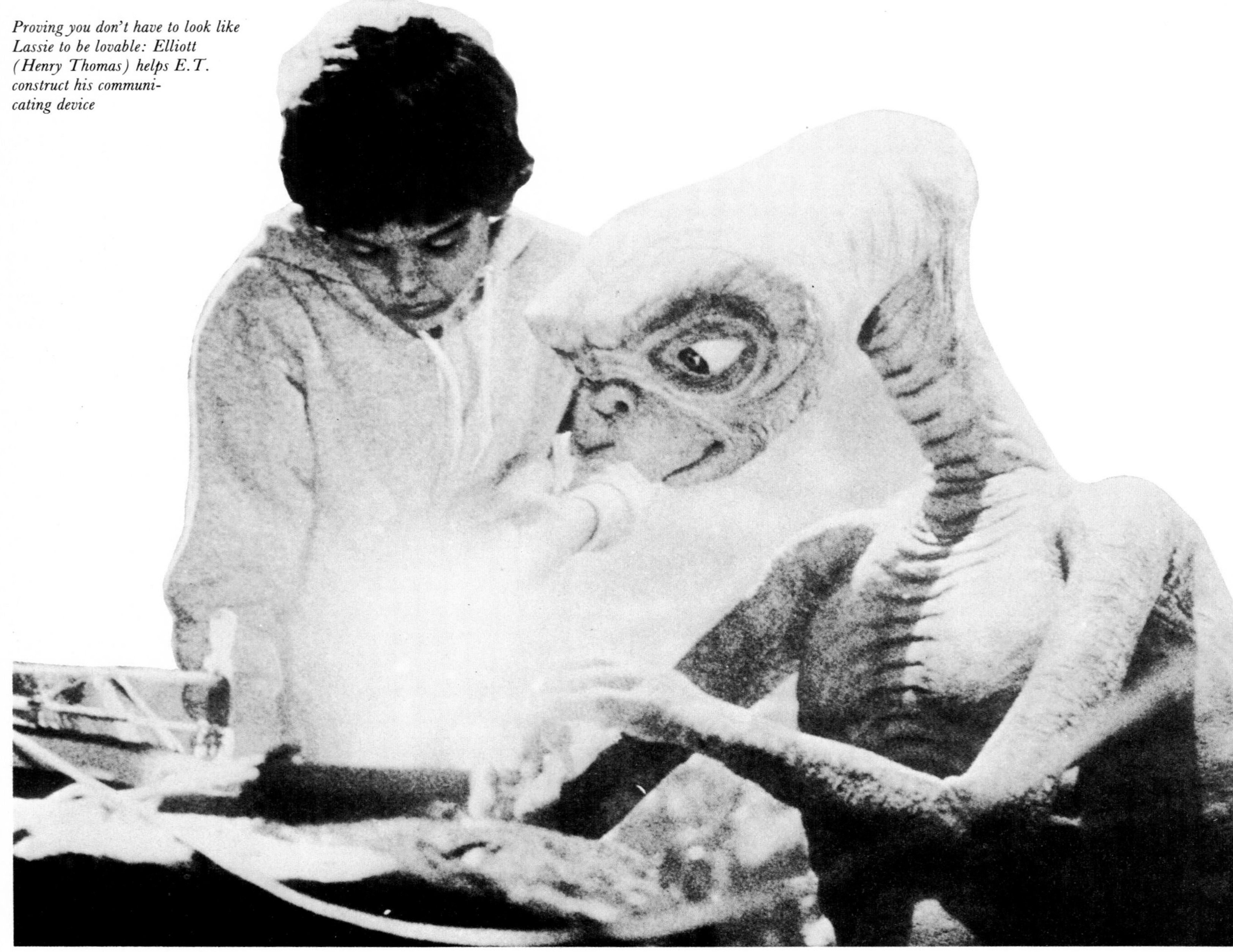

Proving you don't have to look like Lassie to be lovable: Elliott (Henry Thomas) helps E.T. construct his communicating device

A piece of contemporary science-fiction which, according to its co-producer and director Steven Spielberg, is about the understanding, love and compassion people feel towards one another, **E.T. The Extra-Terrestrial** smashed all existing box-office records for Universal and, within just three months of its initial release in 1982, was well on the way to becoming the top money-making film of all time. As every schoolboy knows, it is the story of a young lad called Elliott (Henry Thomas, above) who befriends a strange looking extra-terrestrial after the creature is accidentally abandoned on Earth when his space ship takes off, in a hurry, without him. In a sense, Elliott has also been abandoned—by his father, who has left his mother and is living with another woman in Mexico, so he knows exactly the way poor E.T. (here with Elliott) feels, and that if the creature is to survive, he has somehow to return home. Just how E.T., with Elliott's help, succeeds in returning to his people, provided scenarist Melissa Mathison with her story, and audiences with a cinematic adventure as pure, as innocent, and as entertaining as Dorothy's trip to the Land of Oz and back. Basically a children's story which, like all the best children's stories, also has immense adult appeal, the reason for the film's phenomenal success lay less in Dennis Muren's visual effects (which were good but not extraordinary) than in the enchanting development of the friendship that grows between Elliott and E.T., and in director Spielberg's imaginative grip on the material. What one remembered best about the picture was its more intimate and humorous moments, such as E.T. becoming intoxicated after drinking beer and learning how to communicate with Elliott. For lump-in-the-throat emotion, however, nothing surpassed the finale when earthling and extra-terrestrial finally take their leave of one another. 'Stay' says a weepy Elliott as the two friends embrace. 'Come' replies E.T. Each knows, though, that unless Spielberg decides to bring them together again in a sequel, they will never meet again. With young master Thomas and E.T. giving the story its centre of gravity, there wasn't much chance for the rest of the cast to make much impression. Dee Wallace played Elliott's mum; Robert MacNaughton and Drew Barrymore were his brother and sister, and Peter Coyote a compassionate scientist who has waited ten years to witness the arrival on Earth of an E.T. It was co-produced by Kathleen Kennedy, scenarist Mathison was associate producer, and Frank Marshall the production supervisor. Allen Daviau photographed it, James Bissell designed it (though E.T. himself was created by Carlo Rambaldi), and the music was by John Williams.

· THE · SHAPE · OF · THINGS · TO · COME ·

When it opened in February 1936, **Things to Come** (London Films) was the most expensive British film ever made. It is an exception to the rule, that, before *2001: A Space Odyssey* (1968), science-fiction films were generally cheaply made and popular in their intention. **Things to Come** is every inch a prestige production, and one of only two films actually to be scripted by H. G. Wells. It opens in 1940, the year which Wells predicted (with disturbing accuracy) would bring the 'great war'. It then switches forward to 1970, when the brutish inhabitants of Everytown are visited by a clean, idealistic young airman (Raymond Massey), who points the way forward to technocracy and co-operation. It ends up in the year 2036, with the launching—despite the rabble-rousing activities of an anti-progressive sculptor called Theotocopulos (Cedric Hardwicke, in a part which was written for Ernest Thesiger)—of a giant rocket to the stars. 'Is it that,' asks the hero, pointing to the skies, 'or this?' (pointing back at the Earth). 'All the universe—or nothing?' The tone of Wells' screenplay—he allegedly insisted that no word could be changed without his approval—is frequently a little preachy, especially in the young airman's part, who keeps exclaiming, 'I am wings over the world'; and the special effects are distinctly amateurish. But the sets, by William Cameron Menzies (who also directed), are superb, and the opening air raid of the Endless War is as impressive as it is frighteningly prophetic. Edward Chapman, Ralph Richardson, Margaretta Scott and Ann Todd also starred, and Korda's regular cameraman, Georges Périnal, shot it all. For all its flaws, **Things to Come** is a major landmark in the history of the science-fiction film.

A unique spectacle was presented by a normal sized, black-and-white film. **The World, the Flesh and the Devil** (1957), sponsored by Harry Belafonte and Sol C. Siegel and made at MGM. It showed the vast canyons of Manhattan emptied by some super-weapon, and only Belafonte left alive. These sequences, brilliantly photographed by Harold Marzorati in early mornings before New York crowds and traffic got too thick to keep out of camera range, gave way to a bizarre triangle story when Inger Stevens and Mel Ferrer brought the city's population to three. Scripted and directed by Ranald MacDougall, from Ferdinand Reyher's adaptation of an M. P. Shiel tale; produced by George Englund.

The vision of a world in which a sophisticated technology completely absorbs mankind's humanistic values, outlaws sex and insists that everyone look alike, was interestingly realized in **THX 1138** (1971)—written and directed by George (*Star Wars*) Lucas, with Walter Murch assisting on the screenplay. Originally a short made by Lucas in his college days, but expanded into an 88-minute feature (in Technicolor and Techniscope), the points it raised about enslavement of individuality, dehumanization and computerized regimentation more than echoed Orwell's *1984*, and, despite a dullish script, it was visually absorbing, nourishing both the intellect and the imagination. Produced for Francis Ford Coppola's American Zoetrope Productions by Lawrence Sturhahn, it starred Donald Pleasence and Robert Duvall (above), with Don Pedro Colley and Maggie McOmie (with Duvall).

Future shock: left: Harry Belafonte in The World, the Flesh and the Devil*; top:* Things to Come, *and above right: Robert Duvall and Maggie McOmie in* THX 1138

One of the decade's most controversial films, and a marvellous artistic as well as technical achievement for its empirical writer-director Stanley Kubrick, **A Clockwork Orange** (Warners, 1971) adapted from the novel by Anthony Burgess, was either welcomed by critics as a bold cinematic experiment, or condemned as a pretentious bore. Audiences were equally divided in their assessment. It was, in fact, a frighteningly prophetic vision of a Britain of the future whose censure and appeal resulted directly from Kubrick's chillingly imaginative deployment of violence, typical of which was the sequence in which a keep-fit addict (Miriam Karlin) is bludgeoned to death with a giant sculpture of a phallus. The boy guilty of the atrocity is Alex (Malcolm McDowell, illustrated), a brutal teenage hood who talks in a patois known as Nadsat, and is hooked on 'a little of the old ultra violence' without which he cannot seem to function. Sent to prison for murder, Alex becomes a guineapig in a rehabilitation programme based on aversion therapy and, in the course of being cured of his addiction, emerges rather like young Alan Strang was to emerge in Peter Shaffer's play *Equus*–'as decent a lad as you'd meet on a May morning', with only one thing missing: his soul. Kubrick's ability to draw the very best from his actors (Patrick Magee, Michael Bates, Adrienne Corri, Aubrey Morris, Clive Francis, James Marcus, Warren Clark, Sheila Raynor, Philip Stone) helped to impart a strong sense of credibility to his shocking fantasy, while his brilliantly apposite choice of music helped to offset the brutalities with a power that was almost macabre. The use of Gene Kelly singing *Singin' In The Rain*, introduced as a counterpoint to violence, was only one of the many highly original master strokes which gave this astonishing film its repellent appeal. Kubrick produced, Bernard Williams was associate producer, and the executive producers were Max L. Raab and Si Litvinoff. The film grossed a heartening $15,400,000.

Westworld was the top moneymaker for MGM in the 1973 output—although well down in the all-companies hit list. It was something really new in Westerns. Here, tourist Richard Benjamin (watched by another, James Brolin) shoots and kills Yul Brynner, or so he thinks. But Yul is just a robot worked by computers, like all the natives of this fake Western holiday resort. Writer-director Michael Crichton couldn't maintain the audience's suspension of disbelief when the robots ran wildly out of control. Good try, though. Produced by Paul Lazarus III. Also cast: Norman Bartold, Alan Oppenheimer, Victoria Shaw and Dick Van Patten.

Soylent Green (MGM) was Edward G. Robinson's last movie; he died the same year (1973), 50 years after his film debut and 80 after his birth. This original thriller pictured the horrendous future of a New York in which pollution and over-

Below: Harrison Ford in action in Blade Runner*; left: Charlton Heston feeds Edward G. Robinson in* Soylent Green. *Facing page, top: Malcolm McDowell in* A Clockwork Orange, *and bottom: Yul Brynner being taken away for a refit in* Westworld

population had made everything scarce except people. Harry Harrison's story, scripted by Stanley Greenberg, hinged on the discovery by hero Charlton Heston that the staple food for the masses, processed by a monopoly, was made from human corpses. Strong action and mob scenes; lively box-office response. Also cast: Leigh Taylor-Young, Joseph Cotten, Brock Peters, Paula Kelly, Mike Henry, Roy Jenson, Whit Bissell, Celia Lovsky. Director, Richard Fleischer; production, Walter Seltzer, Russell Thacher.

The follow-up to *Alien* (1979) by director Ridley Scott, **Blade Runner** (1982) was both more ambitious and less successful. It was based on a science-fiction novel by Philip K. Dick, with the wonderful title *Do Androids Dream of Electric Sheep?*, but departed widely from it to tell a tale of mayhem and violence in Los Angeles in the year 2019. A retired 'blade runner' (a policeman licensed to kill), played by Harrison Ford at his most battered, is set the task of tracking down a group of superior robots, who have escaped from the space colonies and returned to earth, where such 'replicants' are banned. Deckard, the blade runner, achieves his goal, but falls in love with Rachael (Sean Young), a beautiful woman who turns out to be a replicant (though one capable of emotion). In the end, Deckard risks his own life to flee the corruption of the city with Rachael. Rather uncertainly endowed with a Raymond Chandleresque voice-over—'I didn't know how long we'd have together,' Deckard's voice growls at the end. 'Who does?'—**Blade Runner**'s strength, like *Alien* before it, came from its overall look. The Los Angeles of the future, designed by Lawrence G. Paull, was a mind-blowing mish-mash of decay and soaring technological achievement. People in the downtown sections talked a multi-lingual patois called Cityspeak, and the streets were dense with car wrecks, smoke and human derelicts. Somewhat marred by its ultra-violent scenes—Deckard's elimination of the replicant Pris (Daryl Hannah) is a particularly excessive example—**Blade Runner** is basically a futuristic thriller with a massive budget and a look to match. Jordan Cronenweth filmed it, and Michael Deeley produced it for one of those production labels that characterized the early 1980s: Blade Runner Partnership, for the Ladd Company, in association with Sir Run Run Shaw.

· SWEET · DREAMS ·

The circles of hell were not without their attractions for the producer of the Hollywood epic, and few studios made more spectacular use of their charms and terrors than Fox with its 1924 epic, **Dante's Inferno**. It was directed by Henry Otto, a filmmaker whose imprint on the history of cinema is otherwise less than impressive. The Inferno in question occurs in a dream had by one Mortimer Judd (Ralph Lewis), an avaricious millionaire, after he has been given a copy of Dante's masterpiece as a pointed present by a business partner whom he has ruined. The book turns out to have a curse on it, and Judd finds himself visiting Dante's delights. Delights was, in fact, the word for it as far as contemporary audiences were concerned, since the most memorable thing about the Fox Inferno was the number of half-naked sinners who lay around in it in poses of total abandon, presumably on the grounds that, once you're actually in hell, the time for keeping up appearances is past. At all events, as a contemporary reviewer remarked, some of the sinners were clad 'in little more than a shadow'. The film also boasted some superior special effects, of which the finest was a rain of fire. Other denizens of the nether regions included Dante himself (Lawson Butt) and Virgil (Howard Gaye), while William Scott won good reviews as Judd's gallivanting son. Fox revisited the Inferno in 1935, this time with a moral tale about a stoker (Spencer Tracy) who rises ruthlessly to power in contemporary San Francisco.

Jimmy Cagney plays the ass to Anita Louise's Titania in A Midsummer Night's Dream; *below: Dante visits his Inferno*

Max Reinhardt's screen version of **A Midsummer Night's Dream** (1935) was Warner Bros.' burnt offering to culture in general and to Shakespeare in particular. It combined the sublime with the ridiculous, and was nothing if not a heated talking point for years after its release. The production was dogged by problems. William Dieterle, an erstwhile student of the great Reinhardt, was recruited to assist the maestro when it became evident that Reinhardt's lack of film experience was about to jeopardize the entire, expensive undertaking; and photographer Ernest Haller was replaced after Jack Warner complained that the majority of the forest scenes were barely visible—a literal case of not seeing the wood for the trees. Hal Mohr, Haller's replacement, hacked his way through the studio-built foliage (each tree had real leaves which were glued on separately then sprayed with silver paint), and thinned Anton Grot's sets to allow for the installation of additional lighting equipment. As a result, much of the film, particularly the ending, was visually sublime, as indeed were the special effects, which turned the dawn retreat of the fairies into something quite magical. Less than magical, however, were many of the performances—most notably James Cagney cast as Bottom, the Hermia of Olivia de Havilland and the Lysander of Dick Powell. Mickey Rooney was a nimble Puck until he broke a leg during shooting and had to be wheeled around by unseen stage-hands behind the bushes on a bicycle. Victor Jory offered a suitably sinister Oberon and Anita Louise a rather beautiful, though pallid Titania. Surprisingly, the best performance of all came from Joe E. Brown as Flute the bellows mender. Others cast were Jean Muir as Helena, Ian Hunter as Theseus, and Frank McHugh as Quince. Reinhardt also engaged the noted Viennese composer Erich Wolfgang Korngold to arrange the Mendelssohn music and, happily for the brothers Warner, Korngold remained at the studio, where, over the next few years, he was to compose some of the greatest film scores of all time. The ambitious production was under the supervision of Henry Blanke.

Walt Disney's historic **Snow White and the Seven Dwarfs** (seen below) premiered at the Carthay Circle Theatre in Los Angeles on December 21, 1937. From there it swept through America—and the world—inspiring an avalanche of critical and customer approval wherever it played. The full-length animated feature, adapted from Grimm's Fairy Tales by Ted Sears, Otto Englander, Earl Hurd, Dorothy Ann Blank, Richard Creedon, Dick Rickard, Merrill de Maris and Webb Smith, had been a sizeable gamble on Disney's part, requiring three years, $1,500,000 in production expenses, 570 artists and 250,000 drawings to complete. But it paid dividends that were beyond even its creator's expectations. Besides attracting a record-breaking $8,500,000 in gross film rentals, the picture became a merchandizing bonanza, with Snow White dolls, toys, books, records and other novelties flooding the nation. Although RKO did not profit from the subsidiary marketing, it was more than happy to be the distributor of this Technicolor blockbuster. Using multiplane animation techniques that set a standard of excellence for the entire field, the Disney staff brought to life a host of memorable characters—Snow White, the wicked queen, the prince and, of course, the redoubtable dwarfs. They were the most recognizable folklore figures in the world for years after the film's release. Though it is impossible to enumerate all the important contributors to **Snow White**, here are a few major names: David Hand (supervising director); Perce Pearce, Larry Morey, William Cottrell, Wilfred Jackson and Ben Sharpsteen (sequence directors); Hamilton Luske, Vladimir Tytla, Fred Moore and Norman Ferguson (supervising animators). Walt Disney's formula for success, as evidenced by **Snow White**, was simple. He gave the public quality entertainment no matter what the cost. RKO's executives could have learned a good deal from their new associate's show-business philosophy. Songs included: *Some Day My Prince Will Come, Snow White, Whistle While You Work, With A Smile And A Song, I'm Wishing*, Frank Churchill, Larry Morey, Paul J. Smith.

In another part of the forest: Snow White and the Seven Dwarfs

Fantasia (RKO), the third full-length Walt Disney feature in 1940, was the most daring cinematic experiment since Warner Bros.' *The Jazz Singer* thirteen years earlier. Filmed in dazzling Multiplane Technicolor and 'Fantasound', it was introduced by Deems Taylor with Leopold Stokowski and the Philadelphia Orchestra in charge of the music, and offered a once-in-a-lifetime experience that, if anything, has gained in stature over the last 40 years to become one of the cinema's undisputed works of art. Setting out to marry images to three kinds of music (music that tells a story, music that paints a picture, and 'absolute' music for music's sake) the film, which opened with a brilliant abstract realization of Bach's Toccata and Fugue in D Minor, was a miraculous blending of animation and musical sound. The item that perhaps best illustrated Disney's achievement in synchronizing the two, was the sequence to 'The Sorcerer's Apprentice' (Dukas) in which Mickey Mouse was featured as the adventurous apprentice who, after his master retires for the night, invokes some magic of his own. The spell, involving a broom which comes to life, goes completely out of control, and it is only after the sorcerer's lair has been flooded that order is finally restored. Less programmatic was 'The Nutcracker Suite' (Tchaikovsky), whose lilting melodies conjured up an enchanted forest, illuminated by fairies of light and inhabited by mushroom Chinamen and dancing flower Cossacks. A feast for eye and ear, it was matched in its invention and graphic detail by Disney's vision of the 'Pastoral Symphony' (Beethoven) set in an idyllic mythological kingdom of nymphs and satyrs, and in whose best moment the Goddess of Night skims across the sky with her cloak of black. **Fantasia**'s comic highspot was a spirited interpretation of 'The Dance Of The Hours' (from Ponchielli's *La Gioconda*), performed by prancing hippopotami, undulating crocodiles, ostriches engaging in *entrechats*, and light-footed elephants. Stravinsky's 'Rite Of Spring' graphically evoked the Creation, with belching craters of fire and warring prehistoric monsters, while the powers of Good and Evil were strikingly contrasted by 'Night On The Bare Mountain' (Mussorgsky)—with grotesque and frightening images of floating skeletons and satanic cauldrons—and Schubert's sublime 'Ave Maria' with its cleansing vision of light-infused landscapes. Joe Grant and Dick Huemer were in charge of the story direction, and the production was supervised by Ben Sharpsteen.

Musical moments: Fantasia *(left) and Robert Montgomery and Claude Rains in* Here Comes Mr. Jordan.

Here Comes Mr Jordan (Columbia, 1941) is a neat reversal of that favourite Hollywood story about an angel who comes down in human form and sorts things out for us mere mortals. In this case, the mortal goes to heaven when an over-zealous messenger called 7013 (Edward Everett Horton) takes him up a little prematurely. When the reluctant corpse (Robert Montgomery) complains, he is referred to Mr Jordan (Claude Rains). There has indeed been a mistake, and Montgomery is returned to earth in a series of available bodies, with manifold amusing consequences. After being a millionaire he ends up what he'd always wanted to be: heavyweight boxing champion. (This is what he was just about to be before his plane crash.) The best scene is the one in which Montgomery, as the millionaire Farnsworth, sets about persuading his ex-manager (James Gleason) that he is in fact himself. There is a nice ending, too, when the boxer K. O. Murdock (Jordon having now erased all previous memories) half-recognizes Bette (Evelyn Keyes), the girl he had loved as Farnsworth, and they go off arm-in-arm. Columbia boss Harry Cohn was at first reluctant to tackle a fantasy, but was talked into it by writers Sidney Buchman and Seton I. Miller. They ended up with Oscars, and the film was a hit. To confuse matters, it was based on a play called *Heaven Can Wait* by Harry Segall (who also got an Oscar), and *that* title was used by Fox for a 1943 film with a similar theme, as well as by Paramount for the 1978 remake of **Here Comes Mr Jordan** with Warren Beatty! Columbia made a musical sequel in 1947 called *Down to Earth*, with Rita Hayworth as a muse. Rita Johnson and John Emery completed the 1941 cast, Everett Riskin produced and Alexander Hall directed.

THRILLS & SPILLS

• THRILLS • AND • SPILLS •

In the last few years, the 'small' film has all but disappeared from the American film industry. As the day-to-day costs of film-making escalate, it seems that it is only those films which offer something of the Barnum & Bailey principle—bigger, longer, more extravagant—which are able to attract a large enough slice of the dwindling audience to recoup their production costs. As one executive recently put it, 'every studio knows every year that its profits are going to come from two or three films; the rest will break even if they're lucky'. So, since the recession finally hit America in the mid 1970s, Hollywood has been living in the age of the blockbuster.

Quite a few of these blockbusters—films like *Star Wars* and *Close Encounters of the Third Kind*—have been discussed in earlier chapters. This one is really about films whose main aim in life is to get the audience gasping—films designed to have people on the edges of their seats during the showing and to send them rushing out afterwards to buy the tee-shirt and the album, the toys and the special-issue comics. And, of course, to tell their friends. Word of mouth, for all the effort that is put into marketing, is still the main reason why people go to the pictures.

This chapter is about films that give pleasure rather than films that make you think, though there is a section of 'serious' films in the middle, among the more 'innocent' pieces of spectacle. First of all there is a collection of movies which features acts of bravado and bravery. With one exception they are innocent and light-hearted, thrilling us without ever threatening us. But, just to add a note of balance and to show that the quest for excitement can often have far from innocent consequences, there is John Boorman's *Deliverance* (1972) about a group of city guys—pretty much like the average male member of the audience, in fact—who decide to canoe down a wild river. It all goes wrong: ordinary guys should sit back in the cinemas and let the heroes of the Hollywood screen carry out their feats of daring for them.

Such feats abound in *Tarzan, the Ape Man* (1932), *Treasure Island* (1934), Errol Flynn's masterpiece *The Adventures of Robin Hood* (1938) and in a couple of films which feature his swashbuckling successors, Stewart Granger in *Scaramouche* (1952) and, in the same year, Robert Taylor in *Ivanhoe*. Then the age of innocence receded, and we are left with the equally thrilling but rather more tongue-in-cheek escapades of James Bond (in *Dr No*, 1962 and *Never Say Never Again*, 1983), *Superman* (1978) and Indiana Jones (*Raiders of the Lost Ark*, 1981). Just to show that larger-than-life adventure is not entirely dead, though, there is John Huston's marvellous *The Man Who Would be King* (1975).

There is also comedy in this chapter. Comedy is no longer really a proper Hollywood genre, since the film whose sole aim is to make the audience laugh is about as rare nowadays as the film which has no laughs in it at all. The films that are included here are the comedies pure and simple, with the emphasis on pure. They are the films which, like the gasp-makers, relied on a fairly simple response. Straddling the changeover from silence to sound, we have a string of gems. They are the sort of film which the modern cinema no longer makes: the films of Chaplin (*The Gold Rush*, 1925, and *Modern Times*, 1936) and Keaton (*The Cameraman*, 1928), the Marx Brothers (*A Night at the Opera*, 1935) and W. C. Fields (*The Bank Dick*, 1940), which have probably given more pleasure

to more people than all the collapsing buildings and capsizing ocean liners in the history of the cinema.

Man's battle with the sea (it was rarely woman's battle, the film industry being most conservative in the sort of action it thought fit for women) has always been a mainstay of Hollywood. Three things characterized the Hollywood ocean: it was stormy, it was mysterious and it was full of strange beasts. *The Poseidon Adventure* (1972) had as much storm as one could wish for—enough to turn a liner turtle.

The little clutch of disaster movies needs no introduction: sitting comfortably while you watch something get wrecked has always proved irresistible to film-goers, from the San Francisco earthquake in MGM's 1936 movie to its Los Angeles successor in Universal's 1974 *Earthquake*. This latter came complete with Sensurround—a low rumbling noise which is first used just when the cinema audience has been lulled into a sense of security by watching someone on the screen go into a cinema. Warners' 1929 *Noah's Ark*, was an early forerunner of this type of film, and the same studio's *The Towering Inferno* (1974) was by far the best of the bunch.

On a more serious note, there are Hollywood's war movies, starting with the greatest anti-war film of all time, Lewis Milestone's 1930 masterpiece *All Quiet on the Western Front*. MGM also gave serious consideration to the ethics of war in the (financially disastrous) *The Red Badge of Courage* (1951) as did Francis Ford Coppola in *Apocalypse Now!* (1979), one of the great American war films. But the deeds that men do when given a gun and a legitimate enemy generally led to more exuberant pictures, such as John Ford's desert adventure, *The Lost Patrol* (1934).

American epics, other than in the form of Westerns, are surprisingly rare in Hollywood. The film business has shied away from any film which might appear in some way political, thus dividing its audience in their response to the problem. John Ford's celebratory *The Iron Horse* (1924), is, however, a straightforward story which showed audiences just how their great country had been built, and how proud they should be. Nevertheless, problem pictures about America seem to belong here along with the celebrations and the war adventures. MGM's *The Crowd* (1927) is about the difficulty of surviving in the city rat race; Warners' *Black Legion* (1937), about the threat of right-wing racist organizations in the late 1930s; RKO's masterly *The Best Years of Our Lives* (1946), about the intense problems of postwar adjustment; Stanley Kramer's *The Wild One* (1954) about the rebellious youth of the 1950s.

Finally, to ease the transition between such serious matters and the final little clutch of comedies, there is a group of heartwarming tales about people who believe in something and won't give up. This includes the boxers of *Kid Galahad* (1937) and, 40 years later, *Rocky* (1976) (plus, with *The Set Up*, 1949, a more cautionary tale about a boxer who *should* give up and, finally, does). And, finally, that terribly British film about those two chaps in baggy shorts who left the world standing, *Chariots of Fire* (1981).

With this array of adventure flicks and comedies, the cinema somehow rejoins the tradition from which it grew—the popular entertainments of the late 19th century, the fairs, the melodramas, the big barnstorming theatrical hits. It seems an apt way in which to round off a selection of some of the world's great movies.

• DERRING • DO •

A box-office sensation of 1932 was **Tarzan the Ape Man**, which spawned a highly profitable series for MGM. It was the best of the dozens of movies about Edgar Rice Burroughs' hero made from 1918 to the present. Johnny Weissmuller, US swimming champion, displayed a magnificent torso and a fetching way with lines like, 'Me Tarzan, you Jane'. (Ivor Novello came from London to write the dialogue for Cyril Hume's scenario.) Maureen O'Sullivan's 'Jane' had so much charm that Mayer gave her a long-term contract. W. S. Van Dyke artfully blended a studio jungle with authentic leftovers from his *Trader Horn* trek, and peopled it with good actors like Neil Hamilton, C. Aubrey Smith, Doris Lloyd and Forrester Harvey.

Treasure Island was one of 1934's biggest MGM hits, produced on the grand scale by Hunt Stromberg and directed with panache by Victor Fleming. Wallace Beery yo-ho-hoed lustily as Long John Silver (below) with Jackie Cooper as Jim Hawkins, supported by Lionel Barrymore, Otto Kruger, Lewis Stone, Nigel Bruce, Charles 'Chic' Sale, Dorothy Peterson and Douglass Dumbrille. All caught the true Stevenson spirit of adventure, as did John Lee Mahin's script and the scenic sweep of no fewer than three top cameramen: Ray June, Clyde DeVinna and Harold Rosson.

Errol Flynn's most popular film, and the one on which his reputation for athleticism squarely rests, was **The Adventures of Robin Hood**, one of the top moneymakers of 1938. Originally planned for James Cagney (with Guy Kibbee as Friar Tuck), Jack Warner changed his mind during one of his frequent disputes with the star, and shelved the idea—until he saw Errol Flynn in *Captain Blood* (1935). Convinced that he had at last found the right man for the part, he set aside a budget of $1,600,000, the highest ever for a Warner Bros. picture until that time (it finally came in at $2 million), and put the directional task in the hands of William Keighley. However, Warner changed his mind midway through production and transferred the job to Michael Curtiz whose sense of style and previous action epics had usually spelled H.I.T. at the box office. Happily the film proved a winner in every department, bringing in both money and prestige. With its simple but strongly delineated message that good usually triumphs over evil (a maxim that coursed

Above: Johnny Weissmuller as Tarzan; below: Wallace Beery and Jackie Cooper in Treasure Island

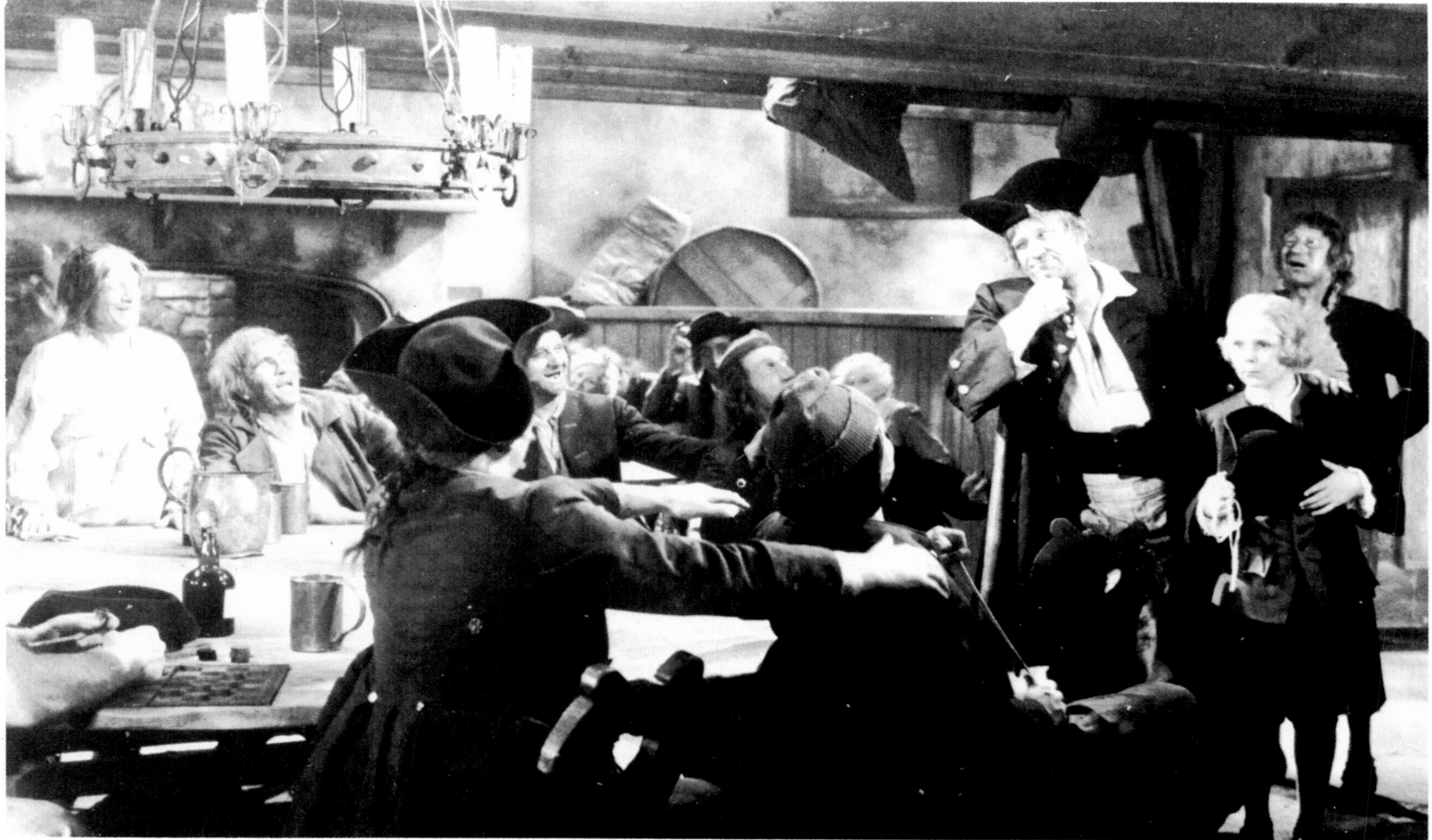

through the veins of the studio's Depression-era products), its rousing story (screenplay by Norman Reilly Raine and Seton I. Miller), and a rumbustious finale in which a polished Basil Rathbone cast as the villainous Sir Guy of Gisbourne perishes on the edge of Robin's sword, the film had enough high-spots to furnish half-a-dozen adventure yarns. Other delights included Erich Wolfgang Korngold's roisterous and inventive score, the use of the new three-colour Technicolor which immeasurably enhanced the majestic look of the film, and Carl Jules Weyl's magnificent sets. As well as Flynn, who did all his own stunts, and whose particular qualities were resourcefully explored by Curtiz (even though the two men disliked one another), the fine cast included Claude Rains as Prince John, Olivia de Havilland as Maid Marion, Patric Knowles as Will Scarlet, Eugene Pallette as Friar Tuck, Alan Hale as Little John, Melville Cooper as the Sheriff of Nottingham, and Ian Hunter as King Richard. It was even better than the silent Douglas Fairbanks version in 1922, and one of the great adventure films to emerge from Hollywood. Henry Blanke was the associate producer. (First National.)

Scaramouche (MGM, 1952) cut a dash, both in the person of Stewart Granger (in Ramon Novarro's 1923 role) and at the box office. Janet Leigh (seen below elegantly riding side saddle) was one of his lady-loves, Eleanor Parker the other; Mel Ferrer was his splendidly sword-swinging foe. They were supported by Henry Wilcoxon, Nina Foch, Richard Anderson, Lewis Stone (who was also in the original), Robert Coote, Elisabeth Risdon, Howard Freeman, John Dehner, John Litel. Carey Wilson supplied a Technicolorful production, briskly directed by George Sidney and rewritten by Ronald Millar and George Froeschel from the old Rex Ingram version of Sabatini's story.

Above: Errol Flynn and his Merry Men in The Adventures of Robin Hood*; below: Janet Leigh and Stewart Granger in* Scaramouche

MGM at last broke through with its first British-made box-office smash since prewar days with **Ivanhoe** (1952). Admittedly, it had to import four stars, producer and director from Hollywood: Robert Taylor, Elizabeth Taylor, Joan Fontaine and George Sanders; Pandro Berman and Richard Thorpe. But three of those were British-born. Not to mention Sir Walter Scott. Or adapter Aeneas MacKenzie, scripter Noel Langley, an army of technicians and a platoon of West End actors: Emlyn Williams, Finlay Currie, Felix Aylmer, Robert Douglas, Francis de Wolff, Norman Wooland, Basil Sydney, Harold Warrender, Patrick Holt, Guy Rolfe, etc. They all fell to with a will, stirring up a fine storm of Technicolored derring-do.

Mike Todd (real name Avram Goldenbogen) was the classic American showman. In 1953, in partnership with Joseph M. Schenck of Loew's Inc., the former parent company of MGM, Todd formed a company to exploit a new widescreen process known as Todd-AO, which used

Above: Robert Taylor, Elizabeth Taylor (no relation) sharing a moment in Ivanhoe*; right: David Niven and Cantinflas sharing a flight in* Around the World in 80 days

65mm film. Their first success was *Oklahoma!* (1955), but it was their 1956 follow-up, **Around the World in 80 Days** (produced in association with London Films) which was the box-office smash, the success within the industry (it won the Oscar for Best Picture) and the film for which Todd will be remembered. (He died in a plane crash on the way to pick up a Showman of the Year Award in March 1958.) Directed by Michael Anderson and lasting a mind-boggling (by 1956 standards) 175 minutes, the film was a lavish all-star version of Jules Verne's adventure yarn about Phineas Fogg (David Niven) accepting a turn-of-the-century bet that he couldn't make the titular voyage. He was accompanied by his servant Passepartout, played by the Mexican comedian Cantinflas (whom Hollywood twice tried unsuccessfully to turn into an international star). Other landmarks along the way were John Gielgud, Noel Coward, Shirley Maclaine, Robert Newton, Marlene Dietrich and some 35 other star cameos, who alone made the trip worthwhile. So, too, did the extraordinary photography, much of it from the air, by Oscar-winner Lionel Lindon, the multitude of sets—Todd hired sections of virtually every backlot in Hollywood—and the general air of wealth and extravagance. Every dollar of the $7 million the film cost was up on the screen, and all of it and more was earned back. Other Oscars went to James Poe, John Farrow and S. J. Perelman for the Best Adapted Screenplay, Gene Ruggiero and Paul Weatherwax for Best Editing, and Victor Young (who died before he could collect it) for Best Score.

Along with the studio hack who noted on Fred Astaire's screen-test card the words 'Can't act, slightly balding, dances a little', a special place must be reserved in the book of non-starters for the manager of a drive-in in Texas who, having been sent **Dr No**, wrote indignantly to the distributors, 'I just can't sell this Limey detective to people in the South.' Since **Dr No**, there have been 14 more Bond films and, whatever one may feel about them, one can say with a fair degree of certainty

that selling them has never been a problem. Produced by Harry Saltzman and Albert R. ('Cubby') Broccoli (direct descendant of the man who crossed spinach with cauliflower) in 1962, **Dr No** was the first, starring Sean Connery as 007, the agent with a licence to kill. Ursula Andress was The Girl and Joseph Wiseman was The Villain. (In Bond films, the names and the actors have come and gone, but the idea of The Girl and The Villain have remained.) Terence Young directed his first of a trio of Bond films, and Richard Maibaum (responsible for a dozen Bond scripts), Berkley Mather and Johanna Harwood put together the screenplay from Ian Fleming's best-selling novel about the wicked Doctor who steals space rockets and takes them to Jamaica—all of which meant there could be lots of shooting, lots of hardware and lots of nice big beaches for Ursula Andress to disport herself on in her stunning white bikini. As with many of the later films, one of the best things about this one was Ken Adam's brilliant sets. It all lasted a restrained 111 minutes, and Bernard Lee and Lois Maxwell were already in harness as M and Moneypenny.

Producer-director John Boorman's powerful and disturbing adult adventure **Deliverance** (Warners, 1972), charted the traumatic course of four city-dwelling buddies from Atlanta who take time off to spend a weekend canoeing in the Appalachians. However, their initially harmless encounter with the forces of nature turns sour with the arrival of some local hillbillies, one of whom has a penchant for sodomy. Though the latter half of the film resembled little more than a Boy's Own adventure, as the quartet of intrepid canoeists battled rapids and scaled cliff-faces in their flight from the sinister locals, Boorman extracted as much suspense from the situation as he could, using the men's frightening predicament to make a broader statement about urban man's rape of the wilderness and his inability to understand his own nature until pushed to extremes. James Dickey's screenplay (from his own novel) was less profound than the material demanded of it and left Boorman to convey the entire burden of its message—which he did with stunning cinematic force. Jon Voight, Burt Reynolds, Ned Beatty and Ronny Cox were the weekenders; and Bill McKinney, Herbert 'Cowboy' Coward, author James Dickey and Ed Ramey were also cast. It was filmed in Panavision and yielded a box-office gross of $22,400,000.

Water sports: top left: Ursula Andress and Sean Connery in Dr No*; below: Jon Voight and Burt Reynolds in* Deliverance

Director John Huston's 1975 film, **The Man who would be King**, is taken from a story by Rudyard Kipling. And Kipling, played by Christopher Plummer, appears in the film, working as a young newspaper editor in Lahore, where he meets the footloose soldiers of furtune, Daniel Dravot (Sean Connery) and Peachy Carnehan (Michael Caine). Peachy and Dravot set off for remote Kafiristan, where no white man has set foot since Alexander the Great. Taken for immortal when an arrow does not kill him (it sticks in his bandolier), Dravot is made king and the pair prosper. But they stay too long, and Dravot is thrown into a ravine when his imposture is discovered (he bleeds, which gods aren't supposed to). Peachy returns alone to Lahore, bearing Dravot's head, still with its crown, as evidence of the truth of his tale. John Huston had been obsessed since the 1950s with making a film version of Kipling's story, which deftly interweaves a rousing adventure yarn with a more complex reflection on empire and responsibility. His first plan had been to cast Bogart as Peachy and Gable as Dravot. But Bogart died. Then it was to be Brando and Burton, but Burton was never available. Finally, producer John Foreman sent the screenplay to Connery and Caine, and the project got under way, with each giving one of his finest performances. Filmed mainly in Morocco, **The Man who would be King** is a magnificent tableau of dusty landscapes and primitively opulent settings, particularly the holy city of Sikandergul. Cinematographer Oswald Morris and veteran art director Alexandre Trauner both got Oscar nominations. The script was by Huston and Gladys Hill, and the resulting film was 129 minutes of exciting, old-fashioned adventure and pleasure.

Conceived by the father-and-son production team of Alexander and Ilya Salkind, and Pierre Spengler, in a sidewalk café in Paris. **Superman: The Movie** (Warners, 1978) took two years to complete, with location work being done in New York City, Gallup, New Mexico, Alberta, Canada, and at Shepperton and Pinewood Studios in England. The first public intimation of the scope of the no-expense-spared undertaking (whose final budget topped a record $40 million) came with the announcement that Marlon Brando had been signed to play Superman's father Jor-El (a role with a thirteen day shooting schedule) for $3 million—which, calculated on a nine-hour day schedule—worked out at roughly $27,000 an hour, or $8 a second (generously, Brando offered to do an extra day of retakes without payment). For the key role of Superman himself, the Salkinds' first choice was Robert Redford, but he declined after failing to agree on money, and because of the absence, during negotiations, of a final shooting script. Paul Newman was then approached, but he too declined. (Newman was then offered the part of villain Lex Luthor but again said no. It finally went to Gene Hackman whose payment was a cool $2 million). Other stars initially sought or considered for the title role were Clint Eastwood, Steve McQueen, Charles Bronson, Ryan O'Neal, Sylvester Stallone, Burt Reynolds, Nick Nolte, Jan-Michael Vincent, David Soul, Kris Kristofferson and Robert Wagner. But with Brando and Hackman signed, a big name was no longer deemed essential. Salkind now actively sought an unknown whose personality would not be associated with an established superstar. The lucky contender was Christopher Reeve (seen below), a stage actor who immediately embarked on a strenuous fitness programme that included two hours of weightlifting every day, roadwork in the mornings, and 90 minutes on the trampoline! The part of *The Daily Planet* girl reporter Lois Lane was won by Margot Kidder after stars such as Jill Clayburgh, Jessica Lange, Liza Minnelli, Shirley MacLaine, Natalie Wood and Carrie Fisher were unavailable or rejected as unsuitable. Best-selling author Mario Puzo was paid $350,000 plus a promise of five per cent of the gross to devise the film's storyline (based on characters and concepts created

Assorted heroes: top left: Saeed Jaffrey, Michael Caine and Sean Connery in The Man who would be King*; below: Christopher Reeve as Superman; top right: Harrison Ford as Indiana Jones in* Raiders of the Lost Ark*, and bottom right: Sean Connery as James Bond in* Never Say Never Again

way back in 1933 by Jerry Segal and Joe Shuster—though it wasn't until 1938 that the first *Superman* comic strip appeared) and came up with a plot that had the 'man of steel' pitting his Kryptonian wits against malignant Luthor's diabolical plan to create an earthquake which will cause everything west of California's San Andreas fault to sink into the ocean, but not before Luthor buys up all the arid land east of it in order to make a real-estate killing as the owner of a new coastline! Puzo also had a hand in the screenplay; so did David Newman, Leslie Newman and Robert Benton. The project's creative consultant was Tom Mankiewicz, the production was designed by John Barry, scored by John Williams, edited by Stuart Baird, photographed by the late Geoffrey Unsworth (to whom the movie is dedicated) and directed with not the slightest trace of 'camp' by Richard Donner. The associate producer was Charles F. Greenlaw. It also featured Ned Beatty and Valerie Perrine as Hackman's useless assistants, Glenn Ford and Phyllis Thaxter as Ma and Pa Kent (Superman's earthly parents), Jeff East as the young Clark Kent, Jackie Cooper as the editor of *The Daily Planet*, and, from the planet Krypton, Susannah York as Superman's real mother Lara, together with Trevor Howard, Jack O'Halloran, Maria Schell, Terence Stamp, Sarah Douglas, Marc McClure and Harry Andrews. Song: *Can You Read My Mind?* (by John Williams and Leslie Bricusse). **Superman** is, to date, the most profitable film in the history of Warner Bros.

Paramount's **Raiders of the Lost Ark** (1981) was a solid gold, super-colossal, one hundred percent blockbuster. From the opening sequence—a perilous escape from a cave booby-trapped in fiendish ways—it kept up a breath-taking pace for 115 minutes. George Lucas, who conceived it, wrote the story with Philip Kaufman and shared executive producer duties with Howard Kazanjian, admitted that the old movie serials were his inspiration. The story, of an adventurous American archaeologist beating the Nazis to it in a search for the magical power-giving chest said to contain the Ten Commandments tablets, was virtually a non-stop succession of thrills, uninhibited by logic. When the heroine, last seen in a van blown to smithereens, turned up unscathed a reel or so later, the hero remarked, 'I thought you were dead', and changed the subject. Soon they were in a pit with 6,000 snakes, then in an exploding plane, then trapped in a submarine base, and so on, to an eye-popping special effects climax. Shot mostly at the EMI Elstree Studios near London, with location trips to France, Tunisia and Hawaii, it cost $20 million, looked it, and returned about ten times as much. Frank Marshall produced the Lawrence Kasdan screenplay and Steven Spielberg directed it with zest. It was the first collaboration of Spielberg (*Jaws, Close Encounters of the Third Kind*) and Lucas (*Star Wars, The Empire Strikes Back*), making their score five of the top box-office hits of all time. Harrison Ford headed a cast that also included Karen Allen, Paul Freeman and Ronald Lacey.

After *Diamonds are Forever* in 1971, Sean Connery, the man who (with one brief interlude) had been Bond since the start, quit the cycle and the part was taken over by Roger Moore. With Moore, the Bond films became different—lighter, more cynical—though the audiences continued to grow. **Never Say Never Again**, distributed by Warner Bros. and whose production consortium is made up of six firms with nothing whatsoever to do with cinema, marks the return of Connery. Its title allegedly refers to his 1971 vow never to play the part again and his $1 million fee was donated to a Scottish educational charity. The screenplay, by Lorenzo Semple Jr, is based on *Thunderball*—a film whose rights were long disputed by producer Kevin McClory. The 1983 movie, directed by Irvin Kershner, is the result of McClory's long drawn-out battle, though by the time it came to be made he had sold out to Jack Schwartzman, and the latter's Taliafilm (named after his wife, Talia Shire, who played Rocky's first girl friend) handled production. Given the complexity of the project, it is something of a pleasure to find that the film turns out to be 134 minutes of pure entertainment, with Connery bringing back to the role of Bond all the brio and the intelligence that had gradually drained from the cycle. Klaus Maria Brandauer made an engaging villain, ably backed up by Barbara Carrera, and Kim Bassinger is a first-rate Domino—all grace and health. The special effects do not, for once, take over, but the set pieces are as fine as ever, with underwater sequences handled by Ricou Browning.

• ALL • AT • SEA •

Tired of playing so many 'scented, bepuffed, bewigged and ringletted' characters as John Barrymore himself put it, he asked Warner Bros. to star him as Captain Ahab in a screen version of Herman Melville's *Moby Dick*. The result was **The Sea Beast** (1926) which, in the end, bore little resemblance to the novel, retaining in Bess Meredyth's screenplay only Ahab's search for the great white whale. Love interest and a happy ending were added, with Priscilla Bonner originally chosen to supply the former. Barrymore's first choice however was Mary Astor, who was unavailable. He settled, instead, for a relative unknown called Dolores Costello, whom he considered the most preposterously lovely creature in all the world. Meantime, the thwarted Miss Bonner sued the studio and an out-of-court settlement was reached. Other problems surfaced during the shooting of the $800,000 epic, not least of which was Barrymore's heavy drinking. All the same, **The Sea Beast** was a huge success, with critics and public alike responding particularly to the chemistry between Barrymore (above right) and Miss Costello (on his left), whose love scenes were so authentic they gave director Millard Webb an unusual problem. He was unable to decide which of the many brilliant takes to

choose, so, for the final embrace, he spliced them all together to create a love scene of unprecedented length and passion. The photographer was Byron Haskin. Also cast were Mike Donlin, Sam Baker, Sam Allen, George Burrell, Frank Nelson and James Burrows.

Three stars at their zenith were box-office insurance for **China Seas** (MGM, 1935), which hardly needed it. Thalberg's meticulous production of a good story, loaded with spectacular action sequences and zestfully directed by Tay Garnett, would have been a hit anyhow. With Wallace Beery as a modern pirate, Jean Harlow given pithy lines to snap and a loose-top-tight-bottom gown to fill, and Clark Gable in command of the ship and the screen, it became a record-breaker. Others on board were Rosalind Russell rather overdoing an English milady, Robert Benchley as a very funny drunk, Lewis Stone, Dudley Digges, C. Aubrey Smith, William Henry, Lillian Bond, Edward Brophy, Donald Meek, Emily Fitzroy and Akim Tamiroff. Screenplay by James K. McGuinness and Jules Furthman from Crosbie Garstin's novel.

MGM climaxed a remarkable year with a great film from Irving Thalberg, released towards the end of 1935. **Mutiny on the Bounty** was one of the biggest successes of Thalberg's career, and winner of the best picture Oscar. He bought screen rights of the book by Nordhoff and Hall from Frank Lloyd along with his services as director, and assigned Talbot Jennings, Jules Furthman and Carey Wilson to write the script. Perfectly cast were Clark Gable, splendid as Fletcher Christian—American accent regardless; and Charles Laughton as Captain Bligh, providing mimics with material for decades to come. Their conflict had even the most blasé moviegoers tense with excitement, so strong was the narrative drive and so colourful (in black-and-white) its depiction by all hands. Arthur Edeson's camerawork and editing by Margaret Booth, the studio's perennial cutting genius, were outstanding. Cast included Franchot Tone, Dudley Digges, Eddie Quillan, Herbert Mundin, Donald Crisp, Spring Byington, Henry Stephenson, Douglas Walton and Ian Wolfe.

Top: John Barrymore as Ahab (with Dolores Costello) in The Sea Beast*; below: Gable and Laughton in* Mutiny on the Bounty. *Facing page: the three stars of* China Seas

John Huston's version of Herman Melville's **Moby Dick**, the third to reach the screen in 1956, was by far the best of the trio. Captain Ahab's grim obsession to seek revenge for his previous encounter with the great white whale by killing him, unfolded with all the power and mysticism of Melville's novel intact, and with a surging sense of doom that was positively awesome. Huston had originally planned the role of Ahab for his father Walter who died in 1950. Instead, the director cast Gregory Peck with Richard Basehart as Ishmael, Leo Genn (Starbuck), Harry Andrews (Stubb), James Robertson Justice (Captain Boomer), Friederich Ledebur (Queequeg) and Orson Welles (Father Mapple). Also among the distinguished cast were Bernard Miles, Gordon Jackson and Seamus Kelly. Huston and Anthony Veiller worked on the adaptation of the novel, with Ray Bradbury responsible for the screenplay. The film was shot in Portugal, the Canary Islands, the Azores and Wales, with real oceans and natural weather conditions taking the place of wind machines, studio tanks and back-projection, the only faking being in the deployment of latex whales. It was photographed by Oswald Morris in a colour process which combined black-and-white with Technicolor to give an unusual and effective sepia tint to the proceedings, and the excellent music score was by Philip Stainton. The film, a Moulin Picture for Warner Bros., was also produced by Huston.

Below: Ahab (Gregory Peck) spears Moby Dick; Right: Gene Hackman and Shelley Winters battle against the odds in The Poseidon Adventure

'We have,' said producer Irwin Allen—who, in his time, has laid waste half the globe—'the perfect set-up of a group of people who have never met before and who are thrown together in terrible circumstances. In the first six minutes, 1,400 people are killed and only the stars survive.' He was referring to **The Poseidon Adventure**, the 1972 film about the ship that is turned upside down by a tidal wave, leaving a motley band of stellar survivors to struggle upwards to the hull, where a rescue team lets them out. Audiences are kept on the edges of their seats as the group battles through the fiery hell of the engine room and the underwater obstacle course of the submerged companion ways. The big set-piece, though, was the capsizing. It had one of the biggest Hollywood stunt calls in years—125 stunt persons—and entire sections of the set were built on an axle, so they could be flipped over. Mainly, however, **The Poseidon Adventure** was about figures—very large ones as it turned out, since its $5 million budget has led to a $40 million return in domestic rentals alone. Among the survivors of the tidal wave are Gene Hackman as a cheerleading priest ('God loves triers', he is constantly admonishing his flock), Red Buttons as the timid little man who discovers bravery, Ernest Borgnine as the loud-mouth ex-cop who discovers humility, Stella Stevens as his ex-callgirl wife who discovers God, and Carol Lynley who is discovered throughout in a brief pair of shorts. The story was taken from a Paul Gallico novel adapted by Stirling Silliphant and Wendell Mayes and the film, which lasted 117 minutes, was directed by Ronald Neame, with Allen doing the disaster scenes and L. B. Abbott doing the model work.

Jaws (Universal, 1975) cost $12 million to make, was almost abandoned because of production difficulties and, so far, has earned over $133 million in domestic box-office rentals, making it one of the top-grossing films of all time. Set in an East Coast holiday resort, it told the simple story of a community terrorized by a man-eating shark, and the efforts to bring the killer to bay. That, basically, was all there was to the screenplay Peter Benchley and Carl Gottlieb fashioned from Benchley's best-seller of the same name. So skilfully, however, did director Steven Spielberg create suspense by concentrating on man's primeval fear of both the known and the unknown terrors of the deep, that audiences were positively mesmerized by the horrific events they witnessed. Far more effective than the climactic destruction of the shark itself, were the opening scenes on the beach to which audiences were able to relate on a real, instantly recognizable level. And they confirmed Spielberg as a director blessed with a remarkable ability to convey menace. Roy Scheider was top-billed playing the small community's chief of police. Robert Shaw was cast as a grizzled shark hunter brought in to kill the monster (in the process of which he, himself, is killed), and Richard Dreyfuss an oceanographer who alerts the unsuspecting mayor (Murray Hamilton) to the gravity of the situation. Lorraine Gary played Scheider's wife, with other parts going to Carl Gottlieb and Jeffrey Kramer. Author Benchley made a token appearance as a TV newsman. Robert A. Mattey was in charge of the special effects which, despite the fact that his killer shark seemed to get bigger and bigger everytime it appeared, were, on the whole, outstanding. Richard D. Zanuck and David Brown were the financially well-rewarded producers.

Town meeting: Murray Hamilton, Roy Scheider and Richard Dreyfuss in Jaws

• THE • END • OF • THE • WORLD • TWICE • NIGHTLY •

One of Warner Bros.' most ambitious films to date, and also its longest (it ran 135 minutes), **Noah's Ark** (1929) was a retelling of the biblical story paralleling, at the same time, a World War I romance. A part-talkie, (the first 35 minutes were silent), the bizarre combination of narratives was directed by Michael Curtiz with immense panache and a thorough grasp of the epic style. Particularly memorable were Anton Grot's sets and the amazing and spectacular scenes depicting the cataclysmic flood. Cameraman Hal Mohr, however, had misgivings about these scenes when he learned that one of Grot's massive temples was expected to collapse, not only on the stuntmen but on the hundreds of extras supplied by Central Casting as well. So he resigned, and Barney McGill took his place. Mohr's fears were not unfounded. In the shooting of the flood scene no shots were faked, and several extras did, in fact, drown. Adapted by Anthony Coldeway from a treatment by Darryl Zanuck, the film starred Dolores Costello (Miriam), Noah Beery (King Nephilim), Louise Fazenda (as a tavern maid), Guinn Williams (Ham), Paul McAllister (Noah), Myrna Loy (as a slave girl) and Malcolm Waite (Shem). Song: *Heart O' Mine* (by Billy Rose and Louis Silvers).

Noah's Ark; *building the boat (bottom) and, checking out the passengers, Paul McAllister as Noah*

Just when you thought it was safe to go back in the lift: The Towering Inferno

The best of all the disaster movies, **The Towering Inferno** (1974), co-produced by Warner Bros. (who released it outside North America) and 20th Century-Fox, was a towering smash which grossed $50 million at the box office. Scripted by Stirling Silliphant from two novels—Richard Martin Stern's *The Tower* and Thomas M. Scortia and Frank M. Robinson's *The Glass Inferno*—it adopted the familiar 'disaster' format of first introducing us to a set of characters then abandoning them to their dreadful fate; in this instance a brand new 138-storey hotel which, due to faulty wiring, goes up in flames on the night of its dedicatory ceremony. Struggling to survive the holocaust were Paul Newman (the building's architect), Faye Dunaway (a magazine editor), Richard Chamberlain (the man responsible for the defective wiring—and a brute to his pretty wife, Susan Blakely), Robert Vaughn (a US senator), Robert Wagner (the building's PR man), Fred Astaire (an ageing con-man) and Jennifer Jones (a widowed art dealer). Co-starring with Newman was Steve McQueen as the brave fire chief but for whose ingenuity even more lives might have been lost; William Holden received third billing to Newman and McQueen as the building's so-called developer-builder. As there is a stronger likelihood of one's being involved in a fire than being a victim of a disaster, at sea, in the air, or on land in an earthquake, the sense of horror at the film's core made it a more involving experience than its predecessors in the genre, and a decidedly more frightening one. It was directed (in Panavision, and as if it were a military manoeuvre) by John Guillermin with producer Irwin Allen taking over the hot seat in the action sequences. Song: *We May Never Love Like This Again.*

Just when you thought it was safe to go back to the stairs: Earthquake *(Charlton Heston in action)*

Earthquake was Universal's second attempt of 1974 to cause havoc among the general public and, unlike *Airport 1975*, the special effects were terrific (see illustration), credit for which must go to Frank Brendel, Jack McMasters, Albert Whitlock, Glen Robinson and John Daheim. The stars in front of the camera were Charlton Heston (top-billed), Ava Gardner, George Kennedy, Lorne Greene, Genevieve Bujold, Richard Roundtree, Marjoe Gortner, Barry Sullivan, Lloyd Nolan, Victoria Principal, Monica Lewis, Gabriel Dell and, in a brief cameo appearance as a drunk, Walter Matuschanskayasky, better known as Matthau. Following the usual pattern of disaster movies, the story gave audiences a chance to take a peek at the disparate lives of the *dramatis personae* before the actual disaster strikes, as well as during, and after it. George Fox and Mario Puzo's original scenario, set in Los Angeles, was better scripted than one had come to expect on such occasions, so that, in a refreshing sort of way, audiences actually cared about the fate of the humans as well as the hardware. Using 'Sensurround' to simulate the sound of an actual earthquake, producer-director Mark Robson heightened the overall impact of the brilliant special effects, and turned the whole experience into quite a cinematic adventure. The cast was completed by Pedro Armendariz Jr, Lloyd Gough, John Randolph, Kip Niven, Scott Hylands and Tiger Williams.

• THE • WINDS • OF • WAR •

Although King Vidor's silent, *The Big Parade* (MGM, 1925), had taken a non-heroic look at World War I, it had a happy ending that sent audiences home with hope in their hearts. In Lewis Milestone's altogether superior **All Quiet on the Western Front** (Universal, 1930)—the most uncompromisingly bleak statement about the nightmare of trench warfare the cinema had ever attempted—there was no comfort at all except, perhaps, in the film's justly celebrated penultimate scene when, in the midst of the surrounding carnage, young Lew Ayres sees beauty and the wonder of creation in a butterfly. Spontaneously reaching to touch it, he is killed by a sniper's bullet. It was the most poignant of moments in a film memorable for the compassion it brought to the story of a group of young men (particularly Paul Baumer, so well played by Ayres, below left) who, one by one, are maimed or killed in action. For an American film it was unique in showing war from the German trenches, underlining that war is hell for both sides. George Abbott's economical screenplay (from the novel by Erich Maria Remarque) eloquently reinforced this point in what was perhaps the film's most moving scene of all: Ayres, finding a Frenchman (Raymond Griffith) in a shell-hole, stabs him, then agonizes over what he has done. No film, before or since, has managed to capture the futility of war with such quiet simplicity, and it remains one of the masterpieces of the American cinema. Louis Wolheim (right) played a seen-it-all-before veteran whose own strength gives Ayres the will to cope, and was superb; and there were fine performances, too, from Arnold Lucy as the schoolmaster exhorting Ayres and other pupils to enlist, John Wray as a once meek postman who turns into a sadistic corporal, and Ben Alexander as Ayres' buddy. Also in the excellent cast: Russell Gleason, Owen Davis Jr, William Bakewell, Joan Marsh, Beryl Mercer (as Ayres' mother), Slim Summerville and, in a small role, Fred Zinnemann. The film was produced by Carl Laemmle Jr, the studio's production head. Interesting sideline: Miss Mercer replaced ZaSu Pitts after the first preview where audiences laughed at Miss Pitts, then fast establishing herself as a comedienne. The film was withdrawn and all her scenes reshot. Interesting too, was the fact that the film was poorly received in Germany, and banned in Berlin where it was considered to have a demoralizing effect on Germany's flowering youth. Re-issued in 1939 with an opening commentary on the horrors of war added to it.

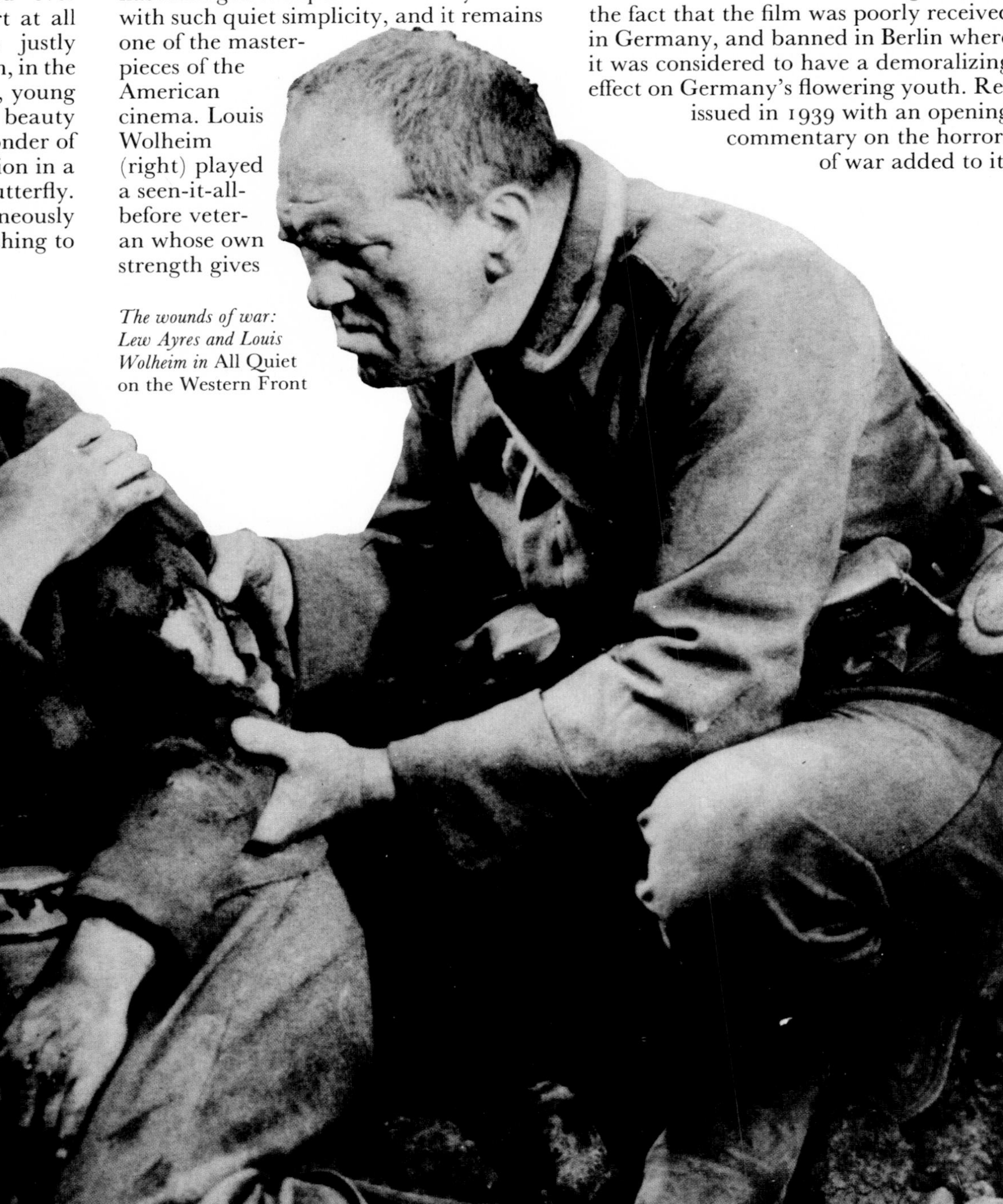

The wounds of war: Lew Ayres and Louis Wolheim in All Quiet on the Western Front

John Ford's first production for RKO in 1934, **The Lost Patrol**, was another reflection of executive producer Merian C. Cooper's preference for adventure stories set in faraway locales. The Dudley Nichols screenplay (adaptation by Garrett Fort) originated as a story by Philip MacDonald about a British patrol that loses its bearings in the Mesopotamian desert and is slowly picked apart by unseen Arab sharpshooters. Victor McLaglen (centre), Boris Karloff (left), Wallace Ford (right), Reginald Denny, J. M. Kerrigan, Billy Bevan, Alan Hale, Brandon Hurst, Douglas Walton, Sammy Stein, Howard Wilson and Paul Hanson comprised the all-male cast. Unlike most of Ford's work—and the escapist tendencies then predominant in Hollywood filmmaking—**The Lost Patrol** was absolutely unremitting in its sense of hopelessness and futility. Even the solace of religion, so prominent in the director's canon, is missing here. Karloff, who mouths Biblical phrases throughout, finally loses his mind and, dressed as John the Baptist, marches out to meet the Arabs. They gun him down without a moment's hesitation. Despite its depressing tone, the picture proved to be a modest financial and critical success, perhaps because its unusual subject matter and approach made it stand out from the log jam of homogenized American pictures. Cliff

Faraway adventures: below: The African Queen; *above:* The Lost Patrol

Reid was the associate producer, and variations of the basic plot would later appear in *Bad Lands* (RKO, 1939), *Bataan* (MGM, 1943) and *Sahara* (Columbia, 1943). A silent version of the tale released by British International in 1929, had used Cyril McLaglen, brother of Victor, in the same starring role.

MGM reached its peak as self-appointed publicist for Britain with a Hollywood movie, **Mrs Miniver** (1942); Churchill said its propaganda was worth many battleships. It was supposed to portray a typical English couple in World War II. It didn't: the Minivers were nobler and nicer than any typical couple anywhere, and well over the average income line. But what a marvellously effective movie it was, and what a sensation it caused! It swept the board in public and exhibitor polls as 1942's most popular picture, won cheers from even the crustiest critics and seven Oscars from the Academy: Best Film, Best Actress (Greer Garson), Best Director (William Wyler), Best Supporting Actress (Teresa Wright), Best Script (Arthur Wimperis, George Froeschel, James Hilton, Claudine West), Best Photography (Joseph Ruttenberg) and Best Producer (Thalberg Memorial Award to Sidney Franklin). Shown here are Miss Garson and Walter Pidgeon as Mrs Miniver and her husband in their air-raid shelter, one of the film's more authentic sets. Also cast: Dame May Whitty, Reginald Owen, Henry Travers, Richard Ney, Tom Conway, Helmut Dantine, Christopher Severn, Brenda Forbes, Henry Wilcoxon, Clare Sanders, Rhys Williams.

The inspired casting of Humphrey Bogart as the rough, drunken boatman and Katharine Hepburn as the spinster missionary lightened the basically serious script of **The African Queen** (produced by Romulus, released by United Artists, 1951) written by director John Huston and James Agee from the novel by C. S. Forester. The story of the unlikely couple who fall in love as they negotiate the perils of an African river on their way to sink a German battleship is funny and touching by turns with nicely judged comic performances by the stars. The picture made some unusual demands on the special effects department—the shooting of the rapids was accomplished with a miniature model and tiny likenesses of the stars. But when the script called for a swarm of attacking mosquitoes, the specially bred insects refused to co-operate. The solution was found by using tea leaves stirred into the clear water of a small aquarium, with an accompaniment of high-pitched buzzing! Katharine Hepburn was nominated for an Oscar and Humphrey Bogart won one. Robert Morley, Peter Bull and Theodore Bikel supported.

Stiff upper lips and a nice cup of tea: Walter Pidgeon and Greer Garson in Mrs Miniver

Martin Sheen as Captain Willard in Apocalypse Now!—*a complex and deeply thought provoking film about the horrors of war*

Having made a fortune with the two *Godfather* movies (1972–4) and won a great deal of critical acclaim with *The Conversation* (1974), director and producer Francis Ford Coppola refused to play it safe like certain of his contemporaries. Instead he launched into one of the most costly and ambitious personal projects in the history of cinema. Produced by Coppola's own Omni-Zoetrope company and with a script by himself and John Milius, **Apocalypse Now!** is nothing more nor less than an attempt to come to terms with the Vietnam war and its impact on America. The story is loosely based on Joseph Conrad's *Heart Of Darkness* (which was set in Africa). It tells of the quest by Captain Willard (Martin Sheen) to find the legendary Colonel Kurtz (Marlon Brando), who has set up his own private army in the jungle. With a budget that gradually escalated to a rumoured $30 million and a schedule which dragged on and on, halted at one stage when Sheen had a heart attack, **Apocalypse Now!** is probably the masterpiece of American cinema in the 1970s. It is a brave, complex and brilliantly executed picture of a hopeless war where, even more than usual, there are no winners and where those caught in the process are inexorably coarsened. The film is a searing nightmare of a movie whose final effect, however, is deeply thought provoking. At its centre are three extraordinary performances by Sheen, Brando and Robert Duvall (as the manic Lt. Colonel Kilgore who loves 'the smell of napalm in the morning'). In addition, there is some virtually unique cinematography by Vittorio Storaro and some magnificent designs by Dean Tavoularis.. Coppola invoked a lot of hostility by the slant of his story and his grandiose vision of the project (it was presented at the Cannes Film Festival in 1979 as a 'work in progress'), but the film easily overcomes this. All the same, it won only two Oscars—for Cinematography and Sound—the jury preferring the smaller pleasures of *Kramer vs. Kramer*.

· AMERICA · AMERICA ·

Despite his reputation for bringing a personal touch and a hint of depth to action pictures, director John Ford stuck to spectacle for **The Iron Horse** (Fox Film Corp., 1924), his 102-minute saga of the building of the transcontinental railroad in the 1860s. There is a kind of plot, involving the villainous Deroux, a landowner played by Fred Kohler at his most melodramatically wicked, who leads the savages in an attack on the honest construction workers. There is also a boy-meets-girl situation involving George O'Brien and Madge Bellamy. But the film is really about tracks, trains and terrain. The climax is the moment when the Union Pacific tracks meet up with the Central Pacific at Promontory Point, Utah, on May 10, 1869. The movie marshalled an impressive set of forces: 5,000 extras, made up of a regiment of US Cavalry, 3,000 railway workers, 1,000 Chinese labourers and 800 Pawnee, Sioux and Cheyenne. Also on hand were 2,000 horses, 1,300 buffalo and 10,000 cattle. With a cast like that, audiences could do little more than sit open-mouthed in wonder at the achievements of the railway pioneers, noting as the *New York Times* reviewer put it, 'the fact that Americans have had more to battle against than any other nation'. The script was by Charles Kenyon, the photography by George Schneiderman and Burnett Guffey, and such folk heroes as Abraham Lincoln (Charles Edward Bull), Buffalo Bill Cody (George Wagner) and Wild Bill Hickock (John Padjan) were seen to pass by.

King Vidor's **The Crowd** was one of the most highly praised pictures in the whole history of MGM. A far cry from his *Big Parade* in scope, it was similar in that it centred on an average man pitted against situations he could not control. James Murray, an extra who was walking by when Vidor was looking for an unknown lead, was amazingly good as the clerk with a little job in a huge office, and a little apartment in a vast city. Eleanor Boardman gave the performance of her life as his wife. Vidor wrote the story early in 1926 and worked on the film intermittently until the end of 1927. It was scripted by him with Harry Behn and John V. A. Weaver. Much of it was shot in New York with scenes of a realism not seen before.

The long, painstaking production was so unhurried that Miss Boardman (Mrs Vidor) took time out to have a baby, between scenes as it were, and Murray acted in a few lesser movies. Seven different endings were shot and it went into release with two; one left Murray as a cipher in the crowd, the other 'happy' ending gave him an unexpected windfall: exhibitors could take their choice. Although regarded as an artistic triumph with no pay-box appeal, the film returned twice its cost. Minor successes were scored by Bert Roach as the boy's office pal, Del Henderson and Lucy Beaumont.

Above: John Ford supervizes Charles Edward Bull as Abraham Lincoln in The Iron Horse*; below: James Murray and Eleanor Boardman in* The Crowd

Insidious secret societies in general and the Ku Klux Klan in particular were under attack in **Black Legion** (Warner Bros., 1937). Humphrey Bogart (below) starred as a disillusioned factory worker who joins the 'pro-American' Klan when he loses the factory foremanship to a foreigner, only to discover—after it is too late—just how evil and corrupt the organization he has sided with really is. Directed by Archie Mayo with frightening realism, the film's thesis that bigotry, mob terrorism and violence were 100 per cent un-American activities was forcefully conveyed in Abem Finkel and William Wister Haines' often chilling screenplay (from an original story by Robert Lord, who was also associate producer). This was especially notable in a lengthy courtroom oration delivered by a judge before passing sentence on the Legionnaires. Hitting audiences with tremendous force, **Black Legion** also won praise and respect from most of the major critics and became a subject of controversy for months after its release. The uniformly well-drilled cast included Dick Foran, Helen Flint (with Bogart), Erin O'Brien-Moore, Ann Sheridan, Robert Barrat, Paul Harvey, John Litel and Eddie Acuff.

Pre and postwar: below: Black Legion*; above:* The Best Years of our Lives

Samuel Goldwyn's **The Best Years of our Lives** (1946) became the most honoured release in RKO history, winning seven Academy Awards (including Best Picture) and innumerable other accolades. The picture weighed in solidly at 170 minutes—a fairly hefty dosage of moral uplift deftly written by Robert E. Sherwood from a novel by MacKinlay Kantor, and masterfully directed by William Wyler. The plot follows the story of Fredric March, Dana Andrews and Harold Russel: three military veterans who meet on a plane taking them back to their home town. Each is returning to a woman he loves—March to his wife, played by Myrna Loy; Dana Andrews to Virginia Mayo, his bride whom he left years before (after only a few weeks of marriage) when he departed overseas; Russell (an actual veteran who lost both hands during the war), maimed and handicapped by combat, to his childhood sweetheart Cathy O'Donnell. Each faces a crisis upon his arrival, and each crisis is a microcosm of the experiences of many American warriors who found an alien world awaiting them when they came marching home. This film had everything: laughs, tears, romance, anger, compassion, steadfast love, wrenching drama, social message. In short, it was emotional dynamite and audiences were emotionally shattered by it. Others fortunate enough to be associated with producer Goldwyn, for whom **The Best Years** was the apogee of a long and distinguished show-business career, were director of photography Gregg Toland, art directors Perry Ferguson and George Jenkins, film editor Daniel Mandell, music composer Hugo Friedhofer, and supporting players Teresa Wright, Hoagy Carmichael, Gladys George, Roman Bohnen, Ray Collins, Minna Gombell, Walter Baldwin, Steve Cochran, Dorothy Adams, Don Beddoe, Victor Cutler, Marlene Aames, Charles Halton, Ray Teal, Howland Chamberlin, Dean White, Erskine Sanford and Michael Hall.

Among other things, the 1950s in America was the beginning of youth culture. While rock 'n' roll may briefly have diverted America's screen children away from the true values of home and High

School diploma, it was a temporary aberration and the kids were generally pretty wholesome. Juvenile delinquents were different. And motor cycle gangs were the worst kind of 'j.d.'s, taking advantage of the new economic freedom and rebelling against their elders in a way that, for once, posed a real threat. **The Wild One** (Stanley Kramer), directed by Lazslo Benedek in the autumn of 1953, was the classic motor cycle picture. It was also the film which gave us the single most famous image of Marlon Brando, in cross-zippered leather jacket and cap, leaning quizzically on his motorcycle, a statuette strapped to the handlebars. The film's real selling point was the rebellious image of Brando and his gang—and, of course, the rival gang led by an even more threatening Lee Marvin as Gino, a bearded, leather-fringed, cigar-chewing Hell's Angel. Johnny (Brando) is quite a nice kid beneath the bluster, and he ends up being humanized by the small town and the small-town girl, Cathy (Mary Murphy), who is the terrified victim of the roaring circle of bikes when the gang first hits town, but who spots the 'something good' in Johnny. However, despite this process of humanization and a strong moral message at the beginning, describing it as 'a public challenge not to let it happen again', the British Board of Film Censors refused to certificate the film, and it remained banned in Britain until 1968. Maybe the BBFC had a point: for all its soggy bits, **The Wild One**, written by John Paxton and photographed by veteran Hal Mohr, is genuinely subversive in its picture of compulsive revolt.

Brando in/as The Wild One

Candy Clark, Charlie Martin Smith and Ronny Howard (left to right) in American Graffiti

One of the key films of the Seventies, and one of the best films of the decade, **American Graffiti** (Universal, 1973) though set in a small Northern Californian town in 1962, evoked the Fifties and remains unchallenged as the most authentic retrospective look at that period and its pastimes. Relying on a collage of events rather than an on-going narrative line, director George Lucas, in his second feature, brought an extraordinary concentration of time and milieu to his film by following the fortunes of four buddies during a twelve-hour period one warm summer's night in the town of Modesto. Curt (Richard Dreyfuss), the intellectual of the group, is going to college in the East next day; so is his mate Steve (Ronny Howard, above right). Both are worried about leaving the town of their boyhood. And while Curt, on his last night, is picked up by a gang of local hoods called The Pharoahs, and almost loses his life in their company, Steve spends the last few hours in town breaking up, then making up with his girlfriend Laurie (Cindy Williams) who happens to be Curt's sister. The third member of the group is John (Paul Le Mat), an aimless 22-year-old drag racer who refuses to leave his teens behind him; while the final representative of the quartet, Terry (Charlie Martin Smith, centre), is a bespectacled walking compedium of gaucheries who spends the night in a borrowed Chevy clumsily trying to seduce a blonde swinger called Debbie (Candy Clark, left). Shot (mostly at night) in 28 days and at a cost of $750,000, the film captured not only the look of the period, with its emphasis of Fifties' cars ritualistically cruising the streets of Modesto, but also its sound. The continuous background throb of contemporary pop music was supplied by disc jockey Wolfman Jack, hitherto a sort of god to the young citizens of Modesto. When, however, Curt finally meets this enigmatic local hero in person, he is so disillusioned by what he sees (an ordinary, middle-aged man eating a Popsicle from a vintage refrigerator) that he no longer feels any apprehension about abandoning his home town for a new life in the East. Director Lucas' screenplay, which he wrote with Gloria Katz and William Huyck, brilliantly captured a generation's last moments of innocence, the loss of which was so touchingly conveyed in all the performances, and which became the underlying theme of a remarkable piece of film-making. It was photographed without recourse to gimmickry by Haskell Wexler, who managed to find a poetry in the garish chrome and neon backdrops which characterized the way the film looked; and was produced by Francis Ford Coppola, with Gary Kurtz as co-producer. The large cast also included Mackenzie Phillips, Harrison Ford, Bo Hopkins, Manuel Padilla Jr and Beau Gentry. The film's initial investment returned a handsome profit of $10,300,000.

• KEEP • RIGHT • ON •

Of the several boxing films made by Warner Bros. (most of which contained the word 'kid' in the title), **Kid Galahad** (1937) was by far the best. The story of a fight manager (mesmerically played by Edward G. Robinson, below left) who turns a bellhop (Wayne Morris, centre) into a prize-fighter, it showed its director, Michael Curtiz, brilliantly supervising some effective fight scenes with a gentle, almost mellow approach to the personal relationships explored in the scenario. Bette Davis as Robinson's mistress didn't have much to do in Seton I. Miller's screenplay (from a story by Francis Wallace), and apart from Robinson, acting honours were shared by Humphrey Bogart (below right) as a crooked promoter, Harry Carey, Jane Bryan and Wayne Morris. Like several previous Robinson vehicles, the actor died in the last reel. The film, which Hal Wallis produced and Sam Bischoff supervised, suffered no such fate, and though its title has since been changed to **The Battling Bellhop** to avoid confusion with a later Presley remake also called *Kid Galahad* (United Artists 1962), it is still a classic of the genre, and was remade in 1941 as *The Wagons Roll at Night*. Song: *The Moon Is In Tears Tonight* (by M. K. Jerome and Jack Scholl). (First National.)

Lassie Come Home (MGM, 1943), the classic boy-and-dog story, was a bonanza from Dore Schary's unit. Roddy McDowall was the star, but there were also two other young performers starting even more famous careers: Lassie (real name, Pal; real sex, male), the first top dog at the box office since Rin-Tin-Tin; and Elizabeth Taylor, already a beauty at 11 and, like McDowall, a London-to-Hollywood wartime evacuee. Other top names: Donald Crisp, Nigel Bruce and Elsa Lanchester. Also featured in Hugo Butler's potent screenplay from the Eric Knight novel were Dame May Whitty, her husband Ben Webster, Edmund Gwenn, Alan Napier. Produced in Technicolor by Samuel Marx and directed by Fred Wilcox, risen from publicist, script clerk for King Vidor, and test director—and not hindered by being Nicholas Schenck's brother-in-law.

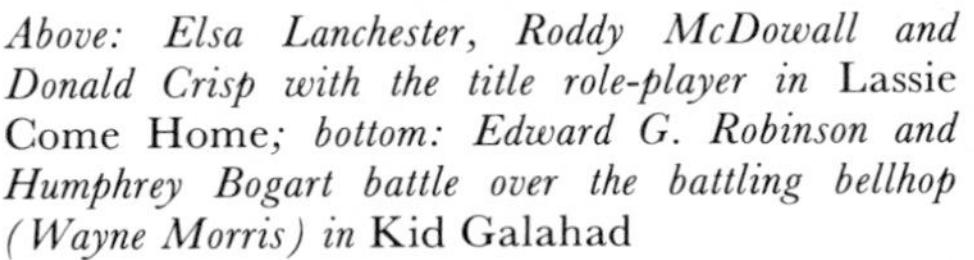

Above: Elsa Lanchester, Roddy McDowall and Donald Crisp with the title role-player in Lassie Come Home*; bottom: Edward G. Robinson and Humphrey Bogart battle over the battling bellhop (Wayne Morris) in* Kid Galahad

National Velvet (1944) had been on Pandro Berman's must-do list since he tried to buy it for Katharine Hepburn at RKO in 1935, but Paramount grabbed the Enid Bagnold best-seller, couldn't cast it, and sold it to MGM in 1937. By 1941 Berman and **Velvet** were under the same roof; three years later a hit was born. Also a star: Elizabeth Taylor was hardly a jockey type, but she played the horse-loving title character with such 'burning eagerness tempered with sweet, fragile charm' (*N.Y. World Telegram*) that not even a splendidly restrained Mickey Rooney, in his last film before army service, could steal scenes. Donald Crisp and Anne Revere, who won an Oscar (as did film editor Rober Kern), together with Angela Lansbury, Juanita Quigley, Jackie Jenkins, Reginald Owen, Arthur Treacher, Norma Varden, Terry Kilburn

and Arthur Shields also reflected the warmth of Clarence Brown's direction of the Theodore Reeves–Helen Deutsch screenplay. And it had a thundering Grand National climax—the best movie horse-race ever.

One of the finest fight films ever made, **The Set-Up** (RKO, 1949) covered 80 minutes in the life of third-rate palooka Stoker Thompson. Just before leaving for a bout, Stoker has a quarrel with his wife over his refusal to abandon his hopeless career in the ring. Later, in the stadium dressing room, he watches ring-scarred battlers return from their matches, recognizing in them phases of his own unhappy life. In the meantime, unknown to Stoker, his manager has made a deal with a gambler to throw the fight. During one of the most brutal ring encounters ever filmed, Stoker learns that he is supposed to take a dive. His pride surfaces; he knocks out the opponent, then must pay the piper for his act of rebellion. Everyone associated with this searing screen experience deserved the highest plaudits. Robert Ryan (seen below), himself an undefeated pugilist during his four years at Dartmouth College, made Stoker a wholly believable character—a weary, inarticulate bum who gains heroic stature in the course of the events. Audrey Totter (borrowed from MGM) as the wife, George Tobias as the manager, Alan Baxter as the gambler and Hal Fieberling as the opponent all played their roles with

Parental authority and wifely comfort: Donald Crisp and Elizabeth Taylor in National Velvet; *below Robert Ryan and Audrey Totter in* The Set-Up

remarkable acuity, while Wallace Ford, Percy Helton, Darryl Hickman, Kenny O'Morrison, James Edwards, David Clarke, Phillip Pine and Edwin Max added to the local colour. Robert Wise, in one of his finest directorial efforts, demonstrated an extraordinary eye for detail, exploring the dark and dingy world of tank-town boxing with withering verisimilitude; Art Cohn wrote the screenplay from Joseph Moncure March's famous narrative poem, and Milton Krasner was responsible for the highly-charged photography. The producer was Richard Goldstone.

'His whole life was a million to one shot,' boasted the publicity slogan for **Rocky**, an old-fashioned tale about a minor league boxer who takes on World Heavyweight Champion, Apollo Creed, and wins, through sheer guts and determination. It could have gone either way: a melodrama derided by audiences, or the sort of thing to warm the hearts of the world. It turned out, as we all know, to be the latter. Shot in a mere 28 days for the derisory sum of $960,000, it was the year's best-loved picture. It made a fortune at the box office ($56 million to date in the US and Canada) and won three Oscars: Best Picture for producers Irwin Winkler and Robert Chartoff, Best Director (John G. Avildsen) and Best Editing (Richard Halsey and Scott Conrad). The one person not to get an Oscar—though he was nominated for both Best Actor and Best Screenplay, something previously achieved only by Orson Welles—was the man we all associate with Rocky, Sylvester Stallone. Battered, sweaty, aggressive, sensitive and massively sincere, Stallone created a one-man legend with his portrayal of Rocky Balboa, the little guy (even the impressive-looking Stallone was dwarfed by Carl Weather's Creed) who wins through against all the odds. There were nice performances from Burt Young as his buddy at the meat-packing plant (the film was set and filmed in Philadelphia), Burgess Meredith as his trainer and Talia Shire as Adrian, his oddly-named girl, but Stallone dominated the film. He has gone on to forge himself into a kind of one-man image of American resilience in films like *F.I.S.T.* and *Paradise Alley* and *First Blood*, not to mention *Rocky II* (1979) and *Rocky III* (1983). Number One was made in 1976, ran for 119 minutes and was released by United Artists.

Some movies belong to their directors, some movies belong to their stars.

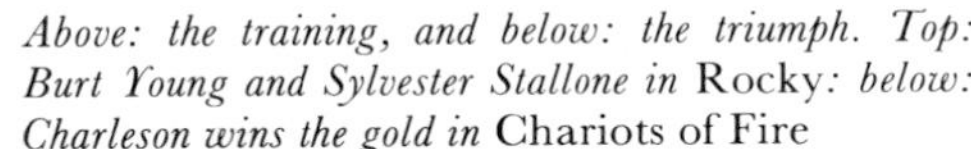

Above: the training, and below: the triumph. Top: Burt Young and Sylvester Stallone in Rocky*: below: Charleson wins the gold in* Chariots of Fire

Chariots of Fire (Enigma Productions for 20th Century-Fox and Allied Stars) belongs to its producer, David Puttnam. The man who more or less held the British film industry together through the 1970s, Puttnam was convinced he had found the perfect subject in the story of two British runners, one a Jewish student at Cambridge, the other a Scottish missionary's son, who both won Golds at the 1924 Paris Olympics. It seems hard to believe, given the extent to which the film has been hailed as the saviour of the British film industry, but Puttnam was unable to raise the money for it in Britain, and the film was finally made with a combination of American and Egyptian finance. At the 1982 Oscar ceremonies, it was triumphant, winning the Awards for Best Film and Best Screenplay (Colin Welland). It is in many ways a simple tale of effort and determination being rewarded—a story of *Rocky* in running shoes—but it has more serious themes, notably the anti-Semitic prejudice which Harold Abrahams (Ben Cross) encounters at Cambridge, and the uncertainties that plague Eric Liddell (Ian Charleson) as to whether his personal will to succeed is not in conflict with his duty to God. The film's success at the box office, though, is due to the heroics of the running track, made up of slow motion photography (by David Watkin) and an unforgettable score by Vangelis, both of which have been repeatedly parodied ever since. Cheryl Campbell, Alice Krige, Sir John Gielgud and director Lindsay Anderson also figure, and direction was by former commercials director Hugh Hudson, whose first feature it was.

• MAKE • 'EM • LAUGH •

On August 15, 1925, a massive crowd braved the heat of a New York summer night and the warning of a 2.30 am curtain down to see the film that Charles Chaplin had laboured eighteen months to make. Not only did he direct and star in **The Gold Rush**, but he also produced it for United Artists, the company he had founded with Mary Pickford and Douglas Fairbanks some six years earlier. Seen by many as Chaplin's most perfect work, **The Gold Rush** was his third full-length feature. The storyline is, as usual, simple: the Little Tramp goes up through the Chilkoot Pass to the Gold Fields. Finding no minerals, he almost starves to death but, of course, comes through in the end. As in most Chaplin films, though, it is not the plot which is memorable: it is the sustained comic invention. **The Gold Rush** is a treasure trove of invention. There is the scene in which, to stave off starvation, Charlie cooks his boot for himself and his partner, Big Jim McKay (Mack Swain), tenderly prising off the uppers as though carving a turkey, and consuming the bootlaces as though they were succulent spaghetti. To balance matters out, Big Jim fantasizes that Charlie is a turkey and pursues him ravenously round the hut and out into the snow. Then there is the Christmas party that Charlie dreams of, with the beautiful girl who promises to come but doesn't—a part which Georgia Hale took over from Lita Grey when Chaplin married the latter in November 1924. The film balances farce and sentimentality more perfectly than any other Chaplin movie. It was reissued in 1942 with music and a commentary in Chaplin's own voice.

Top: Chaplin in The Gold Rush*; below: the Marx Brothers in* A Night at the Opera, *and facing: Keaton in* The Cameraman

Buster Keaton returned to MGM as a contract star in 1928, having released a few pictures through United Artists. It was the first time he had relinquished control over his own productions, and the effect was ultimately disastrous. But **The Cameraman**, which inaugurated his new contract, was completely successful. Edward Sedgwick directed the funny, fast-moving movie by Clyde Bruckman, Lew Lipton and Richard Schayer. It told of a tyro photographer trying to cover news events for the Hearst newsreel: the

gags and stunts were, as ever, Keaton's own. Marceline Day played the girlfriend, Harry Gribbon and Harold Goodwin had bit parts.

A Night at the Opera (1935) was a smashing success, reversing the financial decline of the Marx Brothers' preceding pictures. Irving Thalberg knew what he was doing when he got the Paramount clowns to move over (dropping 'straight' brother Zeppo en route) to MGM, where they were given more opulent production and more elaborate gags, tested in a pre-filming stage tour, than ever before—although some Marx buffs deplored their yielding footage to romantic subplot and musical numbers. Sam Wood directed the George Kaufman–Morrie Ryskind script that bristled with laugh lines for Groucho. Left to right: the monumental Margaret Dumont, singers Kitty Carlisle and Allan Jones (their hit song was *Alone*). Chico, Groucho, Robert Emmet O'Connor, Harpo, Purnell Pratt, Walter Woolf King and Sig Rumann completed the cast.

Modern Times (1936), for which Charlie Chaplin wrote the music and the script, and which he directed, produced and starred in for United Artists, represents two crucial changes in his career as a comic filmmaker (which, by the mid-1930s, was showing signs of waning). Firstly, after resisting it for nearly a decade, he admitted the existence of sound, to the extent of having his tramp sing a little song in gibberish. Secondly, he made a film with two centres, instead of one, by working with an actress (Paulette Goddard) who could preserve some sort of individual identity beneath the battering ram of Chaplin's control. The idea for the film was apparently given to Chaplin by a young reporter, who told him about the production line system in Detroit, which was turning its workers into nervous wrecks. In the film, Charlie becomes literally trapped in the machine and, in one of his finest patches of comic invention, is battered and buffeted by an automatic feeding machine introduced by the bosses to save time and money. Cured after his breakdown, he is arrested when he picks up a red flag that has fallen off the back of a lorry, and runs down the street to return it, exactly the same time as a left-wing demonstration comes round the corner. He meets 'The Gamine' (Paulette Goddard) in the back of the police van. Chaplin always denied that the film had left-wing leanings, but it was coldly received in the States and banned in Germany and Italy, where the Fascist regimes saw it as a Communist tract. Henry Bergman and Chester Conklin were also in the cast, with Rollie Totheroh and Ira Morgan behind the camera.

W. C. Fields made a welcome return to form in **The Bank Dick** (Universal, 1940), a typically Fieldsian brew of laughter and mayhem in which he played Egbert Souse (pronounced Soo-zay), an impecunious inebriate who, in the small town of Lompoc, inadvertently effects the capture of a hold-up man, and is rewarded with a bank guard's job. On the premise that if at first you succeed, there's no reason why you shouldn't succeed again, Fields (below) is given a second chance to prove his worth when a second bank robber happens along at a most advantageous moment. As scripted by the great man himself (alias Mahatma Kane Jeeves), the laughs were plentiful, a surplus supply giving Franklin Pangborn, Una Merkel, Cora Witherspoon, Grady Sutton (below left) and Shemp Howard a fair crack of the comic whip. It all added up to a delightfully expansive entertainment that pleased the customers hugely. Edward Cline (veteran director of the Keystone Kops) directed, his big set-piece being a mountainside auto chase that climaxed the film.

The first in a series of such offerings, **Francis** (1950) was huge money-spinner for Universal. All about the havoc caused by a talking mule (called Francis) in the Burma Command, it was dedicated to the belief that a four-legged creature is far superior to most army personnel, and proved its point through a screenplay by David Stern (from his own novel) that had its fair share of belly-laughs. However, by the law of diminishing returns, it tended to run out of steam towards the end. Though the loquacious quadruped was the undoubted hero of the enterprise, the film top-starred Donald O'Connor (right) as a

Top left: Charlie in jail in Modern Times*; below: Fields in trouble in* The Bank Dick. *Opposite page top: donkeys—the star and Donald O'Connor in* Francis*—and dudes: Gene Wilder and Cleavon Little in* Blazing Saddles

newly-commissioned lieutenant who is rescued by Francis while lost behind enemy lines. The plot had O'Connor spending quite a bit of time in the booby hatch because of his who-would-believe-it? encounters with the mule (in which he is fed top-secret information), and generally overworked what was a one-joke situation. Patricia Medina was a spy, ZaSu Pitts (welcome back ZaSu!) was wasted as a nurse, and Eduard Franz and Howland Chamberlin were in it too; the director was Arthur Lubin and it was produced by Robert Arthur who, in a moment of inspiration, chose Chill Wills to supply Francis' voice.

Encouraged by the box-office oats, Universal brought Francis back seven more times. In 1951, he went to the races, and in 1952 to West Point; in 1953 he 'covered Big Town', then joined the WACS (1954) and went into the Navy (1955), all with O'Connor. The year 1956 found him 'in the haunted house' with Mickey Rooney. Four years later, his first cousin, *Mr Ed*, let it be heard for horses on TV.

Mel Brooks' **Blazing Saddles** (Warner Bros., 1974) was a casserole of a comedy whose chief ingredients were sight-gags, one-liners, black-out sketches, satire, parody and all-out farce. On being brought to the boil it tasted delicious—provided, of course, one's particular taste-buds weren't all that discriminating. For, as written by Brooks, Norman Steinberg, Andrew Bergman, Richard Pryor and Alan Uger (story by Andrew Bergman) it was an anarchic and anachronistic hodge-podge which sometimes worked and sometimes didn't. Fortunately, there were more good things in it than bad, with the narrative (about a black sheriff and his white sidekick saving the Western town of Rockridge from unscrupulous speculators) providing ample opportunities for mickey-taking and merry-making. An elongated cliché of every Western you've ever seen. Cleavon Little (below right) was a black railroad worker promoted to sheriff, Gene Wilder (left) as the Waco Kid, Harvey Korman as business shark Hedley Lamarr and Alex Karras as desperado Mongo. Madeline Kahn appeared as Lily von Shtupp and gave a devastating impression of Marlene Dietrich à la Destry which was one of the film's many highlights. Brooks (who also appeared in it as a territorial governor and a Jewish Indian Chief) directed, and it was produced (in Panavision) by Michael Hertzberg for Crossbow. The total box-office gross was $35,200,000. Songs included: *I'm Tired, The French Mistake, I Get A Kick Out Of You* and *Blazing Saddles.*

· AND · FINALLY...

CITIZEN KANE

Bernard Herrmann's ominous music begins as the camera ventures past a wire fence complete with 'NO TRESPASSING' sign, across the grounds of a darkly imposing mansion and into the room of an exhausted old man who utters one cryptic word ('Rosebud')—and dies. A boy is seen through a closed window, playing with his sled in the snow while his parents and a lawyer cement the arrangement that will transfer responsibility for the child's upbringing from the mother and father to a financial concern. In a series of breakfast table vignettes, the growing gulf between a newspaper tycoon and his wife is shown, the couple moving further and further apart physically until they sit at opposite ends of a huge table, she reading a rival newspaper. These are among the scenes one remembers from **Citizen Kane**. There are dozens of others, equally memorable; taken together, they comprise the most audacious, iconoclastic jigsaw puzzle of a movie ever produced in Hollywood. Though he had many talented collaborators, Orson Welles was the major creative force behind the production. Recklessly combining expressionistic, deep-focus photography (by Gregg Toland), a complex plot structure that utilized five narrators, the most inventive manipulation of sound heretofore attempted in a motion picture and a cluster of radio and stage actors, most of whom had never performed in front of a camera, Welles made a film about egomania and unnatural obsession that stripped bare the American love affair with power and materialism, and revealed the emptiness within. Gossip columnist Louella Parsons believed that Charles Foster Kane, the protagonist, was just a thinly-veiled, slanderous portrait of her boss, William Randolph Hearst. As a consequence, the Hearst newspapers declared war on RKO, disrupting the film's release and damaging its box-office performance. Critics tried to help, working overtime to come up with proper words of appreciation for the extraordinary achievement, but it still ended up a $160,000 loser (subsequent re-issues brought it into the black). However, no American motion picture (with the possible exception of *The Birth of a Nation*) has had more lasting influence; indeed, a poll of international critics conducted by the highly respected British film journal *Sight and Sound* in 1971 named it the best picture of all time. Besides producing, directing and playing the role of Kane, Welles (illustrated) deserved his co-authorship credit (with Herman J. Mankiewicz) on the screenplay. Film critic Pauline Kael argues otherwise in a 50,000 word essay on the subject, but her case against Welles is one-sided and unsupported by the facts. Also cast: Joseph Cotten, Dorothy Comingore, Agnes Moorehead, Ruth Warrick, Ray Collins, Erskine Sanford, Everett Sloane, William Alland, Paul Stewart, George Coulouris, Fortunio Bonanova, Gus Schilling, Philip Van Zandt, Georgia Backus, Harry Shannon, Sonny Bupp and Buddy Swan. Robert Wise edited, Vernon L. Walker supervised the special effects, Van Nest Polglase and Perry Ferguson designed, and John Aalberg took charge of sound. RKO co-produced with Welles' Mercury Productions company. Other films come and go but in the critics' polls carried out by *Sight and Sound* magazine (see below) **Citizen Kane** has topped the list for three decades.

1962 TOP TEN 1972 TOP TEN 1982

1962

1 Citizen Kane/Welles 1941
2 L'Avventura/Antonioni 1960
3 La Règle du Jeu/Renoir 1939
4 Greed/von Stroheim 1924
4 Ugetsu Monogatari/Mizoguchi 1953
6 Battleship Potemkin/Eisenstein 1925
6 Bicycle Thieves/De Sica 1949
6 Ivan the Terrible/Eisenstein 1943-46
9 La Terra Trema/Visconti 1948
10 L'Atalante/Vigo 1933

1972

1 Citizen Kane/Welles 1941
2 La Règle du Jeu/Renoir 1939
3 Battleship Potemkin/Eisenstein 1925
4 8½/Fellini 1963
5 L'Avventura/Antonioni 1960
5 Persona/Bergman 1967
7 Passion of Joan of Arc/Dreyer 1928
8 The General/Keaton 1926
8 The Magnificent Ambersons/Welles 1942
10 Ugetsu Monogatari/Mizoguchi 1953
10 Wild Strawberries/Bergman 1957

1982

1 Citizen Kane/Welles 1941
2 La Règle du Jeu/Renoir 1939
3 Seven Samurai/Kurosawa 1954
3 Singin' in the Rain/Donen & Kelly
5 8½/Fellini 1963
6 Battleship Potemkin/Eisenstein 1925
7 L'Avventura/Antonioni 1960
7 The Magnificent Ambersons/Welles 1942
10 Vertigo/Hitchock 1958
10 The General/Keaton & Bruckman 1927
10 The Searchers/Ford 1956

KANE

A-Z OF THE STARS

From the ancient Greeks, who looked to their gods on Olympus, through the ballad heroes of the Middle Ages, to the real-life national heros of the Elizabethan age, there have always been larger-than-life figures, who can be identified with in moments of stress and happiness. The 20th century has adopted *stars*—movie stars, pop stars, football stars. Stars are ordinary people with something extraordinary about them: better looking than the rest of us, more likely to win and more liable to get what they want. Stars are real people, but stardom is a fabricated condition, fulfilling *our* needs rather than projecting *their* personalities. Being a star has its consolations, of which money is the foremost. But it has its drawbacks too: a star is a public person, not a private one. And the same kind of fascination that makes the public want to set a star on a pedestal can very easily turn into an overwhelming desire to bring him or her crashing down again.

Of course, there are stars and stars. Some of them, like Cagney, are slightly larger than life. Some of them, like Douglas Fairbanks, Clark Gable and John Wayne, are much larger. Others still, like Charlie Chaplin, are a little bit smaller, ground down more than the rest of us but showing a resilience that can reassure. Female stars are a rather different matter: they are for the men to admire rather than the women to emulate. Within the code of accepted beliefs assumed by moviemakers, they are not, generally, the kind of girl a boy is supposed to want to marry.

You don't have to be able to act to be a star. But you do have to have something very special, which will carry through from film to film, irrespective of the name of the character played or the nature of the story involved. Audiences, after all, did tend to go and see a Mae West movie rather than, say, *She Done Him Wrong*. Similarly, when the chips are down, they watch Charlton Heston (with a degree in electrical engineering) struggle to get Ava Gardner out of the flooded storm drain in *Earthquake*, rather than someone called Stuart Graff trying to rescue his high-strung wife Remy. But there are quite a few stars in the pages to come who have won their fame, not for their ability to dominate the story, but by their skill at submerging their own personalities in role after role. Laurence Olivier, Paul Muni and Dustin Hoffman are actors who have become stars, and it seems somehow appropriate that the pictures of them included here show them in character rather than posing for the portraitist or the stills photographer.

Although the movie star is inextricably linked in the public mind with the movies, stardom took ten or fifteen years to become a part of the motion picture industry. In the very early days of the cinema, actors were either unknowns or else they were stage actors who were slumming from their true vocation and did not want to be named. As time went by, however, the public began to form an attachment to the 'Biograph Girl', the regular female star of a string of shorts produced by the long-since vanished company of that name. But it was not until Carl Laemmle, the independently minded head of the new Independent Motion Picture Company (or 'IMP' for short), lured her away from Biograph in 1910, that she was named as Florence Lawrence. Florence Lawrence was the first movie star.

Over the next decade, stars became one of the major drawing factors in the new and rapidly growing American film industry. In the years between 1910 and 1930 they were able to command fabulous salaries. Whereas in 1912, Mary Pickford was getting $500 a week, by 1916, this had gone up to $15,000 a week. That was only the start, and that was before the days of inflation. In the years that followed, million-dollar guarantees were not unusual, and the American film industry stood or fell by its stars.

During the 1920s the growth of the American movie industry was meteoric; but it crashed, like everything else, in 1929. The need to save money meant smaller budgets, and one way of achieving this was to pay lower salaries to the stars, particularly those who could be persuaded that they couldn't make the transition to sound.

The stars of Hollywood's golden age—the Gables and the Garbos, the Flynns and the Fondas, the Bogarts and the Bacalls—were stars who were *marketed*. The battles that Bette Davis had with Warner Bros. are legendary, and we perhaps too readily fall in with the rather romantic view of the glittering movie star as a slave of the mercenary studio. But there can be no doubt that the star's bargaining power in the Golden Age of Hollywood was nowhere near as great as it had been in the silent era, nor that stars were a much smaller part of the whole machinery of the movies. They remained the most glamorous part, however, and the studios devoted enormous amounts of time and money, not to catering to their whims, but to making sure that the stars were the ones the audience wanted.

In the disarray that Hollywood encountered in the years following World War II, hit by television and Federal anti-trust decisions, the old studio system broke down. In a way, the star system broke down, too. The studios could no longer afford to keep a roster of actors under permanent contract. What this meant in terms of stardom was that even the somewhat reduced Golden Age version of the Hollywood superstar underwent a further reduction, giving us a series of people who were more human, closer to us, and who more perfectly fitted the less romantic era of the 1950s, 1960s and 1970s.

The age of the great lover and the romantic idol was over. True, there were the sex symbols, like Brigitte Bardot, Marilyn Monroe and James Dean, but the vast majority of postwar stars are, in appearance, more ordinary mortals, not legendary figures in furs and fast cars. They are working (though admittedly very well-paid) actors in casual clothes—the Warren Beattys, the Robert Redfords, the Jack Nicholsons. None of this means, of course, that the place of the star has much changed. It is just that a Valentino or a Gable is not a figure for the postwar generation to identify with.

Our gods may have changed, but we still need them as much. We still want to think they do it just for us, and we are still happy that they should be paid accordingly. Stardom is a jealous god, but it is a generous one too.

• THE • STARS • • WHO • INVENTED • • STARDOM •

Born in Brooklyn in 1905 with an accent to match, **Clara Bow** was the daughter of a Coney Island waiter. She escaped poverty by winning a fan magazine beauty contest in 1921 and became the cinema's first sex symbol. It was, she said later, 'a heavy load to carry, especially when one is hurt, tired and bewildered'. It was as the '*It* Girl' (from the 1927 movie of that name, 'it' being sex appeal) that she is remembered. She didn't survive the transition to sound, and her personal life was wrecked by a lurid trial in the early 1930s. In 1931, she ran off with cowboy star Rex Bell, who later became Lieutenant Governor of Nevada. Retiring in 1933, Clara spent much of her later life in clinics. She died in 1965. She made over 50 films, including *This Woman* (1924), *Eve's Lover* (1925), *Dancing Mothers, Runaway, Mantrap* (1926), *It, Wings* (1927), *The Wild Party* and *Dangerous Curves* (1928). Her cupid's bow mouth still typifies the image of the silent film star.

C Alonso (Lon) Chaney was born in Colorado Springs, Colorado, on April Fool's Day, 1883. His parents were deaf-mute. Rumour—or studio handout—has it he learned his pantomimic skills from communicating with her. At 17, he went into vaudeville ending up, broke, in Los Angeles in 1912. Then began an extraordinary career brought to an end with his death in 1930. From playing hideous heavies, Chaney, the 'man of a thousand faces', became the star of a series of films in which his physically punishing make-up and his combination of loathsomeness and pathos made him one of the strangest (and biggest) stars of the silent screen. Among these roles were *The Hunchback of Notre Dame* (1923), *He Who Gets Slapped* (1924), *The Monster, The Unholy Three, The Phantom of the Opera* (1925), *The Black Bird* (1926), *The Unknown, London After Midnight* (1927), *Laugh, Clown, Laugh* (1928) and his only sound film, a remake of *The Unholy Three* in 1930.

Born in the East End of London on April 16, 1889, **Charles Chaplin** was the son of a musichall entertainer. He first went on the road at the age of five. At 17, he joined Fred Karno's company, and it was on a trip to the US that he was spotted by Keystone's Mack Sennett. From a movie career that started in 1914, the 'little tramp' went on to become Hollywood's most bankable star, with popular as well as intellectual appeal. In 1919, he consolidated his power by founding United Artists with Mary Pickford, Douglas Fairbanks and D. W. Griffith. Married four times (to Mildred Harris, Lita Grey, Paulette Goddard and Oona O'Neill), his private life was surrounded by controversy. Rather than submit to an 'inquiry' into his morals, he left America in 1952 and settled in Switzerland. Knighted in 1975, he died two years later. He made over 80 films, only about a dozen feature length. These were: *The Kid* (1921), *A Woman of Paris* (1923), *The Gold Rush* (1925), *The Circus* (1928), *City Lights* (1931), *Modern Times* (1936), *The Great Dictator* (1940), *Monsieur Verdoux* (1947), *Limelight* (1952), *A King in New York* (1957) and finally *The Countess from Hong Kong* (1967) with Marlon Brando and Sophia Loren.

F Born Douglas Elton Ulman in Denver, Colorado, on May 23, 1883, **Douglas Fairbanks** (right) in fact grew up with the name that he made famous because his mother reverted to her first husband's name when she left her second. One-time minor stage actor, soap company executive (his first wife's family business) and finally Broadway star, Doug went on to become America's favourite leading man—handsome, agile and debonair. In the mid teens of the century, he fell in love with Mary Pickford and married her in 1920. The couple and their home, Pickfair, became the centre of Hollywood's social life. Doug's swashbuckling hits were *The Mark of Zorro* (1920), *The Nut*, *The Thief of Baghdad* (1924), *Don Q, Son of Zorro* (1925), *The Black Pirate* (1926), *The Gaucho* (1927) and *The Iron Mask* (1928). When sound came, he was 47 and his hairline was receding. His first talkie, *The Taming of the Shrew* (1929) was a flop. He and Mary divorced in 1935; three months later, he married Lady Sylvia Ashley. He died in his sleep of a heart attack in the last month of the decade, December 1939.

G **Lillian Gish** (left) must be the most enduring actress in the history of the movies. Born on October 14, 1896, in Springfield, Ohio, Lillian De Guiche was, along with her sister Dorothy, closely chaperoned by their mother but firmly pushed into the movies, where she became the 'First Lady of the Silent Screen'. Her first big-screen appearance was in D. W. Griffith's *An Unseen Enemy* (1912); and she was still at it some 70 years later in *A Wedding* (1980) directed by Robert Altman; *Hambone and Hillie* (1983) and various TV appearances. She still travels widely, appearing at special screenings of her great silent films. Her chief silent roles were in *The Musketeers of Pig Alley* (1912), *Judith of Bethulia* (1914), *Birth of a Nation* (1915), *Intolerance* (1917)—as the 'hand that rocked the cradle', *Broken Blossoms* (1919), *Way Down East* (1920), *Orphans of the Storm* (1922), *Romola* (1924), *The Scarlet Letter* (1926) and, her finest performance, *The Wind* (1928). In the 1940s, 1950s and 1960s she played character parts, and was particularly memorable in Charles Laughton's *Night of the Hunter* (1955). Her autobiography, *The Movies, Mr Griffith and Me*, was published in 1969.

Above: Douglas Fairbanks
Left: Lillian Gish

J

Al Jolson has gone down in movie history as the man to speak the cinema's first words. But, before and after that moment in *The Jazz Singer* (1927), Jolson was an established musichall star and an actor who could bring great sincerity to the tearjerking vehicles to which he seemed irresistibly drawn. Born Asa Yoelson in Sprednik, Lithuania, on May 26, 1886, Jolson actually *was* the son of a cantor. But, as a blackface singer, he soon became America's most popular recording artist. He entered films in 1926 in an experimental Warner Bros. sound short called *April Showers*. *The Jazz Singer*, his first film, sold as much on his reputation as on the innovation of sound. After that, he made *The Singing Fool* (1928), *Sonny Boy* (1929), *Mammy* (1930) and, in 1934, starred in the Busby Berkeley musical *Wonder Bar*. He had four wives, of whom Ruby Keeler (1928 to 1939) was the most famous. He did the voice-over for the 1946 screen biography, *The Jolson Story* (he was played by Larry Parks), and died of a heart attack in 1950 after returning from singing to the troops in Korea.

Above: William S. Hart
Below: Al Jolson

H

With his stern face and his serious approach to acting, **William S. Hart** (the 'S' stood for Surrey not, as some have claimed, Shakespeare) was the first great Western star. Born in Newburgh, New York, in 1870, he spent his adolescence working (among other things) as a cowboy, and always regarded himself thereafter as a man of the West. He started off on Broadway, where he was soon playing Western roles, then transferred to the movies at the invitation of his friend, the director, Thomas H. Ince. He brought a genuine concern for accuracy to the parts he played. Between 1917 and 1919, he directed his own films, including *The Silent Man* (1917), and *Shark Monroe* (1918). His later roles included *Square Deal Sanderson* (1919), *O'Malley of the Mounted, White Oak* (1921) *Wild Bill Hickock* and *Singer Jim McKee* (1924). *Tumbleweeds* (1925) was his last and best film. After that, he retired to write Western novels and his autobiography. He died in 1946.

K The greatest screen clown of all, **Buster Keaton**, is one of the first of a series of great artists whose career was mangled by Hollywood mismanagement. Born Joseph Francis Keaton on October 4, 1895, in Piqua, Kansas, while his parents were on the road with a medicine show, he apparently got his stage name from Harry Houdini, who saw him fall down a flight of stairs unscathed at the age of six months. He began his theatre career in vaudeville and after scoring a success, he entered films in 1917 in a series of shorts directed by Roscoe 'Fatty' Arbuckle. Between 1919 and 1928, in association with producer Joseph M. Schenck (whose sister-in-law he married), Keaton formed his own film company and proceeded to produce a string of masterpieces, which included *The Saphead* (1919), *The Paleface* (1921), *The Balloonatic, The Navigator* (1924), *Seven Chances* (1925), *The General* (1927) and *Steamboat Bill Jr* (1928). After that, he made the disastrous decision of selling out to MGM and his career went into a nosedive, though his first MGM picture, *The Cameraman* (1928), was successful. His private life also went badly. His marriage collapsed and he became an alcoholic. In 1947, the Keaton legend was revived with a series of stage performances. In 1965, he appeared in Samuel Beckett's *Film*, which was written for him. His last major performance was in *A Funny Thing Happened on the Way to the Forum* (1966), a rather sorry affair. He died on February 1, 1966 of cancer.

P Billed as 'America's sweetheart' (or 'the World's sweetheart' abroad), **Mary Pickford** was never quite able to escape the role of the sweet young thing. Born Gladys Smith in Toronto on April 8, 1893, she first won fame as 'Baby Gladys' on the stage, then stormed her way on to Broadway in 1906 and into films with D. W. Griffith in 1909. This was before the days of stardom, and she was known as 'Little Mary'. That did not last long, though, and by 1916 she was on $10,000 a week. She had three husbands: she married Owen Moore in 1911, Douglas Fairbanks in 1920 (she formed United Artists with him, Griffith and Chaplin in 1919) and Charles 'Buddy' Rogers in 1936. By 1912, she had made 82 films, of which *The New York Hat* (1912) is probably best remembered. Other major roles were *Rebecca of Sunnybrook Farm* (1917), *Pollyanna* (1920), *Tess of the Storm Country* (1922), *Dorothy Vernon of Haddon Hall* (1924) and *The Taming of the Shrew* (as Katherine) in 1929. She quit films in 1933, became a successful businesswoman and received a special Academy Award in 1975. She died in 1979.

Left: Buster Keaton
Below: Mary Pickford

S **Gloria Swanson** was the silent screen's greatest vamp, and one of the top female box-office stars of the 1920s. But the transition to sound was not a successful one for her, not because she couldn't talk (and sing), but because her style of comedy and sex appeal was passé. She was born Gloria Josephine Mae Swenson on March 27, 1897, to a prosperous Swedish-Italian family in Chicago. She got a job as an extra when she visited the Essanay Studios in Chicago and she married their star, Wallace Beery, in 1916. Her most memorable silent features—some comedies, some melodramas—were *Male and Female* (1919), *The Affairs of Anatol* (1921), *Her Gilded Cage* (1922), *Zaza* (1925), *Madame sans Gêne* (made in France in 1925, where she married her third husband, the Marquis de la Falaise), *Queen Kelly* and *Sadie Thompson* (1928). She made a major comeback with *Sunset Boulevard* in 1950, and another with *Airport 1975* (in fact made in 1974). She died in 1983.

Left: Gloria Swanson
Right: Rudolph Valentino

V Every year, for more than 50 years after the death of **Rudolph Valentino** from a perforated ulcer in 1926, a veiled woman in black used to lay a wreath at his grave. She died in 1983. The greatest screen lover of all time was born Rodolfo Alfonzo Raffaele Pierre Philibert Guglielmi in Castellanata, Italy, on May 6, 1896. Failing to become a naval officer, he set off for Paris, then New York, where he worked as a landscape gardener, then became a taxi dancer. His first film was *Alimony* in 1918, but the ones for which he is remembered are *The Four Horsemen of the Apocalypse, Camille, The Sheik* (1921), *Blood and Sand* (1922), *Monsieur Beaucaire* (1924), *The Eagle* (1925) and *The Son of the Sheik* (1926). His male charm was taken in hand by his second wife, Natasha Rambova (born Winifred Shaughnessy), who developed an effeminate screen image for him (the *Chicago Tribune* labelled him 'the Pink Powder Puff'). Effeminate or not, his death was surrounded by mass female hysteria. In 1977, the inimitable Ken Russell made a screen 'biography' with that modern male sex symbol, Rudolph Nureyev, in the title role.

• STARS • OF • THE • • GOLDEN • AGE •

Above: Fred Astaire
Right: Lauren Bacall

A Up until 1932, **Fred Astaire** was very much the junior partner in the brother-and-sister team which made its Broadway debut in 1917. Adele Astaire was the star, Fred her dancing partner. But, in 1932, Adele married Lord Charles Cavendish and retired. Fred (born Frederick Austerlitz in Omaha, Nebraska, on May 10, 1899) was on his own. After a Hollywood screen test (verdict: 'Slightly balding. Can't act. Dances a little.'), he got a small part opposite Joan Crawford in *Dancing Lady* (1933). Later the same year, however, he was paired with Ginger Rogers in *Flying Down to Rio* and, although they were billed fourth and fifth, one of the great screen partnerships had begun. Ginger was good but Fred was a genius—elegant, inventive and perfectly poised, as convincing in the dialogue scenes as he was on the dance floor. He had other partners like Lucille Bremer, Rita Hayworth and Eleanor Powell, but—unless it is for his pairing with Cyd Charisse in *The Band Wagon* (1953)—it is with Ginger that he is always remembered. Their films were: *Flying Down to Rio* (1933), *The Gay Divorcee* (1934), *Roberta, Top Hat* (1935), *Follow the Fleet, Swing Time* (1936), *Shall We Dance?* (1937), *Carefree* (1938), *The Story of Vernon and Irene Castle* (1939) and *The Barkleys of Broadway* (1949). He was also distinguished as a straight actor, in *On the Beach* (1959) and *The Towering Inferno* (1974).

B Who writes about **Lauren Bacall** without writing about Humphrey Bogart? Theirs was one of the great romances of the cinema, lasting from the day they met until the day he died, with her nursing him through the final days of his cancer. Inevitable though the linking is, it is unfair to Miss Bacall, who is very much a star in her own right. Born Betty Joan Perske on September 16, 1924, in New York City, she played Broadway roles and modelled for *Harper's Bazaar*. She shot to stardom opposite Bogey in *To Have and Have Not* (1944), where her eyes suggested more than the dialogue would allow, and she could smoke a cigarette like there was no tomorrow. With Bogart, she appeared in *The Big Sleep* (1947)—their masterpiece—*Dark Passage* (1947) and *Key Largo* (1948). She was particularly fine on her own in *Young Man with a Horn* (1950: UK, *Young Man of Music*), *The Cobweb* (1955), *Written on the Wind* (1957) and *The Shootist* (1976). More recently, she has been a Broadway star again (in *Applause*, 1970) and has written an autobiography called, appropriately enough, *Lauren Bacall by Myself*.

For many people, **Ingrid Bergman** was the postwar Garbo: the same Swedish background, the same intensely personal private life, the same rather brooding beauty. Born in Stockholm on August 19, 1915, she was a stage and screen actress in her native Sweden. David O. Selznick took her to Hollywood to do an American version of *Intermezzo* (1936) in 1939, and stardom followed: in *Dr Jekyll and Mr Hyde* (1941), in which, against type, she played a prostitute, in *Casablanca* (1943), the film for which she will always be remembered, *For Whom the Bell Tolls* (1943) and as RKO's fated *St Joan*. Her popularity took a dive when she ran off with Italian director Roberto Rossellini, for whom she made *Stromboli* (1949) and other films, and she was banned from the US for a time. She returned with an Oscar-winning role in *Anastasia* (1956). After that, she worked mainly in Europe, most recently with compatriot Ingmar Bergman (no relation) in *Autumn Sonata* (1978). In her last role she played Israeli leader Golda Meir in a television mini series. She died of cancer in August 1982.

production chief at Warners. Within two years, Wallis had turned Bogart into a star in *The Petrified Forest* (1936), though he had been in films since 1930. Through the late 1930s he played mainly second-lead villains, but hit his stride in *The Maltese Falcon* (1941) and *Casablanca* (1943) and never looked back. He was the definitive incarnation of private eyes Sam Spade and Philip Marlowe and was equally fine in *The Treasure of the Sierra Madre* (1948), *The African Queen* (1952) (for which he won an Oscar) and *The Caine Mutiny* (1954).

Despite the hard-bitten image, Bogart came from a comfortable middle-class home (his father was a surgeon). Born in New York City on January 23, 1899, he got his strange expression and lisp from a World War I accident in the Navy. His film break at Warners came because Leslie Howard, who had played with him on Broadway, insisted Bogart play Duke Mantee in the screen version of *The Petrified Forest*. His fairy-tale romance with Lauren Bacall ended when he died of cancer of the aesophagus on January 14, 1957.

Left: Joan Blondell
Below: Humphrey Bogart

Facing page, top: James Cagney
Facing page, below: Maurice Chevalier

During the 1930s, which threw up more blondes—dumb, smart and just plain brassy—than any other decade in world history, there can have been few who combined a sharp sense of humour and a genuine warmth more successfully than **Joan Blondell**. Born on August 30, 1909, in New York City, she had a theatrical childhood and became a stage star with another unknown, James Cagney, in *Penny Arcade* in 1929. She was a mainstay of Warners throughout the 1930s, sometimes appearing in ten films a year, including *Blonde Crazy* (1931), *Gold Diggers of 1933*, *Three Men on a Horse* (1936), *The Kid from Kokomo* (1939) and *Topper Returns* (1941). She was married three times, always to film people—cameraman George Barnes (1933–1935), actor Dick Powell (1936–1945) and showman Mike Todd (1947–1950). She never really stopped working, one of her most memorable recent roles being with Eve Arden in *Grease* (1978). She died in 1980.

Deep in the corporate files of Warner Bros., there is a small addendum to a 1934 memo whose real subject is something else: it reads 'Who is this man **Bogart**? I want to know more about him.' and it is signed Hal B. Wallis,

Born in Paris on September 12, 1888, the youngest of nine children, **Maurice Chevalier** began as an acrobat, but after an accident he was forced to take up singing. His suave (and not terribly musical) delivery, and his invariable cane and straw boater, helped make him the most distinctive Frenchman of the 20th century. He made a dozen movies in France between 1908 and 1924, most of them shorts, then hit Hollywood in 1929, starting off with French versions of American pictures. He won stardom in *The Love Parade* (1929) and *The Merry Widow* (1934) but quit Hollywood in 1935 after an argument with Irving Thalberg. His later years were surrounded by political controversy—he was accused of collaborating, then exonerated—but he became a star for a new generation in *Gigi* (1958). His last role (voice only) was singing the title song in *The Aristocats* (1970) two years before his death.

C Of all the actors who rose to prominence in the 1930s, none now appears more modern than **James Cagney**: his low-key, slightly self-mocking style of playing has that rare quality, which can span a 50 year gap, leaving most of his contemporaries looking mannered and old-fashioned. Born on July 1, 1899, Cagney came from much the same background as the characters he played: his father was a bartender, and he grew up on the Lower East side, New York. Through the 1920s, he rose to prominence in vaudeville and, in 1930, was signed to a contract by Warners, playing tough gangsters like the Tommy Powers of *The Public Enemy* (1931), and using his other skills to play the hoofers of *Footlight Parade* (1933) and *Yankee Doodle Dandy* (1942), in which he was George M. Cohan. One of his most striking roles was as the psychopathic, gangster in *White Heat* (1949), but he was equally adept at comedy, as in Billy Wilder's 1961 *One, Two, Three.* He then retired, but was coaxed back to play the police commissioner in Forman's *Ragtime* (1981).

During the 1930s and the 1940s, one actor summed up the ordinary, solid, unflamboyant American values: **Gary Cooper**. Cooper's stock in trade was his relaxed attentiveness and air of abstraction (partly caused by the fact that he had a hearing problem). Born in Helena, Montana, on May 7, 1901, his first ambition was to be a cartoonist, which took him to Los Angeles. Instead, he became a salesman, then an extra. He got his big break when he played the second lead in *The Winning of Barbara Worth* (1926). His roles in the 1930s were those of bluff, action heroes, but he eventually graduated to parts that made more of a demand on him, particularly his 1941 duo, *Meet John Doe* and *Sergeant York* as the World War I hero, a role for which he won his first Oscar. He is probably best remembered, though, for his other Oscar-winning role, as Sheriff Will Kane in *High Noon* (1952), the Western that even Western-haters love. He died of cancer on May 13, 1961, shortly after James Stewart had accepted a special Academy Award on his behalf.

A slightly larger than life figure from the very start, with her coat hanger shoulders and her extraordinary eyes, **Joan Crawford** achieved the status of full-blown monster in her daughter Christina's autobiography, *Mommie Dearest*, published in 1978 and filmed in 1981 with Faye Dunaway. Born Lucille Fay Le Sueur on March 23, 1904 in San Antonio, Texas, she was in the first instance a fabricated star (the name 'Joan Crawford' came from a nationwide publicity contest). She graduated from flapper (*Our Dancing Daughters* 1928), to sensitive gold digger (*Grand Hotel*, 1932), and played a string of major roles at MGM in the 1930s: *Rain* (1932), *Sadie McKee* (1934), *The Bride Wore Red* (1937). At Warners, she had her greatest role in *Mildred Pierce*, for which she won an Oscar in 1945. Her first three husbands were Douglas Fairbanks Jr, Franchot Tone and Philip Terry. Then, as the wife of Pepsi-Cola chairman Alfred Steele, she became a successful businesswoman, promoting the product at sales conferences. She became notorious as an actress again in *Whatever Happened to Baby Jane?* (1962) and ended her career in the execrable *Trog* (1970). She died in 1977.

Above: Gary Cooper
Right: Joan Crawford

D

Sometime around 1934, Warner Bros. realized that **Bette Davis** was not just another starlet—a belief which had determined the kinds of roles in which she was initially cast. In 1934, she won her fight to play the unattractive Mildred in RKO's *Of Human Bondage*, and after that Warners gave her better and better parts. These ranged from *Bordertown* (1935) to *Marked Woman* (1937) to *Jezebel* (1938), for which she won an Oscar, to *Dark Victory* (1939), the most moving of all her 1930s roles, in which she plays a woman with a fatal disease. Born in Lowell, Massachusetts, on April 5, 1908, her determination to get into show-business was not blunted by a string of rebuffs and failures, and it was this determination which brought her into head-on confrontation with Warners in the late 1930s. Technically, she lost her fight with the studio, but in fact she won, as she was given ever-better roles. She received another Oscar in 1950 for *All About Eve*, the gloriously bitchy role for which she is best remembered, but has continued ever since to bring distinction to major movies (such as, *Whatever Happened to Baby Jane?* 1962), minor movies and telefilms. In 1977, she received the American Film Institute's Life Achievement Award.

In 1934, the great German stage director, Max Reinhardt, descended on Hollywood. Always one for spectacle, he decided to stage *A Midsummer Night's Dream* in the Hollywood Bowl. For the role of Hermia, he chose an 18-year-old college freshman, **Olivia De Havilland**. She went on to play the role in the film and from there to stardom at Warner Bros., but generally in sweet, rather than dominant parts as in her greatest role of the 1930s, Melanie in *Gone with the Wind* (1939), where she was inevitably overshadowed by Vivien Leigh's Scarlett. When her seven year contract with Warners came to an end, she sued them for claiming that a six-month suspension should be added on, and won. She played more major roles for a variety of studios—*Hold Back the Dawn* (1941), *To Each His Own* (1946), *The Snake Pit* (1948) and *The Heiress* (1949). Then, in 1955, she married Pierre Galante, editor of *Paris Match*, and moved to France, only making occasional trips back to Hollywood for such dubious causes as *Lady in a Cage* (1964), *Airport '77* (1977) and *The Swarm* (1978). She was born on July 1, 1916, in Tokyo, educated in California and her sister is actress Joan Fontaine.

Top: Bette Davis
Above: Olivia De Havilland
Right: Marlene Dietrich

One of the best guarded secrets of half a century was **Marlene Dietrich**'s date of birth: it was December 27, 1901, the place was Berlin and her father was an officer in the Prussian police. She was well educated and studied under Max Reinhardt. She entered films and became quite successful in Germany during the 1920s. But she became an international star when Josef von Sternberg cast her as Lola Lola in *The Blue Angel* (1930), one of the most sexually provocative roles in the history of cinema. She was signed by Paramount, and dominated the early 1930s with a series of highly-charged, stunningly lit roles in Sternberg's films: *Morocco* (1930), *Dishonored* (1931), *Shanghai Express*, *Blonde Venus* (1932), *The Scarlet Empress* (1934) and *The Devil is a Woman* (1935). In the roles after Sternberg, she is always memorable (even in films like *Destry Rides Again*, 1939), but the magic was not as strong Postwar, she registered strongly in *Stage Fright* (1950) and *Witness for the Prosecution* (1958). Her most recent film was *Just a Gigolo* (1978).

Too mild-mannered to become a journalist, which is what he studied to be at the University of Minnesota, **Henry Fonda** became an insurance clerk, then was encouraged to go on the stage. Born in Grand Island, Nebraska on May 16, 1905, he first appeared on the Broadway stage in 1929, but did not make his first film until 1935. He specialized in diffident, gentle, honest heroes, but his great roles were the ones slightly against type: the 'three-time loser' in *You Only Live Once* (1937), Frank James in *Jesse James* (1939) and, in the same year, his most memorable early part, the title role in *Young Mr Lincoln*. The role he loved most was *Mr Roberts*, which he played on the stage in 1948, and on the screen in 1955. He had a distinguished war record, winning a Bronze Star and a Presidential Citation. His most surprising role was as the cold-blooded murderer in *Once Upon a Time in the West* (1969) and his last was in *On Golden Pond* (1981), for which he won an Oscar. He died after a long, wasting illness (whose effects may be seen in *On Golden Pond*) in 1983.

Above: Henry Fonda
Right: Errol Flynn

F

To a quite remarkable degree, **Errol Flynn**'s private life echoed the flamboyance of his screen roles—wine, women and fisticuffs. He was not as studio publicists liked to pretend, Irish, nor even English (though he was educated in Britain and began his stage career there). He was, in fact, born in Hobart, Tasmania on June 20, 1909. He spent his youth and early manhood on a variety of colourful adventures in New Guinea, got a part in an Australian film, returned to England, went on the stage and ended up in a British Warner Bros. film. Through the mid- to late-1930s, he was Warners' chief male star, appearing in pirate and other costume roles: *Captain Blood* (1935), *The Charge of the Light Brigade* (1936) *The Private Lives of Elizabeth and Essex* (1939) and *The Sea Hawk* (1940). It is as Robin Hood in *The Adventures of Robin Hood* (1938) that he will always be remembered. His career went downhill in the 1940s, as did he, though there was a brief and memorable revival in *The Sun also Rises* (1956). He died of a heart attack on October 14, 1959 and an excellent autobiography, *My Wicked, Wicked, Ways* was published posthumously.

At first overshadowed by her sister Olivia, Joan de Beauvoir de Havilland was born in Tokyo on October 22, 1917. She made her stage and screen debut as Joan Burfield, then became **Joan Fontaine** in *Quality Street* in 1937. Refinement was her stock in trade, demure in her early films, sharp and even bitchy in the later ones. Her first real break was in Hitchcock's *Rebecca* (1940), for which she got an Oscar nomination, and she won the Award itself for the same director's *Suspicion* the following year. She was equally memorable in *Letter from an Unknown Woman* (1948), *Born to be Bad* (1950), *Ivanhoe* (1952) and *Beyond a Reasonable Doubt* (1956). She made three films in the 1960s, of which the last was a British horror movie, *The Witches* (1966). Her autobiography, *No Bed of Roses,* which was written in 1978, also told of her skills at golfing, flying aeroplanes, piloting balloons and tuna fishing.

G

Probably one of the half dozen greatest stars in movie history, it took **William Clark Gable** a few years to get started. Born in Cadiz, Ohio, on February 1, 1901, he worked in a great variety of jobs including in a tyre factory, as a lumberjack, then as a tie salesman before getting a Broadway break in 1928. But both MGM and Warner Bros. turned him down after screen tests (the story has always persisted that Darryl F. Zanuck considered Gable's ears were too big). By 1938, however, he was the 'King of Hollywood'. *'Dear Mr Gable—You Made Me Love You,'* sang the 16-year-old Judy Garland in *Broadway Melody of 1938* (it was, of course, an MGM picture, and Gable was an MGM star). In 1939, he played Rhett Butler in *Gone with the Wind*, allegedly against his will, and at an estimated cost of $25 million to David O. Selznick. His best roles of the 1930s were *Red Dust* (1933), *It Happened One Night* (1934), *China Seas*, *Mutiny on the Bounty* (1935), *San Francisco* (1936), *Test Pilot* (1938) and *Boom Town* (1940). He had a distinguished war record in the US Air Force and a triumphant return to Hollywood ('Gable's back—and Garson's got him!' was the slogan). His last film was *The Misfits* released in 1961. He died of a heart attack in 1960.

Ava Gardner, born on January 24, 1922, on a tenant farm in Smithfield, North Carolina, hit Hollywood almost by mistake in 1940. For the first five years, the only notable thing she did was marry Mickey Rooney (from 1942 to 1943). Later marriages were to jazz trumpeter Artie Shaw (1945–47) and singer Frank Sinatra (1951–57, though they separated in 1954). On screen, she was, once she got a part big enough to show it (in *The Killers*, 1946) a sensuous beauty who could exude sexuality more than any other star of the late 1940s and early 1950s. This she did in such films as *One Touch of Venus* (1948)—she did the touching—*Show Boat, Pandora and the Flying Dutchman* (1957), *The Naked Maja* and *On the Beach* (1959). In the 1960s, she graduated to playing powerful older women, a lot of them bitches, and many of them punished with a vengeance for their sins (as she was, quite spectacularly, in the 1974 film *Earthquake*.

Above: Greta Garbo

Right: Ava Gardner

If there is one person who sums up all the magic and the mystery of the movie star, it is **Greta Garbo**, with her distant, soulful look, her deep, lightly accented voice and her always fiercely private private life. Born Greta Louisa Gustafson on September 18, 1905, in Stockholm, she won a scholarship to the Royal Dramatic Theatre school in Sweden, and was 'discovered' for the cinema by Mauritz Stiller. When Louis B. Mayer wanted to get Stiller to the States, Garbo was part of the package, much to Mayer's disapproval. But her first American film, *The Torrent* (1926), made her a star. Her reputation as the greatest star of all time and her invariable epithet of 'divine' was based on only 22 films, including *Flesh and the Devil* (1927), in which she falls in love with John Gilbert in front of the cameras, *The Kiss* (1929), *Anna Christie* (1930), *Mata Hari* (1931) and *Queen Christina* (1933), *Anna Karenina* (1935), *Camille* (1937) and *Ninotchka* (1939). She retired from the screen following the failure of *Two-Faced Women* which she made in 1941, and since then has kept herself more than ever very much to herself.

One of Hollywood's favourite stories is the one about a publicist who sent a telegram asking 'HOW OLD **CARY GRANT**?' The reply came back 'OLD CARY GRANT FINE HOW YOU?' The real answer to the question can be found by taking January 18, 1904, as the starting point, which is when Archibald Alexander Leach was born in Bristol. He ran away from home, became an acrobat, a lifeguard, a song and dance man and a billboard carrier. He was finally spotted by Arthur Hammerstein, who put him in the New York run of *Golden Dawn*. He signed a Paramount contract and played opposite two of Hollywood's most fatal *femmes*, Marlene Dietrich in *Blonde Venus* (1932) and Mae West in *She Done Him Wrong* (1933), playing a Salvation Army man in the latter. The fact that he held his own did wonders for his reputation, but it was at RKO and Columbia that his talent for light comedy was most perfectly used: in *Topper, The Awful Truth* (1937), *Bringing up Baby* (1938), *His Girl Friday* (1940) and *The Philadelphia Story* (1941). He was also the perfect lead in two Hitchcock comedy thrillers, *To Catch a Thief* (1955), in which he was a cat burglar, and *North by Northwest* (1959), in which he ended up hanging around on Mount Rushmore. His private life was riddled with scandals, and he retired from the screen in 1966.

Above: Paulette Goddard
Right: Cary Grant

For an actress who was one of Paramount's top stars of the 1940s, in films like *Second Chorus* (1941), *Reap the Wild Wind* (1942), *The Crystal Ball* (1943), *I Love a Soldier* (1944) and *Kitty* (1945), **Paulette Goddard**'s career began and ended rather inauspiciously. Born Marian Levy at Great Neck, Long Island, on June 3, 1911, she began as a Ziegfeld Girl called 'Peaches' at 14 and then became a Goldwyn Girl in *The Kid from Spain* (1932). In between she had become a millionaire's wife at 16 and divorced in Reno. At the other end of her life, she reigned over a series of B features, from Edgar G. Ulmer's *Babes in Bagdad* (1952), to a Hammer cheapie, *The Stranger Came Home* (US title, *The Unholy Four*), directed in England by Terence Fisher in 1954. After that, she retired, making a brief comeback in an Italian-French co-production called *Time of Indifference* in 1964, in which she played Claudia Cardinale's mother. The other thing she did, of course, was marry Charlie Chaplin, secretly, at sea, in either 1933 or 1936, and appear with him in *Modern Times* (1936) and *The Great Dictator* (1940). She divorced Chaplin in 1942, married Burgess Meredith in 1944, divorced him in 1950 and finally married novelist Erich Maria Remarque.

Above: Katharine Hepburn

Only two female stars really held their own as independent forces during the 1930s: Bette Davis and **Katharine Hepburn**. Hepburn was born into the best of families in Hartford, Connecticut, on November 9, 1907, and educated at Bryn Mawr. Her breeding showed, not only in the way she dealt with the studios—she got her first contract by naming a sum she thought was absurd and having it accepted—but also in the way she played the roles, notably in *The Philadelphia Story* (1941). Her debut was in *Bill of Divorcement* (1932), and her other great roles of the decade were *Christopher Strong* (1933), *Alice Adams* (1935) and *Holiday* (1938). Her romance with Spencer Tracy lasted for 27 years, until his death in 1967. They never married, but appeared together in such films as *Woman of the Year* (1942), *Adam's Rib* (1949), *Pat and Mike* (1952) and *Guess Who's Coming to Dinner?* (1967), the last one completed a few weeks before Tracy's death. Probably her finest role though, was opposite Humphrey Bogart in *The African Queen* (1951). The modern period has also been a good deal less lean for her than for many actresses of her generation, comprising *The Lion in Winter* (1968), for which she won an Oscar, *Rooster Cogburn* (with John Wayne) in 1976, and *On Golden Pond*, for which she won yet another Oscar in 1981.

When Hedwig Eva Maria Kiesler—**Hedy Lamarr**—arrived in Hollywood in 1938, she was billed as the 'most beautiful woman in the world'. This was mainly as a result of the ten-minute nude sequence in Gustav Machaty's 1933 Czech film, *Exstase* (*Ecstasy*), a few copies of which survived her millionaire husband's mission to buy up and destroy all the existing prints. Born in Vienna on November 9, 1913, she was a Max Reinhardt protégée whom Hollywood did little more than look at, in films like *White Cargo* (1942) and *The Heavenly Body* (1943). Her best early film was *Ziegfeld Girl* (1941), in which she made up a trio of young hopefuls with Lana Turner and Judy Garland. In later years, she played legendary beauties: Delilah in *Samson and Delilah* (1949), Helen of Troy in *L'Amante di Paride* (*The Face that Launched a Thousand Ships*, 1954) and Joan of Arc in *The Story of Mankind* (1957). She retired from the movies in 1957, and was arrested on a shoplifting charge in 1965. She was later acquitted.

No talent search in the history of Hollywood is more famous than the one carried out by David O. Selznick for the role of Scarlett O'Hara in *Gone with the Wind* (1939). The part went to **Vivien Leigh**, a convent-educated English girl who had been born in Darjeeling on November 5, 1913, and won fame opposite Laurence Olivier in *Fire over England* (1937). She married him after a long and much-publicized romance in 1940. After her Oscar for *Gone with the Wind*, she played in *Waterloo Bridge* (1940), *That Hamilton Woman* (1941), *Caesar and Cleopatra* (1945) and *Anna Karenina* (1948), playing the title role in each case. Her other truly memorable role was opposite Brando in *A Streetcar Named Desire* (1951), in which she brought intensity and frailty to the role of Blanche Dubois. A sufferer from tuberculosis throughout her life, she died in 1967, having divorced Olivier in 1960. Her screen career is slight, partly because of the Selznick contract and partly because she never really left the stage.

Middle: Hedy Lamarr
Left: Vivien Leigh

Peter Lorre (right) was an actor whom Hollywood never really knew how to use: that a performer cited by Bertold Brecht as one of the best he had ever seen should end up playing almost exclusively in horror movies is, to say the least, ironic. Born Laszlo Löwenstein on June 26, 1904, in Rosenberg, Hungary, he was a little known stage actor when Fritz Lang cast him in (and as) *M* (1931). His wide-eyed portrayal of a child murderer helped him get work in Hollywood when he fled Hitler's Germany, and he played in *Mad Love* and *Crime and Punishment* (as Raskolnikov) in 1935. But then he went into Mr Moto films, almost a dozen of them between 1937 and 1940. After that, he played some memorable heavies, especially in *The Maltese Falcon* (1941), *Casablanca* (1943) and *Beat the Devil* (1954). Back in Germany, he directed *Der Verlorene* (*The Lost One*, 1951). But after that, it was the horrors, ending with a cameo in *Muscle Beach Party* and a role in Jerry Lewis' *The Patsy*. He died of heart seizure in 1964.

Above: Carole Lombard
Below right: Paul Muni

When **Carole Lombard** was killed in a plane crash in January 1942, not only was she mourned by millions of fans, but the President himself, Franklin D. Roosevelt, sent a telegram of condolence to her husband, Clark Gable. It was one of the legendary screen romances, and it affected Gable's career for years. But Lombard was very much a star in her own right. Born Jane Alice Peters on October 6, 1908, in Fort Wayne, Indiana, she got a contract with Fox at the age of 17 (though she appeared, aged 12, in *A Perfect Crime* in 1921), but nothing much came of it. After a spell of two-reel farces with Mack Sennett, she hit the big time opposite John Barrymore in *Twentieth Century* (1934). It was the film which finally gave her the chance to show her talents as a comedienne, and it led to more screwball comedies, including *My Man Godfrey* (1936), *Nothing Sacred* (1937), *Fools for Scandal* (1938), *Mr and Mrs Smith* (1941), and her last film, Ernst Lubitsch's hilarious *To Be or Not To Be* (1942). She was one of Hollywood's most popular stars, on screen and off, and she was universally mourned.

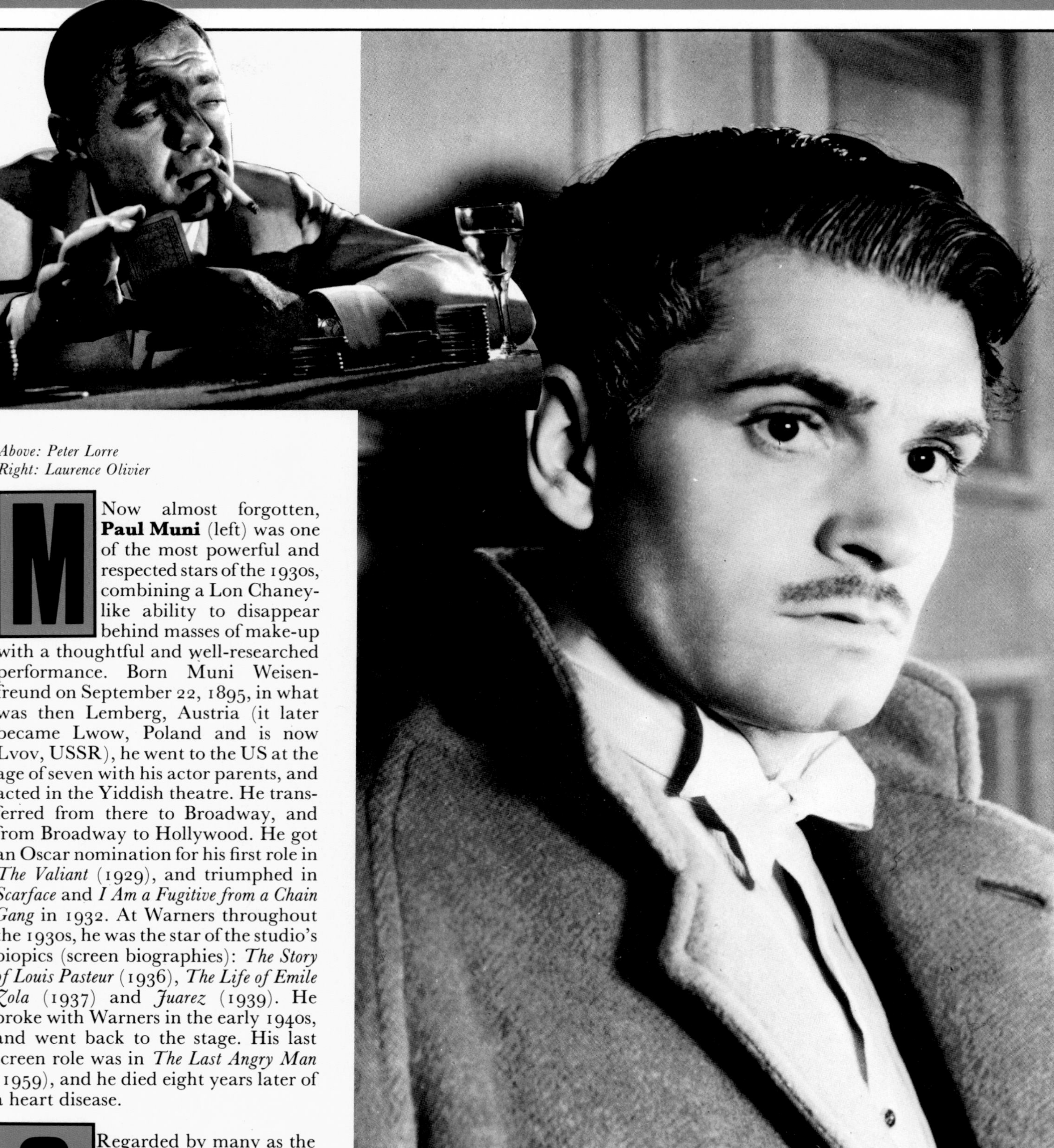

Above: Peter Lorre
Right: Laurence Olivier

M Now almost forgotten, **Paul Muni** (left) was one of the most powerful and respected stars of the 1930s, combining a Lon Chaney-like ability to disappear behind masses of make-up with a thoughtful and well-researched performance. Born Muni Weisenfreund on September 22, 1895, in what was then Lemberg, Austria (it later became Lwow, Poland and is now Lvov, USSR), he went to the US at the age of seven with his actor parents, and acted in the Yiddish theatre. He transferred from there to Broadway, and from Broadway to Hollywood. He got an Oscar nomination for his first role in *The Valiant* (1929), and triumphed in *Scarface* and *I Am a Fugitive from a Chain Gang* in 1932. At Warners throughout the 1930s, he was the star of the studio's biopics (screen biographies): *The Story of Louis Pasteur* (1936), *The Life of Emile Zola* (1937) and *Juarez* (1939). He broke with Warners in the early 1940s, and went back to the stage. His last screen role was in *The Last Angry Man* (1959), and he died eight years later of a heart disease.

O Regarded by many as the greatest actor of his generation, **Lord Olivier** (he was, in 1971, the first actor ever to be elevated to the House of Lords) had parallel careers for a while: as a romantic lead in such films as *Fire over England* (1937), *Q Planes*, *Wuthering Heights* (1939), *Rebecca* and *That Hamilton Woman* (1940); and as a Shakespearian actor, mainly on the stage, but also on film (in, for example, *As You Like It* in 1936). What really established his cinema reputation, however, and probably led to his special Oscar in 1970, were his three Shakespeare films, in which he starred and which he directed: *Henry V* (1944), *Hamlet* (1948) and *Richard III* (1955). In the postwar years, his main creative talents were devoted to the theatre, first as director of the Old Vic, then as the first director of the National Theatre in 1963. But there have been some distinguished roles on the big screen: *Oh! What a Lovely War* (1969), *Sleuth* (1972) and *Marathon Man* (1976) among them. Still, it is hard to escape the conclusion he now does it mainly for the money.

Left: Ginger Rogers
Above: Barbara Stanwyck
Right: Spencer Tracy

R

Along with Romeo and Juliet, Samson and Delilah and Abelard and Heloise, one of the great all-time partnerships was that of Frederick Austerlitz and Virginia Katherine McMath. Miss McMath, better known as **Ginger Rogers** (Austerlitz, of course, became Astaire), was born in Independence, Missouri, on July 16, 1911. Her mother, a powerful woman who exercised great influence over her career (and, during the McCarthy era, the careers of others), scotched a plan for her to become a child star. But before the RKO musicals, she was a mainstay of Busby Berkeley musicals *42nd Street* and *Gold Diggers of 1933* (in the former, she was Anytime Annie: 'the only time she said no was when she didn't hear the question'). With Astaire, she was in *Flying Down to Rio* (1933), *The Gay Divorcee* (1934), *Roberta, Top Hat* (1935), *Follow the Fleet, Swing Time* (1936), *Shall We Dance?* (1937), *Carefree* (1938), *The Story of Vernon and Irene Castle* (1939) and, much later, *The Barkleys of Broadway* (1949). Her career continued without Fred, and she won an Oscar for *Kitty Foyle* (1940). In the 1960s, she returned to the stage, taking over *Hello, Dolly*! from Carol Channing and starring in the London production of *Mame*.

S **Barbara Stanwyck**, as those who have seen *Double Indemnity* (1944) will know, can put more expression into an ankle than many actresses can into their whole body. Born Ruby Stevens on July 16, 1907, in Brooklyn, she had a tough childhood and a tough climb to the top, via the chorus, the Ziegfeld Follies, the lead in a 1926 Broadway production of *The Noose* and non-exclusive contracts with Columbia and Warners. By the year of *Double Indemnity*, she was the highest paid woman in the United States. She shone in a number of cheap movies like *Night Nurse* (1931), was magnificent in *Stella Dallas* (1937), for which she was nominated for an Oscar, and showed the range of her talents as the serious-minded reporter in *Meet John Doe* (1941) and the jive-talking Sugarpuss O'Shea in *Ball of Fire* the following year. Her voice was always a little harsh and her looks were never quite perfect, but she was every inch the professional actress. When her movie roles started to dry up, she switched to TV with *The Barbara Stanwyck Show* and *Big Valley*. In 1983, at 76, she could still be convincing in a love scene in *The Thorn Birds* with a man 30 years her junior.

T **Spencer Tracy** was one of the great *movie* actors, with the emphasis on movie: his intense, toned-down style was ideally suited to the close-up. Watch him suffer in *20,000 Years in Sing Sing* (1933) and *Fury* (1936), and it is not hard to see why Laurence Olivier said, 'I've learned more about acting from watching Tracy than in any other way'. He was born in Milwaukee on April 5, 1900, served in the Navy during World War I, studied acting, and finally got a Hollywood contract in 1930. He was nominated for three Oscars in the 1930s, and won two: for *Captains Courageous* (1937) and *Boy's Town* (1938) (the one that got away was *San Francisco*, 1936). He is best remembered, though, for his roles opposite Katharine Hepburn, but his Catholic faith wouldn't allow him to divorce his wife and marry her. His career kept right on going through the 1950s and 1960s, with such films as *Bad Day at Black Rock* (1955), *The Mountain* (1956), *The Old Man and the Sea* (1958), *Inherit the Wind* (1960) as Clarence Darrow, *Judgement at Nuremburg* (1961), *It's a Mad Mad Mad Mad World* (1963)—he was the pursuing cop—and *Guess Who's Coming to Dinner?*. He died just after shooting of the last was completed.

At the very start of *They Won't Forget* (1937), a trainee typist in a Southern town is trailed by the camera and murdered by an unseen assailant. We never find out who did it, but this was definitely not the last we would see of **Lana Turner** (whose debut role it was). Her given names were Julia Jean Mildred Frances, and she was born in Wallace, Idaho, on February 8, 1920. But she grew up in California, attended Hollywood High and was (allegedly) spotted at the soda counter in Schwab's. Known as 'the sweater girl', she was a World War II pin-up. But she could act, too, a fact demonstrated in (among other films) *The Postman Always Rings Twice* (1946), *The Bad and the Beautiful* (1952), *Peyton Place* (1957) and *Imitation of Life* (1959). The most bizarre piece of casting was when she played the sweet, demure girl to Ingrid Bergman's whore in *Dr Jekyll and Mr Hyde* (1941). She has been married seven times, No. 4 being Tarzan Lex Barker. In 1958, she was in the headlines for some considerable time after her teenage daughter Cheryl stabbed her lover, gangster Johnny Stompanato, to death and got off on a plea of justifiable homicide. Her last good role was in *Madame X* made in 1966.

W

There can't be many actresses who have given their name to a piece of military equipment, which is what **Mae West** did to an inflatable life-jacket, whose effect, it was claimed, was to give men her shape. In fact, as Miss West has pointed out, that shape was a triumph of willpower and engineering. Born on August 17, 1892, in Brooklyn, the daughter of a heavyweight boxer, she started in vaudeville, then became the toast of Broadway with her play, *Sex* (1926), which she followed up with *Drag* (1927). Her screen roles were virtually all vehicles for her unique combination of sex appeal and self-parody. As she put it herself, 'Goodness had nothing to do with it' (originally an answer to the question, 'My goodness, where did you get that diamond?'). On screen, she was in *Night After Night* (1932), *She Done Him Wrong*, *I'm No Angel* (1933), *Belle of the Nineties* (1934), *Goin' to Town* (1935), *Klondike Annie*, *Go West Young Man* (1936), *Every Day's a Holiday* (1938), *My Little Chickadee* (1940)—a sort of on-screen duel with W. C. Fields—and *The Heat's On* (1943), most of which she also wrote. She came back at the age of 78 in *Myra Breckinridge* (1970) and again at the grand old age of 86 in *Sextette* (1978). She died, glamorous to the last, in November 1980.

Above: Mae West
Left: Lana Turner

• MORE • RECENT • METEORS •

A

Julie Andrews' film career has been a series of surprises separated by long spells of predictability. Just when it looked as though all she was ever going to do was exude sweetness and light, her portrayal of Gertrude Lawrence in *Star*! (1968) reminded us she could dance with the best of them. And just when she had come to epitomize sexual safety, she was doing torrid love scenes in *10* (1979) and drag acts in *Victor Victoria* (1981). Born Julie Elizabeth Welles on October 1, 1935, in Walton-on-Thames, she grew up in show-business, played on Broadway in *The Boy Friend* in 1954, then got the lead in *My Fair Lady* two years later. The film role was played by Audrey Hepburn, but Andrews' debut in *Mary Poppins* (1964) disproved for ever the adage about not playing a scene with animals. Since then, she has alternated musicals—*The Sound of Music* (1965), *Thoroughly Modern Millie* (1967) and *Star*!—with straight roles: *The Americanization of Emily* (1964), *Torn Curtain* (1966) and *The Tamarind Seed* (1974). She married director Blake Edwards in 1970.

Above left: Julie Andrews

Above right: Brigitte Bardot

B

A recent French TV documentary revealed **Brigitte Bardot**, at just short of 50, looking every bit as wild, young and beautiful as she did when she shot to stardom in *Et Dieu Créa la Femme* (*And God Created Woman*, 1956). She had been groomed for that film by director/husband Roger Vadim, who had brought in Curt Jurgens as the ostensible star. When Jurgens saw a rough cut, he insisted Bardot share the billing with him. Born on September 28, 1934, she studied ballet, worked as a model and had played some minor roles before Vadim launched her. Against all the odds, she survived Vadim's grooming (married in 1952, they divorced in 1957) and the constant attention of news photographers to become a sensitive movie actress in *La Vérité* (*The Truth*, 1960), *Le Repos du Guerrier* (*Love on a Pillow*, 1962), *Le Mépris* (*Contempt*, 1963), *Viva Maria* (1965) and *Shalako* (1968). She no longer acts and is now an art collector and a campaigner on various issues.

If movie stars stay young longer than the rest of us, none has held on to youth longer than **Warren Beatty**. He was born on March 30, 1937, in Richmond, Virginia, with the same name (but spelt with only one 't'). His mother was a drama coach. He dropped out of school, then started in TV. His movie debut was unforgettable: in *Splendor in the Grass* (1961), with which he seemed to launch the 1960s almost single handed. He played two major parts for director Arthur Penn, the experimental *Mickey One* (1965) and the epoch-making *Bonnie and Clyde* (1967), which he also produced. He was excellent in *McCabe and Mrs Miller* (1971) and *The Parallax View* (1974), but of late has come to be seen increasingly as a champion of the movies in which he is involved: he produced and co-wrote *Shampoo* (1975), co-wrote, co-produced and co-directed *Heaven Can Wait* (1978) and starred in both. With *Reds* (1981), he gambled everything on a story which seemed out of tune with the times—the life and times of an American communist, John Reed. The film cost a fortune and, luckily, was a triumph. Beatty wrote, produced, directed and starred in it, earning much admiration for his refusal to play it safe.

During the 1960s **Dirk Bogarde** made a transition that few actors achieve: from juvenile lead to mature star. In London on March 28, 1920, Derek Van Den Bogaerde was born of Dutch parents. He started out as a designer, then entered the theatre after World War II. He was taken on as potential star material by Rank, and appeared in a series of truly awful films, becoming, however, quite popular. He made his reputation in the 'Doctor' films in the 1950s, starting with *Doctor in the House* in 1954. At the end of the decade, the parts got better—*A Tale of Two Cities* (1958), in which he played Sidney Carton, *The Wind Cannot Read* the same year, and *Victim* (1961). The decisive turning point, however, was Joseph Losey's *The Servant* (1963). Since then, Bogarde's look of quizzical suffering has brought further distinction to a number of distinguished films all over Europe, including *Justine* (1969), directed by George Cukor; Luchino Visconti's *The Damned* (1969); the same director's *Death in Venice* (1971), Alain Resnais' *Providence* (1977) and Rainer Werner Fassbinder's *Despair* (1978).

For the first half of *Apocalypse Now!* (1979), we see only faded photographs of Colonel Kurtz and hear rumours of his exploits; when we finally see him, a huge figure in a shadowy room, he has acquired almost mythic proportions. No actor could better have embodied Kurtz than **Marlon Brando**, not simply because of his skill as an actor, but because he, too, is something of a myth. Born in Omaha, Nebraska, on April 3, 1924, Brando has three periods as a star: young, mean and sexy, as in *A Streetcar Named Desire* (1951), *The Wild One* and *On the Waterfront* (1954); the complete artist, producing his own films (*One-Eyed Jacks*, 1961) and turning in a series of magnetically quirky performances—in *The Chase* (1966), *Reflections in a Golden Eye* (1967) and *Queimada* (*Burn*, 1969); and finally (to date), Brando the myth, larger than life, dominating the film: *The Godfather*, *Last Tango in Paris* (1972), *The Missouri Breaks* (1976), *Superman* (1978) and *Apocalypse Now!* That is Brando the star; of Brando, the actor, trained at the Actor's Studio in New York and burying himself in his role to a quite exceptional degree, there is a whole different story to be written.

Left: Warren Beatty
Middle: Dirk Bogarde
Right: Marlon Brando

Born Richard Walter Jenkins on November 10, 1925, at Pontrhydfen in South Wales, **Richard Burton** is a star whose stardom has tended to come into conflict with his acting. After a distinguished stage career which began in 1949, he became a Hollywood star in 1952 with *My Cousin Rachel*, following it up in 1953 with *The Robe* in America and *The Desert Rats* in Britain. By the early 1960s, he could command $1 million a picture, but the parts were not that good and the pictures sometimes worse. His romance with Elizabeth Taylor, which started on *Cleopatra* (1963), kept him permanently in the public eye. They were married in 1963, divorced, remarried and finally divorced again in 1976. His finest performances are in *Look Back in Anger* (1959), *Becket* (1964), *The Spy Who Came in from the Cold* (1965), *Who's Afraid of Virginia Woolf* (1966) and *The Assassination of Trotsky* (1972). The period after that was less distinguished until his triumphant return as O'Brien in *1984*, his last role before his death in August that year.

C

One of the biggest surprises of 1972 was **Michael Caine**'s performance in *Sleuth*, a two-hander in which Caine held his own with, and at times outplayed, Sir Laurence Olivier. Born Maurice Micklewhite on March 14, 1933, in the East End of London, Caine had been playing small parts for almost a decade, when he attracted attention in *Zulu* (1964). He followed this up by playing Harry Palmer in *The Ipcress File* (1965), a rundown private eye more worried about paying the bills than getting a licence to kill, and the lead in *Alfie* (1966). International stardom followed, and Caine became a tax exile, preferring Beverly Hills to England. His relaxed charm and sardonic delivery have registered particularly strongly in *The Italian Job* (1969), *Get Carter* (1971), *The Black Windmill* (1974), *The Romantic Englishwoman*, *The Man Who Would Be King* (1975) and *California Suite* (1978).

Born in Assam, India, on April 14, 1941, on her father's tea plantation, **Julie Christie** has lately been using her box-office appeal to back projects in which she believes, e.g. the film version of Doris Lessing's *Memoirs of a Survivor* (1981), in which she starred and the propagandist *The Animal's Film* (same year), which she narrated. She trained at drama school (LAMDA), entered films in 1962 and became a star in *Billy Liar* (1963), as the beautiful girl who gets out. She followed this up with *Darling* (1965), in which she played the archetypal 1960s 'bird', a fashion model whose pursuit of hedonism finally leads to unhappiness. International stardom followed with *Doctor Zhivago* (1965), *Far from the Madding Crowd* (1967) and *The Go-Between* (1971). In the 1970s, she picked her projects carefully: Robert Altman's *McCabe and Mrs Miller* (1971), Nic Roeg's *Don't Look Now* (1973), and two more parts with and for Warren Beatty, with whom she had starred in *McCabe and Mrs Miller*: *Shampoo* (1975), which wasn't really worthy of her, and *Heaven Can Wait* (1978), which was. In 1983, she played the liberated modern woman in James Ivory's *Heat and Dust*, confirming her reputation as a star who sees stardom as carrying a certain responsibility.

Top: Michael Caine
Right: Julie Christie

Left: *Clint Eastwood*

Below: *James Dean*

D Born on February 8, 1931, in Marion, Indiana, **James Byron Dean** soon shook off his reputation as a Marlon Brando clone to become the most enigmatic and enduring youth symbol of the 1950s. This status was enhanced rather than damaged by his death in a car crash on September 30, 1955—a date which carries such an automatic association with that event in the United States that it became the title of a 1977 film about Dean's effect on a generation of American kids. Dean appeared in only three films (not counting three bit parts between 1951 and 1953): *East of Eden* and *Rebel Without a Cause* (1955), and *Giant*, released after his death in 1956, for which his friend Nick Adams had to do some of the sound recording. In all three films, he gives excellent performances, but it is his moody presence and extraordinary charm that accounted—and still accounts—for his fame. More than any other actor of the postwar period, Dean is not just a star, he is a phenomenon.

E 'Clint is the kind of guy,' says a friend, 'you *feel* you know the first time you meet him. To get to know him *properly* takes years.' It is an image that **Clint Eastwood** has cultivated from his days as a spaghetti Western hero through to his reign as America's biggest male box-office draw. Born in San Francisco on May 31, 1930, he was a drifter's son who himself drifted from job to job before using his physique to get into Hollywood in 1955. He was a lab technician in *Revenge of the Creature*, flew a fighter in *Tarantula* (both 1955), then played Rowdy Yates in *Rawhide*. From 1964 to 1966, he was in Italy, where he rather improbably became internationally known for his 'man with no name' roles in *A Fistful of Dollars* (1964), *For a Few Dollars More* (1965) and *The Good, the Bad and the Ugly* (1966). Back in the US, he played action parts, then impersonated Inspector Harry Callahan in *Dirty Harry* (1971), *Magnum Force* (1973), *The Enforcer* (1976) and *Sudden Impact* (1984). Starting with *Play Misty for Me* (1971), he has also directed some memorable films, of which the best is *The Outlaw Josey Wales* (1976), for his own Malpaso Productions. True to his image, he lives in Carmel, California, on the fringes of Big Sur.

From anti-war protests with her husband Tom Hayden, former radical leader and now Democratic politician, to her syndicated Work-Outs, **Jane Fonda,** Henry's daughter, has contrived to keep in the limelight. Born on December 21, 1937, in New York City and educated at Vassar, she then became a model, studied under Lee Strasberg, and hit Hollywood with *Walk on the Wild Side* (1962). She married Roger Vadim in 1965, and he tried to turn her into a sex symbol, most memorably in *Barbarella* (1968). She also starred in Jean-Luc Godard's *Tout Va Bien* (1972). Back in the US, her films improved immeasurably: *Klute* (1971), *Steelyard Blues* (1973), *Julia* (1977), in which she played writer Lilian Hellman, *Coming Home* (1978), *The Electric Horseman, The China Syndrome* (1979) and *On Golden Pond* (1981) in which she appeared with her father.

Above: Jane Fonda
Left: Audrey Hepburn

H Born in Brussels on May 4, 1929, of Dutch and English parents, **Audrey Hepburn** was educated in England, spent the war in Nazi-occupied Holland, studied ballet in London after the war and played bit parts in British movies from 1951 to 1952. She played *Gigi* on Broadway, allegedly at the insistence of author, Colette, and made her first Hollywood film, *Roman Holiday* (1953), winning an Oscar. Her charm came from a beautiful face and a *gamine* body. It seemed, by the time she played Eliza Doolittle in *My Fair Lady* (1964) that she would be eternally a teenager. She was 35 at the time, however, and in 1967 retired from the cinema for nine years, returning to play an ageing, disillusioned Maid Marian in Dick Lester's underrated *Robin and Marian* (1976), opposite a grizzled Sean Connery. Her 'youthful' roles were in *Sabrina* (1954), *War and Peace* (1956), *Funny Face* (1957), *The Nun's Story* (1959) and *The Unforgiven* (1960). In 1961, she played the part most perfectly suited to her: Holly Golightly in *Breakfast at Tiffany's.*

Throughout a career in which his rock-like profile has led to him being cast in a series of rock-like roles, **Charlton Heston** has remained determined to prove that he can *act. Antony and Cleopatra* (1972), which he adapted and directed as well as starred in, was the most extreme example. Born Charles Carter on October 4, 1923, in Evanston, Illinois, Heston really hit the big time as Moses in Cecil B. DeMille's remake of *The Ten Commandments* (1956). He played in a few other epics, notably *Ben-Hur* (1959) and *El Cid* (1961), in both of which he played the title role. He was the victim in *Touch of Evil* (1958), and the granite-faced heavy in *The Big Country* (same year). He was the original visitor to *The Planet of the Apes* (1968), and tended to spend the 1970s in a series of spectacular movies: *Earthquake* (1974) *Airport 1975*, and *Two Minute Warning* (1976). Of late, he has been involved in political activity for the Screen Actors' Guild, and has shown himself a determined man of the Right.

'My friends kept telling me I get handsomer the older I get,' **Dustin Hoffman** once remarked. 'I have no doubt that's true. I had nowhere to go but up.' Born in Los Angeles on August 8, 1937, the son of an avid movie fan who named him after cowboy star Dustin Farnum, Hoffman owes his stardom almost exclusively to his acting ability—a virtually unique distinction. The big break came with *The Graduate* in 1967, in which he played the archetypal adolescent on the edge of adulthood, falling hopelessly and dangerously in love with his girlfriend's mother. Resisting offers to repeat the role, he then played the crippled, aggressive Ratso in *Midnight Cowboy* (1969), the 100-year-old Indian fighter in *Little Big Man* (1970), a myopic convict in *Papillon* (1973), comedian Lenny Bruce in *Lenny* (1974), Watergate reporter Carl Bernstein in *All the President's Men* (1976), petty crook and large-scale loser Max Bembo in *Straight Time* (1977)—his only real commercial failure—the abandoned father in *Kramer vs. Kramer* (1979), and the actor who can only succeed by playing in drag in *Tootsie* (1983). Most stars remain the same. But with Hoffman, it is not possible to talk of a Hoffman film: there is just a minutely researched, overpowering performance.

Below left: Dustin Hoffman

Below right: Charlton Heston

L

Burton Stephen Lancaster—Burt for short—was born in New York City on November 2, 1913, and was one of the first stars to realize the importance of controlling his own career, for which purpose he set up Hecht/Hill/Lancaster with agent Harold Hecht and producer James Hill. A capable acrobat, he made a stunning debut as an actor in *The Killers* (1946), and followed it up with Jules Dassin's *Brute Force* (1947), where he combined the two attributes that would characterize most of his early roles: toughness and sensitivity. He was a major star through the 1950s and 1960s, in such films as *Vera Cruz* (1954), *The Rose Tattoo* (1955), *Gunfight at OK Corral* (1957), and *Sweet Smell of Success* (1957), in which he played a gossip columnist, J. J. Hunsecker. In 1963, he went to Italy for Visconti's *The Leopard*, in which he effortlessly transferred from action roles to a thoughtful one: he was, in fact, every inch novelist Giuseppe di Lampedusa's Sicilian Prince. He played in Visconti's *Conversation Piece* (1975) and was the patriarch in Bernardo Bertolucci's epic *1900* (1976). He won his only Oscar for playing the con man preacher in *Elmer Gantry* (1960) and, in 1983, played the Texan oil tycoon in *Local Hero*.

Below: Burt Lancaster

Above: Rock Hudson

Rock Hudson's screen career is a triumph of looks and determination over native talent. Born Roy Scherer Jr in Winnetka, Illinois, on November 17, 1925, it was his height and his classic, chiselled profile that got him his first parts (in *Fighter Squadron*, 1948, his one-line role allegedly required 38 takes). But by *Bend of the River* (1952), he was likeably competent. And by the time he played the lead in Douglas Sirk's two Universal International melodramas, *Magnificent Obsession* (1954) and *All that Heaven Allows* (1955), there was a genuine power in his acting. In the latter, he plays a gardener who falls in love with an older, richer woman (Jane Wyman) and manages to combine ruggedness with sensitivity. He was equally good in *Giant* the following year (he got an Oscar nomination for it), and at his best in the three comedies he made with Doris Day: *Pillow Talk* (1959), *Lover Come Back* (1962) and *Send Me No Flowers* (1964).

Of late, **Sophia Loren**'s screen career has been rather overshadowed by the legal and religious ins and outs of her marriage to producer Carlo Ponti (the couple were exiled from Italy because Italian law did not recognize Ponti's previous Mexican divorce). But for a while she embodied Italian sex appeal, both in fifteen Italian-made movies, and in a string of American ones, like *The Pride and the Passion* (1957), *Heller in Pink Tights, The Millionairess* (1960) and *El Cid* (1961), in which she played a succession of Latin beauties in scoop-necked blouses or their period equivalent. Born Sofia Scicolone on September 20, 1934, in Rome, she grew up in poverty with an ambitious mother, who entered her in beauty contests and brought her to the attention of producers. Inevitably, perhaps, her two finest roles have been in Italian films: as the mother in De Sica's *La Ciociara* (*Two Women*, 1961), and as the housewife caught up in the events of everyday fascism in Ettore Scola's *Un Certo Giorno* (*One Fine Day*, 1977), set on the day Hitler visited Mussolini.

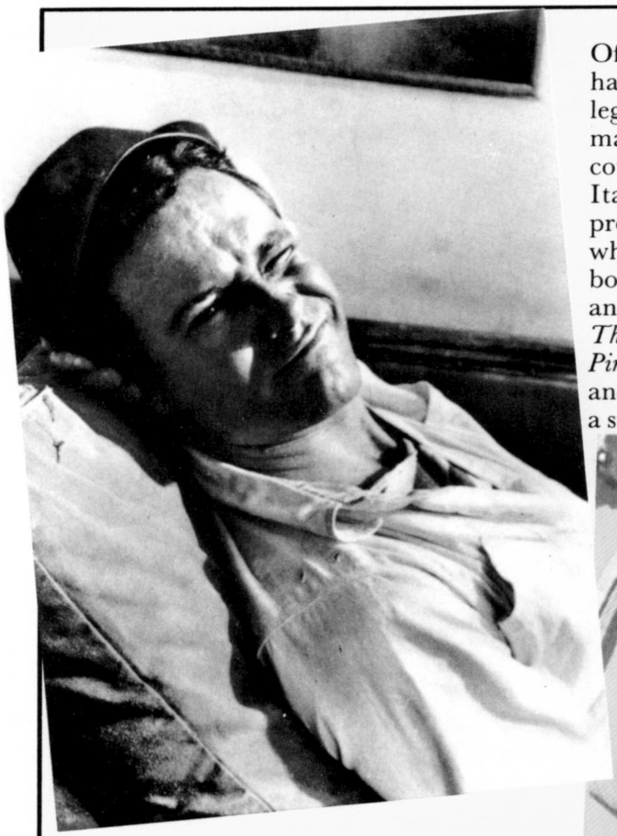

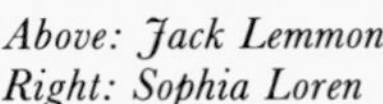

Above: Jack Lemmon
Right: Sophia Loren

Though **Jack Lemmon** (born John Uhler Lemmon III in Boston on February 8, 1925) seemed eternally typecast in variations on Felix, the neurotic, sneezing divorcé he played in the film version of *The Odd Couple* (1968), he was always more than just a comedy actor. He won an Oscar for his (timely) portrayal of a middle-aged, middle class man in crisis in *Save the Tiger* (1973), but long before that he had established a solid career as a serious actor: in *Mister Roberts* (1955), for which he got a Best Supporting Actor Award, in *Cowboy* (1958), in which he played the greenhorn, and above all *Days of Wine and Roses* (1962), in which, opposite Lee Remick, he provided one of the screen's two definitive portraits of alcoholism (the other being Ray Milland in *The Lost Weekend*). The comic roles were never without a strong hint of pathos, especially in *The Apartment* (1960), *The Fortune Cookie* (1966, UK title *Meet Whiplash Willie*), *The Odd Couple, Avanti!* (1972) and *The Prisoner of Second Avenue* (1975). His best roles have so far been, in comedy, *Some Like It Hot* (1959) and, in serious movies, *The China Syndrome* (1979) and *Missing* (1982), where he was not afraid to put his radical principles on the line.

M

Shirley MacLean Beaty, born in Richmond, Virginia, on April 24, 1934, is Warren Beatty's older sister. She started dancing at the age of two, was performing at four, and appeared in several Broadway chorus lines. But her entry into movies is one of those classic tales: she was understudying Carol Haney in *The Pajama Game*, Miss Haney broke her leg, Miss MacLaine went on, producer Hal Wallis was in the audience . . . The first movie part was in Hitchcock's *The Trouble with Harry* (1955). She had major roles in *Some Came Running* (1959), *The Apartment* (1960), *Irma La Douce* (1963), and scored a hit dancing in *Sweet Charity* (1969). In the 1970s, she was more a personality than an actress, doing stage shows and visiting China but she returned in 1983 to take an Oscar for *Terms of Endearment*.

Above: Shirley MacLaine
Right: James Mason

Typecast in Britain as a suave villain, then as top British box-office star of the 1940s, and finally in Hollywood as a soft-spoken romantic lead, **James Mason** has begun to emerge in retrospect as one of the screen's finest actors, notably for his portrayal of Norman Maine in the 'restored' version of the 1954 *A Star is Born*. Born in Huddersfield on May 15, 1909, he studied architecture at Cambridge, went on the stage, then into a string of British 'quota quickies'. His best British role was in *Odd Man Out* (1947), where he played Johnny, the dying gunman on the run. In 1956, he appeared in and also produced *Bigger Than Life*, a propaganda melodrama about the harmful effects of cortisone. From the rest of his vast filmography, it is worth singling out his Captain Nemo in *20,000 Leagues under the Sea* (1954), his elegant villain in *North by Northwest* (1959), Humbert Humbert in *Lolita* (1962), his ever-present Polidoro in the made-for-TV *Frankenstein: The True Story* (1973) and his Mr Jordan in *Heaven Can Wait* (1978). His recently published autobiography is called *Before I Forget*. He died of a heart attack at his home in Switzerland in July 1984.

Marilyn Monroe's life and death are the perfect example of the advantages and the drawbacks of movie stardom. Born Norma Jean Mortenson in Los Angeles on June 1, 1926, she spent part of her childhood in an orphanage, while her mother spent much of it in mental institutions. Norma Jean married at 16 and made her first suicide attempt at 17. With her hair shortened and dyed blonde, she got a contract at 20th Century-Fox in 1946. Her first notable role was in *The Asphalt Jungle* (1950), in which she wasn't very good. She was better in supporting roles in *Clash by Night* and *Monkey Business* (1952). Her first starring role was in *Niagara* (1953), which really launched her career and showed what a fine actress she could be. After that came *Gentlemen Prefer Blondes, How to Marry a Millionaire* (1953), *River of No Return, There's No Business Like Show Business* (1954), *The Seven Year Itch* (1955), *Bus Stop* (1956), *The Prince and the Showgirl* (1957), *Some Like It Hot* (1959), *Let's Make Love* (1960) and *The Misfits* (1961). With the first four, she struggled against roles which cast her as dumb and bubbly, but with *Seven Year Itch, Some Like It Hot* and *The Misfits*, she at last had material worthy of her. She married aircraft worker Jim Dougherty in 1942, baseball player Joe Di Maggio in 1954 and playwright Arthur Miller in 1955. In July 1962, she was fired from *Something's Got to Give* for persistent absence from the set, and was found dead from an overdose of barbiturates, on August 5, 1962.

Top: Jack Nicholson
Right: Marilyn Monroe

N

From an unforgettable supporting role as the small-town lawyer who tags along with the bikers in *Easy Rider* (1969), **Jack Nicholson** (born Neptune, New Jersey, April 22, 1937) finally achieved stardom in the 1970s as the sort of hero best suited to the decade: complex, aggressive, insecure and always on the verge of walking away. He had been in B pictures since 1958 (he is, among other things, the dental patient who loves his pain in *The Little Shop of Horrors*, 1961 and the improbable juvenile lead in *The Terror*, 1962). His first major role was as the drop-out son of a rich, cultured family in *Five Easy Pieces* (1970), for which he got an Oscar nomination. After turning in a series of fine performances in *Carnal Knowledge* (1971), *The King of Marvin Gardens* (1972), *The Last Detail* (1973), *Chinatown* (1974), *Tommy, The Passenger* and *The Fortune* (1975), he finally got his Oscar for *One Flew over the Cuckoo's Nest* (1975), which probably remains his most popular film. After directing a few scenes in *The Terror* uncredited, he directed his first feature with *Drive, He Said* (about basketball) in 1971, and his second, *Goin' South* in 1978. His other roles since *Cuckoo's Nest* have included *The Missouri Breaks, The Last Tycoon* (1976), *The Shining* (1979), *The Border* (1981) and *Terms of Endearment* (1983).

At times, **Paul Newman** seems almost too good to be true: blue-eyed, talented, sensitive and a US delegate to a UN conference on disarmament. He is very much a star for the 1960s and 1970s, combining all the old star charisma with a commitment that shines through as much in his roles as in his personal life. Born on January 26, 1925, in Cleveland, he studied at Yale and at the Actor's Studio (the home of The Method) before entering movies inauspiciously in 1955. His second role, though—that of Rocky Graziano in *Somebody up there Likes Me* (1955)—clinched it: an actor well able to handle himself, but with *feeling*. He got an award at Cannes for *The Long Hot Summer* (1958), and took over a role intended for Brando in *The Left-Handed Gun* (same year). He has directed four movies, *Rachel, Rachel* (1968), *Sometimes a Great Notion* (1971), *The Effect of Gamma Rays on Man-in-the-Moon Marigolds* (1972), *Harry and Son* (1984) and a TV movie, *The Shadow Box* (1981), three of them with his wife, Joanne Woodward. His own most memorable roles include *The Hustler* (1961), *Sweet Bird of Youth* (1962), *Hud* (1963), *Cool Hand Luke* (1967), *Butch Cassidy and the Sundance Kid* (1969, which he also produced), *The Sting* (1973), *The Towering Inferno* (1974), *Slapshot* (1977) and *The Verdict* (1982).

O

An actor with a reputation for raising hell, **Peter O'Toole** has passed from handsome, blue-eyed hero to larger-than-life character actor almost before one's eyes. Born on August 2, 1932, in Connemara but brought up in Leeds, he had a distinguished stage career, notably at the Bristol Old Vic, before rocketing to stardom in his fourth feature, *Lawrence of Arabia* (1962). Other major roles in a remarkably uneven movie career have included *Becket* (1964), in which he played Henry II to Burton's Becket, *The Night of the Generals, Casino Royale* (1967), *The Lion in Winter* (1968), in which he played Henry II again, *Man of La Mancha* (1972), *The Stuntman* (1978–81) and *My Favourite Year* (1982), in which he played a fading movie star with a drink problem. Perhaps the best measure of O'Toole's career is his 1981 stage portrayal of Macbeth: the show was panned so universally that O'Toole was able to turn it into a personal and commercial triumph, the man once more winning out over the performance.

Above: Peter O'Toole
Left: Paul Newman

P

Eldred Gregory Peck, born on April 5, 1916, at La Jolla, California, and educated at the University of San Diego and, briefly, at the Berkeley Medical School before he turned to acting, is a case of the nice guy becoming a star. He was around at the right time, too: turned down by the military because of a spinal injury incurred while rowing at college, he became a star when many other actors were still in uniform. His first movie was *Days of Glory* (1944), and by the following year he had hit the big time with *Spellbound*. He got his Oscar for *To Kill a Mockingbird* (1962), and has been active in a number of artistic and humanitarian roles. His movie roles have tended towards the stolid, from *Duel in the Sun* (1947) via *The Big Country* (1958), *On the Beach* (1959) and *The Guns of Navarone* (1961) to *I Walk the Line* (1970) and *The Omen* (1976). But his palpable sincerity has always carried him through, even when, in the last mentioned film, he turned out to be foster father to the Devil.

Q

Always a somewhat larger-than-life figure, **Anthony Quinn** has of late slid easily into the role of international patriarch and art patron, making pronouncements on various subjects. Born in Chihuahua of Irish-Mexican parents on April 21, 1915, he played heavies through the late 1930s and early 1940s, despite being married to Cecil B. DeMille's (adopted) daughter, Katherine. Nonetheless, he is memorable as Chief Crazy Horse (Hollywood's Mexicans often got to play Indians) in *They Died with their Boots On* (1941) and *Buffalo Bill* (1944). His first major role was as Brando's brother in *Viva Zapata*! (1952), but his two best roles of the 1950s were as Gauguin in Vincente Minnelli's 1956 *Lust for Life* and as the morose but sentimental strongman, Zampano, in Federico Fellini's *La Strada* (1954). The part for which he will always be remembered, though, is the title role of *Zorba the Greek* (1964).

R

Robert Redford has one of the most important of all star requirements: he can be all things to all people. In pin-up terms, he is a blond-haired, blue-eyed hunk, the ideal product of his birthplace (Santa Monica, California, on August 18, 1937), who went through College on a sports scholarship. For more detailed identification, he is the cool, principled loner, who refuses to compromise. To cap it all, he is an art student, who has ploughed money into ecological and cultural institutions like the Sundance Institute in Utah and who is the author of a history of the West. He first attracted notice in *The Chase* and *This Property is Condemned* (1966), shot to stardom in *Butch Cassidy and the Sundance Kid* (1969) and confirmed it in *The Sting* (1973). Other major roles include *Downhill Racer* (1969), which he produced, *Tell Them Willie Boy is Here* (1970), *The Candidate, Jeremiah Johnson* (1972), *The Way We Were* (1973), *The Great Gatsby* (1974), *The Great Waldo Pepper* (1975), *All the President's Men* (1976), *The Electric Horseman* and *Brubaker* (1979). He directed *Ordinary People* (1980) and got an Oscar.

Left: Gregory Peck. Below: Robert Redford. Above: Anthony Quinn

S At the beginning of *Patton* (1970), the hero of the picture is shown in low angle against a huge American flag, addressing the troops in his usual belligerent tone. It was the perfect role for **George C. Scott**, not because he shared Patton's view of life, but because the film required the kind of bravura performance that has become his trademark. Born in Wise, Virginia, on October 18, 1927, George C. Scott (the 'C' stands for Campbell) spent four years in the Marines, and didn't get into films until he was in his 30s, playing in *The Hanging Tree* and *Anatomy of a Murder* in 1959. He was unforgettable as General Turgidson in *Dr Strangelove* (1964), the jingoistic militarist for whom twenty million American deaths amounted to 'getting our hair mussed'. And he has been repeatedly unforgettable ever since, in *Jane Eyre*, *The Hospital* (1971), *The New Centurions* (1972), *The Day of the Dolphin* (1973), *Islands in the Stream* (1977), *Hardcore* (UK: *The Hardcore Life,* 1979) and *Oliver Twist* (1982). Having denounced Awards as a 'meat parade', he won an Oscar for *Patton* and an Emmy for *The Price*. He refused to collect either. He is married to actress Trish Van Devere.

Watching **Peter Sellers** on a TV chat show was like watching a man in hiding from himself, a man who used funny voices and an enormous range of 'characters' as a barrier against the world. Born Richard Henry Sellers on September 8, 1925, in Southsea, he was a camp entertainer in the RAF, then a household voice in the radio series, *The Goon Show*. He entered films in 1951, but didn't really come to prominence until *I'm All Right Jack* in 1959, the Boulting comedy in which he played a self-important union leader. He was a mainstay of British comedy in such films as *The Mouse that Roared, The Battle of the Sexes* (1959), *Two-Way Stretch, Never Let Go* and *The Millionairess* (1960), playing an Indian doctor in the latter, then he did his first major serious role as Quilty in Stanley Kubrick's *Lolita* (1962), and became a major star in the same director's *Dr Strangelove* (1964), in which he played the title role, an RAF officer *and* the President of the United States. His last film was *Being There* in 1979, but his best partnership was with director Blake Edwards in *The Party* (1968), where he was an Indian again, and in the Clouseau films: *The Pink Panther* (1964), *The Return of the Pink Panther* (1975), *The Pink Panther Strikes Again* (1976), *Revenge of the Pink Panther* (1978) and even a posthumous *Curse of the Pink Panther* (1982), with out-takes and a stand-in.

Robert Stack is going to be remembered for three things: his eyes (he has the most piercing eyes in the business), his screen debut (he was 'the first boy to kiss Deanna Durbin' in *First Love* in 1939) and his long-running performance as Eliot Ness in *The Untouchables*, 114 episodes of which were aired on ABC-TV between October 1959 and September 1963, and which have been repeated late-night ever since. Born in Los Angeles on January 13, 1919, he has been in over 40 films, including a TV spin-off, *The Scarface Mob* (1962). He played the lead in *John Paul Jones* (1959), got an Oscar nomination as the ineffective husband with a closet full of mental skeletons in *Written on the Wind* (1957) and was memorable also in *The Bullfighter and the Lady* (1951), *House of Bamboo* (1955) and *The Tarnished Angels* (1958). During the 1960s and 1970s he appeared regularly in French and Italian films—but returned to Hollywood for *1941* (1979).

Left: Peter Sellers. Above: George C. Scott. Below: Robert Stack

Ever since he played Brando's older brother in *On the Waterfront* (1954), **Rodney Stephen Steiger** has been turning in performances so intense that every one seems designed to strengthen his grip on a reputation as one of the modern screen's great actors. He was born on April 14, 1925, in Westhampton, New York and *On the Waterfront* was his second film. This was followed by Jud (as in (*Poor Jud Is Dead*) in *Oklahoma*! and with his manic movie producer, Stanley Hoff, in *The Big Knife*, both in 1955. Since then, major roles have been the Southerner who 'becomes' an Indian in *Run of the Arrow* (1957), the title role in *Al Capone* (1959), the corrupt politician Nottola in Francesco Rosi's *Le Mani sulla Citta* (*Hands over the City*, 1963), *The Pawnbroker*, the opportunist Komarovsky in *Dr Zhivago* (both 1965), *The Illustrated Man* (1969), Napoleon in the Russian-Italian co-production *Waterloo* (1970), Mussolini in the Italian *Mussolini: Ultimo Atto* (1974), W. C. Fields in *W. C. Fields and Me* (1976) and the renegade, exorcising priest in *The Amityville Horror* (1979). The strongest image of all, though, is of him as the Southern police chief in *In the Heat of the Night* (1967), for which he won an Oscar.

Barbra Streisand was, for many people, *the* star of the 1970s, as much at home as a singer who could sell out concerts and make gold albums as she was as an actress, producer and general film person. Born Barbara (with the middle 'a') Joan Streisand in Brooklyn on April 24, 1942, she tied with Katharine Hepburn for the Oscar in her very first movie, *Funny Girl* (1968), a repeat of her Broadway role. Since then she has been in musicals *Hello, Dolly*! (1969), *On a Clear Day You Can See Forever* (her only flop, in 1970) and *Funny Lady* (1975), as a comedy actress in *The Owl and the Pussycat* (1970), *What's Up Doc?* and *For Pete's Sake* (1972 and 1974), and in serious roles (*The Way We Were*, 1973, and *A Star is Born*, 1977). In 1982, she finally got the go-ahead on one of her most cherished projects: to produce, direct, star and sing in *Yentl*. Eighteen months in the making, the movie was a triumph proving that one of the most evident characteristics of her screen personality—an obstinate determination not to play it safe—belongs as much to her as to the parts she has played.

Top: Rod Steiger
Left: Barbra Streisand

Above: John Wayne
Left: Elizabeth Taylor

T Perhaps unfairly, **Elizabeth Taylor**'s notoriety as a marriage addict, diamond owner and explosive public personality has overshadowed her career as an actress. Unfairly, because Miss Taylor (born on February 27, 1932, in London) has turned in some truly fine performances in her time. Her American parents returned to the US in 1939, and she grew up in Los Angeles. She began as a child performer in *Lassie Come Home* (1943), *Jane Eyre* and *National Velvet* (1944). At 17, she was in MGM's remake of *Little Women* (1949), as Meg, but her adult roles are the ones for which she deserves to be remembered: *Giant* (1956), *Cat on a Hot Tin Roof* (1958), *Suddenly Last Summer* (1959), *Who's Afraid of Virginia Woolf* (1966), for which she got her second Oscar (her first was for *Cleopatra* in 1963), and *Reflections in a Golden Eye* (1967). Her Martha in *Virginia Woolf* is especially memorable because, perhaps for the first time, she allows herself to appear unattractive (something of a feat) and throws herself into the part. Her last film was *A Little Night Music* in 1977, which passed largely unnoticed. Her marriages have been to Nick Hilton (of the hotels), actor Michael Wilding, showman Mike Todd, singer Eddie Fisher, Richard Burton (twice) and US Senator John Warner.

'Whatever one may feel about **John Wayne**'s political opinions,' said left-wing French director Jean-Luc Godard, 'it is impossible not to love him when he lifts up Natalie Wood in *The Searchers*.' It is that quality, overriding Wayne's public stance as a right-wing activist (and, in *The Green Berets*, 1969, defender of US intervention in Vietnam), which helped make him one of cinema's biggest stars. Born Marion Michael Morrison on May 26, 1907, in Winterset, Iowa, his movie career spanned just under 50 years. As a football star at the University of Southern California, he worked summers on the Fox lot and became friendly with director John Ford. Throughout the 1930s, after starring in *The Big Trail* (1930), he played the lead in 80 B Westerns, before getting back to major stardom again as The Ringo Kid in *Stagecoach* (1939), which Ford directed. From then he was one of Hollywood's biggest stars. He won only one Oscar, as Marshall Rooster Cogburn in *True Grit* (1969), a part which he reprised in his penultimate film in 1975. Known universally as 'The Duke', his favourite film was the one he produced, directed and starred in, *The Alamo* (1960). His last twenty years were dogged by 'the big C' (cancer) of which he died in 1979.

A 'fabricated' star, whose career has similarities with that of Marilyn Monroe (though without the tragic part), **Raquel Welch** was born Raquel Tejada in Chicago on September 5, 1940. She studied drama at San Diego State and played bit parts until ex-child actor and press agent Patrick Curtis took her career in hand, launching her as the sex symbol of the 1960s, starting with *Fantastic Voyage* and *One Million Years B.C.* in 1966. The constant barrage of sexy publicity photos tended to obscure the fact that she could act, which she showed in *Kansas City Bomber* (1972), a somewhat personal project made after she split with Curtis. Despite fair performances in *The Three Musketeers* (1974) and *The Four Musketeers* (1975) as Constance, she has never been able to overcome the early image of a busty pin-up. A world tour to prove she could be a live entertainer in the early 1980s was a disaster, not so much because she was a bad performer as because the press was determined to punish her for trying to be good.

Right: Raquel Welch

INDEX

(Figures in **bold** refer to main entries; figures in *italics* to illustrations. Film titles are also indicated by *italics*.)

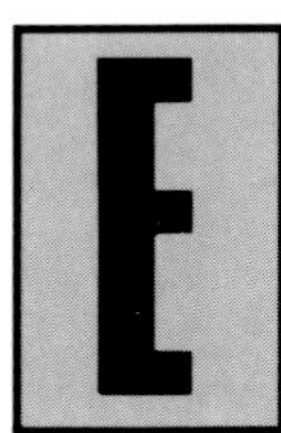

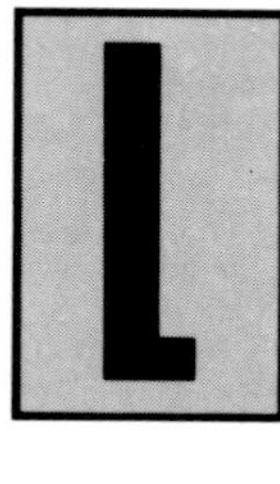

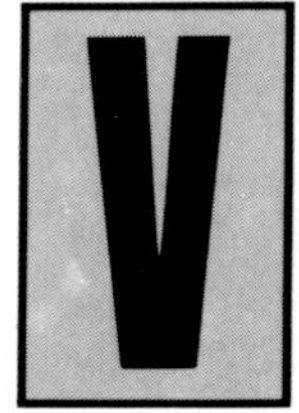

Acknowledgments

The publishers would like to express their thanks to the following individuals and organisations for their kind permission to reproduce the photographs in this book:
Allied Artists, Aquarius Film and Literary Agency, Art Directors Photo Library, Columbia Pictures, Ronald Grant Archive, Joel Finler Collection, The Kobal Collection, London Pictures, M.G.M., Paramount Studios, R.K.O., Twentieth Century Fox, Universal Studios, United Artists, Warner Brothers.
Every effort has been made to trace the copyright holders of the pictures in this book, but the publishers would be pleased to hear from any not listed.

Contents

Picture Credits: R. J. Corbin: cover; I.G.D.A.: 10, 11, 12, 73, 120, 121, 178, 181, 193, 202; M. Bavestrelli: 21, 49, 74, 84, 85, 102, 114, 115, 136, 156, 199, 200; C. Bevilacqua: 4, 5, 15, 16, 26, 29, 30, 31, 33, 37, 38, 39, 42, 44, 52, 53, 54, 66, 67, 69, 70, 75, 76, 80, 94, 97, 98, 99, 107, 109, 118, 119, 128, 130, 135, 140, 141, 142, 143, 146, 147, 149, 150, 151, 153, 155, 158, 160, 161, 162, 163, 165, 166, 174, 175, 177, 179, 183, 185, 188, 211; Bravo: 137, 138, 144, 145; E.P.S.: 19, 65, 72, 77, 81, 111, 148, 168, 189, 194, 207; Etrusko: 2, 3, 7, 8, 13, 27, 28, 35, 40, 41, 43, 56, 60, 61, 91, 92, 96, 100, 112, 122, 134, 180, 198; Ingegnoli: 71, 167, 171, 173; P. Martini: 9, 45, 78, 93, 152, 172, 196, 201, 204, 206, 210; G. Mazza: 36, 63, 95, 117; M. Pedone: 1, 14, 57, 68, 89, 90, 110, 123, 132, 133, 157, 176, 184, 208, 209; P 2: 6, 17, 18, 20, 22, 23, 24, 25, 32, 34, 46, 47, 48, 50, 51, 55, 58, 59, 62, 64, 79, 82, 83, 86, 87, 88, 101, 103, 104, 105, 106, 108, 113, 116, 124, 125, 126, 127, 129, 131, 139, 154, 159, 164, 169, 170, 182, 186, 187, 190, 191, 192, 195, 197, 203, 205, 212, 213.

Adapted from the Italian of Uberto Tosco
Edited by Francis C. Stark, Conrad B. Link and Edwin Packer

Printed in Italy by IGDA, Officine Grafiche, Novara

SBN 85613 168 7

Garden flowers

What would surprise many British gardeners who took the trouble to trace the ancestry of the flowers in their garden would be that the majority of plants originated in other countries. This will become apparent when reading the information accompanying the colour photographs that make up the bulk of this book. True, these popular flowers have been acclimatized, and hybrids and many varieties have been grown by horticulturists in this country. The dahlia, for example, originated in Mexico in the high mountains where temperatures are similar to those of the average British summer. And so the dahlia is an outdoor and not a greenhouse plant as one might have expected on learning that it came from Mexico. Many other garden favourites—eschscholtzias, godetias, clarkias and lupins—are from California, another sunny region of the Americas.

Growing in the wild, as most of these plants do in their natural state, they produce flowers that are very pretty but not necessarily either large or with a wide range of colour. Looking at a beautiful flower garden often leads the visitor to give voice to the truism "Isn't Nature wonderful", when in fact he should be paying tribute as well to the skill and patience of the men who have improved on Nature's work.

Plants in the wild usually reproduce themselves by seeding, and so the same characteristics are retained year after year. What the horticulturalist does is to cross-pollinate two species of the same family—possibly from different parts of the world—to produce a hybrid. This is a new flower; usually it is more vigorous in growth and almost certainly more colourful and with larger blooms than the parent plants. Double flowers resulted in this way, for they are not to be seen in the wild. More will be said about this process of selection and hybridization in a later section. The purpose of referring to it here is to remind readers of the great debt we owe first to the botanists who travelled all over the world looking for new plants, and secondly to the horticulturalists who, once they had the seed, spent years producing the many beautiful hybrids and varieties that today add colour to our gardens.

The most ancient writings about garden flowers date back to more than 4,000 years ago. It is known that the Chinese were cultivating chrysanthemums about 2,500 years before the Christian era. It is also known that the Egyptians grew lotus flowers, papyrus, myrtle and pomegranates. The Persians and the Babylonians were well acquainted with the culture of roses and violets. Pliny the Younger in the first century A.D. wrote about the culture of lilies, narcissus, cyclamens and cornflowers.

Although civilization declined in the Middle Ages, an interest in gardening persisted and whenever people returned from voyages to distant lands they brought back information on exotic flowers. And as has been said, botanists and explorers brought back to Europe seeds and bulbs of new plants, so that soon the gardens of France, Italy, Spain and England were ornamented with rare plants from the rest of the known world.

It was thus that our floricultural inheritance slowly grew rich. Alongside European flowers, such as the cornflowers and violets, already improved beyond their wild state, appeared geraniums from South Africa, hyacinths from the Orient, petunias from America and poppies from Asia, as well as those mentioned earlier.

Thus the number of garden flowers—those which we illustrate here, not including woody plants or shrubs—increased rapidly and today continues to increase. The number of species and cultivated varieties (more correctly called "cultivars") runs into tens of thousands.

So we can cater for our varying tastes, but the choice is limited by climatic adaptation of the species, unless the plant's natural conditions can be artificially reproduced. With correct cultural practice and protection it is possible to have tropical plants in gardens located in temperate regions, even though they can live outside, unprotected, for only a short season.

What kind of plants do well in town gardens where air pollution does far more damage to living things than in the country? The list is more extensive than might be imagined: gladioli, hollyhocks, geraniums, calceolarias, dahlias, antirrhinums, June-flowering iris and michaelmas daisies. For shady gardens—and many town gardens come into this category—choose lilies, primulas, blue poppies, hardy ferns, daffodils and hardy cypripediums. Some plants that are usually grown in sunny beds and borders also do well in the shade. Among these are phlox, lupins, senecio, tall aconitums, some campanulas, astilbes and spiraeas.

It is possible in gardens in the south or those that are sheltered from the wind to grow flowers outdoors that bloom in winter, so a winter flower garden can be considered when taking over a garden. Lenten roses (*Helleborus orientalis*) do well in the shade and on the north side of a hedge or wall. The common primrose, planted in groups for effect, gives a show of colour at Christmas as do some primulas such as *Primula Winteri*. The Rob Roy red double daisy is another that can be recommended for winter blooming.

Even a small garden can have a greenhouse or garden frame to maintain suitable temperatures for growing seedlings, unless one wants to grow only the simpler plants that are adapted to germinate and continue all their life cycle outdoors. There are plenty of these, of course, especially annuals such as petunias, poppies, daisies, pansies and many others.

People who buy an old town house often find that the garden is not doing very well. All the goodness in the soil has been used up years ago, or washed away. The soil cannot be restored to good health immediately; it will take several years. A pH test would be advisable in such circumstances before commencing to add the humus, leaf mould and manure that will return fertility to the soil. How this is best done is considered in the next section.

Soil

In addition to ecological and climatic influences, there are two other factors of importance in growing garden flowers: soil and water.

Plants are living organisms, often delicate, and each species performs best in a particular type of soil. The characteristics of the soil determine its water-holding capacity, so that moisture requirements are related to the types of soil in the garden.

So basic to the success of any garden is good soil. Yet the quality of the soil is rarely taken into account when buying or renting a house, and the garden must start with the soil as it is. Some soil problems are the result of building the house when heavy equipment is used on the plot during rainy periods. Spreading of excavated earth over the top soil, and leaving bricks and rubble about are but two building practices that give the gardener a lot of hard work.

The ideal garden soil is a sandy loam, loam, or silt loam, having one per cent or more organic matter and a pH of 6.0 to 6.5. The pH formula is used to express the acidity or alkalinity of the soil; pH7 is the neutral point, below it being acid and above it alkaline.

Some ericaceous plants, such as azaleas, prefer a soil pH of 5.0, although most plants thrive best at pH 6.0 to 6.5. Soils low in pH can be limed for correction, but a pH test should be performed to determine the amount of lime needed. These tests are performed by many agencies; the gardener can get details by writing to a gardening magazine.

Soils having pH 7.0 or higher can be corrected by the addition of sulphur, but the usual thing is to grow those plants that do well on high-calcium soils.

Soils low in organic matter can be improved by the addition of organic materials, but the basic texture of the soil cannot be materially changed except at great expense. Soils are composed of particles of sand, silt and clay. It is the mix of these particles that determines soil texture. A loam will contain about 20 to 25 per cent sand, 20 to 50 per cent silt, and 8 to 28 per cent clay. A sandy loam contains more sand and less silt and clay. A silt loam contains more silt and less sand than a loam. Sandy soils are considered "light" and easiest to manage, while those with higher percentages of clay are called "heavy" and are more difficult to manage. The heaviest soils, the clays and the clay loams, present special problems to the gardener, but can be improved in time by incorporation of sand and organic materials. Sandy soils can best be improved by using practices designed to increase the organic matter content.

Organic materials most commonly used to enhance the soil texture and to increase water-holding capacity are compost, leaves and peat moss.

Compost is made by building a pile of alternate layers of soil and organic matter—leaves, garden refuse, straw, animal manures or any inexpensive organic material. Six to eight months after such a pile has been constructed, it is ready to use. Fertilizers such as superphosphate and some nitrogen forms may be included as the pile is built.

Leaves and peat moss are used as a mulch for the soil, and should be applied thickly enough to inhibit weed growth. When the garden is reworked the following spring for the new crop of annuals, these materials are turned under and a new mulch applied after planting. After a few years, this practice will materially improve most soils.

Watering the garden

That water is indispensable to plants is obvious when one realizes that most vegetative tissues are 85 to 95 per cent water. Water should never be lacking otherwise the plants will wilt, and should wilting be prolonged death of the plant may result.

Annual plants with succulent leaves, such as cinerarias and calceolarias, are especially subject to desiccation, while those with small leaves and stiff stems, such as carnations, are much more tolerant. Those plants with tubers, rhizomes, or bulbs are most tolerant to drought, since their underground stems serve as a reserve for water and minerals.

The amount of water needed by various flowering species is extremely variable. Some plants are hygrophytic (requiring a large amount of water), mesophytic (having a moderate water requirement), or xerophytic (that is, thriving under very dry conditions).

The amount of water needed varies also with the climatic, regional, and seasonal conditions, and depends upon the soil texture and organic matter content as well as upon the nature of the subsoil.

Generally in small gardens the amount of water needed is modest and an inch of rainfall or a watering every five to seven days should be adequate. The soil should be kept loose and permeable by weeding and tilling to prevent the formation of surface crusting.

Hand weeding is best for the maintenance of the water balance of cultivated ground, since the invading plants often absorb more water than the flowering plants. Drought is especially dangerous when seedlings are very small and therefore tender and delicate. Overwatering is equally dangerous.

To avoid extreme transpiration and to inhibit weed growth, a mulch of leaves, peat moss or straw is desirable.

Watering may be done at any time, but mid-afternoon watering should be discouraged in areas of high light intensity. Droplets on the leaves after watering may act like small magnifying glasses and concentrate the sun's rays, resulting in localized leaf burn.

The use of fertilizers

Referring earlier to the various types of soil, organic matter and pH were mentioned as being of importance in the cultivation of plants. But soils contain numerous chemical elements, present in greater or lesser quantities, including calcium, nitrogen, potassium, phosphorus, manganese, iron, sulphur, magnesium, boron, copper, zinc, molybdenum, bromine, tungsten and silicon. Some are indispensable to plant growth, whereas others, such as the last three named, are unnecessary to plants. These compounds are also present in organic residues.

Nitrogen, phosphorus and potassium are the three nutrient elements that are most commonly lacking in soil and so are added as fertilizers. They can be added in a dry form as the soil is prepared or in a liquid form after the plant has been planted. The liquid types are water soluble and should be applied according to the manufacturer's instructions. The inorganic fertilizers, in either the dry or liquid form, may supply only one element or, in certain cases, two elements. Commercial mixtures generally supply the three nutrient elements named and often include one or more of the trace elements such as iron, boron or manganese which, in very minute quantities, are necessary for plant growth.

The inorganic fertilizers are the least expensive to use when based on the amount of nutrients they supply. Organic fertilizers are not available to the plant until they have been decomposed.

Inorganic fertilizer sources are those manufactured especially or are by-products of certain manufacturing processes. These include ammonium sulphate, calcium sulphate, soldium nitrate, ammonium nitrate and urea that supply nitrogen; superphosphate that supplies phosphorus; and potassium chloride or potassium sulphate that supply potassium.

The inorganic fertilizers are produced primarily as a by-product from certain animals. Organic nitrogen sources include horn and hoof shavings, dried blood and fish meal; phosphorus may be supplied from bonemeal; and wood ashes are an organic source of potassium. Organic fertilizers may vary slightly from time to time in the exact amount of fertilizer element they supply, and may actually contribute traces of some other elements when decomposing. This is due to the process employed when making the fertilizer.

Lime is not considered to be a fertilizer; its value is that it makes the soil less acid and helps improve soil structure. Calcium becomes available to the plant from the lime incorporated in the soil.

Animal manures are not easily obtained and vary in fertility value which is influenced by the kind of animal, its diet, the amount of bedding material included and the care of the manure before application to the soil. The greatest value of manure is not as a fertilizer, but rather as a source of organic matter which improves soil structure.

For the average gardener it will probably be convenient to use commercially-prepared fertilizers, which are usually mixtures of materials that supply nitrogen, phosphorus and potassium and are referred to as "complete fertilizers". Three types are available. A dry form is mixed into the soil in advance of planting or is used as a top dressing. Liquid types are water soluble materials that can be dissolved in water and applied to the soil in the concentration required.

A third type is the slow-release or slow-acting kind that is mixed into the soil and remains effective for many months. One form is a soluble material encapsulated in a plastic material which, when in contact with the soil moisture, gradually releases the fertilizer that is then available to the plant.

Seeding

Almost every plant that bears flowers can be reproduced by seed, because this is the natural process for its reproduction. In gardening practice it is often easier to propagate some flowering plants vegetatively, that is by cuttings, grafting or layering; these methods are discussed later.

Propagation by seed is the best way to grow annual flowers. Annuals are the easiest of all plants to grow, and they require no care or space when flowering has ended since they die after completing their life cycle. To this group, with some exceptions, belong the morning glories, marigolds, pansies, petunias, poppies, zinnias and many other beautiful flowers.

Biennial plants—those that complete their life cycle in two years—are also reproduced by seed. In certain cases they live longer than two years and are sometimes propagated by cuttings.

Perennials are hardier plants that usually live for several years and can be reproduced by seed. Often they are increased by cuttings, especially in cases in which flowers do not bear seeds to maturation, such as the fuchsias, or are sterile or do not produce seed.

Some seeds are sown in the area where they are to grow. Plants that do not transplant easily are handled in this way. Among ornamental plants, this method is necessary for only a few kinds of annuals. Most seed is sown in a medium that is loose, porous, well aerated and yet will hold water. Such a medium can be prepared by mixing soil with organic matter and perhaps some inert material. In outdoor beds this may be accomplished by selecting a suitable spot with well-drained soil. Mixtures of materials include peat and perlite, peat and vermiculite, or other mixtures that include soil, sand or similar inert substances.

Seed may be sown in beds out of doors or in the home at a window, in a greenhouse or in protective frames such as a cold frame or hot bed. It should be scattered over the seed bed uniformly and then be lightly covered. Tiny seeds such as those of begonia, calceolaria, petunia or azalea are not covered, but are merely pressed into the soil. For seed of this kind, covering the soil with a thin layer of finely-screened sphagnum makes a good material for the seed. When the seed has germinated, thin out the weak seedlings and those that are crowded to allow those remaining to have greater space for development. When the seedlings have developed their first true leaf they are ready for transplanting. Transplant them to seed beds, spacing them to allow for development and then later transplant them again to where they are to grow. Or they may be transplanted to pots, seed trays or other containers. Rapidly-growing kinds are often transplanted from the seed bed to the place where they are to grow to maturity.

In recent years the use of pelleted seed has grown, both in commercial horticulture and domestic gardening. Pellets make seeds much easier to handle and sow, consequently less thinning is necessary and there is less waste of seed. A prerequisite for success with pelleted seed is moist soil, for moisture causes the pellet covering to disintegrate so that germination can commence. Watering is therefore essential before and after sowing.

Transplanting

When sowing is completed, germination will take place within a few days for annuals, or may require several weeks with certain perennials and woody plants. Just after emerging from the soil the new plants are extremely delicate, and sudden, extreme changes in temperature must be avoided, as should exposure to full sun or excessive water.

As soon as the plants begin to grow they show the morphological characteristics of the species to which they belong. They can be distinguished from any other plants that may surround them which have sprung from seeds already present in the sowing medium or perhaps from seeds mixed with the seed sown.

Weeds must be removed with care; this is most easily done at the time of thinning or transplanting.

Thinning is required to give space to seedlings that spring up too closely to each other. This can be done by transplanting the seedlings into separate pots. Sometimes it is convenient to transplant seedlings to their permanent site outdoors. The operation must be done with some care to avoid bruising or breaking the young plants.

To remove a plant from a pot it is advisable to overturn it, keeping the stem between the fingers and tapping lightly on the sides of the pot in order to remove the ball of soil.

Thinning is best done during the cooler hours of the day. Afterwards, the soil should be firmed gently around the plants and they should be sprinkled lightly. Thinned or transplanted seedlings should be protected from direct sunlight for two days.

Vegetative propagation

Since plants produced from seed may not come true-to-type or may require too long a period of time before coming into flower or developing mature characteristics, a vegetative method is often used. Plants vary in the part of the plant that may be used for propagation; depending on the kind of plant it may be the stem, the leaves or the roots. In some plants vegetative methods merely use the parts of the plant that naturally account for the increase, such as the bulbs, tubers, rhizomes, stolons or off-shoot runners. Propagation may also be achieved by dividing the plant; this involves its separation into smaller parts by layering, by grafting or by budding.

Tubers, bulbs, rhizomes and runners are all essentially modified stems that have the ability to produce new roots when they are separated from the mother plant. When they are removed they already have the beginnings of new roots and are ready for replanting.

Layering is a form of propagation where a branch is bent down to the soil and covered, leaving the tip exposed. Often a wound is made in the stem portion that is covered. After roots develop, the branch is cut at the end nearest the parent and the new plant is replanted. Air layering is a method often used on foliage plants that have become too tall. A wound is made in the stem, a bit of wood is placed in the cut to hold it open and the wound is dusted with a root-promoting hormone. The entire area is covered with moist sphagnum moss and wrapped with plastic or aluminium foil. The moss must be kept moist. After roots have grown into the moss, the stem is severed below this area and the tip (now with roots) is potted as a new plant. Air layering may be used on a few woody plants outdoors.

Cuttings are perhaps the most common method of vegetative propagation. Cuttings are made from strong, healthy stems. The tip is used generally with 3 to 4 nodes, varying with the kind of plant, and often similar sections of the lower portions of the stem can be selected as well. The season of propagation varies with the plant. Soft immature growth is not satisfactory; rather it should be fully developed, although the growth may not need to be fully mature. Such growth is referred to as a soft-wood cutting or as a green-wood or herbaceous cutting. Other cuttings may be semi-woody or fully developed and woody. Cuttings are propagated in sand, peat, perlite, vermiculite or some other inert, pest-free material. Some gardeners make a mixture of these kinds. Loose porous soil is also used especially when propagating outdoors.

In the greenhouse, propagation is done in a shaded location, either by shading the plants or the glass above them. The humidity should be high. The use of a misting system to keep the cuttings moist is recommended. This can be automatic to reduce the attention needed.

During the autumn, winter and spring months the rooting of many cuttings is hastened if the medium is several degrees warmer than the air temperature. Heating pipes located below the propagation bench or the use of an electric heating cable are ways in which this can be done.

Root-promoting chemicals speed up the time of rooting and ensure that a higher percentage of cuttings will root. Commercial preparations of these are available in either a dry or liquid form. The dry form is a hormone powder, and the stem end is dipped into it before it is placed in the propagation medium. The liquid kinds are either ready to use or need to be diluted with water. In either case the stem end is dipped into or soaked in the solution before being put into the medium. These preparations are available in small-sized packages for the home gardener. They contain chemicals such as indole-acetic acid, indole-butyric acid, or salts of these acids with other related chemicals.

The leaves from certain types of plants may be used for propagation. Mature leaves are removed from a plant such as *Saintpaulia* and inserted into a propagating medium in the same manner as a stem cutting. A new plant will develop at the base, and when it is large enough to handle conveniently it is potted as a new plant. Leaves of peperomias may be handled in the same way. Leaves of certain begonias, especially *Begonia Rex*, are laid on a moist propagation medium and new plants will develop at the base as well as at any wound that is made in the large leaf veins. Leaves of the *Sansevieria* may be cut into sections 2 to 3 inches long and treated in the same way.

Division is a simple method of propagation. It is used for those plants that form a cluster of many stems. The plant is removed from the pot, and the stems or crowns cut apart into smaller pieces. Usually this is done when the plant is in its least active period of growth. The practice is the same as that used for perennial plants outdoors.

Grafting and the related technique of budding are seldom used for garden plants. An appropriate understock is selected and a scion of the desired plant is attached or the bud inserted. The methods of taking care of the grafted or budded plants and the season of the year in which it is done vary with the kind of plant. Fruit trees, some azaleas, roses and lilacs are familiar plants that are grafted. Cacti are

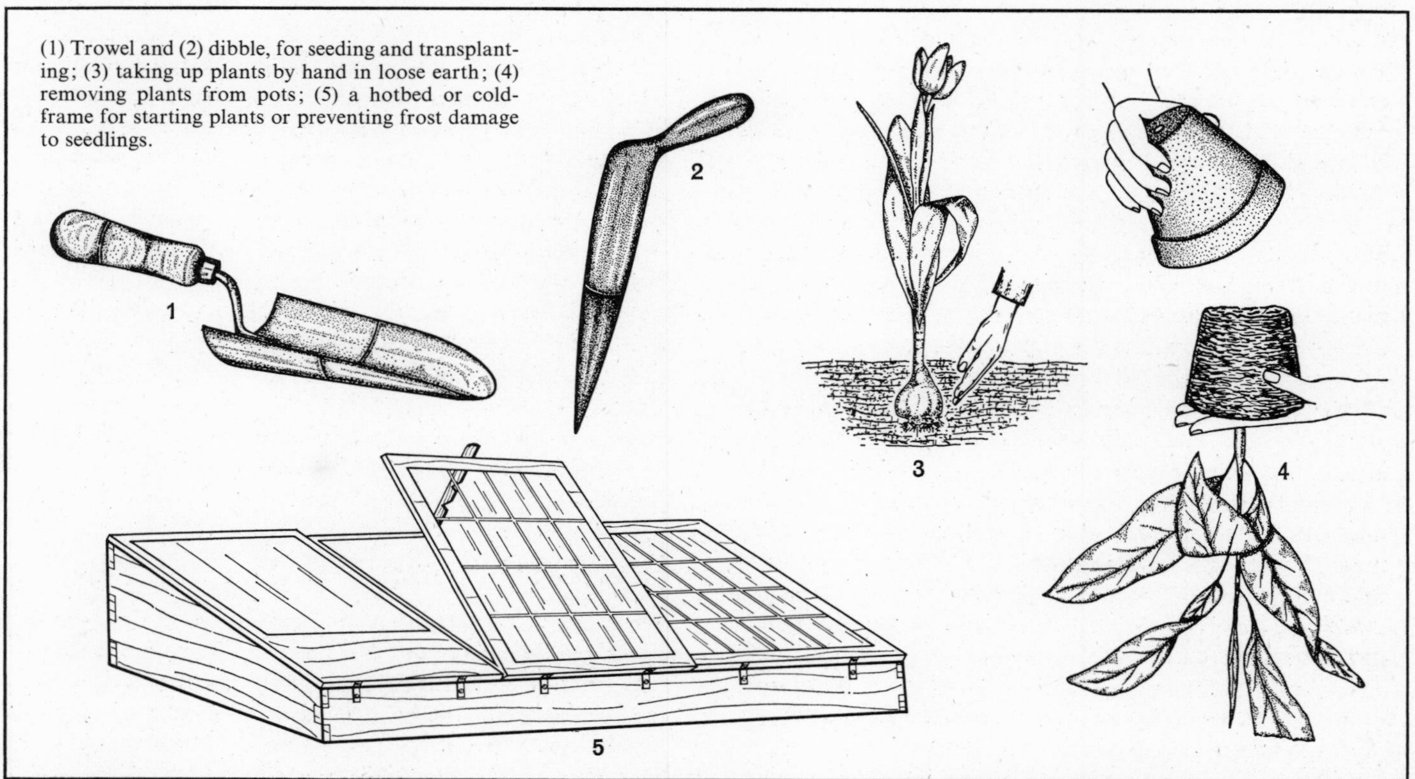

(1) Trowel and (2) dibble, for seeding and transplanting; (3) taking up plants by hand in loose earth; (4) removing plants from pots; (5) a hotbed or cold-frame for starting plants or preventing frost damage to seedlings.

sometimes grafted, to produce odd-shaped plants; an example is the practice of grafting the Christmas Cactus, *Schlumbergera* or *Zygocactus*, onto *Pereskia* to form a tree-like plant.

Selection and hybridization

All plants that reproduce by seed have, in their genetic complexity, the characteristics already present in their parent plants—those that in fertilization produced the seed. It is obvious that all plants emerging from seed which has been produced and self-fertilized by a single plant—and these self-pollinated types are numerous—will be identical in their qualitative characteristics, the form of the leaves and general structure and flower colour, for example.

In a population of flowering plants there are variations. Some have greater or lesser height, some more or fewer flowers. These are quantitative characteristics.

Observing this variability among several individual plants of the same cultivar, gardeners make a primary selection by collecting seed only from the most vigorous and healthy plants. This results in the isolation of special strains, or breeds, of a cultivar that will perpetuate a particular characteristic (for example, early flowering or colour intensity) even though the basic qualitative characters remain unchanged.

As has been said, plants propagated vegetatively will be identical to the parent plant since, without sexual union, genetic variability that can occur with natural hybridization is prevented. Cross-fertilization of one plant with another results in an equal mix of genes from the female and the male parents in the seed. This cross-fertilization is called hybridization, and is employed by plant breeders to develop new cultivars or horticultural varieties. Hybridization may result naturally from cross-pollination effected by wind or by insects, or it may be performed by man to obtain controlled crosses so that the male as well as the female parent is known. Artificial hybridization consists of taking pollen from the anthers of one flower and putting it on the stigma of a flower on another related plant. By this technique the plant breeder induces fertilization and employs his knowledge of Mendelian and cytoplasmic inheritance to induce variation within succeeding generations.

Usually the plants used as parents belong to the same botanical species or at least to the same genus. Crosses between plants of two different genera are rarely successful, and in some cases crosses between two species of the same genus are difficult. For example, the pollen of a zinnia flower (genus *Zinnia*) will fertilize flowers of the same species of zinnia, and an attempt to fertilize flowers of other species of zinnias has a high probability of success. But zinnia pollen will not fertilize the flowers of some other plants similar in appearance, such as asters (genus *Aster*) or China asters (genus *Callistephus*), because the genetic makeup of these distinct genera is very different.

Artificial hybridization can give surprising, often unexpected results since it is not always possible to know the genetic background of the parent plants used for pollination. This is the reason why horticulturists have obtained—often accidentally—hybrids with flowers quite exceptional in colour, shape or size. The range of offerings among the dahlias and chrysanthemums emphasizes the possibilities.

One should be aware, however, that not all pollination results in the production of fertile seed, and if not fertile the seeds, of course, will not germinate. In other cases the plants resulting from hybridization may be less beautiful and less colourful, with smaller flowers than those of either parent. Occasionally these "reversions" are successful, producing strains of dwarf plants or those with tiny flowers (*parviflora* varieties) of particular value.

Artificial hybridization is an operation that can be performed rather easily, especially when the plants have large flowers or a large ovary, a conspicuous stigma and very distinct anthers. In selecting which of two plants to be hybridized to be the female parent, it is better to utilize the more vigorous plant or the one with larger flowers.

One must remove the anthers from the flowers that are to be the female parent before pollen is shed. This is to prevent self-pollination. The flowers thus emasculated are then enclosed in a cloth or paper bag to prevent insect or wind pollination. Frequently the stigma is receptive to pollen before the pollen in the same flower is shed, permitting emasculation and cross-pollination to be done at the same time. In other species it is necessary to delay pollination for from 12 to 24 hours. Pollen is placed on the stigma by direct contact with an anther or by a small brush which has lightly swept a mature anther of the flower selected to be the male parent. For sticky pollen and that gathered in small masses, slender tweezers or wooden splinters are used.

Once pollination is completed the flower is again protected by the bag to prevent outside pollination. If the operation has been successful the ovary will enlarge slowly, and the bag can be removed. The flower should be tagged to identify its parentage when the cross is made.

The seeds are collected when mature and should be stored in paper envelopes on which the parentage of the seed is indicated. The parentage is indicated by writing the name of the female first, followed by an X (meaning "cross-pollinated") and then the name of the male parent.

By international convention, the varieties of plants not naturally found in the wild but developed by hybridization and/or selection are called cultivars—that is, cultivated varieties.

Garden pests

There are several major groups of pests and diseases that attack plants. Plants which suffer from physiological abnormalities often appear as if they had been attacked by an insect or a disease. Leaf damage or irregularities may be caused by a mineral deficiency or excess, especially of the three major elements most commonly lacking from soils (nitrogen, phosphorus and potassium) and on occasion of other elements such as magnesium or boron. A lack of each element produces a distinctive reaction in the plant, yet the deficiency is difficult to diagnose since some diseases may show similar symptoms. Toxic substances in the atmosphere may cause marginal injury to leaves or interfere with normal leaf development.

Improper conditions in the environment such as excess or insufficient sun for a particular species may cause unnatural growth, resulting in foliage that is excessively large or small or an unnatural leaf colour for that plant. Constant excess or lack of water in the soil will influence plant growth, and eventually the size and perhaps flower formation as well. Soil problems are corrected by the proper fertilizer applications, while excess applications can sometimes be leached from the soil by frequent heavy watering provided the soil has good drainage.

Oedemia, the development of swellings or outgrowths on the lower side of the leaf of certain plants, is associated with an excessive supply of water in the soil and high humidity. It is a greenhouse problem and uncommon in the garden.

The more typical diseases include the virus diseases and those caused by bacteria or by fungi.

Virus diseases are caused by a submicroscopic organism that increases rapidly in the sap of the infected plant. They are spread by contact with an affected plant by a healthy one. Because the vascular system is infected there is generally no control. Some virus diseases develop so rapidly that the plant is dwarfed, and shows characteristic leaf patterns of green and yellow. A few virus diseases seem to do little damage and may be present without injury to the plant. This is true for some variegated plants, where the variegation is actually caused by a virus. Most virus diseases are rather specific for a given plant while others may infect many kinds. There are no effective controls for viruses, so use care in selecting propagating material and get rid of infected plants.

Bacterial diseases develop when bacteria enter the plant through a wound. Many rot and decay diseases are caused by bacteria, as well as certain leaf spots, leaf blights and galls.

Fungi cause other types of injury; they may appear as a leaf spot, a leaf blight, as cankers on a stem, as mildew, or as rust on a leaf or stem. Diseases that cause the plant to wilt are also caused by a fungus.

Damping off, the dying of seedlings and young plants by rotting at the soil line or just below, may be caused by several disease organisms. Soil sterilization and seed or soil treatment with a fungicide are effective controls, together with the avoidance of damp, stuffy conditions in the greenhouse.

To control diseases in a garden, first be certain that the soil and environment are correct for the plant, then remove infected parts if possible and use a recommended fungicide, following directions on the label. Disease controls are constantly changing, but currently recommended fungicides are to be found in the catalogues of seedsmen.

Insect pests include the aphids, thrips, scale and leaf-chewing insects and spider mites. White fly may be a problem during periods of low rainfall. Insects may attack many kinds of plants in contrast to certain diseases that infect only one species or closely-related species.

Aphids typically are found on rapidly-growing tips of plants and injure the plant by sucking the juices. Thrips are very tiny and feed on the underside of the leaf, sucking the juices and causing a silvery appearance on the surface. Scale insects are sucking insects that attach themselves to stems and leaves and are covered with a waxy or shell-like covering which makes them more difficult to control. Mealy bugs are soft white insects, "mealy" in appearance, found in the axils of the leaves and at the tip, and cause damage by sucking the plant sap. Control is difficult because of this waxy covering. Cyclamen mites attack the growing shoots of the African violet, cyclamen, begonia, gloxinia and other gesneriads, causing the new growth to be stunted or deformed, and often preventing the plant from developing properly. White Fly is a small white insect from the tropics and can become difficult to control. The adults are moth-like, covered with a white waxy powder, and fly about when the plant is disturbed. This insect lays its eggs on the underside of the leaves of many greenhouse plants and may be transported outdoors with the plants. The immature stages are a pale greenish colour, semi-transparent, and cause damage by sucking the plant juices. Lantana, cineraria, fuchsia, ageratum, tomatoes and poinsettias are favourites of this insect.

The control of insects involves using a spray or dust. The recommended materials change rapidly to conform to acceptable safety standards that commercial preparations have become the most convenient method of control. Many insects are most easily destroyed when immature; plants should be thoroughly covered with the insecticide, both on the top and the lower side of the leaf. It is good practice to inspect all plants before transplanting them and to spray them first. Sometimes a thorough washing of the foliage with warm soapy water will dislodge the pests; this is followed by a clear water wash to remove the suds. Syringing of the plants with water under a spray-like force will dislodge many insects, and should be done routinely.

There is still another group of pests, not true insects but for practical purposes often considered with them, that will cause damage. Woodlice, oval-shaped crustaceans with many legs are among these. Millipedes also have many legs; they are shiny dark brown and move rapidly. These two pests are common in areas where organic matter accumulates, as under a mulch or in a compost pile. Generally they are harmless to growing plants. They may sometimes attack germinating seed and seedlings. Slugs, slimy snails without a shell, and snails with a shell may be a nuisance because they feed not only on decaying matter but on seedlings or on soft succulent leaves and new growth. Control for these is by bait such as slug pellets.

Eel worms are another soil pest that may attack the roots or the leaves. These are also called nematodes; they penetrate the tissue and in the case of roots may cause a swelling or an enlargement. Foliage eel worms create damage by causing spots or sections of a leaf to turn brown, as on begonias or chrysanthemums. For nematodes, soil sterilization is the best control; the planting of pest-free material is of course advantageous. Sprays control foliar types.

Garden design and the lawn

The lawn is an essential part of the design of most gardens. It often is the greatest area of the garden and, when well kept, adds lustre to the other plants, the flowers, shrubs and trees; in short, the lawn is the green carpet.

In designing a garden, plan it in such a way that it will be easy to maintain. Avoid styles or designs with many small areas, isolated specimen plants and beds, or garden ornaments. To obtain a feeling of space, allow as much open unplanted space as possible.

Consider the use of the garden and develop the plan to allow for the activities it can provide. It may be an area for children to play, an area with garden furniture, an area for pets, a place for outdoor games or for a small greenhouse. In your design, include areas where you can grow your favourite plants such as roses, dahlias or gladioli, or for annuals, perennials, a bed of strawberries or a vegetable garden. Take advantage of existing features on your property: for example, if you have large trees and much shade, then develop a woodland garden with plants suitable for these conditions. A low area may suggest a natural-looking pool, or a slope may be the place for a rock garden. Consider the architectural features of the house and develop the garden to fit that style.

Lawns are made up primarily of grasses, generally a mixture of two or more kinds appropriate to the climatic conditions and the purpose to which the lawn is to be put. Choice of grasses is therefore important, equally so is the care taken to prepare the soil and the attention given to the lawn once the seed has been sown. There are at least a dozen grasses commonly used in Britain to produce lawns. Four belong to the Bent Grass species; examples of them can be seen in the stretches of fine lawn that surround the stately homes of England.

Browntop (*Agrostis tenuis*) has the ability to grow on slightly acid soils and it forms a close-textured lawn. Redtop (*Agrostis alba*) can take a lot of treading and so is suitable for playing fields. Creeping Bent (*Agrostis stolonifera*) varies in its characteristics but produces a close-textured turf, and Velvet Bent (*Agrostis canina*) is usually used for ornamental lawns but must have very fertile soil. Chewings Fescue (*Festuca rubra* var. *compacta*) dislikes dry conditions but does well on poor soil. Creeping Red Fescue (*Festuca rubra* var. *commutata*) has dark green foliage and resists cold weather. Yet another Fescue species, *Festuca rubra* var. *glaucesans* has proved to be an excellent turf grass and grows wild on sea-washed turf in Britain, and *Festuca tenuifolia* or Fine-leafed Sheep's Fescue, is found on the moors and mountains of Britain on acid soils.

A species used in mixtures for football pitches is Crested Dogstail (*Cynosurus cristatus*) which stands hard wear but must not experience drought. Couch grass (*Cynodon dactylon*) is known under different names in various parts of the world; it must be cut closely and regularly or it becomes coarse. The famous Kentucky Blue-grass (*Poa pratensis*), free from many of the diseases that afflict grasses, does not need regular cutting and so is used for sports fields. It is able to withstand periods of drought.

The amount of seed per square yard depends on the mixture decided upon; in general 1 oz per square yard of a Bent and Fescue mixture is adequate, or $\frac{3}{4}$ oz per square yard if a Bent species only is used. Soil conditions of course play an important part in deciding quantities, and for this reason the advice of the supplier should be sought.

Soil tests can be made to determine the need for lime and fertilizers. Lawn grasses grow best in a slightly acid soil, pH 6.0 to 6.5. As soil is being prepared for seeding, incorporate liberal quantities of thoroughly decomposed organic matter especially on heavy-textured soils. Add the necessary fertilizer and the lime that may be required to correct the acidity.

Fertilizing an established lawn is generally done by using a complete fertilizer with a high amount of nitrogen and medium levels of phosphorus and potash, unless a soil test indicates otherwise. Such lawns are fertilized in early autumn and again in early spring. More frequent fertilization is done when special attention is given to watering at other seasons. For tired town lawns a sprinkling of sulphate of ammonia, well watered in, is recommended once a month during May, June and July.

Lawns need to be fertilized regularly depending on the growth and climate. Mowing frequently gives a well-groomed appearance if the seed chosen is one that can stand regular cutting. If the lawn has been newly laid, the grass must be at least 2 inches high before the first mowing is attempted. For the first half-a-dozen mowings it is advisable not to cut the lawn in the same direction, but to vary it by cutting horizontally the first time, vertically the second time and diagonally the third time, in rotation. Never cut a lawn when it is wet, and in very dry weather mow less frequently. Fescue lawns should be mowed not shorter than 2 to 3 inches. Water should be applied liberally when the soils become dry to wet it to a depth of 4 to 6 inches. Avoid frequent sprinkling.

Turfing with a good quality turf gives an immediate lawn. To turf a lawn, the soil should be as carefully prepared and fertilized as if seed were to be sown. After the turf has been laid, it is rolled and then watered.

Cut flowers

Many flowers that grow in the garden are suitable for house decoration. To make the best use of those available, someone in the house should study the principles of flower arrangement, an art which has become increasingly popular in recent years. Although the accepted phrase is "flower arranging", other materials contribute as much as flowers to many of the arrangements—bark, grasses, foliage, twigs, branches, pebbles and shells. But in this section we shall consider just those flowers that are good for cutting, and give some advice on the way they should be treated in order to make them last as long as possible.

Cutting a flower stem and leaving it exposed to the air sets in motion a process of sealing; within about 10 minutes this sealing prevents water from passing upwards to the flower head. Bearing this in mind, many flower arrangers take a bucket of water with them when they go into the garden, so that the flowers can have their stems immersed in water immediately cutting takes place, thus retarding the sealing process. This may seem a rather tiresome chore; if you decide against it be sure not to keep the cut flowers out of water for more than a few minutes.

Flower stems vary in texture, and the treatment accorded to them after cutting depends on the type of stem. Woody stems, such as one finds on chrysanthemums, need to be split so that as large an area as possible is in contact with the water. They should be left in deep, warm water for two hours before being placed in the container where they will be on display.

Some flowers, chiefly of the Amaryllidaceae family like daffodils and narcissus, produce a rather slimy discharge after being cut. This should be got rid of by holding the tip of the stem under a hot water tap until the discharge is washed away. Then they too should be left in deep, warm water for two hours before being arranged in the container.

A white, latex substance is exuded by some plants when cut. Both poppies and dahlias belong to this group. The exudation differs from the slime produced by daffodils and, whereas it is necessary to get rid of the slime, it is equally essential to retain the latex substance. This is best done by dipping the stems in very hot water for 15 seconds, and then transferring them to deep, warm water for at least two hours.

The third category of plants suitable for cutting have soft stems. These should be re-cut under water when brought into the house, and then should be allowed to stand in deep, lukewarm water for two hours before being used in an arrangement.

Experience will tell the flower arranger which flowers last the longest after being cut. Some of the most popular are given here, certain species being valued only for their foliage, others for flowers and foliage. The list is by no means exhaustive:

Amaranthus	Kniphofia
Centaureas (foliage)	Lathyrus
Chrysanthemum	Narcissus
Clary	Primula
Cleome	Roses
Covallaria	Rudbeckia
Delphinium	Salvia (and foliage)
Dianthus (and foliage)	Senecio (and foliage)
Hosta	Tulipa
Iris	Viola

When cutting flowers it is always advisable to use a sharp pair of scissors or secateurs; blunt instruments tend to seal the stems. Strip off all the leaves that will be below the water line of the container, as these pollute the water. Use warm water in the container and put the water in before arranging the flowers. Some experts recommend that flowers be cut either in the early morning or in the evening; avoid the mid-day sun. By making good use of cut flowers the beauty of the garden can be recaptured indoors.

Glossary

**see illustration*

*1. **Achene**—a dry, hard, indehiscent, single-seeded fruit with a single carpel.
2. **Acaulescent**—stemless
3. **Acuminate**—tapering to a point.
4. **Adnate**—united, grown together.
5. **Adventitious**—originating at other than the usual place; *roots* originating from any structure other than a root; *buds* arising from a part of the plant other than terminal or node.
6. **Alternate** (leaves)—one leaf at each node but alternating in direction.
7. **Annual**—a plant with a one-year life cycle.
8. **Anther**—that part of the stamen containing the pollen.
9. **Apetalous**—lacking petals.
10. **Apical**—terminal or summit.
11. **Axil**—the angle between a leaf and stem.
*12. **Berry**—a simple, fleshy fruit developed from a single ovule (loosely, any pulpy or juicy fruit).
13. **Biennial**—a plant with a two-year life cycle.
14. **Blade**—the expanded part of a leaf or leaflet.
*15. **Blossom**—the flower of a seed plant.
16. **Bract**—a specialized, modified leaf; of leaf-like structure.
17. **Bud**—a compressed stem; an underdeveloped stem.
18. **Bulb**—underground storage and reproductive organ with fleshy leaves called bulb scales.
19. **Calyx**—the outermost of the floral parts, composed of sepals.
*20. **Campanulate**—bell-shaped.
21. **Capitate**—shaped like a head.
*22. **Capsule**—a dry, dehiscent, multi-seeded fruit of more than one carpel.
23. **Carpel**—a leaf-like structure bearing ovules along the margins; a simple pistil.
*24. **Cauline**—related to an obvious stem or axis.
25. **Comose**—having tufts of hair.
*26. **Cordate**—heart-shaped.
27. **Corm**—an enlarged, underground stem, serving as a storage organ for food reserves.
28. **Corolla**—an inner cycle of floral organs, comprising the petals.
29. **Corymb**—a flat-topped, indeterminate flower cluster, with pedicels originating along a central peduncle; outer flowers open first.
30. **Cotyledons**—the first (seed) leaves of the embryo.
31. **Crenate**—toothed with rounded teeth.
32. **Crispate**—curled.
33. **Culm**—the stem of a grass or sedge.
34. **Cultivar**—a variety developed from known hybridization or origin.
35. **Cuneate**—triangular, wedge-shaped.
36. **Cyme**—a determinate flower cluster in which the central flower opens first.
37. **Deciduous**—plants that drop their leaves at the end of each season.
38. **Dehiscent**—opening of an anther or a fruit, permitting escape of pollen or seeds.
39. **Dentate**—toothed along the margins, apex sharp.
40. **Dichotomous**—divided into pairs; forked branches roughly equal.
41. **Dicotyledonous**—having two cotyledons.

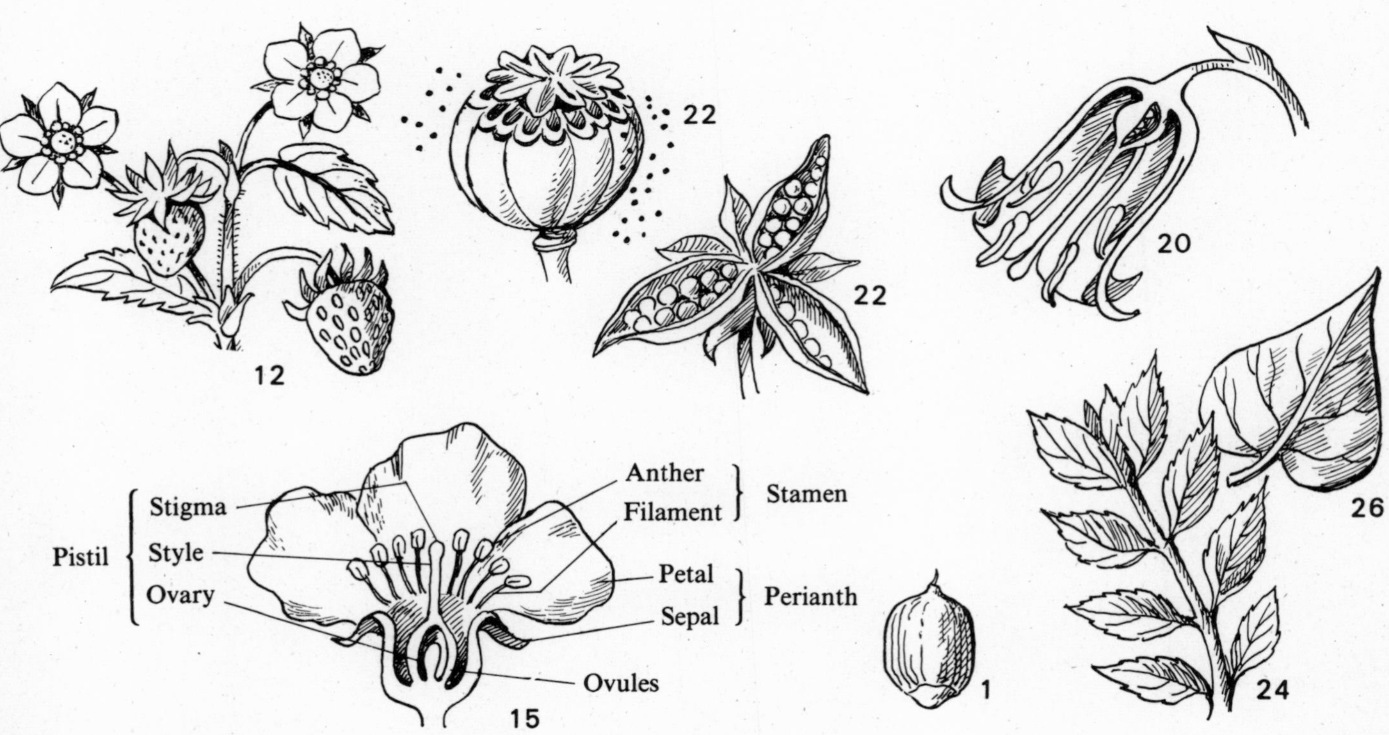

42. **Digitate** (leaves)—with leaflets arising from the apex of the petiole.
43. **Dioecious**—a species having male and female flowers on different, individual plants.
44. **Distichous**—in two vertical ranks, as the leaves of grasses.
*45. **Drupe**—a simple fleshy fruit, single carpel, with a hard endocarp containing the seed, e.g., the peach.
46. **Embryo**—a rudimentary plant.
47. **Entire**—without dentation or division.
48. **Epiphyte**—a plant that grows on another but is not parasitic.
49. **Fasciated**—an abnormally wide and flat stem.
50. **Filament**—the part of the stamen supporting the anther.
51. **Follicle**—a dry, dehiscent fruit with a single carpel, which dehisces along the ventral suture.
52. **Frond**—the leaf of a fern.
53. **Glabrous**—without hairs or pubescence.
54. **Glaucous**—covered with a whitish "bloom."
55. **Habit**—the general appearance of a plant.
*56. **Head**—a short, dense inflorescence, frequently with ray flowers around the margins and *tubular* disk flowers inside.
57. **Herbaceous**—non-woody.
58. **Hirsute**—hairy.
59. **Humus**—incompletely decomposed organic materials in the soil.
60. **Hybrid**—the result of a cross between two parents differing in genetic composition.
61. **Hydrophyte**—water loving; a plant adapted to wet conditions; capable of growing in water.
62. **Imbricate**—overlapping vertically or spirally.
63. **Indehiscent**—fruits remaining closed at maturity.
64. **Inflorescence**—the arrangement of flowers in a cluster; a complete flower cluster.
65. **Internode**—the part of a stem between two nodes.
66. **Involucre**—a cycle of bracts subtending a flower or an inflorescence.
67. **Keel**—the two front, united petals of most leguminous flowers, e.g., pea.
*68. **Lanceolate**—lance-shaped, narrow and tapered at the ends, widening above the base and narrowed to the apex.
*69. **Legume**—dry, dehiscent fruit, single carpel, usually opening along both sutures.
70. **Lenticils**—small, corky areas on woody stems.
71. **Lenticular**—lens-shaped.
72. **Ligulate**—strap-shaped.
73. **Ligule**—a thin membrane at the top of the leaf sheath in the grasses.
74. **Lip**—one portion of an unequally divided corolla; often of different sizes or colors as in orchids.
75. **Monoecious**—having male and female flowers on the same plant.
76. **Morphology**—form, structure, and development.
77. **Needle**—the long, narrow leaf characteristic of the conifers, as pine and spruce.
78. **Node**—point on a stem from which a leaf or branch emerges.
*79. **Opposite** (leaves)—two leaves at each node, opposite each other.
*80. **Palmate**—palm-like, radiating outward from the base.
*81. **Panicle**—a compound raceme.
*82. **Papilionaceous** (corolla)—a pea-like flower, having a standard keel and wings.
83. **Pedicel**—the stem of a single flower.
84. **Peduncle**—the stem of an inflorescence.
85. **Perrenial**—a plant that lives from year to year and does not die after fruiting.
86. **Perfect** (flower)—having both stamens and carpels in the same flower.

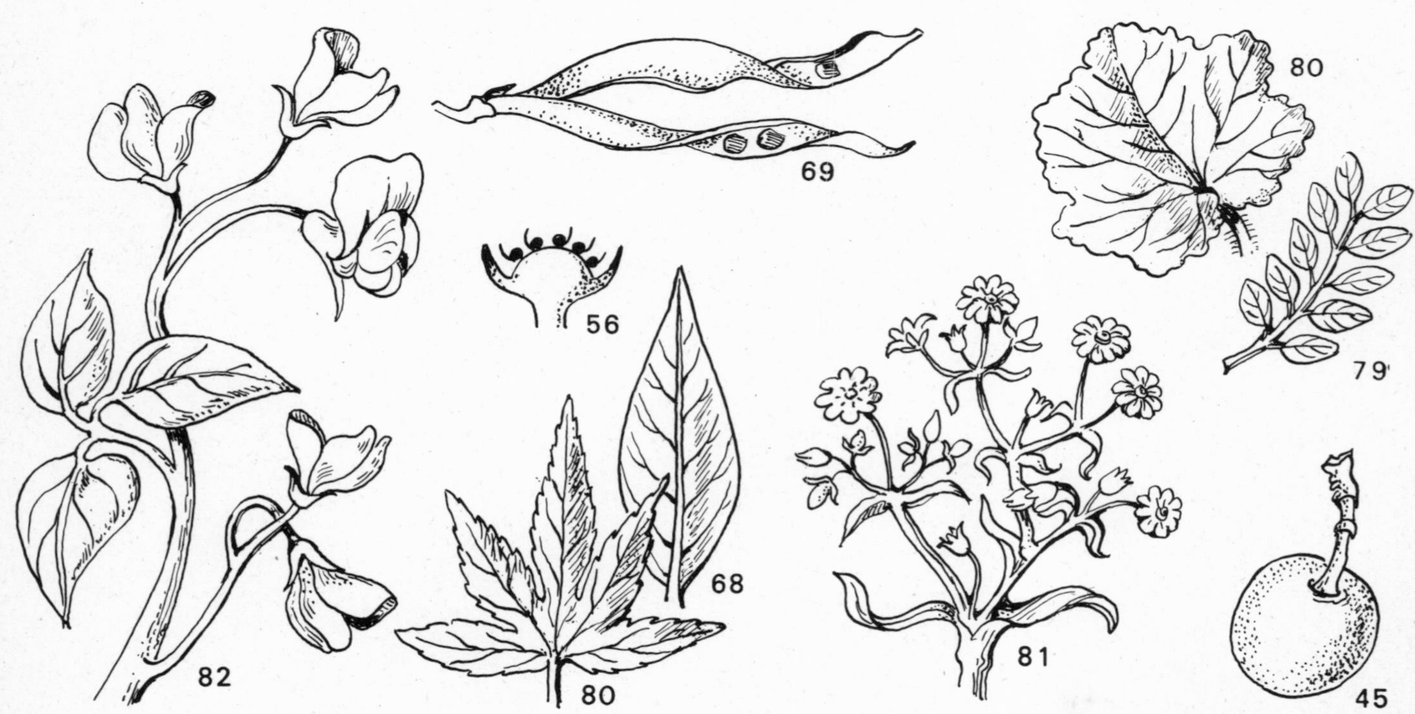

87. **Perianth**—the calyx and corolla.
88. **Persistent**—remaining attached.
89. **Petal**—one member of the corolla.
90. **Petiole**—the supporting stalk of the leaf blade.
91. **Pinnate**—separate leaflets arranged along a leaf stalk.
92. **Pistil**—the female reproductive parts of a flower, comprised of the stigma, style, and ovary.
*93. **Pome**—a fleshy, indehiscent fruit, with a leathery endocarp surrounding the seed, e.g., the apple.
94. **Pseudobulb**—thickened bulblike structure on leaves of epiphytic orchids.
95. **Pubescent**—covered with short hairs; downy.
96. **Raceme**—an elongated, indeterminate flower cluster with each floret on a pedicel.
97. **Rachis**—the axis of a spike.
98. **Receptacle**—the axis of a flower stalk bearing the floral parts.
99. **Reniform**—kidney-shaped.
100. **Reticulate**—as in a network of veins in a leaf.
101. **Rhizome**—an underground stem, usually horizontal, from which shoots and roots may develop.
102. **Rosette**—a cluster of leaves crowded on very short internodes.
103. **Rugose**—wrinkled.
104. **Sagittate**—arrow-shaped.
*105. **Samara**—a dry, indehiscent fruit having a wing, e.g., maple.
*106. **Scape**—a leafless flower stem arising from the soil.
107. **Schizocarp**—a dry, dehiscent fruit in which the carpels separate at maturation.
108. **Sepal**—a single member of the calyx.
109. **Septum**—a partition within an organ.
*110. **Serrate**—with sharp teeth and directed forward.
111. **Sessile**—without a stalk.
112. **Silique**—a dry, dehiscent fruit with two carpels separated by a septum.
113. **Sori**—spore masses on a fern.
*114. **Spadix**—a spike with a thick, fleshy axis, usually enveloped by a spathe.
*115. **Spathe**—a large bract or bracts surrounding an inflorescence.
116. **Spatulate**—spade-shaped; oblong with the basal end narrow.
*117. **Spike**—an inflorescence like a raceme except the florets are sessile to the peduncle.
118. **Stamen**—the male organ that bears the pollen.
119. **Standard** (in a papilionaceous corolla)—the large upper petal.
120. **Stigma**—the receptive part of the female organ.
121. **Stipule**—an appendage at the base of the petiole in some species.
122. **Stolon**—a prostrate stem that tends to root; sometimes called a runner.
123. **Style**—that part of the pistil connecting the stigma and the ovary.
124. **Succulent**—fleshy and juicy.
125. **Terrestrial**—plants growing in soil.
126. **Tomentose**—densely covered with hairs; woolly.
127. **Tuber**—underground storage organ; a stem with buds, e.g., the potato.
*128. **Umbel**—an indeterminate inflorescence in which the pedicels originate at about the same point on the peduncle and are about the same length, e.g., flowers of carrot.
*129. **Undulate**—a wavy surface.
130. **Variety**—a subdivision of a species, naturally occurring.
131. **Whorled**—leaves arranged in a circle around the stem.
132. **Wings**—(in a papilionaceous corolla)—the two side petals.
133. **Xerophyte**—a plant adapted to dry, arid conditions.

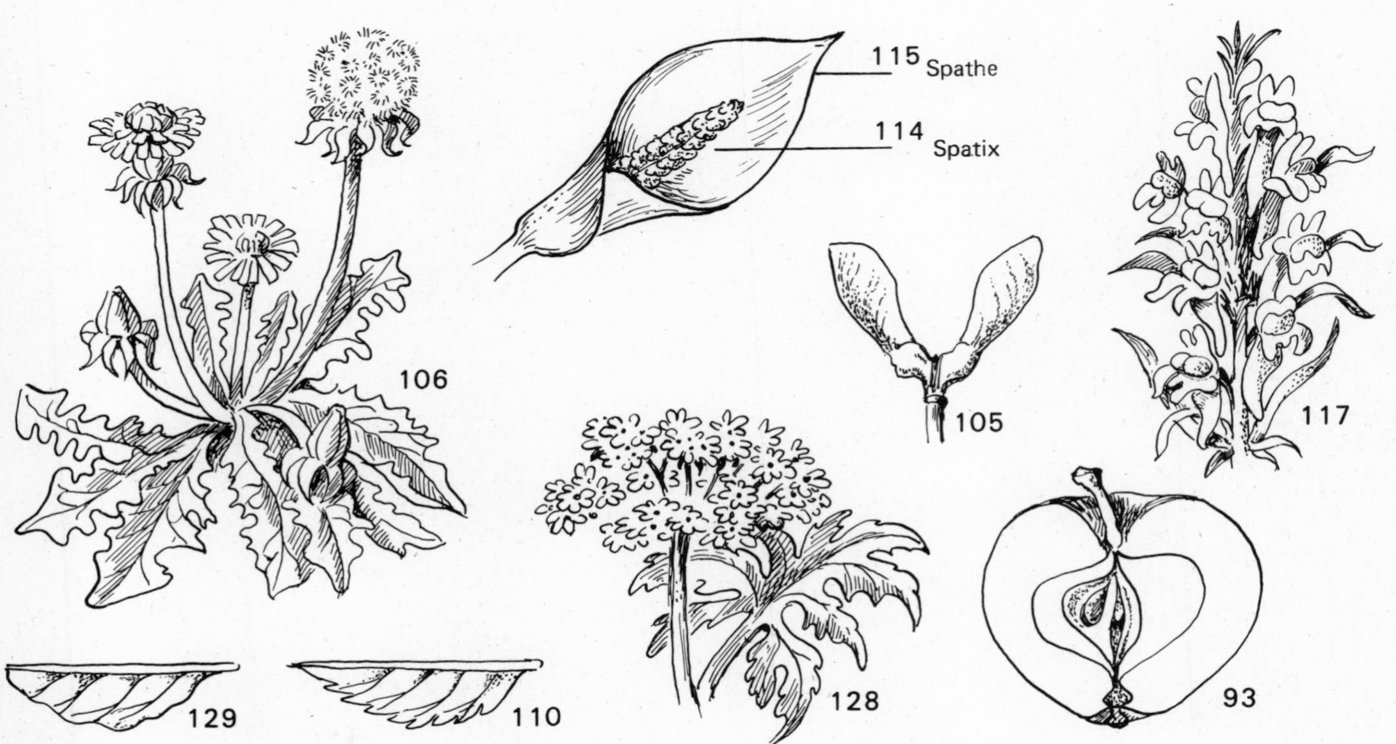

Index of plants mentioned

Small plants for edgings

Flowering plants for edgings are numerous; some are annual, some biennial and some perennial. They should be short and grow in clumps or clusters, in order not to leave empty spaces in the borders. They may have a height and a habit naturally suited to the purpose or they may be pruned and shaped to the desired height. The choice of species should take in consideration the flower colour of the plants near the edging.

Among the most suitable small plants are ageratum (*Ageratum coeruleum* and similar species), daisies (*Bellis perennis florepleno*), forget-me-nots (*Myosotis palustris* and *M. silvatica*), rock cress, (*Aubrietia deltoidea*), candytufts (*Iberis sempervirens* and similar species), small begonias (*Begonia semperflorens*), Sweet Williams (*Dianthus barbatus* and *Dianthus plumarius*), lobelias (*Lobelia erinus* and others) and *Convallaria majalis*.

For taller borders, some species of *Achillea*, *Amaranthus tricolor*, some *Cynoglossum*, *Iris germanica* and *I. florentina*, narcissus, nasturtiums, and some grasses of the *Phalaris* genus are suitable.

The ageratum include a few species (*Ageratum coeruleum* or *A. conyzoides*, *A. Houstonianum*, *A. wendlandii*: Compositae family) all originating in the tropics.

This is a perennial plant but is usually grown as an annual except in climates with no frost. A herbaceous plant 4 to 12 inches high, it has a somewhat woody and branched habit. It has opposite leaves; the lower ones are oval and obtuse, the upper ones are narrower and rather rhomboidal. All of them are dull, light green and with a toothed margin. The blossoms are in branched corymbs that create spots of light blue or lavender and sometimes white. They have a velvety surface because of the stamens and the small, pointed petals. The seeds are small achenes with five corners, overtopped by tiny scales.

Seeds are sown in early spring under glass, transplanted to peat pots, and planted outdoors after all danger of frost is past. Distance between plants should be from 8 to 16 inches. Propagation by cuttings is done in the autumn before frost.

The *Ageratum conyzoides* and the *A. wendlandii* have varieties with white clusters.

Aubretia or sweet alyssum (*Aubrietia deltoidea*: Cruciferae family) is especially suited for edgings on limestone soil; it grows well in rock gardens.

It is a small branched perennial plant, 4 to 8 inches tall, and has alternate triangular, toothed leaves. The many flowers are white, pinkish-purple or lilac, have four petals and grow in thin clusters. The seeds are contained in oval siliques.

Plant seeds in early spring, transplant them to peat pots and plant them outdoors after danger of frost is past, 6 to 12 inches apart. Propagation by division is in the early autumn. The plant prefers light soil, sunny and not too moist locations. It flowers in spring, but both early and late varieties are known. There are also some varieties having smaller but thicker flowers, some with brighter violet colours (var. *Tauricola*), with brighter purple colours (cultivar "Crimson King") and some others much darker (*A. hybrida* cultivar "Dr. Mules" and others).

The forget-me-not, or myosotis, (*Myosotis palustris* and *M. sylvatica*) is classified as belonging to the Boraginaceae family. *M. palustris*, native to Britain, is mainly suited to moist locations, whereas *M. sylvatica* is suited for drier places and it prefers semi-shady locations. Seeds are sown in June to August in the seed bed, and transplanted outdoors in the autumn or early spring. Spacing: 8 to 12 inches.

Forget-me-nots are well known for their tiny, blue flowers, having a yellow "throat" and four rounded petals.

Several species of candytufts may be grown (*Iberis amara*, *I. Jordanii*, *I. sempervirens*, and *I. umbellata*: Cruciferae family). The first three species mentioned have white or pinkish flowers, the fourth has violet. They are sparsely branched, 6 to 14 inches tall, with erect stalks carrying few narrow, pointed, small leaves with few large indentations. The flowers are sweet smelling, grouped in clusters in which the central florets are smaller and the outer ones have bigger petals. The *Iberis* have both annual and perennial species native to Europe, Asia Minor and Africa. They are seeded in autumn, grown over winter under protection, and planted outdoors in early spring, 8 to 16 inches apart. Feeding with weak liquid manure is advisable when the flowers show.

---

1. *Myosotis palustris*.

2. Edging of *Aubrietia deltoidea*.

3

4

5

Wax begonias, violets and violas

In flower beds, it is customary to arrange more or less large groupings of flowers. One of the small plants that serve this purpose well are the wax begonias.

Begonia semperflorens (Begoniaceae family) is native to Brazil and has been known in gardening since 1828. It is herbaceous, perennial if protected from frost, 6 to 14 inches tall, and multibranched. It has somewhat succulent leaves that are light green, often red-edged, bronze or coppery and slightly indented. The flowers are in axillary inflorescences, and are pink, white or red, having four or five petals with a yellow, thick tuft of stamens in the centre.

The wax, or everblooming, begonia can be propagated by seed, and the seedlings will begin to flower when three to four months old. Seed sown in June will produce flowering plants for winter flowering. Sow seed in January or February for plants to be planted outdoors in the spring. This begonia may be reproduced by stem cutting taken in the autumn, using a cold greenhouse. Insert the cuttings into a light soil mixed with peat, or in sand or other propagation media. The plants then are kept in a temperate greenhouse for the winter. To obtain good cuttings, choose branches having a healthy bud at the base. Cold and windy locations are to be avoided. Distance to leave between the plants is from 4 to 8 inches.

The *Begonia semperflorens* variety *gigantea rosea* bears large sterile flowers and is a distinctive bedding plant. The cultivars "Tausendschön" and "Rosanova" have scarlet or pink flowers clustered in thick groups. The "Red Pearl" is one of the shortest in stature, and has deep-red flowers, small stems and few branches. Both "Red Pearl" and the cultivar "Primadonna" have red to red-brown leaves.

Other dwarf plants suitable for creating colour highlights are violets, species of the *Viola* genus (Violaceae family), primarily *V. cornuta* and *V. odorata.* The latter is the Sweet Violet, known for the perfume of its flowers. *Viola cornuta* is native to the Italian, French and Spanish mountains, especially the Pyrenees. Known as the Horned Violet, it is biennial or perennial, 5 to 10 inches tall, little branched and with alternate, oval, spatulate or almost heart-shaped, indented leaves. The flowers are irregular on long peduncles and have a corolla of about 1 inch across, with five petals; the two upper petals are

6

7

larger and erect, the lowest one is wider. Colour varies from a dark violet to a pale purple, or from white to a cream colour to bright yellow.

The viola, *Viola odorata*, has less height and smaller flowers in comparison with *V. cornuta*. It is also a perennial and a few varieties are known, including the well-known Parma violet, with large, scented, dark-blue to purple coloured flowers, the Russian violet, with darker flowers on longer stems and the four-seasons violet, which blossoms continuously. Available also are cultivars having white flowers, hybrids and related species with blue flowers (*Viola Mumbyana*) or yellow flowers (*Viola vilmoriniana*).

Violets and violas may be propagated by seeds, by stolons, or by division. Seeding is done in July and August and seedlings transplanted in September or October for spring bloom.

Another good plant is the alyssum "Basket-of-Gold" (*Alyssum saxatile*: Cruciferae family), which has golden-yellow flowers.

---

3. Flower bed of *Begonia semperflorens*.

4. Close-up of *B. semperflorens* flower.

5. *Begonia semperflorens*, cultivar "Rosanova."

6. *Viola cornuta* (Horned Violet).

7. *Alyssum saxatile*, cultivar "Basket-of-Gold."

8

Portulacas

The portulaca (*Portulaca grandiflora*: Portulacaceae family) is a small plant that originated in Brazil.

It is treated as a half-hardy annual. The plants are only 3 to 8 inches high, are spreading and multibranched. Portulaca is well adapted for use in beds, borders, edges, hanging baskets and rock gardens. It has succulent stems and leaves. The stems are reddish-purple; the leaves are needle shaped, dark green and glabrous or thinly velveted. The flowers are large, isolated and open completely in direct sunlight; in their simple forms they are composed of four to six silky, oval-rounded, slightly heart-shaped petals. The flowers may be of various colours, from white to a cream colour to yellow, from pink to dark lilac, and from red to bright carmine, with all intermediate shades. It is seeded in early spring, outdoors, and the plants are thinned to stand 5 to 10 inches apart. Seed may also be sown earlier inside and transplanted outdoors after the danger of frost is past. Some kinds have double flowers that are very pretty; culture is the same as for the single ones.

Portulacas blossom continuously from about July to autumn. The heterogeneity of their colours provides beds and edgings with a charming mosaic effect.

9

10

11

12

---

8. Bed of *Portulaca grandiflora*.

9-12. Individual flowers of portulaca.

13

14

Gazania

The Gazania (*Gazania splendens*, Compositae family) is probably a hybrid between *Gazania Pavonia* and *G. Uniflora* and comes from South Africa.

It is a small plant with a prostrate habit and has both upright and spreading short stems. The leaves are sessile, almost persistent, opposite, tapered, 2 to 4 inches long, dark green on the upper side and greyish-white below. The flowers are large, solitary blossoms with a diameter of 1 to 2 inches, and are similar to large dasies, having a large ligules with purplish-black or whitish spots at the base.

A half-hardy perennial it blossoms copiously from May to October. It is sown indoors in the early winter and planted out after frost danger is past. It prefers warm climate, full sun and loose soil, and it can be propagated by cuttings in a cold frame from July to September.

Other species used are *Gazania rigens* var. *citrina* with flowers with yellow rays and greenish crown and *G. longiscapa* with very large blossoms. A cultivar with variegated leaves is rare and not vigorous. A number of cultivars having flowers ranging from yellow to red are grown as *Gazania Hybrida*.

13. Bed of *Gazania splendens*.

14, 15. *Gazania longiscapa*.

16. *Gazania rigens* var. *citrina*.

17

18

19

Primroses and polyanthus

Primroses (*Primula* genus: Primulaceae family) include a large number of species, most of which grow well outdoors. *Primula sinensis* and *P. obconica* are suited only for potting. The cowslip (*Primula veris*) and two garden species, *Primula polyantha* and *P. hortensis* deserve mention. *P. polyantha* is related to the wild *P. vulgaris* of woods and shores, having yellow flowers. *P. hortensis* is related to *P. veris* and to *P. auricula* which grows wild in the mountains.

The well-known *Primula veris* grows 2 to 6 inches high, is perennial, and without a distinct stem has a tufted appearance. The leaves, all basal and arranged as a rosette, are large (2 to 4 inches), oblong-spatulate, rugose, with indented margins, and generally have a festive green colour. In the centre of the rosette of leaves, the flowers are produced; they are numerous and tightly gathered as in a nosegay. The floret is round and has five petals. The calyx is slightly swollen with five ridges. Flower colour varies greatly among the many different cultivars, being yellow in wild *Primula vulgaris*. Flowers may be unicoloured, or bicoloured with either a yellow centre or one that is at least lighter than the rest of the corolla, which may be pink, purple, red, violet or blue. The plant produces ovoid capsules with a large number of seeds.

Primula are sturdy plants suitable for edgings, thickets and rock gardens. Seed is sown in spring or early summer in the seed bed in the shade, transplanted into loose-textured soil in early autumn or in the following spring. Distance between the plants: 6 to 10 inches. Plants may be propagated by dividing the clumps in the summer. They do not require a special culture or soil.

A large number of cultivars with double or single flowers are available; those with bicoloured flowers are also known as "owl's eyes."

Horticulturalists have done much to improve the polyanthus strains and varieties, and the gardener today has more than 100 from which to choose. Some of the best known modern strains are: American Wine Red, very robust even in eastern maritime regions with large crimson-black flowers.

Barkby, of compact habit and useful for bedding, has a wide colour range.

Blue Polyanthus bears dark blue flowers with a yellow centre.

Brilliance, much favoured for cloche cultivation, has a vivid colour range and is good for cutting.

Deep Orange, with flowers so vivid that the plants lose little by being in shady borders.

Festival, free flowering and in a wide colour range.

Giant Yellow, another for the shady garden.

Kelmscott, with blooms measuring $2\frac{1}{2}$ inches in diameter and as many as 20 to the truss.

Sutton's Superb, suitable for bedding, has brilliant colouring.

17-21. *Primula vulgaris* flowers, illustrating the interesting range of colour.

22

23

Pansies

The pansy includes many cultivars all derived genetically from *Viola tricolor* (Violaceae family), a native of Europe, the little white, yellow and blue-purplish violet of the fields. The most commonly grown pansy today is either *Viola tricolor* var. *hortensis*, or *V. tricolor* var. *grandiflora*.

It is a hardy perennial plant, 2 to 12 inches high with an open habit. It has oval-lanceolate, indented leaves each bearing two finger-like stipules. The nonodorous flowers may be as large as 2½ inches in diameter; they are irregular and with a posterior spur, and have five rounded velvety, unicoloured or variously bordered or tinted petals, with markings or spots. The throat of the corolla is usually yellow. The range in flower colour is quite wide, from pink, to red, to blue, to purple, to almost black. The numerous tiny seeds are contained in a three-valved, dehiscent capsule.

The pansy is a sturdy plant that is used for edges, bedding, hanging baskets and for cut flowers. It should not have too much shade or dampness. It is sown outdoors from July to August in the seed bed in light soil, and the young plants are transplanted from September to October to the garden or to a cold frame leaving 6 to 12 inches between plants. It may also be propagated by division.

Pansies are subject to several diseases, including powdery mildew and violet rust. All may be controlled with appropriate fungicides.

Among the well-known kinds are the Swiss Giants: Alpenglow, rich cardinal shades; Berna, violet blue; Coronation, golden yellow; Swiss Blue, medium blue; Swiss Orange, orange to golden yellow; Rhinegold, yellow with dark blotch and Raspberry Rose, a pink. In addition to these there are many excellent mixtures such as Oregon Giants, Roggli Swiss Giants, Steeles Jumbo, and Butterfly hybrids. For the early riser, the sweet fragrance of the pansy is at its best when the dew is on the plants.

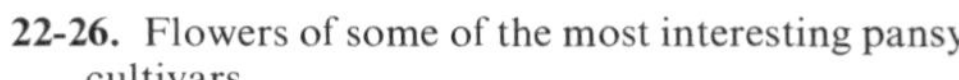

22-26. Flowers of some of the most interesting pansy cultivars.

24

25

26

Cinerarias

The cineraria (*Senecio hybridus*=*Cineraria hybrida*: Compositae family) is developed from the *Senecio cruentus* which it resembles; it is native of the Canary Islands and it has been used in gardens since 1777.

It is a biennial plant (perennial if protected), 10 to 20 inches high, erect and branches at the top. It has large, heart-shaped, variously toothed and dull leaves that are also velvety; they are rugose and light green on top. The flowers are in clusters of large heads that resemble large daisies with wide petals. The plant flowers profusely. The flower heads have a central reddish, dark-brown or purple-violet disc and rays of different colours that range from lilac-pink, to red, to violet, to blue, with very intense and bright gradations. There are many cultivars with bicoloured flowers, usually having a light central crown.

The seeds are brown, oblong achenes. Some cultivars with tubulous ligules that are improperly called double-flowered cinerarias, also exist, and there are some that actually have double flowers.

Seeds are sown from June until August for flowering in the greenhouse in the winter, and are transplanted into well-drained pots as soon as the first true leaf appears. In most locations they can be sown outdoors. For the cultivars in which one wants to maintain a particular characteristic, the propagation is by cuttings using basal branches with buds. Cinerarias bloom from winter to early spring.

Cinerarias are subject to wilting and leaf browning caused by the bread mould organism, and to powdery mildew. The former disease shows up first as pale spots on the leaves, which become yellow and then brown, and, in moist conditions will be covered with a grey mould; often the plants wilt and die. It is advisable to ventilate the plants if they are in the greenhouse or under glass, to reduce the applications of nitrogen fertilizer if they have been excessive, and to treat the plants with fungicides. Soil disinfection also gives good results. Powdery mildew usually develops during periods of cool, moist nights, and can be checked by application of suitable fungicides.

Related species include *Senecio grandiflora* introduced to Europe from Mexico in 1844, having yellow flower heads, and from which some taxonomists believe *Cineraria hybrida* is derived; *Senecio pulcher*, from Argentina, with flowers having a yellow disc and lilac rays; and *S. Petasitis* from South America, with golden flowers. *S. adonidifolius*, has orange flowers and grows from 8 to 12 inches; *S. aurantiacus*, with orange-yellow blooms is slightly larger, growing to 18 inches. *S. incanus*, another hardy species, has silvery-grey cushions of foliage. *S. Smithii* originating in Cape Horn, grows to 3 feet and has white flowers.

27

28

29

30

31

27. Plants of *Cineraria hybrida* in their most characteristic colours.

28-30. Examples of colours in some cultivars.

31. Close-up of a cineraria blossom, showing detail.

Calendulas, or pot marigolds

The calendula (so named because it blooms any month of the year) is also called the pot marigold and is derived from the original botanical species named *Calendula officinalis* (Compositae family). A native of Southern Europe, it has been cultivated for decorative purposes since the mid-sixteenth century.

It is an annual herbaceous plant, 8 to 15 inches tall that has a particular, aromatic fragrance. It is erect and branched at the top. The leaves are alternate, rather thick, glandulous, and lightly sticky, have an oblong shape and a light green colour. The blossoms consist of large flowers (up to 2½ inches in diameter) that are solitary, apical, and contained in a global rosette; the tubular flowers of the central disc are yellow, orange or brownish. The ray flowers are numerous and range in colour from yellow to bright orange.

The seeds are oblong, curved achenes, and are dark yellow.

Calendulas may be used in flower beds, for edging and for hanging baskets. They are very suitable for use as cut flowers, and bloom during summer and autumn.

They can be sown indoors or in a greenhouse in the seed bed during March and April and transplanted outdoors in April or May. It is also possible to sow them directly outdoors. They require rich soil and a sunny location. The calendula has been used by herbalists because its blooms have anti-emetic and wound-healing properties. The juice of the leaves and stems, extracted at the time of full bloom, has been used to treat warts.

Variations other than those for colour are known. The double calendulas have attracted favourable attention. Multibranching cultivars form plants shaped like bouquets. The two most important cultivars are "Ball's Gold" with yellow flowers and "Ball's Orange" with bright, red-orange flowers.

Calendulas have also been grown from seed in the house, sprouting in a pot in a quiet corner.

32

33

34

32. Bed of *Calendula officinalis*.

33. A flower of the cultivar "Ball's Gold" showing some detail.

34. Blossoms of the cultivar "Ball's Orange."

35

36

37

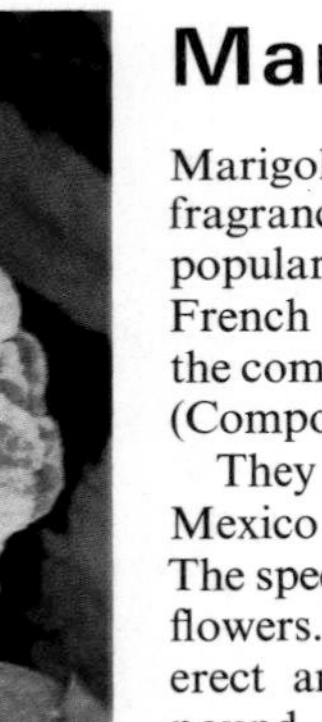

38

39

Marigolds

Marigolds are characterized by their strong fragrance, unpleasant to some people. Two popular species are *Tagetes patula*, also called French Marigold and *T. erecta* also known by the common name of Aztec or African Marigold (Compositae family).

They are half-hardy annuals introduced from Mexico to Europe during the sixteenth century. The species differ both in height and shape of the flowers. *Tagetes patula* is from 5 to 20 inches tall, erect and bushy, with mostly opposite compound dark leaves. The blossoms are either single or double flowered, and from 1 to 2 inches in diameter. The disc flowers are tufted and yellow or orange. The ray flowers vary greatly in number and are yellow to reddish, or spotted with purple-brown toward the centre of the blossom. Some cultivars are basically orange, yellow, brown or purple in the centre. The ligules are either flat or tubular. Some dwarf cultivars are particularly suitable for edging.

Tagetes erecta is taller (20 to 40 inches) and has larger flowers (2 to 3 inches in diameter) that are yellow (*T. erecta flore Pleno*, cultivar "Yellow Supreme"), or double golden or orange (*T. erecta flore pleno* cultivar "Guinea Gold"). It is suitable for beds and as a cut flower. In both species the seeds are elongate, black, shiny achenes.

Marigolds are very rugged, and prefer sunny locations; they may be seeded in early spring, transplanted to peat pots and planted outside after danger of frost is past. Distance to leave between the plants is from 10 to 15 inches for *Tagetes patula* and from 12 to 24 inches for *T. erecta*. They bloom from June to October. Plant African Marigolds in groups of three or six as an alternative to planting them in rows. French Marigolds can be planted singly.

Related species include *Tagetes tenuifolia* or Indian carnation, and *T. lucida*. Both were introduced from Mexico during the eighteenth century.

Among the cultivars of *T. patula* are *T. patula nana flore pleno* cultivar "Light Lemon Yellow," with double yellow flowers, and cultivar "Robert Beist" also double, but with red-brown to purple colours. The cultivar "Harmony" has a big tuft of yellow twisted flowers in the centre, with a crown of wide purple ligules around the edge.

Tagetes tenuifolia, var. *pumila* is a dwarf plant with small leaves and tiny blossoms that are solitary and completely yellow.

---

35. Bed of *Tagetes tenuifolia* var. *pumila*.

36. Blossom of *T. patula* cultivar "Naughty Marietta."

37. Bed of *T. patula flore pleno* hybrid.

38. Blossom of *T. patula flore pleno* cultivar "Robert Beist."

39. Blossom of *T. erecta flore pleno* cultivar "Guinea Gold."

40 41

Calceolarias and nasturtiums

These two plants have great ornamental qualities. They have interesting and unusual flower shapes, extremely different in the two species and perhaps only associated by their colours, which range from all gradations of yellow and orange to red and purple.

The calceolaria (*Calceolaria hybrida*: Scrophulariaceae family) is genetically linked to *C. integrifolia*, *C. arachnoidea*, *C. corymbosa* and *C. crenatiflora*.

Calceolaria is perennial if not exposed to frost, but is grown as an annual. It is 8 to 15 inches high, sometimes reaching 25 inches, with erect and sparsely branched stems; the leaves are alternate or opposite, oval or oblong with a winged stalk, wrinkled and rugose above, wavy and toothed. Its flowers characteristically exhibit the shapes of a swollen kidney and a small flattened bag, due to the two lips of the corolla: the upper one is smaller and shaped like a hood and the lower one is expanded, swollen, and very wide, like the labellum of some orchids. The flowers may have one colour or be variously dotted or spotted. The seeds, grain-shaped, are numerous inside capsules. Blossoming occurs in late winter and spring.

42

The calceolarias are propagated by seed, which is sown from May to September in a fine soil; the young plants are transplanted when they are large enough to handle. Certain kinds are propagated by cuttings in a temperate greenhouse in September; they will have to spend the winter in a cool greenhouse and flower in the spring. Distance between plants: 10 to 16 inches. Cuttings are made with branches that are still herbaceous, rooted in sandy, acid soil. The cultivars are unicoloured, striped and spotted.

Hybrids with other species are grown, including *Calceolaria fruticohybrida* (derived from *C. amplexicaulis*). *C. alba* has white flowers. *C. polyrrhiga* is a perennial, dwarf species, 3 to 5 inches high, a native of Patagonia and used for beds and rock gardens.

The species are subject to infestation by aphids and red spider mites which should be controlled by appropriate insecticides.

Nasturtiums (*Tropaeolum majus*) and their variations belong to the Tropaeolaceae family. They originated in Peru.

T. majus, also called the Tall Nasturtium, is annual, with a trailing habit, and with dwarf or semi-dwarf cultivars.

The plant is smooth and waxy; the leaves are round with the petiole attached at the centre of the blade. The large flowers have a corolla formed by five wide, free, oval petals with a thin and ciliated throat, and with a spur in the back. Colour, always velvety, varies from yellow to orange to red and to brownish-purple. The seeds are large, kidney-shaped and dark yellow. The buds and the fruits are used, like capers, to make pickles; the flowers are quite edible and are used to brighten salads.

Nasturtiums are seeded in February and March indoors for subsequent transplanting or they may be seeded directly in the bed after danger of frost is over. They should be planted or thinned 12 to 18 inches apart. Special types, such as the double-flowered cultivars, may be propagated by cuttings.

Related species include *Tropaeolum minus*, with smaller, orange or red flowers (cultivar "King of Tom Thumb"), *T. peregrinum*, with very small, yellow flowers and lobed leaves, *T. peltophorum* with large orange flowers.

The cultivar "Gyldenskar" is one of the most beautiful with its golden, overdoubled flowers.

40, 41. Appearance of *Tropaeolum majus* in blossom.

42. *Calceolaria hybrida*.

43

44

Petunias

The garden petunia (*Petunia hybrida*) is derived from the two species *Petunia nyctaginiflora* and *P. violacea* (Solanaceae family).

The petunia is a perennial, although it is often grown as an annual. It grows 10 to 20 inches tall and has an erect but disorderly habit. The whole plant is light greyish-green and velvety. The leaves are alternate or opposite, rounded or oval. Flowers are large, trumpet-shaped and tubular with united petals having an expanded and circular edge, observation of which allows one to distinguish the five joined petals. Flower colour varies from white to red to purple to a dark violet. It may be of a single, uniform colour or with spots that often design a star. Some cultivars are single, some are double, some have a curled corolla that resembles a carnation. The seeds, globular and tiny, are in an oval capsule.

Petunias bloom all summer, generally from May to October. They are seeded in early spring, transplanted to peat pots, and planted outside at a spacing of 12 to 20 inches after the danger of frost is past. Plants with double flowers are propagated by cuttings in order to maintain their characteristics. Such propagation is done in spring inside pots under glass and in not too sunny locations. They require little moisture; excessive water will cause yellowing and death.

Among the most interesting cultivars are "Himmelsroschen" with single flowers having a bright pink colour with a white throat; the "Bla Vidunder" with lavender flowers; "Satellite," with purple petals and a white star having a narrow point; "Glitters," similar to Satellite but with larger white points; and "Canadian Wonder" with a large, crinkled, purple corolla.

43. Bed of *Petunia hybrida* with red flowers.

44. Cultivar "Satellite."

45. Cultivar "Glitters."

46, 47. Cultivar with crinkled flowers.

45

46

47

Verbenas

The colourful garden Verbena, *Verbena hybrida* (Verbenaceae family) may be derived from such American species as *Verbena chamaedryfolia* from tropical regions, *V. incisa* from Panama, *V. phlogiflora* from Brazil, and *V. teucrioides* also from Brazil. All the species cited and the hybrids have been cultivated since the mid-eighteenth century.

The verbena is a perennial but is normally grown as an annual. It is erect, with branches often prostrate, and branched at the top of the plant. The leaves are opposite, oval to oblong, small and indented. The flowers are scented and grouped in large numbers into umbrella-shaped clusters, similar to round bouquets. They have a united corolla, about $\frac{1}{2}$ inch in diameter that is round and has five petals. Colour varies from white to pink to red, to blue to purple, and even to brown and grey. The flowers may be uniform in colour, variegated or striped. The throat is always white or yellowish-green and always lighter than the petals. The seeds are small, cylindrical, and wrinkled.

Verbenas blossom from June to October, and are used in edgings, mass plantings, and beds. They may also be grown in pots, and the flowers used for cutting. Sow seeds in August to September outdoors, transplant seedlings into pots, and keep over winter in a cool greenhouse. Then when the plants begin to flower, transfer them outdoors. The distance to leave between plants is from 6 to 12 inches. Seeds may also be sown in February and March in the greenhouse, the seedlings later transplanted, and the young plants set outdoors in May. The direct propagation by cuttings in the winter and spring is possible, using fresh, mature, herbaceous branches, or in the autumn with selected cuttings from plants outdoors. Verbenas prefer well-prepared garden soil and need a sunny location. They can survive mild winters outdoors.

A large number of cultivars are available. The group called Italian are unicoloured, variegated flowers with a large throat of a different colour.

Verbena hybrida, cv. *candidissima* has white flowers and a dwarf habit, the cultivar "Defiance" is bright red, "Dannebrog" has red flowers and a large white and shaded throat, and "Royal Blue" has dark, violet-blue flowers.

Among the related ornamental species are: *Verbena canadensis*, (= *V. Aubletia*) with dark red flowers; *V. pulchella* and *V. tenera* with lilac-violet flowers; and *V. rigida*, lilac or blue-violet forming a pyramidal cluster and having wrinkled leaves.

V. bonariensis from South America grows to between 4 and 5 feet and has summer-blooming purplish-lilac flowers. *V. laciniata* from Peru has a trailing habit and produces lilac flowers, and *V. peruviana*, also from Peru, has a similar trailing habit but produces scarlet flowers. *V. radicans*, another with a trailing habit, originates in Brazil and bears lilac flowers in summer. *V. teucrioides*, also native to Brazil, grows to 1 foot and has yellowish-white or pink flowers.

48

49

50

51

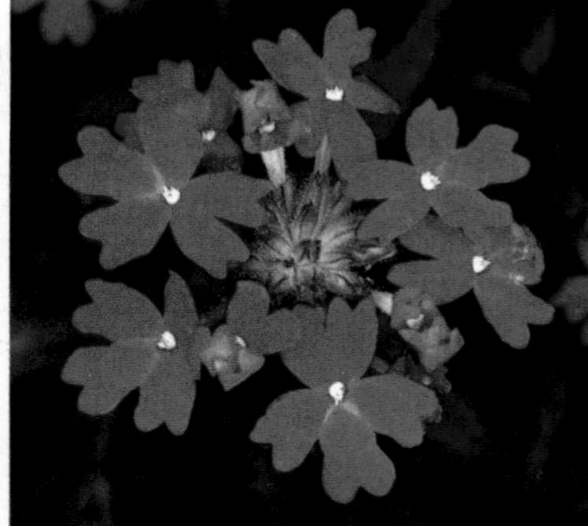

52

48-51. Some cultivars of *Verbena hybrida*.

52. Hybrid of *Verbena chamaedrifolia* with velvety red flowers.

53

55

56

54

Snapdragons

Snapdragons (*Antirrhinum majus*: Scrophulareaceae family) are extremely popular flowers and are unusual because of their large tubular and swollen corollas whose throat, when the walls of the corolla are pressed together, opens up wide. In Europe the plant is sometimes called the "Mouth of the Lion". Snapdragons originated in the Mediterranean countries and they have been cultivated since at least the sixteenth century.

It may be an annual, biennial or perennial, grows 12 to 30 inches tall, is erect and not greatly branched. The leaves are opposite or alternate, lanceolate, narrow and entire. The flowers, blooming in spring and summer, are numerous and grow on an erect and terminal cluster. The corolla is united and ranges from white to yellow to light pink, or salmon to red to copper and even to reddish-violet; it generally has a yellow spot at the opening of the throat. Seeds are small, brown and numerous, and develop in a capsule.

Snapdragons are sown in a greenhouse or indoors in February or March for planting outdoors in the spring; distance between the plants should be from 12 to 20 inches. Seeds can also be sown outdoors from April to May. Fine seeds need to be covered to once their depth in soil, and very fine seeds merely pressed into moist soil.

To flower in a greenhouse in the winter, sow from July to October. From sowing the seed to bloom takes 16 to 18 weeks. The propagation of double or selected kinds is possible by cuttings. The snapdragon prefers slightly acid soil, and a sunny situation.

It is a sturdy plant, having dwarf, semi-dwarf and tall types. The dwarf and semi-dwarf types may be grown in beds or rock gardens; the tall types do well in beds or for cut flowers. There are also cultivars with bicoloured, shaded and spotted flowers. Hybrid types are available either in separate or mixed colours. Popular types are: Rocket Snapdragons, 30 to 36 inches tall; Floral Carpet Snapdragons, 6 to 8 inches; Tetra Snapdragons, 24 to 30 inches; Butterfly Snapdragons, with open-face florets, and doubles.

Antirrhinum Asarina from South West Europe has a trailing habit and bears large yellow flowers in summer. It is suitable for hanging baskets; *A. glutinosum*, originating in Spain has a prostrate habit and produces cream and yellow flowers in June; *A. Orontium*, growing to 1 foot is native to Europe and bears purple flowers in the summer. It is usually treated as an annual for summer bedding.

A. Fastigatum Max, the little "Tree Snapdragon" as it is sometimes called, grows to 3 feet and in suitable conditions can produce an enormous bush of orange-red flowers. *A. Poggenhagen bicolor* grows to 2 feet and produces ruffled flowers in contrasting colours, such as vivid pink blotched with yellow, brick-red with gold, and orange with pink throat.

53, 54. Groups of snapdragons in blossom, showing the beauty of mixed colours.

55, 56. Close-up of snapdragon flowers.

57

58

Wallflowers, stocks and nemesias

Mathiola incana (Stocks) and *Cheiranthus Cheiri* (Wallflowers) came originally from Mediterranean Europe (probably the islands of Greece). Varieties with double flowers have been developed. Both belong to the *Cruciferae* family.

M. incana is an annual, biennial or perennial plant, 12 to 30 inches tall, and is branched at the top. The column stock is unbranched. It has alternate, oblong, narrow, entire leaves, silvery-green and velvety. Its flowers are large and either single with four petals, or more commonly double. They are brightly coloured in pink-lilac, white, purple or yellow, and are very fragrant. The seeds are disc-shaped, reddish, winged and develop in long, cylindrical siliques.

C. Cheiri is quite similar to *M. incana*. The plant is dark green and the flowers are yellow or orange; they may also be unicoloured, or striped or spotted with red or brown. They are mostly single and bloom in the spring.

They are sown from January to April under glass and are transplanted a first time when the plants have three or four leaves. Seed may be sown in October or November and young plants carried over the winter in cold frames. The cultivars of *Cheiranthus* can be considered perennial plants; those of *Mathiola* may be biennial or perennial. *M. incana* var. *annua* is annual and blooms about three months after sowing. Both dwarf and tall varieties exist, as well as some that bloom in the autumn of the year following sowing.

Wallflowers prefer a sandy soil with high pH, and grow best in full sun. Among the alpine wallflowers recommended are *Cheiranthus Allionii* (=*Erysimum asperum*) which grows rapidly and has small, single, yellow flowers, and *C. alpinus* which should be planted in spring and given a top-dressing of manure.

Nemesias, *Nemesia floribunda*, *N. strumosa*, *N. versicolor*, and their hybrids (Scrophulariaceae family) were introduced from South Africa in the eighteenth century. They are annuals, 10 to 15 inches tall, branched from the base. They have opposite leaves; the lower ones are oval and the upper ones narrow. The flowers are about 1 inch in diameter with a round but slightly irregular corolla. They are whitish, shaded, and rayed in yellow and violet, or they may be yellow, red or purple, and dotted or streaked. The seeds are small and winged, and are in a bivalved capsule.

These plants are suitable for borders and beds and blossom from May to August. Seed is sown in September; seedlings are transplanted to a cold frame or cool greenhouse for the winter and planted in March or April outdoors. It is also possible to sow them indoors in February or March and later transplant them outside, thinning to a distance of from 6 to 12 inches. They require light soil and good sunny locations.

57. *Cheiranthus Cheiri.*

58, 60. *Nemesia floribunda.*

59. Bed of *Cheiranthus Allionii.*

59

60

61

62

63

64

Sweet williams and garden pinks

Sweet Williams (*Dianthus barbatus*; Caryophyllaceae family), have been cultivated since about 1750, and are native to Europe and Asia.

The plant is biennial or perennial, 12 to 20 inches tall, erect with strong stems and opposite, lanceolate, dark green leaves. The flowers grow in a corymb. The corollas are regular, round (about 1 inch in diameter) and are formed by five triangular petals having a very narrow throat and a toothed margin. Colours vary from white to pink to dark purple; sometimes the flowers are unicoloured, but more often they have a darker rayed halo. Some are "eyed," spotted or streaked.

Sweet Williams are used in flower beds and edges and can be cut for house decoration. They bloom from April to July during their second year. They are sown in July to August in the seed bed, transplanted to a garden frame or greenhouse in September or October and to the garden in the spring. In mild climates they may be transplanted to the garden in the autumn. Cultivars with double flowers are available and have a very decorative effect in flower beds.

Sweet Williams should not be planted where they are overshadowed by bushes or trees as they like direct light. If exhibition specimens are desired it is advisable to have the pH of the soil tested, for these plants do not thrive on an acid soil. If in doubt, sprinkle lime before digging commences. The distance between the plants varies. If they are to be removed after flowering, then 15 inches or less is sufficient. If the intention is to allow the plants to remain for three or four years then at least 18 inches between them is advisable. When transplanting, take a ball of soil with the roots and make sure it is wet by soaking the ball in water.

If Sweet Williams are grown in a cold greenhouse the rooted layers are planted in September in 3 inch pots, repotting to a 5 inch pot in October or November. The final repotting takes place in February when a 7 inch pot is used.

Garden Pinks or Cottage Pinks (*Dianthus plumarius*) are native to Britain and southeastern Europe. The plant is perennial, but it is commonly cultivated as an annual. It has a bushy habit, reaching a height of about 12 inches. It is multibranched and the stems and leaves are waxy and light green. The leaves are opposite and lanceolate. The fragrant flowers are white, pink or purple, and have narrow, triangular petals with fringed margins. Cottage Pinks bloom throughout the summer and are excellent for borders and for rock gardens. Both single- and double-flowered types are available, some unicoloured or streaked or dotted. The culture is similar to that for Sweet Williams.

Other species of the Caryophyllaceae family recommended for the home garden are *Dianthus Caryophyllus*, the Clove Pink, in various colours; and *D. chinensis*, the Chinese or Indian Pink, a biennial in a variety of colours and growing from 6 to 12 inches in height.

61-64. Beds and single plants of *Dianthus barbatus* showing the variety of colour.

65

6

67

68

Daisies

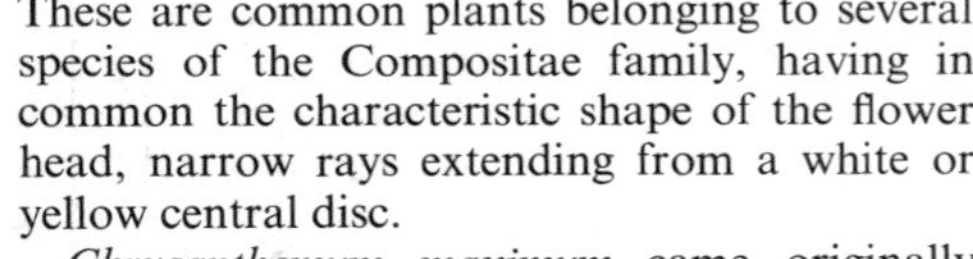

These are common plants belonging to several species of the Compositae family, having in common the characteristic shape of the flower head, narrow rays extending from a white or yellow central disc.

Chrysanthemum maximum came originally from the Pyrenees and the horticultural form is known as Shasta Daisy. It is perennial, has an erect and bushy habit, 20 to 30 inches tall, and has oblong and toothed leaves. The flowers are 2 to 3 inches in diameter with a yellow disc and white rays, sometimes on two rows. It is used for mass plantings and its flowers can be cut. It needs a rich soil and a sunny location.

Chrysanthemum frutescens, the Marguerite or Paris Daisy, is native to the Canary Islands and has been grown since about 1700. It is perennial, bushy, and grows about 30 inches high. It has oblong leaves, toothed or deeply pinnate. Its flowers are smaller than *C. maximum*. Cultivars with double and with yellow flowers are available. It may be grown from seed with adequate protection but is customarily propagated by cuttings. It blooms from late spring until autumn and is very ornamental as a specimen plant.

Daisies with attractive flowers include *Chrysanthemum coronarium* with laciniate-toothed leaves and yellow or white, mostly double flower heads; *C. segetum* with yellow flowers; *C. coccineum* with white and double flowers (White Queen Mary) or with carmine rays (James Kelway) or pink rays (Eileen May Robinson).

Among the other attractive hardy species cultivated are *C. alpinum* from the Alps, with white flowers; *C. arcticum* from the Arctic whose white flowers are tinged with lilac; *C. azaleanum* in numerous colours, with double flowers and a cushion form; *C. Leucanthemum*, the Oxeye Daisy, native to Europe that grows to 2 feet and has white flowers; and *C. uliginosum*, the Giant Daisy, growing to 5 feet and also with white flowers.

English Daisy is the common name of *Bellis perennis*, a familiar plant in European meadows, having shaded white ligules. Normally single-flowered in nature, there are double-flowered cultivars (*Bellis perennis flore pleno*), with white, pink, or carmine flower heads, and some kinds with globular heads. It is perennial and native to Europe. It blooms from April to June, is 2 to 5 inches high and has a basal rosette of spatulate, toothed leaves. The flower heads are single, apical, on peduncles without leaves. It is used for edging and as a bedding plant, being seeded in July or August and planted outdoors in autumn or early spring. It is also possible to seed it directly. Especially valuable cultivars are propagated by division. *B. rotundifolia caerulescens* has white flowers tinged with blue. *B. sylvestris*, has bright red flowers with a yellow disc.

65, 66. Flower bed and flower head of *Chrysanthemum maximum*.

67. *Bellis perennis flore pleno*.

68. *Chrysanthemum frutescens*.

9

0

71

72

Asters and gaillardias

Asters are species of the *Aster* genus (Compositae family) and are sometimes called Michaelmas Daisy or Starwort. They are herbaceous, tall and bushy, and either with numerous flower heads in a delicate violet colour (purple asters), or with large single flowers, sometimes white and similar to daisies. Purple asters include: *Aster Amellus* having a yellow disc and lilac-blue rays; *Aster novae-angliae* and *A. novi-belgii* with white, pink, lilac, or purple rays and yellow discs.

A. Amellus is indigenous to Europe; the other two originated in North America. They grow from 3 to 6 feet tall, are bushy, with lanceolate, entire and shiny leaves. They are planted in groups and are useful for cut flowers. They may be seeded in February indoors and transplanted outdoors, but the usual propagation is by division.

Aster Amellus cultivars "Wonder of Staffa" and "Kobold" have violet flowers, "Sonia" is pink, and "October" is violet. *Aster alpinus*, the Rock Aster, is the dwarf Alpine aster that has varieties among which var. *superbus* has large violet-lilac rays.

Other attractive species cultivated are *A. acris*, with lilac-purple flowers, that grows to 3 feet; *A. alpinus*, the Rock Aster, a dwarf variety; *A. diplostephioides*, flowers a rich purple, originating in the Himalayas, and its variety *Eichtlinii*, with pale blue blooms; *A. ericoides*, the Heath Aster, native to North America, that bears white flowers in October; the hybrid *A. Frikartii*, that produces lavender blue flowers from August to October; *A. lateriflorus* (synonymous to *A. diffusus*) with white flowers, and its variety *horizontalis* that has long spreading branches; *A. Thomsonii* from the Himalayas, that produces pale blue flowers from July right up to November; *A. yunnanensis* with lilac-blue flowers, growing up to 1 foot; and *A. cordifolius* that has mauve flowers.

An *Aster hybridus* derived from *A. novi-belgii* has very small leaves and numerous, double lilac-red flowers.

The so-called China Asters are either single or double flowered and belong to the species *Callistephus chinensis*.

The gaillardia, *Gaillardia pulchella* or *G. aristata* (Compositae family), is of North American origin. It may be annual, biennial, or perennial. Plants grow about 15 inches tall, have oblong leaves on the higher part of the plant, and irregularly lobed and toothed leaves on the lower. The flower heads, shaped like daisies, have reddish-yellow discs and rays of golden-yellow at the periphery and purple at the base. These robust plants are seeded in spring, transplanted to pots, and planted outdoors in April or May. Variety *grandiflora* is the most beautiful.

---

69. An *Aster* with white rays.

70. *A. Amellus.*

71. A group of double China Asters.

72. A flower bed of gaillardias.

Centaureas

The most common of the centaureas is the Cornflower or Bachelor's Button (*Centaurea Cyanus*: Compositae family). Cultivars with white, pink, lilac and blue flowers have been developed. The cornflower is an annual or perennial herbaceous plant, originating in Europe and the Middle East. The plant is quite common, is very sturdy, and is used for mass plantings and cut flowers.

Seeds are sown outdoors in April where plants will flower, or they can be sown indoors in February or March and transplanted outdoors in April when the plants have reached a good level of development, spacing them from 12 to 18 inches. The cornflower will also reseed itself. It requires loose soil and a sunny location.

Its roots and flower heads are sometimes used by the herbalist for making eye-drops or to alleviate coughing.

Many related species are very ornamental: *Centaurea oxylepis*, which has pink flowers with finely-fringed rays; *C. americana* (Basket Flower) with lilac flowers; *C. moschata* (Sweet Sultan) with yellow, fragrant flowers; and *C. macrocephala* with yellow blossoms.

Centaura montana (Mountain Bluet) has much larger blossoms in blue and pink-lilac. Native to the Caucasus and the Pyrenees, it is possible to grow it in gardens where it can flower in the autumn and spring.

C. babylonica from Asia Minor grows to 7 feet and produces yellow flowers in July; *C. dealbata*, from the Caucasus, in contrast grows to 18 inches and produces rose-coloured blooms. Its variety *Steenbergii* grows to 2 feet and has rose magenta blooms; *C. glastifolia* carries yellow flowers and grows from 4 to 6 feet; *C. macrocephala* from the Caucasus has yellow flowers and grows from 3 to 5 feet; *C. nudicaulis* is a small plant growing to 6 inches that is native to Asia Minor with pink flowers; *C. orientalis* from Europe grows to 3 feet and bears yellow flowers; *C. ruthenica* from Siberia and the Caucasus has pale yellow flowers.

Among the tender species cultivated, *C. Cineraria* has greyish foliage and is one of many plants called by the name Dusty Miller. It grows to about 18 inches and produces yellow or purplish flowers, but is grown chiefly for its foliage as are three other tender species, *C. Clementei*, native of Spain, that grows from 2 to 3 feet; *C. gymnocarpa* (synonymous to *argentea*) from Southern Europe that grows to 2 feet; and *C. ragusina*, also from Southern Europe, that grows up to 2 feet.

The tender species can be grown from seed sown in the greenhouse in spring and transplanted to pots. Another method is by using cuttings planted in the cold frame in the summer, potting them in the greenhouse and planting them outdoors in May.

73, 74. *Centaurea Cyanus.*

75. *C. oxylepis.*

76. *C. macrocephala.*

74

75

76

73

Cosmos

The best-known species of Cosmos is the Purple Mexican Aster, *Cosmos bipinnatus* (Compositae family), an annual that blooms from July to October and grows usually from 3 to 4 feet tall but under very good conditions to 5 feet. It has erect, branched stems, and its leaves are opposite, bipinnate, and with very narrow leaflets that make the plant bushy. The flowers are 2 to 4 inches in diameter, have a central yellow disc, and rays of not too many ligules that are wide and toothed at their tips. The plant has a wide colour range, and the flowers may be pink, rose, purple, crimson, lavender or white.

Cosmos is a versatile plant that can be put to a number of uses. Its height makes it suitable for temporary hedges, and it is also used for mass plantings.

Best results are obtained by sowing under glass in March and planting out the seedlings to their permanent position in May. For sowing, the soil should be light and the temperature from 50° to 55° F. These plants like a sunny position in the garden, a warm, dryish border being admirable. The soil should be ordinary; too much manure results in excessive vegetative growth. Distance between the plants should be between 2 and 3 feet, although some authorities stipulate from 15 to 24 inches. It is possible to sow the seeds directly at the site where the plants are intended to flower, this being done in late April or early May but, to obtain the longest possible flowering season and vigorous plants, seeding under glass is recommended.

Cosmos has received the attention of horticulturalists not only in this country, where the plant was first introduced in the late eighteenth century, but also in America and India. As a result several striking varieties have been introduced in recent years.

Of the species available the following can be recommended: *Cosmos bipinnatus*, mentioned earlier, is an early flowering strain. American horticulturalists have produced a variety "Pink Sensation" that has large rich pink flowers, and a crimson disc at the centre instead of the yellow one common to the species. In India a variety "Single Alipur Beauty" has been introduced with rose-pink flowers and a crimson disc.

C. diversifolius, sometimes known as *Bidens dahlioides*, also flowers in September, producing lilac coloured flowers. It grows to 3 feet.

C. diversifolius atrosanguineus, also known as *Bidens atrosanguinea*, is popularly called Black Cosmos. It carries velvety dark-red flowers and grows from 15 to 18 inches.

Especially suitable for British gardens is *C. sulphureus* in its variety "Orange Ruffles". This has semi-double, rich orange flowers, that appear very soon after planting out in May. The plants grow to 1½ feet, although *C. sulphureus* grows to between 3 and 4 feet and produces pale yellow flowers from July to August.

77-79. Various cultivars of *Cosmos bipinnatus*.

80. *Chrysanthemum carinatum*, another member of the Compositae family.

78

79

80

77

81

82

83

84

85

Peonies and buttercups

Peonies and buttercups belong to the same family, Ranunculaceae.

The peony (*Paeonia albiflora* also known as *P. lactiflora* and *P. edulis*) is a beautiful plant originating in Siberia and China. It is perennial, 2 to 3 feet tall, with fleshy thickened roots. It has many stems, giving the plant a bushy appearance. Leaves have three to six leaflets, each small and oval. The flowers are slightly fragrant; they are large, double or single, white shaded with pink, yellowish, or bright pink to carmine. Flowers consist of many rounded unequal petals that often are wavy or laciniate. In the centre of some cultivars a tuft of stamens with yellow anthers surrounds an ovary of three carpels that contains two to five large round seeds resembling small peas.

Peonies are normally propagated by division. They can be grown from seed, but do not then produce blossoms for about five years or more. They are suited for mass plantings, although isolated plants can have an aesthetic effect if planted at least 3 feet apart.

Many species are cultivated; among the best known are *P. anomala*, bearing crimson flowers in May; *P. arietina* with dark, purplish-red flowers; *P. cambessedesii*, producing deep rose blooms; *P. festiva* (synonymous with *P. officinalis*, a hybrid that has deep red double flowers; *P. obovata*, with colours ranging from white to rose-purple; *P. Potaninii* (synonymous to *P. Delavayi*, var. *angustiloba*), with deep maroon flowers, and its varieties *alba* with white flowers and *trollioides* with yellow blooms; and *P. Wittmanniana*, native to the Caucasus, producing bright yellow flowers in May.

The florist's ranunculus is derived from *Ranunculus asiaticus*, a native of Eastern Europe, Asia Minor and China. It is a perennial, 5 to 15 inches tall, with large and fascicled roots, large and slightly indented basal leaves and toothed upper leaves. The flowers are single, formed by five petals, or doubled, in whitish or yellow, red, lilac-pink or violet. The stamens are numerous with grey-brown or almost purple anthers and surround the carpels. The seeds are in achenes.

The buttercups blossom in May and June and are used for edges, masses, rock gardens and for cut flowers. They are propagated by root division. These are planted in autumn and are dug after they bloom. It is possible to grow them from seed, but then will bloom only after two years. They prefer loose soil and half shade with adequate moisture, and benefit from a mulch of decayed manure in spring.

The cultivars with double flowers (*Ranunculus asiaticus flore pleno*) have an extraordinary resemblance to little roses.

81-83. Variety of *Paeonia albiflora* with double flowers.

84. Buttercup with double flower.

85. Buttercups of the cultivar *Ranunculus asiaticus flore pleno*.

6

7

88

9

0

Poppies

Even though sometimes a pest, the common field poppy (*Papaver Rhoeas*)—also called the Corn or Shirley Poppy—has a beautiful flower. Related species are decorative for their large, brightly coloured or white flowers.

The most important species are *Papaver nudicaule*, *P. orientale* and *P. Rhoeas* (Papaveraceae family).

Papaver nudicaule or Iceland poppy is of arctic-alpine origin, and is suitable for Alpine and rock gardens. It is biennial or perennial, 12 to 16 inches tall, and blooms from May until autumn. It has thin, laciniate-toothed leaves. Its flowers are large, with four or five white, orange or yellow petals, and they grow on long, thin stems. It is propagated by seed and needs well-drained soils and sunny locations.

Papaver orientale or Oriental Poppy, is native to the Caucasus. It is perennial, grows from $1\frac{1}{2}$ to 3 feet tall, is rough, erect, and has pinnate-toothed leaves. The flowers are large (up to 4 to 8 inches in diameter), normally red with a black throat, but cultivars with white, orange, or pink as well as with double flowers exist.

It is seeded in May or June in the seed bed using light soil; seedlings are thinned and later transplanted in August or September for flowering in the spring. Distance between plants should be from 15 to 24 inches. It is possible to propagate it by dividing the root clumps in the autumn, or by root cuttings inside the greenhouse during the winter.

Other perennial species cultivated include *P. alpinum*, the Alpine Poppy, that grows to 6 inches and has yellow, orange, white and salmon coloured flowers; *P. californicum*, native to California, that grows to 1 foot and produces orange flowers in June; *P. pilosum*, from Greece that has orange flowers; and *P. rupifragum*, the Spanish Poppy that produces unusual terra-cotta flowers in summer.

The Opium Poppy (*P. somniferum*) may not legally be grown in some countries but its cultivation as a flower is permitted in Britain, although the manufacture of opium is, of course, illegal. It is native to Mediterranean Europe and Northern Africa.

The Shirley or Corn poppy (*P. Rhoeas*) is widely distributed throughout Europe and the Near East. Seed is sown early in the spring where it is to flower, and plants are thinned to 6 to 8 inches apart. Flower colour is red, pink and white. The plant will commonly reseed itself if seed is allowed to ripen.

Species among the annuals that also deserve mention are *P. glaucum*, the Tulip Poppy, native to Syria that grows to 18 inches and produces scarlet flowers; *P. laevigatum* from Greece that has white, black and scarlet flowers; and *P. pavoninum* from Afghanistan, called the Peacock Poppy, that has scarlet and black flowers.

86, 87. *Papaver nudicaule.*

88. *Papaver orientale.*

89, 90. *Papaver somniferum.*

91

92

Celosias

Within this group are the species of *Celosia* (Amaranthaceae family). The most commonly grown are *Celosia argentea* cv. *plumosa* (plumed cockscomb) and *C. argentea* var. *cristata* (crested cockscomb).

Plumed cockscomb produces conical and feather-shaped flowers. The crested cockscomb flower resembles a thick, crested and wavy fan. In both species, the colours range from yellow to fire-red, from pink-purple to a dark carmine, and in some cultivars silver shades are seen.

These are greenhouse annuals, 15 to 24 inches tall (although dwarf cultivars may be only 8 to 12 inches), erect, little-branched, with alternate, wide, oval-lanceolate, dark green leaves. The flower cluster consists of numerous tiny flowers grouped together into a very compact mass.

They are used for edges (dwarf cultivars), for mass plantings and for cut flowers.

Seeds are sown in March or April indoors, the seedlings transplanted to small pots, and the young plants planted outdoors in May or June, 8 to 15 inches apart. They require full sun and bloom from July to September.

The *Celosia argentea* var. *cristata*, form *fasciata*, has large and unusual clusters.

91, 92, 94. Cultivar of *Celosia argentea* cv. *plumosa.*

93. Group of *C. argentea* var. *cristata.*

95. A close view of the crested form, *C. argentea* var. *cristata* form *fasciata.*

94

93

95

96

Phlox

There are many species of phlox but two of the most interesting are *Phlox Drummondii* and *P. paniculata* (Polemoniaceae family), both native to North America. They grow from 1 to 3 feet tall with rigid stems. The basal leaves are oval-lanceolate and the upper leaves are large and rounded. The flowers are gathered in apical and axillary corymbs. Each flower is on a pedicel, and has a tubular corolla with a plain, round edge formed by five petals. Cultivars with double flowers have been developed. Flower colours can be white, pink, purple, yellow (rare), red, violet and blue. Flowers can be one colour, shaded, spotted or striped.

Phlox drummondii is the original of the common annual phlox. It is seeded in February or March and planted outside in April or May to bloom from May or June to September.

Phlox paniculata is a perennial, a little taller than the annual and blooms in August. It can be increased by division in late autumn or early spring. It can be seeded during winter and planted outdoors when danger of frost is past. A colourful perennial cultivar is "Frau Alfred von Mauthner," with red blossoms.

---

96. Patch of *Phlox paniculata.*

98. *Phlox paniculata* var. *alba grandiflora.*

97, 99. Annual phlox, *P. Drummondii.*

100. Flowers of *P. paniculata.*

97

98

99

100

101 

102 

103

104 

105 

Columbines and bleeding hearts

The *Aquilegia vulgaris* or Common Columbine (Ranunculaceae family) is native to Europe, America and Asia and probably the Algerian mountains as well.

It is a perennial, 1 to 3 feet tall, grows in clumps, and has thin, erect stems. The leaves have two to three leaflets with slightly or deeply toothed lobes. The flowers are formed by five sepals coloured like the five petals, which elongate at the base into a spur. The colour of the flowers varies from white to light pink, to lilac to blue, to blackish-violet. There are cultivars with double flowers, with the petals one inside the other, or with simple flowers, with very open almost nonexistent spur petals or those with very long spurs. The small and shiny black seeds are contained inside follicles in large numbers.

Aquilegia canadensis or American Columbine has yellow and red pendulous flowers. Other species, with less flashy flowers, are cultivated for the beauty of their colours, often mixed with different shades. *Aquilegia caerulea* (Colorado Columbine) is bluish-white; *A. Skinneri* (Mexican Columbine) has yellow and red flowers; all have multi-coloured hybrids.

Other popular species cultivated are *A. akitensis*, native to Japan that has purple and cream flowers and grows to 9 inches; *A. atrata*, with dark violet flowers that grows between $1\frac{1}{2}$ to $2\frac{1}{2}$ feet; *A. Bertolonii*, a small plant growing up to 6 inches, with deep blue flowers that appear in early summer; *A. chrysantha*, an American species, with yellow flowers, that grows to 2 feet; *A. discolor*, possibly the smallest species cultivated that grows to 3 inches and bears blue and white flowers; *A. ecalcarata*, native to China, with purplish maroon flowers; *A. flabellata* another species that originated in Japan, that grows to $1\frac{1}{2}$ feet and has pale purple or white flowers; *A. oxysepala* from Asia that has reddish-violet and yellow flowers; and *A. viridiflora* that originated in Siberia and has chocolate and green flowers in early summer.

Columbines bloom in early summer and are interesting in natural or rock gardens especially as isolated plants. They are seeded in early spring, transplanted to peat pots and planted outdoors either in spring or in autumn. They prefer sandy soil and semi-shade. Distance between plants should be from 12 to 20 inches. It is important to remember that these plants are poisonous if eaten.

Bleeding Heart (*Dicentra spectabilis*: Fumariacaea family) is very ornamental; its heart-shaped and swollen, white and pink flowers are all in-line and pendulous from a long peduncle. It is perennial, a native of China and Japan, and blooms in May and June. It is used to make groups in semi-shade, particularly under trees and along slopes. It is seeded in autumn; the plants spend winter under glass and are planted outdoors in spring at a 20- to 24-inch spacing.

101-104. Flowers of some cultivars of *Aquilegia vulgaris* (columbine).

105. *Dicentra spectabilis* (bleeding heart).

106

107

108

109

Foxglove, cleome, and acanthus

The foxglove (*Digitalis purpurea*: Scrophulariaceae family) is a native of Europe. It is a biennial plant, 1½ to 5 feet high, erect and rigid, not branched. The basal leaves are in a rosette and those on the stem are alternate; all are oval-lanceolate, rather wide, coarse, and velvety on the upper surface and on the edges. The flowers are large, tubular in shape somewhat resembling a thimble as their corolla is of one piece. Colour varies from lilac-carmine to pink to white. They are on a one-sided spike or raceme. The tiny, brown seeds are in bivalved capsules.

Foxgloves bloom from June to August. They are robust plants and are used for patches of colour in flower beds and for herbaceous borders. Seeds are sown in the spring or late summer and will bloom the following year. Spacing between plants should be from 15 to 24 inches.

Species cultivated are *Digitalis dubia* (synonymous *D. ambigua*), which has yellowish flowers and is very ornamental, and *Thapsii*, with rosy-purple flowers. The foxglove leaves are poisonous.

The cleome (*Cleome spinosa*, Capparidaceae family), commonly called Spider Flower, is native to South America. It is an annual plant, grows from 3 to 4 feet high, and has one spiny erect main stem that is branched. Leaves are alternate, palmate-compound with five to seven leaflets. Flowers are in large, erect apical racemes. Each flower has four oblong petals with long claws turned upward, and six long and thin stamens coloured in purple with yellow anthers, giving a spidery appearance. The petals are pink-lilac or pinkish-white or white and sometimes with purple stamens. The seeds are small, yellowish, oblong-truncated and irregular, in cylindrical capsules.

It blooms from mid-summer until autumn and looks good in groups. Seed is sown in a heated greenhouse or frame in March or April, the seedlings being transplanted into peat pots. Young plants can be planted outdoors in very warm regions. Distance between plants should be from 15 to 20 inches.

We include some species of the *Acanthus* genus (Acanthaceae family) of which the *Acanthus mollis* is the most common and the sturdiest. Another is *A. spinosus* with spiny leaves.

Acanthus is native to Europe, perennial, height 3 to 4 feet with large basal, oval, and lobate-toothed leaves in a thick rosette (spiny in *A. spinosus*). The large, irregular, labiate flowers are in large, thick spikes. Colour varies from pinkish-white to lilac-rust, with some striping and a darker, hood-shaped upper edge.

It is used as an isolated plant or in groups. Propagation is by division in spring or autumn. It needs a well-drained, rich soil and full sun. It should be heavily mulched in the north to protect it during the winter.

106, 108. *Digitalis purpurea.*

107. *Acanthus schottii.*

109. *Cleome spinosa.*

110

113

111

112

Salvia, delphiniums, and sweet peas

Three unrelated plants are included here, all having very ornamental flowers.

Salvia or Scarlet Sage (*Salvia splendens*: Labiatae family) is native to Brazil. It is cultivated as an annual, but it is perennial in the greenhouse. It grows from 15 to 30 inches tall although there are some dwarf types that reach only about 1 foot. It has opposite, oval and cordate, toothed leaves dark green above and greyish on the underside. The flowers are in apical spikes, each flower having a long, tubular, lipped, red corolla, with a large calyx of the same colour. The seeds are small nutlets.

It blooms from July to September and is excellent for edges (dwarf varieties), borders, and for mass or bed planting. It is seeded in March or April under cover, the seedlings being transplanted to peat pots, and the young plants planted outside when danger of frost is over, at a spacing of from 12 to 20 inches. It does best in sunny locations but may be grown in semi-shade. Cultivars with white, pink, red, violet or dark purple flowers have been developed.

Among the hardy species cultivated are *S. bicolor* with bluish-violet and white flowers that originated in the Mediterranean areas of North Africa and Spain; *S. Bulleyana* from the Himalayas that grows to 2 feet and has yellow flowers; *S. grandiflora* (also known as *S. Pitcheri*) that grows to 3 feet and has sky blue flowers; and *S. pratensis*, called Meadow Sage, native to Britain, that has violet flowers and grows to 3 feet.

Within the *Delphinium* genus (Ranunculaceae family), we illustrate two species. The perennial delphinium is *Delphinium cultorum*; the annual is the larkspur, *Delphinium Ajacis*.

The larkspur is an annual herbaceous plant originating in Europe and the Orient, grows from 1 to 3 feet tall, has erect and rigid stems, with round leaves at the base of the plant and oblong above. The flowers are in apical spicate racemes. They are not large and are irregular with the receptacle the same colour as the corolla, which is formed by five petals, the highest being extended into a long spur. The seeds are small, round, and black, in follicles. The colour varies from white to pink to blue to violet.

The larkspurs are suited for borders and for cut flowers. They are seeded indoors during spring, the seedlings being transplanted to pots and the young plants planted outdoors after the last frost. They may also be directly seeded either in early spring or in autumn. Distance between plants should be about 12 inches.

Delphiniums are perennial plants derived from both European and Asiatic species. They grow to 25 to 40 inches or more, and have palmately-lobed leaves. The flowers are larger than larkspur and often wrinkled, and they form taller and bigger clusters. Flower colour varies from blue to violet, to pink-lilac with white, pink, and light blue types.

Delphiniums prefer sunny locations, and moist, well-drained, friable soils. They are seeded indoors in the early spring and then the young plants are transplanted outdoors. Seed sown in mid-summer produces plants ready for transplanting in September to flower the following spring.

Other popular perennial species cultivated are *D. cardinale* from California that produces scarlet flowers; *D. elatum*, native to the Alps, with blue flowers; *D. Pylzowii* of small habit, growing from 6 to 10 inches, with blue and violet flowers; and *D. Zalil*, native to Afghanistan, that grows to 6 feet and produces yellow flowers.

Among the annual species are *D. Consolida*, native to Europe, that grows to 2 feet and has blue flowers; and *D. orientale*, known as Rocket Larkspur, that grows to 2 feet and has either rose, violet or white flowers.

The Sweet Pea (*Lathyrus odoratus*: Leguminosae family) is grown for its large, butterfly-shaped, fragrant, multicoloured flowers, that bloom from June to September. It is annual and is normally seeded directly outdoors very early in the spring. A related species is the *Lathyrus latifolius*, the perennial sweet pea that has smaller flowers in white, pink or carmine. It is sown in the spring and is transplanted in early summer.

---

110. *Salvia splendens*, scarlet sage.

111. *Delphinium cultorum*, delphinium.

112. *Delphinium Ajacis*, larkspur.

113. *Lathyrus latifolius*, a perennial sweet pea.

Anemones

Anemone coronaria, the Poppy Anemone (Ranunculaceae family), is a common species grown in gardens and used as a cut flower by florists. It is a perennial, native to Central and Eastern Mediterranean countries. Erect and branched, it grows from 12 to 20 inches. Leaves are palmate, laciniate, and toothed; flowers have a cup shape and are formed by five to ten petaloid sepals which are wide and round, in white or red, lilac, violet, purple or blue, of a uniform colour or variegated; the actual petals are missing. In the centre of the flower is a thick crown of stamens with black or purple anthers that surround the carpels. The seeds are achenes.

Anemones bloom from April to June and are used for beds, borders and edgings or for cutting. They may be seeded in the autumn and carried over winter under protection, but they are usually propagated by planting rhizomes, remembering to plant the bud up. Division of the clumps is also possible. Spacing should be from 6 to 12 inches. These plants suffer from excessive cold and must be protected in northern areas. Double and semi-double flowered cultivars are available.

In addition to *A. coronaria*, there are many species cultivated by horticulturalists: *A. albana* from Asia has flowers that range from white to light blue; *A. alpina*, from Europe, has white flowers, and many varieties such as *sulphurea*, yellow flowers; *A. appeninina* has blue, rose and white flowers; *A. baldensis* from Europe with white flowers tinged pink; *A. blanda* from Asia Minor with blue flowers that bloom from January to March; *A. canadensis* from America that grows to 2½ feet and produces white flowers in June; *A. Fanninii* from South Africa that grows to 4 feet and has white flowers; *A. fulgens*, the Scarlet Windflower, native to Europe that produces scarlet flowers in May; *A. Halleri*, from Switzerland that grows to 6 inches and has lilac flowers; *A. hupehensis* from China that has rose-coloured flowers; *A. nemorosa*, the Wood Anemone, native to Britain that grows to 6 inches and produces white flowers in March, together with its many varieties of which *alba*, *Allenii* and *Robinsoniana* are the best known; *A. Pulsatilla*, the Pasque Flower, native to Europe that produces purple flowers in April, and has many varieties; *A. verbalis* that has purple flowers with white on the outside; *A. vitifolia*, a delicate species that produces white flowers; and *A. trifolia* that produces white flowers, and has a variety, *caerulescens*, with bluish flowers. Both grow to about 6 inches.

Other ornamental species are *Anemone japonica* (Japanese Anemone), a tall growing perennial with pink or white flowers and yellow anthers; *A. hortensis* (Garden Anemone) with lilac, pink or red flowers that are similar to *A. coronaria*, of which there are several cultivars; and *A. sylvestris*, the Snowdrop Windflower that grows to 1 foot.

114-116. A few examples of *Anemone coronaria*.

117. *A. coronaria*, a semi-double.

115

116

117

114

118

11

12

121

122

Fuchsias

Fuchsia (Onagraceae family) are grouped into the long-tube and the short-tube types, as well as into those having drooping flowers and those with erect flowers. Native to tropical America, they are showy shrubs; their leaves are simple, oval-oblong, entire or slightly toothed, opposite or alternate or in whorls of three. The flowers are solitary or in groups in axillary or terminal clusters, mostly with long peduncles. The flower has a long, tubular calyx in red, lilac or purple, with four fleshy sepals usually curved backwards; the corolla is formed by four wide, rounded petals. There are double-flowered cultivars of great beauty, having a corolla of pink, lilac, purple or white.

Among the less shrubby species, *Fuchsia magellanica* var. *globosa* grows about $1\frac{1}{2}$ to 3 feet tall. It is used in borders, hanging baskets and in pots and tubs.

Other varieties of *F. magellanica* are *conica* that bears scarlet flowers; *discolor*, with purple and red flowers; *gracilis*, flowers scarlet and purple; and *Riccartoni* with scarlet flowers.

Propagation is usually by cuttings in early spring under glass, which can then be transplanted into pots and protected over winter for planting outdoors the following spring.

Fuchsias need semi-shade, and sandy soil high in organic matter. Pruning is done during the autumn. Fuchsias are generally injured by cold. They should be protected in winter with a layer of leaves or moss.

The most beautiful species are undoubtedly those grown in the greenhouse. Here the choice is wide both as regards the range of colour and the height of the shrub. *F. alpestris*, native to Brazil, grows from 12 to 18 feet and produces crimson flowers in summer; *F. arborescens* bears pink flowers in summer, grows to between 10 and 15 feet and is native to Mexico; *F. bacillaris*, from Chile, grows to 5 feet and has rose-coloured flowers; *F. cordifolia*, of similar height, is native to Mexico and has orange flowers; *F. corymbiflora*, from Bolivia, has deep red flowers and grows to 6 feet; from New Zealand *F. procumbens* has a trailing habit and bears yellow and blue flowers in the summer. In autumn its magenta berries make a good display; *F. serratifolia* from Peru produces scarlet and green flowers; *F. simblicicaulis*, also from Peru, carries scarlet flowers; *F. superba*, a hybrid, has crimson flowers; and *F. triphylla*, growing from 12 to 18 inches, produces cinnebar red flowers.

Other species include: *Fuchsia fulgens* and its hybrids, with autumn and spring bloom, and having flowers in many colours; *F. splendens*, with summer blooming; and *F. speciosa*, with flowers in clusters. The latter has been used in developing many of the present garden cultivars.

---

118. *Fuchsia magellanica* var. *globosa*, cultivar "Ridestar."

119. Cultivar "Melody."

120-122. Some species of fuchsias.

123

124

125

126

127

Zinnias

Most Zinnia varieties are cultivars of *Zinnia elegans* (Compositae family), a native of Mexico. They are annual herbaceous plants 6 to 30 inches tall, erect and only slightly branched with brittle stems. The leaves are rough like the stems, opposite, oval and light green.

Zinnia flower heads are of different sizes (from 1 to 6 inches), are single or double, with a protruding central disc which has a crown of male flowers with yellow anthers around its edge. The rays are numerous ligules in various colours: white, greenish, yellow, orange, red, pink, lilac, purple. The seeds are elongated achenes overtopped by bristles.

Zinnias bloom abundantly from summer to autumn and are used for edges (dwarf varieties), borders, massed plantings and for cut flowers. They are seeded in April or May, the seedlings are transplanted to peat pots, and the young plants planted outdoors when danger of frost is past, with 8 to 10 inches between plants. They may also be seeded directly outdoors. They prefer warm, sunny locations and rich soil.

Cultivars with giant flowers ($3\frac{1}{2}$ to 6 inches in diameter) include "California Giant". Another popular species is *Zinnia Haageana* or Mexicana zinnia, that has orange-scarlet flowers. *Z. pauciflora* has yellow or purple flowers.

128

123-127. Some types of *Zinnia elegans*.

128. Bed of *Z. Haageana*.

129

130

131

132

133

Carnations

Carnations or clove pinks include the cultivars of *Dianthus Caryophyllus* (Caryophyllaceae family).

They are a perennial species, 5 to 30 inches tall, erect or drooping, branched with rigid, light green, shiny stems having long internodes. Leaves are opposite, linear and thick. The flowers are solitary or clustered, scented, with a rigid, cylindrical receptacle having a double involucre and a corolla with many long deltoid petals that have an indented or fringed margin. Colour ranges from white to pink to yellow to red and maroon, and flowers may be of a single colour or shaded, spotted or variegated. The seeds are small, oval, and contained inside a capsule.

Carnations may be grown in gardens or in flower boxes on terraces and porches. A large greenhouse industry exists to sell cut flowers. Seeding takes place in early spring, the seedlings being transplanted to pots when they have five or more leaves. The most common method of propagation is by cuttings, made in the greenhouse during winter. A heavy, fertile soil is preferred. Carnations will not tolerate cold or excessive heat, and they are susceptible to a number of diseases, some of which are encouraged by growers who fail to give the plants sufficient light and air. Wilt and stem-rot are both caused by fungi. The latter occurs at the point where soil and stem meet and unless checked will kill the plant. Carnation wilt blocks the food passages of the plant. Some varieties are now being raised that are resistant to both diseases.

There are a number of other fungus diseases that afflict the plant, including Fairy Ring Spot, Mildew Spot and Rust. Light and air which create a fresh atmosphere are perhaps the best protection the plants can have, for it is a stuffy, humid atmosphere that aggravates these diseases. If fungus disease is noticed in the autumn the affected leaves should be removed and burnt, the plant subsequently being dusted with a proprietary fungicide powder.

During the summer months of June, July and August the red spider is active on carnations and unless checked will cause the leaves to become a rusty colour and to fall off. To lessen the damage the plants should be regularly syringed in hot, dry weather; once the red spider has a hold it can be defeated by using one of the many remedies obtainable from seedsmen. Insecticide sprays are effective against other pests such as green-fly aphis, black-fly and root aphis. Thrip, too, can be dealt with in this way.

Many cultivars of carnations are available, some of which bloom almost continuously. The choice of flower colour is practically unlimited and plant breeders continue to develop hybrids. The hardy garden carnations, as the Enfant de Nice or the Chabaud Giants, are better adapted to garden conditions than the greenhouse cultivars. These hardy plants are grown from seed. A related species *D. plumaris*, the Cottage Pink native to Britain and Eastern Europe, grows to about 12 inches and is available in many colours (see page 31).

129-133. Examples of colour in cultivars of *Dianthus Caryophyllus*.

Small dahlias

Small-flowered dahlias are those varieties with flower heads 1 to 2 inches in diameter. They may be daisy-like with the central yellow disc surrounded by only one row of ligules, or they may have globose and extra-doubled flower heads formed by very many short, hollow and conical ligules: these latter are known as pompon dahlias. All these dahlias, as well as those with large flowers illustrated on the next page, belong to the hybrid series *Dahlia hortensis* (Compositae family) and derive from some species such as the *Dahlia coccinea*, *D. pinnata*, *D. Merckii* and others, all native to Mexico. They are one of the most popular garden plants.

Dahlias are perennial, grow from 2 to 6 feet tall, and have oblong-spindle-shaped, fleshy storage roots. Stems are erect and branched. Leaves are opposite and may be simple, pinnate or bipinnate; leaflets are oval, toothed and dark-green. The flower heads are terminal on axillary peduncles, have a large involucre formed by two series of green bracts and by a halo of rays; ligules are wide or narrow, plain or twisted (conical) in the various cultivars. The tubular central disc, which is visible and yellow in the simple forms, is practically nonexistent in the doubled flowers formed largely of ray flowers.

Dahlias flower from July to October. They are excellent in groups, in borders (dwarf species with small flowers), and for cut flowers. In early spring the storage roots are placed in a warm and moist location. The roots generally are planted outdoors directly after danger of frost is past in May or June. They may be propagated by cuttings, taken in the spring from the young shoots sprouting from the storage roots. As soon as the cuttings have rooted, they are planted into pots until they have grown large enough to be planted outside. They are usually propagated by division of root clumps. These clumps are dug up in October and placed in a cool, dark, humid area, preferably in dry sand. There are many classes of dahlias based on the flower size and type, such as Show, Fancy, Peony-flowered, Charm, Decorative, Cactus, Pompon, Collarette and Single. Of the several small-flowered types included, the Pompons have flowers that are small and circular with florets, and the Charm and Miniature Peony-flowered have semi-double flowers with broad and somewhat flattened florets, the plants being bushy and branching, with a very wide range of colours that make the two types extremely popular.

134

134. Group of dwarf single-flowered dahlias.

135, 136. Two pompon dahlias.

137. Cultivar with slightly larger flowers.

5

6

137

139

138

140

141

142

Large dahlias

Dahlias with large flowers reaching 10 inches in diameter belong to the same species mentioned on the previous page, *Dahlia hortensis*, and have the same origins. The plants do not differ substantially from the small-flowered types except that they grow from 6 to 8 feet tall and have larger flowers. The flowers are of various types; sometimes with from eight to twelve simple, flat ligules, sometimes with many ligules making semi-doubled flower heads (like peony flowers), and sometimes doubled or extra-doubled.

The Show types grown for exhibition have circular flowers, with quilled florets, and colours all of one tint. The Fancy types have large circular flowers, with quilled florets, the florets being tipped, striped or flaked in a contrasting tint to the basic flower colour. The Cactus types have a flower that is high in the centre, with long, narrow florets that are pointed and reflexed at the edges.

The ligules may be of a single colour or shaded darker towards the centre of the flower. In other cases, the ligules are bicoloured lengthwise (for example, white in the centre and red at the edge) and are called "flamed."

A particularly interesting group of these large flowered dahlias is the Cactus Dahlia, derived from *Dahlia Juarezii*. Their flowers are doubled and the ligules are long and twisted lengthwise, simulating long and rigid tubular petals.

The colours are variable in all large dahlias, having all the gradations of white, yellow, golden, orange, pink, red, carmine, lilac, dark purple and violet; only blue is missing.

Of these Cactus Dahlias whose flowers exceed 10 inches in diameter the following varieties can be recommended: Arab Queen, growing to 4 feet with flowers that are pale apricot with a yellow centre; Gladys Reynolds, up to 4 feet 6 inches with flowers a reddish-orange; Graf Folke Bernadette, growing to 6 feet and with white flowers; G. W. Leak, up to 4 feet 6 inches, with white flowers; Herbert Apps, golden blooms and growing to 5 feet 6 inches; Peculiar, crimson flowers that shade away to rose, height 6 feet; Royal Rothesay, up to 4 feet in height and bearing deep crimson flowers; and Searchlight, growing up to 5 feet in height and bearing yellow flowers.

Of slightly smaller flower diameter, but retaining the colour range are these varieties of the Cactus Dahlia: Aristos, growing to 4 feet, with purple flowers, tipped white; Ballego's Surprise, also 4 feet, and with white flowers; Bunny, bearing yellow flowers; Janet Beckett, also carrying yellow flowers; Pride of Holland, with pink flowers; Rocket, growing to 4 feet 6 inches and with red flowers; The Colonel, yellow flowers; and Victory Day, growing to 5 feet and bearing red flowers.

---

138. Cactus Dahlia.

139. A large single-flowered dahlia.

140, 141. Two large double dahlias.

142. A dahlia with flamed petals.

143

144

145

146

147

Chrysanthemums

On this page chrysanthemums other than the Korean types are described, in particular the cultivars of *Chrysanthemum hortorum*, which might have derived from *C. indicum*, *C. sinense*, and perhaps from other species as well.

C. hortorum is perennial, somewhat shrubby, erect, 1 to 3 feet tall, and has rigid stems. The leaves are aromatic, oval or oblong, indented-lobous or pinnatifid, more or less toothed, green-grey above and lighter coloured on the underside. The chrysanthemums of this group produce large flowers, solitary or in clusters, or in corymbs. The heads have numerous ray flowers, more or less narrow but mainly ribbon-shaped and curved towards the centre of the head to form a beautiful globose mass. In many cultivars they are twisted or ruffled and then the whole flower head will look twisted and ruffled. The central disc can be seen but is always very small, greenish or yellow, or it may be absent.

They bloom from August through November. Seedlings for planting can be purchased in the spring, or species can be propagated by cuttings. Chrysanthemums need a light pruning in June or July to remove side branches so only one or two stems remain to bear large blossoms; it is important to remove the side buds on each stem leaving only the central bud. The pompon or hardy kinds have the tips of the shoots removed to induce branching and are not disbudded.

Chrysanthemums suitable for greenhouse culture form a large part of the horticulturists' annual programme, and there is a steady demand from florists for the blooms. The compost is usually made up of three parts loam, one part manure, one part decayed leaves, one part coarse silver sand, half-part ground bones and one part charcoal or wood ashes.

Seedlings are potted for the first time in 3 inch pots in March and are transferred at the end of April into 5 inch or 6 inch pots. At the end of May they are repotted in large pots of 8 to 10 inches. If exhibition plants are required then the main stem has to be stopped in March—the distance from the base depending on the variety and this information can be obtained usually from the seedsman's packet or from his catalogue. To obtain bushy plants for general use it is usual to stop the main stem about 4 inches from the base.

Chrysanthemums have numerous cultivars. Colours range from white to yellow to pink to carmine to golden brown to purple-rust.

They are susceptible to aphids, which may be controlled with appropriate insecticides. Foliar nematodes may also damage the plants, but may be controlled by disinfecting the soil. Among the diseases, mildew and rust can be problems, but can be dealt with by using approved fungicides.

---

143. Example of a Japanese chrysanthemum.

144-146. Standard chrysanthemums.

147. A spider chrysanthemum.

148

Garden chrysanthemums

Within this group are included the chrysanthemums that have a more dwarf and bushy habit than those described on the previous page. The Korean types have smaller and thicker leaves and usually have many flower heads in large corymbs. They have been developed from *Chrysanthemum koreanum* and *C. hortorum*. The flowers can be single, semi-double or double. The single flowers resemble daisies. The doubled types resemble the Japanese chrysanthemums, both in the shape and in the colour, but are smaller. The cultivars with tiny button-like flowers are quite attractive.

These chrysanthemums are grown similarly to the larger flowered types. They are used in edges, beds, or for mass plantings, and may be grown in pots as porch or house plants. If large blooms are required, the plants should be disbudded, leaving only the central bud.

148. Garden chrysanthemums mixed with Japanese chrysanthemums.

149, 150. Garden chrysanthemums, showing the large, central disc.

151. Garden chrysanthemums with daisy-like flowers.

152. Cultivar of chrysanthemum with tubular ray flowers.

Lupins

Both perennial and annual lupins belong to the genus *Lupinus* (Leguminosae family).

The prototype of the perennial lupin is considered to be *Lupinus polyphyllus*, a native of California. It is from 2½ to 5 feet tall and has erect stems. Leaves have long petioles, are palmately-compounded, formed by 10 to 16 lanceolate leaflets, dull green on top and pubescent underneath. The flowers, resembling a pea flower, are numerous and arranged on long, terminal racemes. Flowers are white, cream coloured, pink, red, violet or blue, of a single colour or with the standard petal (the petal turned upward) differently coloured from those of the wings and the keel.

The perennial lupins flower from June to September and are especially suited for massed groups. They are seeded in spring in pots or directly outdoors; the plants germinated in pots should be planted outside when they show the first leaves, taking care to avoid root damage.

A related species, *Lupinus Hartwegii*, of Mexican origin, has blue flowers with white or pink standard. It is generally grown as an annual.

Many species belong to the annual lupins: *Lupinus mutabilis* (also var. *Cruckshanksii*), *L. hirsutissimus*, *L. luteus*, *L. pubescens* and its several varieties, and at least 10 others.

L. mutabilis, one of the most decorative, is from Peru. It grows from 30 to 50 inches tall, is smooth and shiny, and has branched stems shaped like a candelabra on the top of the plant. Flowers are scented and form thinner clusters than the perennials, but have the same colour.

Seeds are rounded, yellowish and shiny, and grow in thick pods.

The dwarf lupin, *Lupinus nanus*, grows to about 12 inches, has flowers with a white standard and blue wings, and is suitable for edging.

153-156. Some colours of cultivars of *Lupinus polyphyllus*.

Sunflowers and rudbeckias

These plants belong to the same family (Compositae) and have in common a rugged appearance and yellow flowers.

The Common Sunflower (*Helianthus annuus*) is a large annual, native to North America. It has a rigid and hairy stem with alternate, large and oval, dull and rough leaves, which are light green, toothed and irregular. The flower heads are very large and may exceed 15 inches in diameter. They have a large, flat central disc that may be yellow, orange or brown, large ligules that can also be unicoloured or bicoloured. If the latter they present a darker basal crown around the disc. The seeds are large achenes.

The sunflower blooms from July to September and is suitable for borders, for screening walls and for groups. It may be seeded in late spring and transplanted outdoors after frost danger is past. Usually it is seeded directly outside. Spacing depends on the cultivar. Single and doubled varieties exist, the latter with ligulated flowers even in the central disc. Some resemble gaillardias and have a brown disc, a red crown and a yellow periphery.

The seeds are a source of an edible oil, and are used for feeding birds.

Related species include *Helianthus decapetalus* var. *multiflorus* and *Helianthus rigidus*, also native to North America and, like many other species (*H. atrorubens* and *H. tuberosus*), are perennial by creeping rootstocks. They grow as high as 10 feet and have large, underground rhizomes. Leaves and flowers are smaller than *H. annuus*. The dominant flower colour is yellow.

Helianthus tuberosus, known as Jerusalem Artichoke, has large edible rhizomes. The perennial species can be reproduced by division of the rhizomes in autumn or in spring.

Similar to the smaller sunflowers are the Rudbeckias or Coneflowers (*Rudbeckia* genus), of which there are many species and cultivars suited to gardens. They have flowers with yellow ligules, with a protruding greenish disc (*Rudbeckia nitida*), or a brown-blackish one (*Rudbeckia subtomentosa*).

There are annual and perennial species, both used for borders or edges. Less sturdy than sunflowers, they require a light and well-drained soil. They are seeded either inside for transplanting, or directly outdoors.

The Gloriosa Daisy has been developed from *R. hirta*, and is related to the Black-Eyed Susan. Flowers are single or double, golden yellow with a dark centre, or with mahogany red at base. The plant grows from 2 to 3 feet tall and the flowers are 4 to 6 inches in diameter. Sown indoors and transplanted later, they will flower the first year.

157

158 159

160 161

157. Flower head of *Helianthus annuus* (sunflower).

158. *H. decapetalus* var. *multiflorus* (miniature sunflower).

159. *H. tuberosus* (Jerusalem Artichoke).

160. *Rudbeckia hirta* (Black-eyed Susan).

161. *Rudbeckia subtomentosa* cv. "Goldsturm."

162

163

Hollyhocks

Plants of the botanical species *Althaea rosea* (Malvaceae family) are known as Hollyhocks, and are sometimes called Mallows. They are native to China.

Hollyhocks grow to a height of 5 to 9 feet, even though they are herbaceous. They are perennial and are erect and little branched. Leaves are alternate, on long petioles, large, rough and light green. The flowers are large, axillary, almost sessile, developing along the stem. Each flower, in its simple form, has a large, funnel-shaped corolla, formed by five petals joined only at the base. The stamens are numerous and joined to form a column covering the ovary. The seeds are kidney-shaped.

Hollyhocks grown from seed flower in the second year. They are used for borders, beds and screens. They are normally seeded directly outside and thinned to stand 2 to 3 feet apart. Special types may be started inside, and should be grown in 6 inch pots until planted outdoors. They can be propagated by division of the root clumps, or by cuttings using young growth. They are often infected with rust (*Puccinia malvacearum*), which may be controlled by use of appropriate fungicides.

The flowers and roots are used by herbalists to make soothing medicaments.

Cultivars with single, semi-double and double flowers are available. The extremely doubled types resemble peonies. Dwarf cultivars, as well as the tall variety, are rich in variously coloured flowers: white, pink, lilac, red, crimson, reddish-yellow and yellow.

Althea ficifolia, the Fig-leaved Hollyhock, native to Siberia, has yellow flowers and is seen in gardens all over Europe and North America. *A. cannabina*, from Europe, grows to 6 feet, and has rose-coloured flowers.

164

165

162, 165, 166. Examples of several species of double hollyhock flowers.

163. Hollyhock with single pink flowers.

164. Semi-double flowers.

167

168

169

170

Plants with coloured leaves and fruits

In addition to the flowering plants, colour and interest can be enhanced by using plants having multi-coloured leaves and brightly-coloured fruit.

Among the foliage plants, the most popular is the Coleus (*Coleus Blumei*) of the Labiatae family. It is perennial in the greenhouse but will not withstand frost. It grows from 1 to 2 feet tall, has an erect stem that is square in cross section and little branched. The opposite leaves are oval-pointed, toothed and sometimes laciniate, are yellow, green or purplish and may be uni-coloured, striped, spotted or margined. The flowers are labiate, not showy, and grow in terminal racemes. The seeds are small.

The *Coleus* are generally native to Malaysia and Africa. Because of their attractive coloured leaves, they are used for edgings, borders, mosaic patterns and hanging baskets. It is common to propagate coleus by cuttings in the greenhouse during winter, using stems taken from healthy plants. They are planted outside after danger of frost is past, 1 to 2 feet apart.

There are many named cultivars and several excellent strains grown from seed which are true to colour and habit of growth.

In addition to *C. Blumei*, already mentioned, popular cultivated species include: *C. Autranii*, from Abyssinia, producing lavender flowers in winter; *C. Frederici*, native to Angola, that produces purplish-blue flowers in winter; and *C. thyrsoideus*, the Winter Flowering Coleus, native to tropical Africa that bears blue flowers from January to April.

Coleus are subject to damage from mealy bugs and from aphids; these may be controlled with suitable insecticides.

Species of the *Perilla* genus belong to the Labiatae family too, are native to China, and also have very ornamental coloured foliage. *Perilla frutescens*, with its very pretty red-brown to blackish-purple leaves, is very well known.

Small plants, which produce brightly coloured fruit often of great beauty, include *Capsicum frutescens* and some *Solanum* (Solanaceae family). Within *Capsicum frutescens* is a dwarf pepper that develops very small, finger-shaped, yellow or red fruits, and has dark green leaves. It is particularly good for borders, edging and massed plantings.

Numerous species of the *Solanum* genus have colourful fruit, and most are perennial. They produce red, globose berries about 1 inch in diameter and are suited for flower beds and edgings. *S. Pseudo-Capsicum*, Jerusalem-Cherry, is used as a decorative pot plant for Christmas.

---

167. *Coleus Blumei*, cultivar with reddish leaves and yellow margin.

168. A flower bed corner of *Coleus* showing colourful foliage.

169. *Capsicum frutescens*, small ornamental peppers.

170. A *Solanum* with red berries.

71

172

173

4

75

Clematis and morning glories

Clematis belong to the *Clematis* genus (Ranunculaceae family). They are perennial shrubby vines with thin, ropy stems, trifoliate leaves, and large flowers with four or more petals. One of the most popular is *Clematis lanuginosa*, a native of China and commonly known as the large-flowering clematis. Its thin stem is knotty and multibranched; leaves are almost persistent, woolly and silvery when the plant is young, and becoming dark-green as the plant matures. Flowers are solitary or in groups of three, axillary, large (3 to 6 inches in diameter), formed by four to eight petaloid sepals, variously coloured from white to pink to lilac-blue. The stamens are numerous, whitish, and form a central tuft. The seeds are achenes with a persistent plumose style attached.

A related species is *Clematis patens* native to Japan, with blue flowers, while the hybrid *C. venosa*, has smaller ($1\frac{1}{2}$ to 2 inches in diameter) cream-coloured flowers. Numerous hybrids have been developed from crosses of *Clematis lanuginosa* and *C. patens*, sometimes called *C. hybrida* var. *grandiflora*.

Clematis are rugged plants with abundant bloom, and are suitable vines for covering walls, arbors and treetrunks. They are propagated by cuttings or by grafting to maintain the flower characteristics. Grafts are made in spring or autumn on *C. Flammula* or *C. Viticella* rootstocks. They prefer rich, well-drained soils and a light shade.

Morning Glories are mostly annual (*Pharbitis*, *Ipomoea* and *Convolvulus* genera, often synonymous: Convolvulaceae family). *Convolvulus tricolor* is the common, three-coloured Morning Glory. It is dwarf, growing only to 1 or 2 feet, has pubescent, little-branched and drooping stems. Leaves are alternate, oblong-spatulate. The flowers are solitary, axillary, with long peduncles, funnel-shaped, large, with a corolla blue-violet at the edge and white inside with a yellow throat. Seeds are black, dull, angular and are contained in a capsule.

It is used for hanging baskets and borders and is usually seeded directly outdoors, the seedlings being thinned to 5 inches apart when 2 inches high. It may also be propagated by cuttings. Cultivars are available with white, pink or violet flowers, either single-coloured or bicoloured, and either simple or double.

The most popular of the Morning Glories is *Ipomoea purpurea*, native of the American Tropics, commonly known as Tall Morning Glory. It is climbing, annual, and has heart-shaped leaves. The flowers are like *C. tricolor* but with a wider range of colours. It is seeded in late spring outdoors. Blossoming is continuous from July to September and often is spectacular. There are many related species.

171, 172. Two examples of *Clematis hybrida*.

173, 174. *Ipomoea purpurea* in two different colours.

175. *Convolvulus tricolor*.

176

1

17

17

18

Zonal and succulent geraniums

Commonly known as geraniums, these pelargoniums belong to the species *Pelargonium hortorum* (= *P. hybridum* = *P. zonale* × *inquinans*) and to the Geraniaceae family. They are native to South Africa. The plant is a perennial in the greenhouse, but will not withstand frost. It grows from 12 to 24 inches tall, sometimes higher. It has thick, cylindrical and branched stems with alternate leaves which have a rather thick epidermis, are rounded and somewhat reniform, and have five to twelve lobes and a crenated edge. Leaves are light green or greyish with a concentric red or brown area and are velvety and scented. The flowers have five or more free petals and are in clusters of from five to thirty, in axillary umbels with long penduncles. The fruits are small, and contain five seeds.

Zonal geraniums flower all year round if protected from frost. They are used in pots, as patio or house plants, in hanging baskets and outdoors for beds and edging.

They may be propagated by seed sown from February to April in pots, taking care to regulate the temperature to between 55° and 65° F. The most common method of propagation, however, is by cuttings taken in early autumn and during the winter months and placed in pots with light, well-drained soil, in a cool greenhouse. They may be repotted in spring and placed in warm shelters to force the growth for outdoor planting.

Geraniums are subject to invasion by nematodes, which can be controlled by using sterilized soil. Green aphids also sometimes infest the plants.

The cultivated forms of *Pelargonium hybridum* are numerous; some having single and other double flowers. Colour varies from white to pink to bright red to dark carmine. Some are of a single colour, some are bicoloured. Some cultivars have variegated or white margined leaves.

A related hybrid, *Pelargonium domesticum*, has scented, rounded-palmate leaves that are also toothed around the margins. In addition, it has large flowers (up to 2 inches diameter) in less numerous groups than the previous species. Many cultivars have flowers with a dark black-purple throat; the blooms are sometimes doubled and ruffled.

Succulent geraniums for the greenhouse are given full exposure to the sun and are sparingly watered. Recommended species include *P. Bowkeri*, with yellow and purple flowers; *P. Gibbosum* with greenish-yellow flowers, that has a somewhat gouty stem; *P. tetragonum* that has rather square stems and pale pink flowers; *P. echinatum*, with white flowers spotted red; a hybrid *P. Stapletonii* that has pinkish-white flowers; and *P. triste* bearing brownish-yellow flowers with some dark spots, and its varieties *daucifolium* and *filipendulifolium*.

176, 177, 180. Hybrids of *Pelargonium domesticum*.

178, 179. *Pelargonium hortorum*.

181

182

183

Ivy-leaved and fragrant-leaved geraniums

The ivy-leaved geraniums, *Pelargonium peltatum* (Geraniaceae family) are from South Africa.

Pelargonium peltatum is a perennial plant if protected from frost. It is frequently grown in pots to decorate porches, verandas, terraces, walls and hanging baskets. It has a green stem and branches that are rather woody, rigid and knotty, often hanging. Stems may grow 3 feet long and, are alternate, persistent, rounded but angular, thick, fleshy and hard, and bright green. The flowers, like the zonal geraniums, have five petals in globose umbels with long peduncles; simple and double forms are known. The colour varies from white to all the gradations of cyclamen-pink to purple and to red.

Ivy-leaved geraniums prefer full sun and a soil high in organic matter. It is possible to take cuttings all the year, although the best period is during late summer. The plants are kept indoors during the winter.

Recommended for fragrant-leaved geraniums is a soil mixture of two parts loam, half a part leaf mould and decayed manure with a quarter part sand. For summer flowering, cuttings are taken in August or September and are inserted singly in 2 inch pots, being kept in a greenhouse or frame at a temperature of about 45° F until the following March. They are then repotted into 4 inch pots. The main shoot is nipped off in March, and the side shoots when they are about 2 inches long. Transfer to 6 inch pots in May. Remove the flower buds until 14 days after the final potting, and then water freely and give stimulants. They should be shaded from the sun when they come into bloom. Provided they are not exposed to frost they can be used outdoors for patio plants, in beds and borders, and in hanging baskets.

The best known of the fragrant-leaved species are *Pelargonium capitatum* that grows to 3 feet and has purple and rose-coloured flowers, whose leaves have the fragrance of roses; *P. citriodorum*, a hybrid that grows to 3 feet and has white flowers with leaves smelling of citron; *P. crispum*, growing from 2 to 3 feet with rose-coloured flowers and lemon-scented leaves; *P. fragrans*, growing from 2 to 3 feet with rose-coloured flowers and leaves smelling of nutmeg; *P. graveolens*, growing to 3 feet, with purple and rose-coloured flowers and leaves that are scented like roses; *P. Radula*, similar in height and flower colour to *P. graveolens*, but with balsam-scented leaves; *P. denticulatum* with purple flowers that grows to about 12 inches and has an interesting variety, *filicifolium*, known as the Fern-leaved geranium; *P. odoratissimum* that grows to 18 inches and produces clear white flowers; and *P. tomentosum* with leaves giving off the fragrance of peppermint, and producing white flowers. It grows to 3 feet.

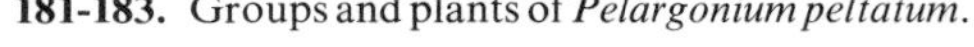

181-183. Groups and plants of *Pelargonium peltatum*.

184. Ivy-leaved geranium cultivar.

185. Double-flowered cultivar of *P. peltatum*.

184

185

186 187

189 188

Hyacinths

The following pages are devoted to some important bulbous or rhizomatous plants especially suited for gardens. One of the earliest of the flowering bulbs to bloom is the Common Hyacinth, *Hyacinthus orientalis* (Liliaceae family), a native of the Eastern Mediterranean region. It has a bulb, is perennial, grows from 4 to 20 inches, with only basal leaves that are upright, linear, thick shiny and shorter than the inflorescence. The inflorescence is a cylindrical-pyramidal raceme, thick, with a long scape. The numerous flowers are delicately scented, have six petals arranged in a star shape and curved backwards, with a corolla swollen at the base. The seeds are few, black, rounded and are contained in three-lobed capsules.

In addition to the Common Hyacinth and its variety *H. orientalis* var. *albulus*, known as the Roman Hyacinth, the Spanish Hyacinth, *H. amethystinus*, is popular. It grows to 1 foot and has blue flowers. Its variety, *albus*, is white. Other species cultivated are *H. candicans* that grows from 2 to 3 feet, has white flowers and considerable fragrance; and *H. ciliatus*, with sky blue flowers that grows to about 9 inches.

Hyacinths flower from February to April and are suitable for flower-boxes, pots, or for forcing in bowls, as well as outdoors where they are very suitable for edges, beds and borders. The bulbs are planted in late autumn, about 4 to 6 inches deep, in loamy soil 4 to 6 inches apart. The bulbs may be removed after flowering when the leaves are dry, and should be stored in a cool, dark place.

To force blooming during winter, the bulbs should be planted sometime between September and November in small pots with a light, rich soil, watered abundantly, plunging the pots into the soil in a cool place. When the bulbs sprout, the pots should be taken into a warm shelter in full light.

Propagation may be by seed, but plants will flower only after four to six years. Commonly, propagation is by planting the small bulblets that develop by the parent bulb.

For convenience hyacinths are divided into two groups: Dutch Hyacinths with large inflorescences, and Miniature Hyacinths with fewer flowers on the spike. The flower colours vary from white to yellow, to pink to carmine-lilac and to violet-bluish with all the intermediate shades. Among the most popular cultivars are "Innocence" with white flowers; "City of Haarlem" (yellow); "Lady Derby" and "Queen of the Pinks," pink coloured; the red carmine, "La Victoire"; and perhaps the favourite of them all, the sky-blue "Grand Maitre".

186, 188, 189. Hyacinths of various colours.

187. Close-up of an inflorescence.

Tulips

These plants offer the largest variety of shapes and flower colours among the flowering bulbs. Most popular are the two species *Tulipa Gesneriana*, the Common Tulip, and *T. suaveolens*, the Duc van Thol Tulip (Liliaceae family).

They are perennial, with oval bulbs having a reddish brown outer tunic. Leaves are oval, elongated, pointed, shiny and light green. The flowers, usually single and apical on a scape, are large, with six petals that form a cup. In the centre of the flower is a short pistil with a large three-lobed stigma surrounded by six stamens with yellow, purple or violet anthers. The seeds are dark and flattened and are contained in a three-lobed capsule.

Tulips bloom from April to June. The bulbs are planted in autumn, 4 to 5 inches deep and 4 to 6 inches apart. They are removed from the ground after flowering when all the leaves have dried. They are propagated by the small bulbs around the parent bulb. Reproduction by seed is possible, but will not come true.

Cultivars of common tulips and the more valuable ones are usually *Tulipa Gesneriana*, including the Darwin Tulips that are of a single colour, and the Rembrandt that are streaked or spotted. None of these is fragrant.

The earliest blooming and smallest flowered tulips, with single flowers, unicoloured or margined, are *Tulipa suaveolens*. These are mostly replaced by types merely called Early Single and Early Double.

The parrot tulips, having flowers with fringed petals, usually bicoloured, are a form of *Tulipa Gesneriana* var. *dracontia*.

Other popular species grown are: *Tulipa Kaufmanniana*, mainly with white petals inside and pink-violet outside; *T. Forsteriana* with elongated flowers; *T. praestans* which is multiflora; and *T. Clusiana* with red, white and black flowers.

It is customary to designate tulips developed by hybridization as *Tulipa hybrida* and to distinguish various cultivars, such as Triumph, Darwin, Cottage, Mendel, etc. Several thousand cultivars have been created by the skilled Dutch floriculturists. Among the best of the cultivars with simple flowers are: "Zwanenburg" (white); "Golden Harvest" and "Yellow Prince" (yellow); "Orange Wonder" and "Telescopium" (orange with thin streaks); "Princess Margaret Rose" (with yellow petals having flames of red on the sides); "Brilliant Star" (red-scarlet); "Cardinal" (red-carmine); "Clara Butt" (pink); "Aristocrat" (dark pink); "Demeter" (violet); and "La Tulipe Noire" (a Darwin hybrid).

Double-flowered cultivars are: "Therose" (early yellow), "Orange Nassau," (flame coloured) and "Peach Blossom," (peach coloured).

Important parrot tulips are the cultivars "Sunshine" (yellow); "Red Champion" (crimson); and "Violet Queen" (violet).

190. A tulip field.

191, 192. Cultivars of single-colour tulips.

193. A double-flowered tulip.

190

191

192

193

194

Narcissus

The genus *Narcissus* (Amaryllidaceae family) includes both the narcissus and the daffodil. The narcissus, with flowers shaped like stars formed by six petals, has a small cup or corona slightly ruffled on the margin in the centre. On the other hand, daffodil is the common name for those that have a large conical or trumpet-shaped corona. Through hybridization it has been possible to obtain all intermediate shapes and sizes and even double types are now common, giving rise to such terms as "small cupped," "medium cupped," "large trumpet," and "double."

Narcissus are perennial plants, originally from Europe. They have a pyriform bulb covered by a yellowish-brown tunic. The leaves are all basal, long and narrow, practically gramineous but more fleshy, and shiny green. The flower scapes are erect, one or more per plant, and have one or more flowers according to the cultivar. The flowers have six petals with a corona in the centre.

Regardless of species or variety, narcissus are suitable for borders, beds and for potted plants. They bloom from March to May, and are cultivated and propagated as hyacinths. Bulbs should be spaced 8 to 10 inches apart. If propagated by seed, they bloom in four to six years.

The common Poet's Narcissus (*N. poeticus*) characterizes the Poeticus group, with fragrant, simple, white flowers having a yellow corona trimmed with red; both early and late cultivars are available. All are single flowered.

N. Jonquilla, commonly known as jonquils, have between five and twelve yellow flowers in an umbel. The Polyanthus Narcissus, *N. Tazetta*, has white flowers with a corona and a medium sized cup that may be yellow or orange.

Hybrids of *N. poeticus*, Poet's Narcissus, and *N. Tazetta* have resulted in the *Poetaz* group of narcissus, with larger flowers and a larger corona; the colours of the perianth vary from white to light yellow, with golden orange or almost red coronas. The "Scarlet Gem" cultivar is multiflowered, yellow with a reddish corona; and the "Laurence Koster" is multiflowered and white.

Daffodils, *N. Pseudo-Narcissus*, are characterized by a well-developed corona with a tall crown and are white, yellow or bicoloured. These are hardy and can remain outdoors throughout the winter.

Hybrids of the Poet's Narcissus and daffodils have produced the "incomparables" group, *N. incomparabilis*, also known as the Chalice Cup Narcissus. They are uniflowered, with a medium large and open corona, ruffled around the edges. "Scarlet Elegance" is a cultivar with red corona.

194. Group of daffodils.

195, 196. Hybrids of *Narcissus Pseudo-Narcissus;* trumpet types.

197. A narcissus of the large-cupped type.

198 199

Various flowering bulbs

The Liliaceae, Amaryllidaceae, and Iridaceae families include bulbous and rhizomatous plants commonly used in gardens.

Three popular species of grape hyacinths are *Muscari botryoides; M. racemosum*, known as the Starch Hyacinth; and *M. comosum*, the Tassel Hyacinth (Liliaceae family). They have a flower scape that rises from the tuft of linear or ribbon-shaped leaves, resembling hyacinths. The bulbs are planted in late autumn and will flower yearly; the small bulblets should be separated in early autumn.

Crocuses belong to the *Crocus* genus (Iridaceae family) and are very low bulbous plants with a very early flowering—from January to March. *Crocus vernus*, a popular species, sometimes called Early Saffron, grows only 2 to 6 inches high and has narrow, linear leaves that are green with white veins. The white, violet or lilac flowers have a chalice-shaped perianth of six petals. The bulbs of the crocuses are planted during September to December, 3 to 4 inches deep and 2 to 8 inches apart.

Freesia (Iridaceae family) are bulbous plants, native to South Africa. They reach 5 to 18 inches in height, have narrow, parallel-veined leaves and the flowers have a tubular, funnel-shaped perianth in a spike inflorescence. The flowers are white, yellow, pinkish, orange, red or violet. They are used for massed plantings, but may be cultivated outdoors only in southern areas. The bulbs are planted in October in light soil, and are dug up and stored after they bloom. Variety *F. refracta* var. *grandiflora* is very popular, as is *F. odorata* that has yellow and orange flowers.

Day Lilies belong to the Liliacaea family and are of the genus *Hemerocallis*. Popular species cultivated are *Hemerocallis aurantiaca major*, the Japanese Day Lily, that has apricot flowers; *H. Dumortieri* with orange-yellow flowers; *H. fulva*, yellow flowers, and varieties *Kwanso* (double flowered), *longituba* and *rosea*; *H. Middendorffii*, golden yellow flowers; *H. minor*, a dwarf variety growing to 8 inches with yellow, scented flowers; and *H. Thunbergii*, also with yellow, scented flowers.

The Plantain Lilies, of the *Hosta* genus (Liliaceae family) are hardy plants; the flowers grow in terminal clusters, first with a tubular, light violet perianth that opens into six petals. *H. plantaginea* the Corfu Lily, a well-known species, has large, white, fragrant flowers that first look spindle-shaped and swollen; then as they open up, they appear with six points at the apex. The leaves are oval-pointed, wide, and with curved veins more pronounced on the lower surface. Perennial, rhizomatous plants, they are used for edges, beds and as specimen plants.

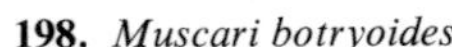

198. *Muscari botryoides.*

199. *Sternbergia lutea.*

200. *Freesia refracta.*

201. *Hemerocallis fulva.*

200

201

202

203

205

206

207

Iris

These plants, well known for the shape and colour of their flowers, belong to the genus *Iris* (Iridaceae family). Bearded irises of the *I. germanica* group and the bulbous irises of the *I. Xiphium* group are among the most interesting.

Both are perennial growing from 1 to 3 feet tall. The bearded iris has a cylindrical jointed rhizome that is often branched. The leaves are distichous, shaped like a sword-blade, shiny and light green. The scapes are erect, rigid and branched at the top to bear a group of flowers. Their perianth consists of six petals joined at the base.

The bearded irises include *Iris germanica* (with violet flowers) known as the Flag Iris, *I. germanica* var. *florentina* (with white flowers); and several others including those grouped as hybrids, *Iris hybrida*. They are characterized by large flowers whose six petals are similar three by three. The external three, the falls, are curved outwards and drooping, and have short, yellow, soft and erect hairs along their middle line. The three interior petals alternate with the outer group, curve inwards, stand erect, and are called the standards.

Colours are various, ranging from white to a cream-colour to yellow to pink-salmon to bright violet to dark blue to purple brown.

The bulbous group includes two species: *Iris Xiphium* and *Iris xiphioides*; the first is known as the Spanish Iris and the second one as the English Iris. They are native to the Mediterranean regions. Their flowers have narrower and more rigid petals, which, with the stamens, acquire a three-pointed appearance.

The rhizomes of irises are best planted in July or August or in early spring at a distance of 15 to 18 inches, and should be left in place until they are crowded. They are propagated by division.

Bulbous irises are planted in the autumn in mild climates, or in early spring in colder areas. Usually they are cultivated in a cold frame.

---

202. *Iris germanica*, or bearded iris; typical flowers.

203-205. *I. hybrida*, bearded iris hybrids.

206. *I. Xiphium*, or Spanish Iris.

207. A garden of bearded iris with several other perennials.

8

209

Gladioli

Included here are the numerous species and varieties of the genus *Gladiolus* (Iridaceae family) often called the Sword Lily. They are bulbous plants, native of Southern and Tropical Africa, the Mediterranean and West Asia. They are perennial, and grow from 1 to 5 feet tall. The corm is globose, with a yellowish-red tunic. The sword-shaped leaves have a strong central vein and are light green. Flowers are large, in tall terminal spikes. Each flower has a rather irregular, almost bilabiate perianth of six oval, wide petals joined at the base and forming a deep throat. The seeds are brown, mostly winged, numerous, inside a three-lobed capsule.

The size of gladioli and the beauty of their inflorescences make these plants suitable for cut flowers. In the garden they are planted in beds, borders and rows. Colours range from white to the brightest shades of yellow, pink, orange, red, purple and violet. Many cultivars have shaded, spotted and streaked flowers.

Gladioli corms are planted in early spring, 3 to 4 inches deep and 8 to 12 inches apart. After blooming, the flower stalks should be cut, and when the leaves have dried the corms should be dug and stored in a dry, cool place. They are often attacked by thrips (*Eliothrips hoemorrhoidalis*); these insects may be controlled by appropriate insecticides.

The gardener has many species from which to choose; among the most popular are *Gladiolus byzantinus*, that grows to 2 feet and has red and purple flowers; *G. Colvillei*, a hybrid, that grows to 2 feet and has red and white flowers; *G. primulinus* or "Maid of the Mist" grows from 3 to 4 feet, has bright yellow flowers and is scented; *G. psittacinus* grows to 3 feet and has scarlet and yellow flowers; *G. Saundersii* grows from 2 to 3 feet and has white, pink and red flowers; *G. tristis* grows to 12 inches and has red and yellow flowers; *G. blandus* grows to 18 inches and bears white, red and yellow flowers in June; *G. cardinalis* grows from 3 to 4 feet and bears vivid scarlet flowers in July and August; *G. communis*, or "Corn Flag", grows from 1 to 2 feet and bears rose-coloured flowers from June to August; and *G. cruentis* flowers in September producing scarlet and white flowers.

208-210. Gladioli cultivars.

211

Cannas and torch-lilies

Here in conclusion are two rhizomatous plants with an erect habit suitable for groups or borders.

Canna (Cannaceae family) are native to Central and Southern America. They are a perennial, 30 inches (dwarf cultivars) to 5 feet tall, with large rhizomes. The stems are erect and rigid, single and bear large, alternate, oval and pointed leaves that are light or dark green and sometimes reddish. The inflorescences are flashy, terminal, formed by two or more flowers that are protected by a green, leafy bract before they bloom. These flowers are irregular and large, with three green sepals, three yellow, orange or red petals (unicoloured or spotted), and two sterile, petaloid stamens. The large, round and black seeds are in a nondehiscent capsule.

Cannas are propagated by division of the rhizomes, although the seed may be planted if desired. Rhizomes are planted each spring at a spacing of 1½ to 3 feet, and must be dug up before frost each autumn. They should be stored over winter in a cool, dry place.

Species cultivated include *C. edulis* that grows from 8 to 10 feet and produces bright red flowers; *C. flaccida* with yellow blooms that grows from 4 to 5 feet; *C. glauca* that grows to 6 feet and has yellow flowers; *C. indica*, known as Indian Shot, that grows to 4 feet and has red and yellow flowers; *C. iridiflora* that grows from 8 to 10 feet and has rose-coloured flowers; and *C. Warscewiczii* that has red flowers tinged with blue and grows from 3 to 5 feet. Many hybrids are also cultivated.

Kniphofia (Liliaceae family), also known as Torch Lilies or Club Lilies, are rhizomatous and perennial, and grow from 3 to 6 feet tall. Leaves are all basal, long, ribbon-shaped and pointed, thinly ciliate around the edges. The striking inflorescences are apical on racemes terminating the scapes, and have a conical shape with a thick tuft of numerous flowers of yellow, orange or red, either unicoloured or shaded. The seeds are black and angular, in three-lobed capsules.

Torch Lilies are seeded in pots in spring and transplanted outdoors after danger of frost is past. They are usually propagated by separating the rhizomes. Excessive cold or water is harmful and a well-drained soil is required. They flower from July to September.

Many species are cultivated, of which the most popular is probably *Kniphofia Uvaria*, the Red Hot Poker plant, with its varieties *erecta* that has coral scarlet blooms, and *maxima* that grows to 7 feet. *K. Burchellii* with scarlet, yellow and green flowers, grows to 3 feet; *K. caulescens* with salmon flowers grows to 5 feet; *K. comosa* grows to 2 feet and has yellow flowers; *K. corallina* grows to 3 feet and has scarlet flowers; and *K. snowdonii* has coral scarlet flowers

211. Canna flower.

212. *Kniphofia Uvaria*, cultivar "Canary."

213. A cultivar of the torch lily with red-orange flowers.